HOMER'S ILIAD

A Commentary
on the translation
of Richmond Lattimore

Norman Postlethwaite

UNIVERSITY
of
EXETER
PRESS

First published in 2000 by
University of Exeter Press
Reed Hall, Streatham Drive
Exeter, Devon EX4 4QR
UK
www.ex.ac.uk/uep/

British Library Cataloguing in Publication Data
A catalogue record of this book is available
from the British Library

Paperback ISBN 0 85989 684 6
Hardback   ISBN 0 85989 683 8

Designed and typeset in 10/12 Sabon
by Mike Dobson, Quince Typesetting, Exeter

Printed and bound in Great Britain
by Short Run Press Ltd, Exeter

CONTENTS

COMMENTARY

PREFACE

This commentary is designed for readers of the *Iliad* who either have no knowledge of Ancient Greek or who may perhaps have begun to learn it alongside their study of ancient texts. It can be read as a continuous commentary on Richmond Lattimore's translation[1] of the poem or consulted on particular points of interpretation of the text. It is hoped that it will be of use to the general reader as well as to the undergraduate and postgraduate student of Classical Civilization, for whom it was originally conceived. It provides the reader with sufficient background information to make sense of the poem's detail, and it seeks to answer the question of how the poet Homer tells his tale, why he chose to tell it in the way he did, and what are the literary devices he uses to do so. It locates each of the 24 books within the structure of the poem, and it shows how each is linked to the previous and the following books. In this way the reader can see how Homer develops his chosen theme, defined in the first two lines of the poem as 'the anger of Peleus' son Achilleus and its devastation', and how he achieves the poem's unity through it.

References within the text of the commentary are kept to a minimum, in the hope that the suggestions for further reading will both lead the reader into more detailed study and reveal the debt owed to the expanse of Homeric scholarship. The study of the ancient world does not stand still, any more than that of other subjects, and the suggestions for further reading in each of the sections of the Introduction and in the body of the commentary offer the reader a pointer to some of the more significant recent studies, as well as some of the long and distinguished history of Homeric scholarship. The

Bibliography contains full detail of all the works referred to by author and date only in the text and in the suggestions for further reading.

The spelling of Greek proper names is a contentious issue. To avoid confusion, I have followed Lattimore's transliteration of Homer's Greek: so, for example, Ajax is written as Aias, and Phoebus as Phoibos (Apollo); see further, Lattimore's Glossary (1951.497–527). Line references throughout are to Lattimore who, with very few exceptions, follows Homer's text accurately.

N.P.
Exeter, September 2000

---

[1] Richmond Lattimore, *The Iliad of Homer, translated and with an Introduction*, University of Chicago Press 1951: this version continues to set the standard, both in its accuracy and in its reproduction of the heavily formulaic quality of the poem's language.

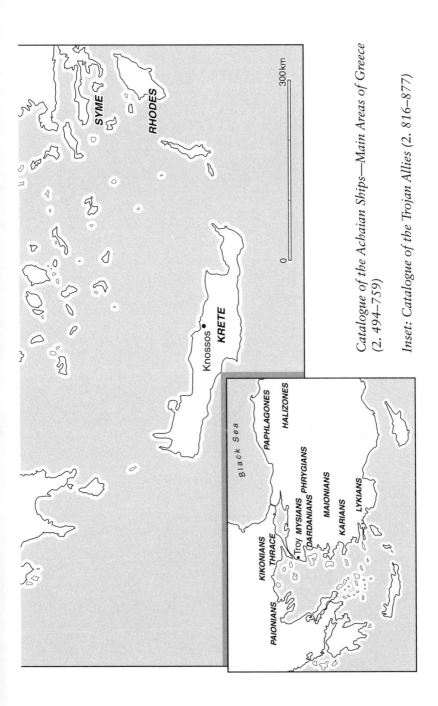

*Catalogue of the Achaian Ships—Main Areas of Greece
(2. 494–759)*

Inset: Catalogue of the Trojan Allies (2. 816–877)

INTRODUCTION

1. Homer

The name of Homer attaches to the two earliest works of Greek, and of European, literature, the *Iliad* and the *Odyssey*. Nothing certain is known about him, although there were various traditional stories in antiquity, for example, that he was born of the union of a river and a nymph, and that he once entered a poetic competition with Hesiod, author of the *Theogony* and the *Works and Days*; in antiquity it was thought that the two poets had been contemporaries, or that Hesiod may even have been the earlier. The Greek dialect of the *Iliad* and the *Odyssey* is predominantly that of Ionia—today the western coast of Turkey and the adjacent islands—and so it is generally assumed that it was in that area that the poems originated; and of the many places laying claim to Homer as its own, the island of Chios was thought to have the strongest case. In part this resulted from the claim of the composer of the so-called *Homeric Hymn to Apollo* (169–73):

> 'Whom think ye, girls, is the sweetest singer
> that comes here, and in whom do you most delight?'
> Then answer, each and all, with one voice:
> 'He is a blind man, and dwells in rocky Chios;
> his lays are evermore supreme'.

In part too it resulted from the later presence in Chios of a group who called themselves the Children of Homer (Homeridai), a guild of rhapsodes (literally meaning 'stitchers of songs'), who claimed to be descended from Homer and who preserved the poems by their recitations of them. The popular tradition that the poet was blind also resulted, in part, from the claim of the composer of the *Homeric*

Hymn; but it was also suggested by the blindness of the singer Demodokos, who performs for Odysseus at the Phaiakian court and who has been thought, without any evidence, to be Homer's own self-portrait (*Odyssey* 8. 64). In fact, the poet reveals little or nothing about himself in his poems, and this allows, indeed compels, the reader to focus more closely on the poems themselves for an understanding and appreciation of them.

Just as many claims were made for the home of the poet, so also many different dates have been suggested for his life, from the time of the Trojan War (thirteenth/twelfth century BC) down to the sixth century BC. It is generally accepted that the *Iliad* is earlier than the *Odyssey*, and the language of the two is sufficiently alike to indicate that they were produced within the life-span of a single poet. A date in the second half of the eighth century BC is accepted by many (Janko 1982), but West (1995) has argued for a date as late as 660–650 BC. Nothing actually prevents their being the products of two different poets, but it is certain that, whatever the resolution of the perennial question, the name of Homer will continue to attach to both poems.

For short introductions to Homer and the poems, see Thorpe 1973; Camps 1980; Griffin 1980b; Silk 1987; see further, Marg 1956; Reinhardt 1961; Vivante 1990; Frazer 1993; Latacz 1996; Conche 1999.

2. The Homeric epics

Writing some four centuries after Homer, Aristotle in his *Poetics* identified unity and compactness of theme as the essential feature of the best kind of epic. The story, he declared

> must be constructed as in tragedy, dramatically, round a single piece of action, whole and complete in itself, with a beginning, middle and end, so that like a single living organism it may produce its own peculiar form of pleasure. It must not be such as we normally find in history, where what is required is an exposition not of a single piece of action but of a single period of time, showing all that within the period befell one or more persons, events that have a merely casual relation to each other
>
> (Aristotle, *Poetics* 23).

For all its mass of detail, the *Iliad* in particular displays a marked consistency and unity of theme. The poet declares in the first word of the first line that the anger (*menis*) of Achilleus is to be the theme of the poem. This theme locates the action of the poem in the tenth year of the Trojan War and, within the 'history' of that war, the end of the poem brings the reader to the point where the Trojan Hektor is killed by the Achaian Achilleus; the poem does not go on to recount the fall of Troy or the death of Achilleus himself, nor does it tell, except occasionally in passing, of events in the previous nine years of the war or of events before the war itself. The *Odyssey* tells of the return from the Trojan War of the Achaian Odysseus to his home in Ithaka and how he takes revenge on a gang of suitors who have been wasting his home and trying to win his wife, a theme which locates the poem in the tenth year following the fall of Troy; in addition, the poem tells retrospectively of the hazards which the hero had to overcome in his wanderings after Troy's destruction, and so it also incorporates some of the intervening period before his return home. Besides the two Homeric epics there were other poems, collectively known as the *Epic Cycle* (Evelyn-White 1967), which covered the events of the Trojan saga not narrated in the *Iliad* and *Odyssey*: the *Cypria* told of the abduction of Helen, wife of Menelaos of Sparta, by Paris prince of Troy, that is, it recounted the cause of the Trojan War; the *Aithiopis* continued the story of the war following the *Iliad*, including the death of Achilleus, as far as the quarrel between Odysseus and Aias over the armour of Achilleus; the *Little Iliad* (*Ilias Parva*) told of the Trojan Horse; the *Sack of Troy* (*Iliou Persis*) recounted the fall of the city and the departure of the Achaians for home; the *Returns* (*Nostoi*) told how the various Achaians reached their homes; and the *Telegonia* told the story of Odysseus, subsequent to the *Odyssey*, until his death. None of these poems is any longer attributed to Homer, and none has survived except in summary form. The very survival of the Homeric epics, on the other hand, is testament to Aristotle's observation above.

See further, Kullmann 1984; Baldick 1994; Sherratt 1992. For representation of the poems in art, see Friis Johansen 1967; Anderson 1997; Snodgrass 1998.

3. The historical background

The Homeric poems are set in a glorious and distant past: a time when the warrior kings, the heroes, though themselves mortal, in some cases had divine ancestors; a time when the gods often played an active role in the lives of mortals; a time when the heroes far surpassed men of Homer's own day in their physical prowess. It is reasonable to suppose that this mythical age of heroes may have had its origins in a dim recollection of the Late Bronze Age of Greece, a period roughly dated between the sixteenth and twelfth centuries BC, and known today as the Mykenaian Age. At the apex of Mykenaian Greece were a number of fortified citadels, such as Mykenai itself and Tiryns in the plain of Argos, and Pylos in Messenia. Each of these citadels appears to have controlled its surrounding territory, in much the same way as is pictured in the Catalogue of the Ships in *Iliad* 2; there is no conclusive evidence that Mykenai exercised control over the other citadels, either politically, economically, or militarily, nor is there evidence for the kind of united national expedition pictured in the poem. It seems more likely that each citadel was an independent political and economic unit, although very clear cultural similarities between them have been identified. It was to these citadels, and to the royal families which were said to have ruled them, that some of the Greeks' most enduring legends became attached: of Oidipous in Thebes; of Atreus and Thyestes, and later Agamemnon, Klytaimnestra, and Orestes in Mykenai; of Theseus in Athens; and of Jason and the Argonauts in Iolkos. The citadels housed royal palaces, administered by extensive bureaucracies which kept close control over, and careful record of, the day-to-day business of the palaces. These records were maintained in a syllabic script, called today Linear B, inscribed in shorthand fashion on clay tablets. The language of these tablets is an early form of Greek; although in theory this means only that the scribes who wrote the tablets were Greek-speakers, it is generally accepted that the Linear B tablets prove that the people of Mykenaian Greece were Greeks. The Mykenaians also had a significant presence outside the mainland of Greece, particularly in Krete and Cyprus; and, from the evidence of pottery, they were trading in the west as far as Italy, in the south as far as the Nile Valley, and in the east as far as Syria and Mesopotamia. They appear to have had dealings with the empire of the Hittites in central and eastern Turkey, who named in their records the land of Ahhiyawa which may well recall Homer's name for the land of the heroes, Achaia. In addition, they had close links to the north with the area of the Black Sea, and in particular the site at modern Hissarlik in north-west Turkey, now conventionally identified as the city of Troy.

Although the story of the *Iliad* may look back to this historical period, it retains very little of the detail which archaeologists and historians have recovered of it. Of the palace organization, the bureaucracies and the clay tablets there is no trace, although it may be that the story Glaukos tells about his ancestor Bellerophontes contains a reference to writing of some sort (6. 168–9). Instead, the poem retains a few details of specific objects which archaeologists have shown to date from the Mykenaian period: most famous of these, Odysseus' helmet made from a felt cap covered with the tusks of a boar (10. 261–5); Aias' great shield like a wall (7. 219–23); the ornate wine cup from which Nestor drinks (11. 631–6); and the universal use of bronze weapons by the heroes, rather than the iron weapons which superseded them in the following Iron Age. In addition, the account of the Achaian forces in *Iliad* 2 seems to recall quite accurately the geography of Mykenaian Greece.

By about 1200 BC this Mykenaian world was at an end. Many of the major sites were destroyed or damaged by attack, although some continued to be occupied with few signs of damage. Greek tradition told of the Dorian invasion, an event which brought Greek speakers of the Dorian dialect from the north, and the end of the Mykenaian era is often blamed on this movement of peoples; but the evidence suggests that the destruction of the Mykenaian civilization was a more protracted affair than can be accounted for simply by invasion, and there is some reason to think that warfare between the different citadels may have played some part in their destruction. The end of the Mykenaian palace culture brought the end of writing in the Linear B script: the use of the script seems to have been limited to the scribes who maintained the palace records, and so the disappearance of the palace culture, if not of the palaces themselves, removed the need for the records and for the script in which they were written. Certainly nothing resembling poetry has survived in the clay tablets and, in any case, the script would not have been suitable for recording it. In effect, until the Greeks borrowed their alphabet from the Phoenicians in the eighth century BC, literacy disappeared from Greece, and it entered a cultural and economic Dark Age.

The disappearance of writing from Greece is one reason why the following three centuries or so are known as the Dark Age of Greece (Snodgrass 1971), but in fact it is only one of a number of signs of a dramatic collapse in both the cultural and economic fabric of the country. It was a Dark Age not just in terms of the comparative absence of evidence for it, but, more importantly, in the impoverished conditions in which the depleted population eked out an existence. The fall of the Mykenaian centres also resulted in the migration of those dispossessed during the destructions to lands overseas, including the western coast of Asia Minor—modern day Turkey—and its adjacent islands. If the *Iliad* and the *Odyssey* did indeed originate in Ionia in Asia Minor, then they may well have been created by the descendants of these original migrants from Greece; and since the migrants would likely have taken with them, besides their goods and chattels, their own beliefs and traditions, there is good reason to believe that the Homeric poems would, despite the centuries which intervened, reflect something of those traditions, and that some of the detail of the events they recounted would ultimately have been derived from the period in which they occurred.

Greece emerged from its Dark Age in the eighth century, an event traditionally associated with the holding of the first Olympiad in 776 BC. The succeeding period, the Archaic Age, the Age of Experiment as it has been aptly called (Snodgrass 1980), witnessed a dramatic transformation of the country, both culturally and economically. Rapid and sustained population increase gives firm evidence of new prosperity, and at the same time it provided the stimulus for overseas colonization to ease the pressure on land at home. The most important development of the period was the evolution of the *polis*, the politically independent unit that took in both urban area and surrounding territory; and it is to this same century, or soon after, that many assign the appearance of the *Iliad* and the *Odyssey*.

See further, Stella 1978; Murray 1980; Finley 1981; Warren 1989; Dickinson 1994; Bennet 1997; Morris 1997; Raaflaub 1997; Fisher and Van Wees 1998.

4. The Trojan War

For the purpose of reading and interpreting the *Iliad*, it does not really matter whether or not the Trojan War was an historical event. Few today would accept the tradition of a ten-year siege, or the traditional cause of the war, the abduction of Helen; those who do accept the war as historical look for more likely causes of it, for example, the Greeks' wish to overthrow Trojan power and supposed economic dominance. Yet for the Greeks the tradition of the Trojan War was the most enduring fixed reference point in their early history, and it was adopted by the Romans too as a fixed point in their foundation legend, for it was a Trojan survivor of the war, Aineias, who, they claimed, led his followers to Italy and founded the Roman line which culminated in the imperial family of the Caesars. However, archaeological evidence suggests that the citadel in northwest Turkey identified as Troy was destroyed by man at much the same time as the Mykenaian citadels in Greece, and so casts doubt on the traditional Greek account of the Trojan War, which tells of the presence at Troy for ten years of the kings of all the leading states of Greece, at the very same time that those states were themselves under attack.

Because it lies beyond the scope of the poem's theme, Homer for the most part suppresses the traditional cause of the Trojan War. It was said that during the wedding feast of the parents of Achilleus, the mortal Peleus and the sea goddess Thetis, the goddess of Discord (Eris) threw amongst the diners a golden apple inscribed 'For the most beautiful'. Paris, prince of Troy, was asked to adjudicate between three goddesses who competed for the apple: Hera, who offered him power in return for his favour, Athene who offered him military strength, and Aphrodite who offered him sexual prowess. Paris awarded the golden apple as prize to Aphrodite and was rewarded with the most beautiful woman in the world, Helen wife of Menelaos the king of Sparta; and having been entertained at Sparta by Menelaos, Paris duly made off with his wife. Menelaos' brother, Agamemnon of Mykenai, raised and led an expedition comprising the principal leaders of Greece and a force of 1,186 ships (cf. 2. 484–93n), and besieged the city of Troy for ten years.

The continuing excavation of the mound of Hissarlik, which was begun by Schliemann in the last century and carried forward more systematically by Blegen in this, has revealed occupation of the site from Neolithic to Roman times: the mound in fact consists of a number of superimposed levels (Manning 1992). Schliemann thought that he had found the Troy of the poems, and the treasure of Priam, in level II, but it is now believed that the level known as Troy VIIA is closest to the traditional date for Troy's fall of 1184 BC. Troy VIIA has been revealed as a city of one-roomed hovels, many with storage jars sunk into their floors, where earlier there had been large, many-roomed palaces, temples and houses; it looks like a city prepared for siege, and in the end it was destroyed by fire. Its appearance is very different from the previous level, Troy VI, with its magnificent city walls and spacious buildings, which show signs of having been destroyed by earthquake, and it has been suggested (Wood 1985) that this earlier, much grander, city is really the Troy of the poems. For those who wish to believe in Homer's version, this has the advantage of placing Troy's destruction earlier than that of the citadels of Greece and so of allowing for the presence at Troy of the kings of those citadels, who then returned home to fight to defend their own land, much as recorded by later writers.

See further, Reinhardt 1960; Foxhall and Davies 1984; Mee 1984; Korfmann 1986; Mellink 1986; Austin 1994; Traill 1995; Korfmann 1998; Allen 1999.

5. Composition

Since the period between the end of the Mykenaian era and the conventional date for the appearance of the *Iliad* and the *Odyssey* in the eighth century BC was, on the evidence, one of total illiteracy, it must be that any recollections of the traditions and folktales of that earlier time were handed on by word of mouth from generation to generation. Oral transmission most likely accounts also for the presence in the poems of the description of those few Mykenaian objects mentioned earlier. By the same token, however, it is clear that much of the substance of the Mykenaian era is not recorded in the poems, and so the picture of society which they present must, if it has any historical basis at all, derive either from the intervening period, the Dark Age, or from the poet's own period, the Archaic Age. It has been argued by Finley (1977) that the society described in the poems is largely that of the Dark Age: for example, disposal of the dead in the poems is by cremation, the practice of the Dark Age but not of the Mykenaians, who buried their dead. Other scholars place much more emphasis on Homer's contemporary society, reasoning that any social institution in the poems must have been recognizable to his audience if it was to be acceptable to them (Morris 1986). In reality, the picture is an amalgam of elements of the Mykenaian, Dark, and Archaic Ages, together of course with those elements the reader might wish to believe were the fictions of Homer himself (Crielaard 1995b).

Some two hundred years ago the suggestion was made that Homer was himself illiterate, within an illiterate culture, and that he composed the poems orally for oral recitation; that the poems were then transmitted orally over a number of centuries and underwent many changes; and that they were subsequently written down by editors who themselves made substantial changes (Davison 1962). However, it is only in the present century that systematic analysis of the language of the poems has finally established that the *Iliad* and the *Odyssey* were indeed the products of oral composition. Although his conclusions, and his techniques, continue to be the subject of debate, the American scholar Milman Parry stands out as a figure of the greatest importance in the history of Homeric scholarship (Parry 1971). His work, and that of his collaborator A.B. Lord (1960; 1991), who continued Parry's work after his premature death, stimulated a reappraisal of the poems which continues to this day (Hainsworth 1969; Rutherford 1996).

A dominant feature of the Homeric poems is the amount of repetition they display: repetition of groups of words, of whole lines, and even of groups of lines; and the repetition of themes, or 'type-scenes', such as the feast and the arming of a warrior. Parry used the term 'formula' to describe the repetition of language, and he defined it as 'a group of words which is regularly employed under the same metrical conditions to express a given essential idea'. He examined the use in the poems of the very distinctive formulas consisting of a personal name with one or more epithets: 'the lord of men Agamemnon', 'swift-footed brilliant Achilleus', 'Diomedes of the great war cry', and the like; and he showed that these personal names make up a pervasive formulaic system, providing the poet with a formula, and normally only one formula, for each major character in each of the principal positions in the Homeric hexameter verse. Parry referred to the 'economy and scope' of this formulaic system: economy, because there was normally only one formula in each case, and scope, because the system covered, as far as was practical, all the principal characters in all the principal verse positions. He argued that it was inconceivable that one poet could have produced, or would have wanted to produce, such a system, and that it resulted from an evolutionary process designed to enable generations of singers to produce rapidly extemporized verse without the help of writing. His own work and that of Lord amongst the contemporary oral bards (*guslari*) of Yugoslavia revealed similar systems in action in a living oral tradition. The model then is of a traditional formulaic diction shared by all composers of Greek oral poetry; using this, the composers extemporized their songs without the aid of writing, by repeating and combining pre-existing groups of words, rather than individual words, within a defined metrical framework, and most likely with quite rudimentary musical accompaniment to aid the rhythm of composition. The tradition was a living one, with formulas ever changing, as new generations of composers experimented and devised new formulas to replace others which fell into disuse.

Since Parry first proposed his model of the Homeric formula and of the oral composition of the poems, a number of necessary adjustments have been made. It was soon realized that the area of the diction on which he had concentrated his greatest effort, the personal name plus epithet formulas, was much more conservative than other areas, and that it was impossible to demonstrate the same fixity in, for example, formulas consisting of a common noun with one or more epithets, where modifications such as mobility, separation, and expansion of the elements are commonplace (Hainsworth 1968). In addition, it is clear that not all areas of Homer's diction are formulaic, except in the most general sense that certain words and phrases are the same metrical shape as others, and occupy the same metrical positions. However, perhaps the most serious problem arises from the implications of 'economy and scope' for the meaning of the formulas: for if, as Parry suggested, a particular formula was chosen because it suited the particular metrical context, if Agamemnon is 'powerful Agamemnon' (*kreion Agamemnon*) in one metrical context, but 'the lord of men Agamemnon' (*anax andron Agamemnon*) in another, it seems clear that little or no significant meaning can be attached to the descriptions 'powerful' and 'the lord of men' within the particular narrative contexts. When Odysseus is described as 'of the many wiles' (*polumetis Odysseus*) no fewer than eighty-one times, it seems clear that the epithet is merely ornamental and contributes nothing to the meaning of a particular context, and so the formula as a whole may mean no more than 'Odysseus'. Foley (1991.141) has suggested the following formulation: that a formula is indeed tied to its usage by its metrical shape, as Parry suggested, and that, when it appears, a formula such as 'swift-footed Achilleus' does not bring to its particular narrative context a particular connotation of Achilleus' swift-footedness, which may well be unsuited to that context; but rather, the appearance of the formula evokes the entirety of the hero's traditional identity, that is, all the separate occasions that character has appeared in the traditional oral tales. It is the audience's experience of the traditional oral story, and in this case of Achilleus' role within it, which is stressed, rather than the immediate poetic context of the story of the *Iliad*; the audience is invited to ponder, not the appropriateness of Achilleus' swift-footedness to a given context, but rather the words and actions of Achilleus in that context, against the background of his entire mythic existence.

It is possible to suggest a similar model for the other main element of oral compositional technique, the theme. This term may be used in the broadest sense, to describe the very subjects of the Homeric poems, the Anger of Achilleus and the Return of Odysseus; or it may refer to a large-scale component of one of the poems, sometimes the length of an entire book, such as the Embassy to Achilleus in *Iliad* 9, the Night Raid of Odysseus and Diomedes in *Iliad* 10, or the Shield of Achilleus in *Iliad* 18; or a theme may be a smaller-scale element, recurring on many different occasions in many different books, such as supplication, feasting, or arming, and in these cases the term 'type-scene' is applied. The repetition, particularly of these smaller-scale themes, throughout the poem allows the composer to foreshadow, or to recollect, one scene by means of another, and, through the changed circumstances of the scenes, to achieve sometimes pathos, sometimes irony, sometimes humour. For example, when his goddess mother, Thetis, visits Achilleus to console him as he grieves for his dead companion Patroklos, she finds him on the sea-shore (18. 67–71); his situation is a repetition of 1. 359–60, where Thetis also came to the sea-shore to console him after his violent quarrel with Agamemnon. The repetition of the theme establishes a link between the two scenes, to show that Patroklos' death and Achilleus' grief in the later book are the direct result of the request Achilleus made to his mother in the earlier one, that the Achaians should suffer a great defeat.

As in the case of the formulas above, it may be suggested that the audience's experience of the traditional oral story embraces the countless separate realizations of each particular theme, and that the individual scene recalls to the audience, and to the composer, the entirety of that experience. The subtlety of variation between scenes— of wording, of setting, of background, of characters—then informs the audience's response to each thematic occurrence. An obvious example is that of the Arming of the Hero (Armstrong 1958): in the *Iliad* four warriors are described putting on their armour, Paris (3. 330–8), Agamemnon (11. 17–44), Patroklos (16. 131–44), and Achilleus (19. 369–91). On each occasion the theme introduces a combat which leads, or appears that it will lead, to a turning point in the narrative; on each occasion the hero puts on essentially the same items of armour and in the same order; but in each case there are subtle variations. In the case of Paris, he borrows the corselet of his brother Lykaon, and so draws attention to the fact that he normally does not have need for one, because he fights at long distance with the less than heroic bow and arrow; in the case of Agamemnon, the lavish detail of the description of his corselet may be intended to mark him as leader, or perhaps to reveal him as one given to empty show, but in either case it is in marked contrast to his unimpressive performance on the battle-field; in the case of Patroklos who puts on the armour of Achilleus, the two spears he takes call attention to Achilleus' great spear, the only item of Achilleus' armour he does not put on, and this in turn points to his inadequacy to take on the role of Achilleus as Achaian champion; and in the case of Achilleus, the armour has been made by Hephaistos the blacksmith god, and its description is closely associated with the fire imagery which becomes an important part of the description of Achilleus in the final books of the poem. On the other hand Aias, who after Achilleus is the greatest of the Achaian heroes and their finest defensive warrior, is not given an arming description as he prepares for his duel with Hektor; instead Homer draws attention only to his great defensive shield like a wall, and thus indicates the new defensive role into which the Achaians have been cast as a result of Achilleus' withdrawal from the battle.

Where Parry and Lord aimed to illustrate Homeric composition by identifying parallels amongst the *guslari* of Yugoslavia, Finnegan (1977) has examined a much broader range of oral traditions from a diversity of geographical areas, and offers a series of observations which make it impossible to propose one single model to explain the composition, transmission and performance of oral poetry; in particular, she observes widely differing degrees of reliance on prior composition and memorization. The result has been to remove the dividing line, within the genre of oral poetry, between works produced wholly by the use of writing, works produced partially by the use of writing, and works produced without the use of writing at all; between works which have been produced prior to performance, and works which are produced during performance itself; and between works which are the product of the performer himself and works which the performer has taken over from some other singer or singers. So, while acknowledging that the Homeric epics were the products of an oral tradition, it seems that they are nevertheless in this, as in all other respects, wholly exceptional works of art, and it would be unwise to base a reading of them on the experience of Yugoslav, or any other, oral poetry, but rather on the criteria which come from the texts of the poems themselves.

Homer himself provides two portraits of the singer (*aoidos*), though neither gives much assistance in understanding their technique of composition; however it is instructive to observe the subject matter of their songs and the setting of their performances. Both are associated with royal houses: Phemios is the resident singer in Odysseus' palace who is forced to sing for the entertainment of Penelope's suitors (*Odyssey* 1. 154), and Demodokos sings at the Phaiakian court for the entertainment of king Alkinoos and his guest Odysseus. Phemios sings of the journeys home from Troy of the various Achaian heroes (*Odyssey* 1. 326-7); Demodokos sings of a quarrel at Troy between Achilleus and Odysseus (*Odyssey* 8. 75-82); he then sings of the adulterous affair of Aphrodite, the goddess of love, with Ares, the god of war, and their discovery by her husband Hephaistos (*Odyssey* 8. 267-366); and finally Demodokos sings of the ruse by which Troy was finally captured, the Trojan Horse, and of the role in it of Odysseus himself (*Odyssey* 8. 500-15). In each case, the subject matter of the song is merely an episode, normally of the Trojan War, chosen from the singer's repertoire, and sung to the accompaniment of a lyre as entertainment at a feast of noblemen; and the most important quality of the song is its accuracy, for which Odysseus praises Demodokos, saying that he has sung it as though he had himself been an eye-witness or had heard it from another who had been so (*Odyssey* 8. 487–91).

See further, Arend 1933; Meister 1966; Fenik 1968; Krischer 1971; Foley 1988; Lord 1995.

6. The Homeric Question

Many believe that the discoveries of Milman Parry have finally put an end to the Homeric question. The debate over the nature of Homeric composition has been long and at times bitter: on the one hand, the Unitarians believe that they can identify the genius of one individual pervading both poems, and on the other, the Analysts feel that only by proposing a number of authors can the inconsistencies within the texts be explained. These range from the trivial to the serious: for example, the appearance of Pylaimenes at 13. 658, long after he has in fact been killed by Menelaos at 5. 576, is no more than the kind of minor mistake to be expected in a poem of the *Iliad*'s length and complexity, and suggests the absence of checking which a written version would allow. More serious is the very real confusion over the number of ambassadors who make up the embassy to Achilleus, since it is specifically stated that two men make their way along the shore to Achilleus' shelter (9. 182), but that three men then address their separate appeals to him. Incongruous too is Achilleus' declaration 'now I think the Achaians will come to my knees and stay there in supplication, for a need past endurance has come to them' (11. 608–9), appearing to ignore the embassy to him in Book 9, which offered just such supplication a few hours earlier. For some readers inconsistencies such as these are incompatible with the belief that a single author could have been responsible for the entire poem; and so an original poem on the subject of Achilleus' anger is identified, and to this, it is argued, subsequent layers of narrative were added.

There was a tradition in antiquity associating the establishment of a definitive text of the *Iliad* and the *Odyssey* with the rule in Athens of the tyrant Peisistratos. In the sixth century BC continuous recitations of the poems by 'rhapsodes' were established at Athens at the four-yearly festival of the Panathenaia, and Cicero (*De Oratore* III.34.137) credits the Athenian tyrant with having been 'the first person who arranged the previously disordered books of Homer in the order in which we now have them'. If correct, this tradition might suggest that the written texts of the poems came into existence at the time of their composition in the eighth century, and that in the intervening period a number of different written versions appeared, and so necessitated the so-called 'Peisistratean recension'. Since the work of Parry and Lord, it has been generally accepted that a feature of the oral composer is his illiteracy, and it has been suggested that the tradition of Homer's blindness might have been symbolic of this. Lord (1953) therefore and, more recently, Janko have offered the view that the texts of the *Iliad* and the *Odyssey* came into being as the oral dictations of the poet, and Janko (1992.38) declares that 'once a poet has adjusted to the slower pace of dictation, he can take advantage of it to create a longer, finer and more elaborate song than he would have been able to sing'. Alternatively, on the basis that the eighth century BC, when the alphabet had only recently been introduced into Greece, was too early for epics of the monumental scale of the *Iliad* and *Odyssey* to have been written down, Kirk (1962.301) has suggested that they may have been entrusted to memory and so passed down from generation to generation—a feat which he claims to be within the capabilities of an oral culture—until they were written down at a later time. More radically, Seaford (1994.153) has questioned the conventional picture of the poems as the creation of an eighth-century master-poet, and has suggested rather that the very complexity of the long oral tradition suggests the work of a school of singers, who were recreating the various elements of that tradition almost until the moment when they were consigned to writing in Athens.

An important period for the establishment of the text of the two poems was the third and second centuries BC. In the library built by Ptolemy I at Alexandria in Egypt, a number of scholars fashioned a composite text from the many versions and excerpts recorded on papyrus which had been brought to that city. Of these scholars the most important contributions came from Zenodotos of Ephesos, Aristophanes of Byzantium and Aristarchos of Samothrace. It was the task of these men to choose between variant readings of words and lines which had come into existence during the previous centuries, and it is as a result of their efforts that we possess an established text of the Homeric poems. How that text relates to the original poems of Homer—however that phrase is interpreted—can never be known.

See further, Heubeck 1974; Turner 1997; Haslam 1997.

7. Some features of style

(a) Simile

Similes both vary and enrich the narrative: in the books containing long descriptions of battles and dying warriors, similes, particularly extended similes, break up the descriptions by adding to them a variety of detail; in contrast, in dramatic scenes where speeches predominate, similes are very rare. Similes establish the closest bond between the poet and his audience: in his narrative, the poet vouches for the truthfulness of the events he is describing and his audience accepts his authority; but in the similes the poet relates his description to the everyday experience of his audience and that experience enhances the description. At times the modern reader may sense his own disadvantage, as much of the world of the similes is foreign to him, except by vicarious experience; but for Homer's own audience, a world in which man contended with nature, where wild beasts attacked his cattle and swollen rivers inundated his land, was real enough. Yet even vicarious experience permits the reader to associate with the images of this poetic world peopled by potters and reapers, hunters and shepherds, and neighbours arguing over a boundary mark. So the similes, for the brief moment of their telling, transform the distant world of the heroes into the living world of the poet and his audience.

In its briefest form the simile draws a single, though often quite complex, comparison: Apollo descending from Olympos to bring his plague of arrows on the Achaian army 'came as night comes down' (1. 47), Nestor declares that his charge into battle was 'like a black whirlwind' (11. 746), and in their duel Hektor and Aias are 'like lions who live on raw meat' (7. 256). Brief similes are often found repeated and, like the formulas, they serve an important purpose in the process of composition (Scott 1974). More striking are the extended similes, which briefly take the place of the dramatic moment in the narrative and impart colour and texture to that moment. For example, the opening of *Iliad* 3 describes the Achaian and Trojan armies marching out to battle: the Trojans are, in a brief simile, like wildfowl, to describe their excited clamour but also to emphasize the variety of foreign tongues contained in this disparate Trojan army, and its lack of proper discipline (3. 2); but Homer immediately extends the simile to describe the attack of one type of wildfowl, the cranes, on the Pygmaian men, and in this way he changes the thrust of the comparison, away from the noise of the birds, to the unnaturalness of their attack on men (3. 3–7). Two more extended similes follow almost immediately, to characterize Paris and Menelaos in advance of their coming duel: Menelaos' joy at encountering Paris is compared to that of a lion which has come across a carcass and, since Paris has just been portrayed in the guise of a leopard, the simile, in which he now takes the form of the victim of a killing, establishes the reversal of his role which the encounter with Menelaos threatens (cf. 3. 23–6n); then the dismay of Paris at encountering Menelaos is compared to a man who has suddenly come upon a snake and steps back with a shudder of fear (cf. 3.33–5n). By contrasting the images in each of the two similes, the lion and the carcass, the snake and the man, and by contrasting the two similes with each other, the joy of the lion and the horror of the man, Homer effectively characterizes the scene in the narrative, and at the same time imports colour and texture from the audience's own world. Balance and contrast of images is achieved, often over very long sections of narrative, by the conscious echoing of similes. For example, the contrast between the cowardice of Paris and the courage of his brother Hektor is a recurring motif of the poem. So the comparison above, of Paris to a man recoiling in fear when he comes upon a snake (3. 33–5), finds its echo when Hektor, determined bravely to confront Achilleus and certain death in defence of his city, is compared to a snake which coils itself around its nest to defend it (22. 93–5). Similarly, when Priam sees Achilleus advancing into battle to kill his son Hektor, Achilleus is like the dog-star which 'is wrought as a sign of evil and brings on the great fever for unfortunate mortals' (22. 30–1); and then, as he closes in on Hektor for the kill, Achilleus is like the evening-star Hesper, which here signals the end of Hektor's final day (22. 317–18).

See further, Fränkel 1921; Moulton 1977.

(b) Metaphor

Like similes, metaphors enrich the narrative by incorporating fresh images and motifs; but unlike similes, where objects are illuminated by comparison or by contrast with others, metaphors often introduce images which, by their very unfamiliarity in a given context, challenge the reader to view that context in a different light or from a novel angle. Metaphors pervade the poem, even more than similes, and there is no reason to suppose that they were any less a part of the traditional oral language Homer inherited than the formulas, the type-scenes and the themes. Indeed metaphor is a common feature of the formulas themselves: for example, the very common 'winged words', suggesting words flying almost without control from the mouth; or 'the shepherd of the people', indicating the caring concern of the military commander for those under his control; in both cases, the metaphors may suggest to the reader a fresh view of the context in which they appear, and yet the frequency with which they are found repeated in other contexts shows that they are part of the poet's formulaic inheritance, rather than his own inventions.

Metaphor is one of the poet's most vivid devices for characterizing individuals, actions and attitudes. For example, during his violent quarrel with Agamemnon, Achilleus characterizes his relationship with him in the words 'I am minded no longer to stay here dishonoured and pile up your wealth and your luxury' (1. 170–1). The metaphor in the word translated by Lattimore 'pile up' is in fact that of drawing liquid, perhaps water from the well or, in the case of the god Hephaistos later in Book 1, drawing nectar from the mixing bowl for his fellow gods at their feast (1. 597–8). Through this metaphor Achilleus is able, at one and the same time, to characterize his own treatment by Agamemnon as that of servant by master, and to highlight and condemn Agamemnon's selfishness and greed in taking for himself the spoils of others. Similarly, amongst many other insults hurled during their quarrel, Achilleus describes Agamemnon as 'wrapped in shamelessness' (1. 149). The clothing metaphor seems deliberately to exaggerate the picture of Agamemnon's shamelessness and to present it, as it were, as his all-enveloping characteristic; at the same time there might even be the suggestion that this trait is Agamemnon's protection, the bravado which he 'puts on' to conceal his inadequacy as hero. The clothing image is taken up in one of the poem's most famous metaphors: claiming that the Trojans are cowards for not punishing Paris' crime in abducting Helen, his brother Hektor says he would otherwise have 'worn a mantle of flying stones' (3. 57), that is, he would have been stoned to death. Again, however, the metaphor adds to the picture: for, by presenting the stones as a cloak, Hektor seems deliberately to allude to Paris' preoccupation with show rather than substance.

As in the case of formulas, themes and similes, the traditional nature of a metaphor need not affect the vividness of its contribution to the narrative; rather, metaphor brings to its context the entirety of the image's meaning from its other appearances in the poem, and in the oral tradition generally, and this in turn enhances the novelty of each particular occurrence.

See further, Moulton 1979.

(c) Ring composition

Ring composition is a device which aids the composer in the organization of his narrative: in its simplest form, a passage is structured to end in just the same way, and sometimes the same words, as it began; and at its most complex, all the elements of the second half of a passage match all the elements of the first half, but exactly reversed. One of the most complete examples is the story of Niobe in *Iliad* 24, which Achilleus tells to Priam to induce him to break his fast and eat with him (24. 599–620). Willcock (1976.273) has analysed the scene as follows:

a	In the morning you may take your son back (599–601)
b	Now let us eat (601)
c	For even Niobe ate (602–3)
d	Her twelve children had been killed (603–6)
e	Niobe's offence (607–8)
d'	Her children were eventually buried (609–12)
c'	She ate food (613)
b'	Let us also eat (618–19)
a'	Afterwards you may take your son back (619–20)

where abcde are precisely balanced, in reverse, by a'b'c'd'e. The aim of the composer is to include additional material, in this case an anecdote, in his narrative, and then to bring his audience back to the narrative by the same route he took them into the anecdote, and so, as it were, to close the ring. Ring composition is often used when a character recalls a past exploit, in order to lend colour to, or provide a precedent for, a present action: as such, it is a technique often associated with the aged Nestor.

See further, Lohmann 1970.

(d) Zielinski's Rule

The directness which is such a feature of Homer's narrative is partly a result of the convention that he describes events successively, even when those events actually occur simultaneously (Whitman and Scodel 1981): this convention is known as Zielinski's Rule (Zielinski 1899). Occasionally Homer will break off his account of a particular scene in order to describe a different, but simultaneous, scene: in such cases he holds the first description in suspension until he has completed the second, and then he reverts to the first scene which has remained exactly as it was left. So, for example, at the end of *Iliad* 11 the Achaians have suffered terrible defeat; the healer Machaon lies wounded in Nestor's shelter, and he is given a cup of wine to help restore him (11. 640); Nestor then persuades Patroklos to hurry to Achilleus' shelter, to try to persuade him to intervene on behalf of the Achaians. At this point the scene in Nestor's tent is interrupted, and Homer turns away to describe the great battle for the Achaian wall in *Iliad* 12 and the Achaian recovery in *Iliad* 13. Not until *Iliad* 14 does Homer return his narrative to Nestor's shelter, where the old man is still sitting cup in hand (14. 1), and Machaon is still waiting for treatment to his wound (14. 6–7), both apparently frozen in time. As in the case of ring composition, the convention is explained by the demands of composing orally for a listening audience, for by telling events successively, the poet is better able to hold its attention.

(e) Foreshadowing and retardation

Telling his audience in advance the outcome of a particular scene, or of a much larger-scale event in the poem, is a technique the poet uses often to engage its attention, which he achieves 'not in spite of the reader's foreknowledge, but by means of it' (Duckworth 1966.53). The technique helps the listener to organize events in his own mind so that, in effect, he is able to locate the narrative at any point within the foreshadowed story pattern. For example, the general introductory statement of the theme of the poem, 'the anger of Peleus' son Achilleus and its devastation' (1. 1–2), is expanded soon afterwards when Achilleus appeals to his goddess mother Thetis to go to ask the favour of Zeus:

> '. . . if perhaps he might be willing to help the Trojans,
> and pin the Achaians back against the ships and the water,
> dying, so that thus they may all have profit of their own king,
> that Atreus' son wide-ruling Agamemnon may recognize
> his madness, that he did no honour to the best of the Achaians.'
>
> (1. 408–12)

In broadest outline, this speech foreshadows the course of the *Iliad* until the moment when Agamemnon finally acknowledges his error and hands over his splendid gifts to Achilleus in token of their reconciliation (19. 78–265). However, the foreshadowing discloses little of the detail of intervening events, and conceals the terrible irony that the culmination of the Achaians' defeat requested by Achilleus will be the death of his dearest companion Patroklos at the hands of Hektor. Furthermore, as the theme of Achilleus' anger moves to its climax, Patroklos begs Achilleus to be allowed to fight in his armour, in the hope that this will rally the Achaians and rout the Trojans; in reality, it will result in his own death, and Homer has no hesitation in foreshadowing this outcome in his comment on Patroklos' appeal: 'So he spoke supplicating in his great innocence; this was his own death and evil destruction he was entreating' (16. 46–7).

Alongside foreshadowing is another important technique, retardation, as Homer raises expectations that the moment he has foreshadowed is approaching, but then defers its fulfilment: so, Zeus may nod his head in formal agreement to Thetis' request that he honour Achilleus by granting victory to the Trojans (1. 528–30), but in fact it is not until *Iliad* 9 that the Achaians make their first approach to Achilleus. And having described in *Iliad* 11 and 12 the Trojan victory which at last fulfils Zeus' promise to Thetis, Homer unexpectedly announces that Zeus' attention now wanders from the battlefield (13. 1–9), and the result is that the Achaians are able to stage a rally during Books 13 and 14 which effectively reverses the situation which the poet has taken the two previous books to establish. For all its obvious artificiality, the technique allows the poet to expand his narrative considerably, but retain the attention of his audience who continue to wait expectantly for the promised outcome.

See further, Morrison 1992.

(f) Focalization

Readers of Homer often observe that his objectivity is a distinctive characteristic of his narrative style. In the sense that only very seldom does he refer to himself, this is true: a famous exception is his declaration that, without the help of the Muses on Olympos, he could not tell of the many leaders of the different parts of the Achaian army at Troy, 'not if I had ten tongues and ten mouths, not if I had a voice never to be broken and a heart of bronze within me' (2. 489–90). However, in the sense that the poet seldom gives his own view and interpretation of events, that is, his own focalization (De Jong 1987), it is clearly not true. As early as the second line of the poem, he describes the anger of Achilleus as *oulomenen*, destructive, translated by Lattimore 'and its devastation': he has chosen not to pass a moral judgment on the anger, he presents it as neither right nor wrong, neither justified nor unjustified; but his choice of description nonetheless is his own characterization of the anger, in that he presents it as the direct cause of the terrible destruction of Achaians and Trojans he is about to recount. As has often been observed, very seldom is there description of the personalities of the poem's characters; instead, they, and their thoughts and emotions, emerge naturally from their actions, words and gestures: that is, the poet continually presents the focalization of his characters also, their view and interpretation of events. It is a part of the audience's role, therefore, to differentiate the focalization of the poet from that of his characters. For example, when Homer tells that Achilleus, having killed Hektor, 'thought of shameful treatment' for his body (22. 395)—that is, his decision to deny him burial and to drag the body behind his chariot around the tomb of Patroklos—it is obviously important that the reader decides whether 'shameful' represents Homer's focalization, that is, his condemnation of the actions of Achilleus, or whether it is Achilleus' own, that is, it describes his motive in thus treating Hektor's body, his attempt to inflict as much shame as possible on his enemy even in death.

See further, Richardson 1990; Rabel 1997.

8. The hero

The story of the *Iliad* is of gods and of heroes: all other characters are secondary, and gain definition only from their relations with the heroes. The status and role of women in the poem is restricted to their kinship with, and their interaction with, the heroes: so, Helen is wife, first of Menelaos, and later of Paris; Andromache is wife of Hektor; Hekabe is mother of Hektor; and Briseis is concubine of Achilleus. Ordinary soldiers appear only in order to be killed by the heroes, although sometimes a brief story may be included to heighten the importance or the pathos of the occasion of their death. The one ordinary soldier to be given a featured role, Thersites, is described in such terms as to make him, physically, the very opposite of the hero (2. 212–19). Old men, Nestor amongst the Achaians and Priam amongst the Trojans, though no longer properly capable of fighting, retain the attributes of heroes and, particularly Nestor, are regarded as their equals because of their past exploits.

Although they are themselves mortal, the heroes attract the attention, and often the protection, of the immortals; and although that attention may often involve the apparently supernatural, the heroes themselves remain firmly in the natural world. In their strength, in their passions, and in their achievements, the heroes far surpass the mortals of Homer's own day (cf. 5. 303–4), yet Homer is careful to avoid any suggestion that their excellence is based on the magical. So there is no place in the *Iliad* for the tradition that Achilleus' body, except for his heel, had been made invulnerable when his mother dipped him at birth into the waters of the river Styx; so too the tradition that Achilleus was raised by the Centaur Cheiron, half-man half-beast, is carefully suppressed, in favour of the story that he was raised by Phoinix who acted as a surrogate father to him (11. 831n).

When Achilleus rejects Agamemnon's offer of compensation for the offence he suffered in *Iliad* 1, he declares, amongst other things, that 'we are all held in a single honour, the brave with the weaklings'

(9. 319). The honour (*time*) that Achilleus speaks of represents the regard, or estimation, a hero is held in by the other heroes, and in his great speech of rejection Achilleus is complaining that, despite his courage in always fighting at the front, he is regarded no differently from the coward and weakling, by implication Agamemnon himself. The hero's aim is to promote his *time*, and, as the indicator of his success, he receives a prize (*geras*) when spoils are distributed: so the cause of the initial dispute between Achilleus and Agamemnon in Book 1 is whether one or other of them is to be deprived of the girl he was given as a *geras*, Agamemnon of Chryseis, or Achilleus of Briseis (1. 133–4). In his pursuit of *time*, the hero is driven by his sense of *aidos*, his sense of what befits his status as hero and of what is a cause of shame. For example, when Hektor declares to Andromache that he is unwilling to stay with her within the walls of Troy and to defend his family and people from a position of security there, he says that 'I would feel deep shame (*aidos*) before the Trojans, and the Trojan women with trailing garments' (6. 441–2).

Although Achilleus, for example, is the son of the sea nymph Thetis, Aineias is the son of Aphrodite, and Sarpedon is the son of almighty Zeus himself, these, and all heroes, are nevertheless mortal and must in time confront their mortality. Yet even in death a hero may surpass ordinary mortals, for the glorious deeds which have brought him to his death may also bring him immortal renown (*kleos*), to be remembered for ever in the songs of men: again in his great speech replying to the ambassadors who bring Agamemnon's offer of compensation, Achilleus, speaking of the fate his mother has predicted for him, says 'if I stay here and fight beside the city of the Trojans, my return home is gone, but my glory shall be everlasting' (9. 412–3), whereas failure to fight at Troy will bring him long life, but anonymity.

It is their very mortality, the inevitability of their death, that drives on the heroes in their quest to be the best (*aristos*). The supreme manifestation of the hero is his *aristeia*, a series of military exploits which, however temporarily, reveal him as the best. In his great affirmation of the heroic ethos, Sarpedon declares to Glaukos:

> 'Man, supposing you and I, escaping this battle,
> would be able to live on forever, ageless, immortal,
> so neither would I myself go on fighting in the foremost
> nor would I urge you into the fighting where men win glory.

> But now, seeing that the spirits of death stand close about us
> in their thousands, no man can turn aside nor escape them,
> let us go on and win glory for ourselves, or yield it to others.'
>
> (12. 322–8)

Since no man, hero or ordinary mortal, may escape death, it is best to encounter it at the forefront of battle in pursuit of *time*, for it is from there that *kleos* will be won. And it is just this which differentiates the hero from a god: for a god there is no death, and so there can be no *kleos*; and because for a hero there can be no immortality, it is only his fame which will be remembered for ever.

Because he has proved himself the best in his community, the hero is honoured by his community and looked on as if he is an immortal: he is given pride of place, the choice meats and filled wine cups at the feast, and the best piece of land for his orchard, his vineyard, and his ploughland (12. 310–14); in return, the hero provides his community with leadership, in particular leadership in war, where he fights always in the forefront (12. 315–21). This principle of give and take, or reciprocity, underpins the hero's relations, not just with the community below him, but with his fellow heroes also. By rendering a favour to another, a hero creates the expectation of a favour in return, by giving a gift he creates the expectation of a gift in return, and by providing hospitality he creates the expectation of hospitality in return. In each case there is an expectation that the return will match the original, that the reciprocity will be balanced, that neither party will seek to gain from the transaction: and the result is an ethical system to which all heroes subscribe, and which binds together their society in trust and mutual dependency. It is precisely this system which underpins the Achaian expedition to Troy, in which each of the Achaian heroes honours the reciprocal debt he owes to Menelaos and Agamemnon. When, for whatever reason, the exchange is not balanced, when one party seeks to gain an advantage over the other, then disruption follows. When Trojan Glaukos and Achaian Diomedes seal the ancestral friendship they have discovered by exchanging armour on the battlefield, and Glaukos gives his armour of gold, worth a hundred oxen, in exchange for Diomedes' armour of bronze, worth only nine, there is such a breach of convention that the poet feels the need to explain that Zeus has stolen away the wits of Glaukos (6. 234–6n). And when Agamemnon, far from exchanging gifts with Achilleus, forcibly removes the gift he has already given, an act, that is, of negative reciprocity, the outrage to convention is such that Achilleus withdraws his services in battle, and none denies his right to do so.

See further, Nagy 1979; Goldhill 1991; Van Wees 1992; Gill, Postlethwaite and Seaford 1998.

9. The gods

It was claimed by Herodotos (2.53) that

> whence each of the gods came into being, or whether they had all for ever existed, and what outward form they had, the Greeks knew not till (so to say) a very little while ago; for I suppose that the time of Hesiod and Homer was not more than four hundred years before my own; and these are they who taught the Greeks of the descent of the gods, and gave to all their several names, and honours, and arts, and declared their outward forms
>
> (Godley 1966.341)

A literal reading of Herodotos' claim may no longer be valid, but his words nevertheless reflect the important role the gods play in the Homeric poems; and, it may be suggested, their role reflects the perception of the gods held by the poems' audiences and in turn helped to mould that perception.

In the Homeric poems the family of the gods comprises a society in parallel to that of humans, sharing, on occasion, their ambitions and reversals, their passions and their experiences. For the most part they inhabit the heights of Mount Olympos, and from there they observe the progress of mortals. At their head stands Zeus, who is known as 'the father of gods and men' (1. 544). Zeus achieved his all-powerful position through his violent overthrow of his father Kronos, and he is set to remain in that position until, and unless, he is himself overthrown. His position has been challenged in the past (1. 396–400), and he remains constantly ready for challenge in the future (15. 174–83). As such, Zeus is the divine counterpart of a mortal hero: Agamemnon, for example, similarly has his authority at home challenged during his absence at Troy by his cousin Aigisthos, and he will be violently overthrown by him on his return to Mykenai; and the position of Odysseus too is continually challenged by his wife's suitors during his absence from Ithaka. Connected with this is the tradition that Zeus' position was inextricably bound up with that of Achilleus himself: that Achilleus' mother, the sea nymph Thetis, was courted by Zeus, but that, when he was warned that she was fated to produce a child who would be greater than his father, Zeus gave her as bride to the mortal Peleus, and the mortal child of the union was Achilleus. Accordingly, the very survival of Zeus as the greatest of the immortals was contingent upon the mortality of the greatest of the heroes, Achilleus (1. 352n): had Achilleus been born a god, he would have overthrown Zeus and become supreme himself.

Throughout the poem the gods interfere in human affairs. In part, this is a consequence of the fact that some favoured mortals have divine ancestors: for example, Zeus is both father to Sarpedon and, via another son Herakles, grandfather to Tlepolemos, and when these two confront each other on the battlefield, Sarpedon kills Tlepolemos with a spear to the throat, while Zeus protects his son Sarpedon from a spear to the thigh (5. 628–62). In part too, the gods' interference results from their taking sides in the conflict, to the extent that they even draw up their own battle-lines and fight a series of single combats against each other (21. 385–520).

On occasion, a god promotes the action by putting it into a character's mind to act in a particular way: for example, Achilleus responds to the plague sent by Phoibos Apollo to devastate the Achaian army by summoning an assembly, 'a thing put into his mind by the goddess of the white arms, Hera' (1. 55), and during this assembly there erupts the quarrel between Achilleus and Agamemnon whose consequences will dominate the poem. Similarly at the end of the poem, Priam's visit to the shelter of Achilleus to ransom the body of his son Hektor is put into his mind by Iris, sent as a messenger to him by Zeus (24. 142–6); and Achilleus' agreement to Priam's request is likewise motivated by a divine visit, that of his mother Thetis (24. 120–37). Yet this is by no means a general rule, and many of the most significant moments of the poem occur with no divine action at all.

A god may appear to a mortal in a dream, as when Zeus sends Dream to deceive Agamemnon into arming the Achaians for battle (2. 1–6); or a god may adopt a disguise in order to walk amongst mortals, as when Hermes takes the form of a young nobleman so that he may assist Priam's passage through the Achaian camp to the shelter of Achilleus (24. 339–48). In either case, the mortal will remain unaware of the god, unless the god chooses to reveal himself; but for the character, and for the listening audience, the divine intervention is real, not simply metaphor. Of these two examples of divine intervention in the mortal world, the second results in the reconciliation of Achilleus with the enemy king, and in a final moment in the poem of peace and harmony, albeit temporary; yet, quite the opposite, the first leads eventually to the violent destruction of the Achaian army, which has the sole purpose of gratifying Achilleus' desire for revenge for the insult he has suffered at the hands of Agamemnon. In neither case does the god's action result from a moral sense of right or wrong, but rather from his wish to repay a service rendered to him: Zeus agrees to the release of Hektor's body and to the safe journey of Priam through the Achaian camp because

> '. . . He [Hektor] never failed of gifts to my liking.
> Never yet has my altar gone without fair sacrifice,
> the smoke and the savour of it, since that is our portion of honour'
> (24.68–70)

Similarly, Zeus agrees to Thetis' request for the Achaians' destruction, because she reminds him of the favour he owes her for past services (1. 503–4); and the reservation he entertains about granting her request derives from his anxiety about his wife Hera's reaction (1. 518–21), not from any distress at the Achaians' resulting fate.

A result of divine intervention may sometimes be a scene which the reader finds repugnant, not least because the intervention appears quite unnecessary. For example, at the climax of his assault on the Trojans, Patroklos comes face to face with Hektor and with his death: yet, far from presenting his death at Hektor's hands alone, Homer describes how Patroklos is first disabled by Apollo, who strikes him on the back, dashes his helmet, shield and breastplate to the ground, and shatters the spear in his grasp (16.788–804). Whether the description is designed to win sympathy or respect for Patroklos, or to enhance the glory of Hektor by means of this show of divine support, the reader may be disturbed by such direct intervention. Similarly, at the moment of Hektor's own death at the hands of Achilleus, the intervention of the goddess Athene, who takes the form of Hektor's brother Deiphobos and persuades him to stand and face Achilleus, is as distasteful to the reader as it appears unnecessary (22.225–37).

The gods' causation of events in the poem comprises one half of what has been termed 'double motivation' (Taplin 1992.99), that is, the belief that gods and humans share responsibility in human affairs. For example when Agamemnon, desperately trying to explain and to excuse his role in the catastrophic quarrel with Achilleus, claims that he himself was not to blame but rather it was the delusion (*ate*) Zeus inflicted upon him, he at one and the same time accepts both his own mistake in antagonizing Achilleus and also Zeus' role in sending it upon him (9. 115–19). Similarly when Achilleus, in the very act of drawing his sword and on the very point of running Agamemnon through, is physically restrained by the goddess Athene, this is not simply a representation of his change of mind: indeed he did change his mind, but it must therefore be concluded that a god must have restrained him (1. 194–8).

Homer's characters do not look to their gods for moral guidance: since the gods are wholly anthropomorphic and since their actions reveal them as wholly amoral, they are in no position to provide it. As Crotty (1994.78) puts it:

> the gods plan out the largest outlines of human affairs without regard to the human misery that will result. The point is not the malice or even the cruel indifference of the gods. Rather, it is a comfort to the distressed to refer the painfulness of emotions to a source having little to do with the emotion.

Instead the characters look to influence their gods, through a system of reciprocal favours: so Priam is able to claim that, even though doomed to die, his son Hektor received the gods' favour, because '[he] never forgot in his halls the gods who live on Olympos. Therefore they remembered him even in death's stage' (24. 427–8). At the poem's end, Achilleus provides Priam with a vivid illustration of the gods' dealings with mortals, when he tells of the two urns that stand on the door-sill of Zeus, the one containing evils, the other containing blessings (24. 527–33). From these urns, Achilleus declares, man receives from Zeus at one time a mixture of evils and blessings, and at another the gift of evils alone, but he gives no indication that this distribution is intended as reward or punishment for human behaviour; instead his unspoken, pessimistic, conclusion seems to be that man receives his gifts at the whim of god. And when a god forsakes a mortal and leaves him to his fate, as when Apollo finally abandons

Hektor, Homer reports the plain fact, without comment and without complaint (22. 213). Longinus (*On the Sublime* 9) concludes:

> In his accounts of the wounds suffered by the gods, their quarrels, their vengeful actions, their tears, their imprison- ment, and all their manifold passions, Homer seems to me to have done everything in his power to make gods of the men fighting at Troy, and men of the gods. But while for us mortals, if we are miserable, death is appointed as a refuge from our ills, Homer has given the gods immortality, not only in their nature, but also in their misfortunes.
>
> (Dorsch 1965.111)

See further, Lesky 1961; Severyns 1966; Kullmann 1985; Erbse 1986; Emlyn-Jones 1992; Bardollet 1997.

ILIAD 1

Homer declares the theme of the poem in the first line, the Anger of Achilleus. The anger results from a violent quarrel between Achilleus, the finest Greek warrior, and Agamemnon, the leader of the Greek expedition to Troy, apparently over the disputed possession of two female prisoners; but in reality the quarrel is about honour and leadership, and reflects a long-standing animosity between the two. The aged Nestor tries, and fails, to settle the quarrel, and Achilleus declares that he will no longer fight for the Greeks; he also persuades his mother, the goddess Thetis, to intervene with Zeus to bring defeat on the Greeks for the dishonour he has suffered. Achilleus retires to his shelter and does not reappear until Book 9 when the defeated Greeks send an embassy to try to persuade him to return to their defence.

1–7 The first seven lines of the poem form a preamble (Greek *prooimion*), in which the poet states his subject. In the Greek, but not in Lattimore's translation, the first word is **the anger** (*menis*), which focuses the reader's attention on this as the theme the poet has chosen from the many tales that make up the saga of the Trojan War. The **goddess** is the Muse, on whom the poet calls for inspiration by inviting her to sing the tale herself using him as her medium.

2   and its devastation. Homer points not just to the devastating effect of Achilleus' anger, but that it was on his own side that he inflicted it. In his anger Achilleus will pray that victory be granted to the Trojans; but it will be his tragedy that the victory will also bring the death of his dearest companion Patroklos. **Achaians** is Homer's more usual name for the Greeks, though he also refers to them as Argives and Danaans.

4–5   the delicate feasting of dogs. The heroes constantly threaten each other that they will give their enemies' body to the dogs, but in fact none suffers this fate. The **will of Zeus** refers to the plan which Zeus hatches with Achilleus' mother, the goddess Thetis, later in this book to bring glory to Achilleus by arranging the defeat of the Achaians; there was a later belief that Zeus sent the Trojan War to cure the problem of the world's over-population.

6   **when first there stood in division of conflict.** Homer indicates to his audience at what point in the ten years of the Trojan War he is beginning his tale: he assumes that his audience knows the saga already, and so does not even mention the war itself.

7   **Atreus' son the lord of men** is Agamemnon the leader of the Greek expedition to Troy. Homer draws the contrast between the two heroes who are soon to quarrel: on the one hand the military and political authority of Atreus' son, Agamemnon, on the other **brilliant Achilleus**, the Achaians' finest warrior. It is Achilleus' unwillingness to accept the authority of Agamemnon which lies at the heart of their quarrel.

9   **the king** is Agamemnon. From the outset Homer makes it clear that the blame for the problems which beset the Achaians lies with him. The god **Apollo** is the principal supporter of the Trojans; **the foul pestilence** he sends takes the form of a nine-day attack with his bow and arrows, causing the death of many Achaians.

11–14   The occasion for the quarrel of Achilleus and Agamemnon is provided by the introduction of **Chryses, priest of Apollo**, who takes his name from his home town of Chryse (37), and in turn gives his name to his daughter Chryseis (111). Chryses begs before the Achaian assembly for the return of his daughter. Homer gives none of the background to his appeal, not even that the girl has been given to Agamemnon as his prize of war (*geras*): the effect is to pare the scene down to its bare essentials, and so to focus exclusively on the exchange of Chryses and Agamemnon. The **ribbons of Apollo** indicate Chryses' role as priest, the **gifts beyond count** his status as suppliant; both emphasize the outrageousness of Agamemnon's rejection of his appeal, and this is understood by the rest of the Achaians, when they demand respect for him as priest and when they recognize the worth of his suppliant's ransom (22–3).

15   **supplicated all the Achaians.** The theme of supplication (Crotty 1994) appears at many of the most important moments of the poem: as well as the present scene, there is the supplication of Achilleus in

Book 9 by Odysseus, Phoinix and Aias; the supplication of Achilleus
by Patroklos in Book 16; and the supplication of Achilleus by Priam
in Book 24. This first supplication, by Chryses for the return of his
daughter, is paralleled by the last, by Priam for the return of his
son Hektor; and the generosity Achilleus shows Priam in the final
scene is in contrast to the roughness of Agamemnon's rejection of
Chryses' supplication here.

24   **this pleased not the heart of Atreus' son Agamemnon.** No
explanation is offered of Agamemnon's rejection of Chryses' appeal,
but during the quarrel he will declare that it would be 'unfitting'
(119) for him alone to be without a prize of war. The prize given to
a hero represents the honour (*time*) in which he is held by the
others, and so loss of his prize represents the loss of honour.

28   The **staff and the god's ribbons** indicate the sanctity of the
supplication Chryses has made, but Agamemnon dismisses them
with such contempt that he does not deign even to name the god,
Apollo. He is an autocrat who cares nothing for the feelings of
either his army or an aged father, or for the possible consequences
from the god: this sets the tone for his quarrel with Achilleus.

30–1   **in my own house, in Argos.** Agamemnon's city is in fact
Mykenai; here he uses the name of the city of Argos to refer to the
Greek homeland generally. There seems to be calculated cruelty as
he three times points up the isolation of the girl from her father—
in Argos, far from her own land and **in my bed.** Agamemnon's
declaration that Chryseis will continue to be his concubine when
they return home shows insensitivity towards his wife Klytaimestra;
when he did in fact return home after the war with a concubine,
Kassandra, his wife exacted full vengeance.

35   **the old man prayed as he walked in solitude.** The repetition of
'old man' from 33 emphasizes the priest's vulnerability and contrasts
with Agamemnon's contemptuous use (26). The image of the
individual alone on the beach is employed on a number of occasions
to convey grief or anger; for example, Achilleus will be alone on
the beach when he too calls upon a god, his mother Thetis (350n).

37   **lord of the silver bow.** Homer emphasizes Apollo's role as archer
god (cf. 'who strikes from afar' 15; 21) because of the plague he is
about to send with his bow and arrows, and also his role as protector
of the Trojan region, represented by the island of **Tenedos** and the
towns of **Killa** and **Chryse**, where Chryses himself is priest; the

curious title **Smintheus**, 'Mouse god', may refer to Apollo's role as protector of crops against the plague of mice.

40   **if ever it pleased you.** Chryses lists the services he has given to Apollo, and so establishes the grounds for the god to return his favour. Paying careful attention to the detail of offerings and ritual was crucial in securing a god's favour, and failure to do so might lead to catastrophe (cf. 64–5); but it by no means guaranteed the favour of the god, and the pathos of the human condition in the poem is reflected in the gods' often casual disregard and dismissal of appeals (cf. 6. 311). The **rich thigh pieces** were the parts of the sacrificed animal offered to the gods, wrapped around in layers of fat laid on the fire, and wafted in the smoke to the gods above; the rest of the animal was shared out as a feast (cf. 458–68).

47   **He came as night comes down.** This is the first of only three similes in this book. It characterizes the menace of the occasion, conveying both the speed and suddenness of the god's approach; it presents too a picture of the all-enveloping nature of the god's presence in the camp, like that of night's darkness (Edwards 1980.10).

54   **Achilleus called the people to assembly.** The Agamemnon–Chryses episode has revealed Agamemnon as the man of authority over the army; the following assembly scene shows Achilleus as the man of the army, aware of its plight and sympathetic to it, and bitterly opposed to Agamemnon. It is significant therefore that it is Achilleus who responds to the crisis by summoning the meeting of the assembly.

55–6 **a thing put into his mind by the goddess of the white arms, Hera.** This kind of direct intervention by a god is a common way of motivating human actions in the poem. Hera is sister and wife of Zeus. Just as Apollo proves to be a leading supporter, not just of Chryses, but of the Trojans generally, so Hera will be an equally staunch supporter of the Achaians. The **pity** she displays for the Achaians' plight reflects the concern of Achilleus himself in calling the assembly.

62–4 **why Phoibos Apollo is so angry.** Achilleus displays considerable sensitivity, since it would be easy enough for him to blame Agamemnon's recent behaviour towards Chryses for their troubles and to advocate the return of the priest's daughter; but it would be easy enough also to predict Agamemnon's response to such a suggestion. However what is unacceptable coming from Achilleus might be acceptable coming from **some holy man, some prophet.**

65   A **hecatomb** is technically the sacrifice of a hundred cattle, but is used of the sacrifice of any type of animal in large numbers.

69–71   **Kalchas, Thestor's son.** The detailed introduction of Kalchas as the best of all soothsayers, whose interpretations are therefore always correct, seems designed to highlight the irrationality of Agamemnon's outburst at him that he only ever predicts evil things for him (106–8). **who guided into the land of Ilion** (Troy) may be an oblique reference to the events at Aulis at the launch of the expedition, when Kalchas persuaded Agamemnon to sacrifice his own daughter Iphigeneia to Artemis.

80–3   **a king when he is angry.** Although Kalchas does not name him, it would be difficult to conclude that this picture of vindictiveness and contempt for underlings refers to anyone other than Agamemnon, who has so recently behaved in just this way towards the priest. Kalchas is inviting Achilleus to draw that conclusion, and his emphasis on power and kingship (of Agamemnon) can only serve to provoke Achilleus: Kalchas knows his leaders well.

86–91   **In the name of Apollo.** Achilleus swears in the name of Apollo, the god to whom Agamemnon has given such grave offence, and his offer virtually to lay down his life in defence of the suppliant seer contrasts with Agamemnon's treatment of the suppliant priest. The addition of **'even if you mean Agamemnon'** shows that he has drawn the natural conclusion from Kalchas' description, but it is a provocation nevertheless. **who now claims to be far the greatest of all the Achaians:** Donlan (1979) has described the conflict between Achilleus and Agamemnon through the nature of authority in the poem: he calls the authority of Agamemnon 'position authority', which he exercises by virtue of his position as acknowledged leader, as commander of the largest section of the assembled forces (cf. 281); he terms the authority of Achilleus 'standing authority', based on his standing as the hero of greatest fighting ability. The norm is where the same individual exercises both types of authority, indeed where the commander's position results from his standing as greatest warrior. Achilleus' dismissive **'claims to be'** highlights the anomaly of Agamemnon's position as commander. On the development of the quarrel, see Pucci 1998.179ff.

99   **without price, without ransom.** Homer's heroes continually strive
to acquire honour (*time*) and the respect of their fellow-heroes
(Adkins 1982). As the tangible symbol of this respect, of his standing
within his heroic community, a hero might point to the prize of
war (*geras*) awarded to him by his community at the sacking of a
city (Introduction, 8). It is in these heroic terms that Agamemnon
will view the coming events: for the girl Chryseis is his*geras*, and
his surrender of her will bring him humiliation, for he will gain no
compensation for her.

103   **the heart within filled black.** The heart was seen as the seat of
the emotions: the contrasting imagery of the blackness of his heart
and the blazing fire in his eyes throws each into dramatic relief.

106–8   **never yet have you told me a good thing.** It is possible that
Agamemnon is here alluding to Kalchas' prophecy at Aulis about
the sacrifice of Iphigeneia (cf. 69–71n), but he is displaying a real
sense of persecution in implying, irrationally, that Kalchas could
ever foretell anything other than the truth.

113–18   **I like her better than Klytaimestra.** Agamemnon may simply
be overstating his case, but again this is gratuitously insulting to his
wife (cf. 30–1n). His previous reference to Chryseis marked her as
merely his slave and concubine, and, for all that he protests his
affection for her, he immediately agrees to surrender her; so it
seems clear that it is his loss of face Agamemnon dreads, not the
loss of the girl herself. He does not insist that he be given another
girl, merely **some prize that shall be my own** to confirm that he is
still held in the same high regard. So he sees it purely as a matter of
honour.

122–9   **greediest for gain of all men.** Achilleus' insult is a
misrepresentation of Agamemnon's stance on a point of honour,
and so a provocation. There is a parallel, and an irony too, in the
experience of the two antagonists, since the advice which Achilleus
urges on Agamemnon, to accept a short-term loss and in return **we
Achaians thrice and four times over will repay you** is the same he
will himself receive from the goddess Athene as he contemplates
killing Agamemnon (213).

134–9   **Are you ordering me to give this girl back?** Achilleus of course
did not, and could not, *order* Agamemnon to give back the girl;
rather he offered him a deal to try to persuade him. So
Agamemnon's language is significant in revealing that he senses a

challenge to his authority from Achilleus. Agamemnon's threat to take **your own prize, or that of Aias, or that of Odysseus** appears to be a general one, but the names he gives are significant: after Achilleus himself, Aias is recognized as the principal warrior of the Achaians, and Odysseus by his record proves that he is their greatest strategist. So there is also something very specific about Agamemnon's threat—not any *geras* will do, only that of one of the foremost heroes. His threat to take another's girl **going myself in person** proves an empty one when in the event he sends two heralds to perform the task (320–1).

145   **Aias** is Ajax son of Telamon, who leads the contingent from the island of Salamis, **Idomeneus** heads the army from the island of Krete, and **Odysseus** brought his army from the island of Ithaka.

146   **or you yourself, son of Peleus.** Even at this moment of apparent conciliation Agamemnon finds it necessary to assert his position of authority, for it can hardly be supposed that he is extending to Achilleus a hand of friendship, or an honour, by suggesting, in the same breath as threatening to take his girl, that he be responsible for taking Chryseis back to her father. Nor is it likely that the phrase *ekpaglotat' andron* is intended as the compliment which Lattimore's 'most terrifying of all men' would suggest: 'most excessive of all men' is nearer the meaning (Kirk 1985.68).

148–9   **looking darkly** is one of the most common gestures in the poem: 'the speaker, whatever his message, transmits by his facial demeanor that an infraction of propriety has occurred; he deplores the willful traducing of rules of conduct governing relations between subordinates and inferiors' (Holoka 1983.2). By accusing Agamemnon of having **your mind forever on profit**, Achilleus again seems to be deliberately misrepresenting the point of honour on which he has taken his stand (cf. 122–9n).

153–5   **to me they have done nothing.** For Achilleus and for the other heroes, fighting for a cause essentially means seeking revenge for personal harm or insult; they do not go to war to fight for the flag. **Phthia** is Achilleus' home in Thessaly.

159   **to win your honour and Menelaos'.** This is the first reference to the cause of the war, and even this remains vague, since there is no mention of Paris' abduction of Helen, the wife of Menelaos. Lying behind Achilleus' words is the story that Helen's father Tyndareus made all her suitors swear an oath (2. 286) that, if ever

she was abducted, they would unite in pursuit (Ps.–Hesiod *Catalogue of Women* 68. 89–100). The reason Achilleus gives is only partially true: regardless of the story of the oath they swore, the heroes would have mutual obligations to lend assistance in times of trouble, but a hero chooses a career of heroic combat as being the most acceptable way of life, granted that he, like all mortals, must one day die anyway (Gill 1996.134); neither Achilleus nor any other hero joined the expedition to win honour exclusively for another, although Menelaos will acknowledge that Patroklos died 'for the sake of my honour' (17. 92).

167–8 **I with some small thing yet dear to me.** 'Achilleus pictures himself as a helpless creature fed on scraps' (Redfield 1975.13). When he is threatened with the loss of even these scraps, Achilleus is faced with exactly the same humiliation as Agamemnon (cf. 99n); but whereas Agamemnon's surrender of his girl will benefit the whole Achaian army, in Achilleus' case it will serve only to gratify Agamemnon.

171 **pile up your wealth and your luxury.** The Greek *aphussein*, 'pile up', has a literal meaning of taking liquid from one vessel to another, perhaps water from the well to the bucket: later in this book it describes Hephaistos drawing nectar from the mixing bowl to serve to the other gods (597–8). So the metaphor suggests the image of Achilleus as inferior, as servant performing menial tasks for his master.

175 **above all Zeus of the counsels.** Agamemnon will prove to be gravely mistaken in believing that Zeus will show him honour, for when Thetis requests Zeus' honour for her son Achilleus (505), Zeus promises to grant it to him (528).

178–80 **if you are very strong indeed, that is a god's gift** Achilleus does indeed have such a gift, as the son of a goddess mother; but his father Peleus is a mortal, and so Achilleus must himself die in time. By saying that Achilleus' greater prowess as a warrior is the gift of a god, Agamemnon is seeking to belittle both it and him. Similarly his declaration **'be king over the Myrmidons'** is designed to give Achilleus a status which is far inferior to his own as leader of the entire Achaian expedition.

184 **the fair-cheeked Briseis** is Achilleus' prize of war; like Chryseis (cf. 11–14n), she too takes her name from her father Briseus (392).

186 By describing himself as **greater** (*pherteros*), Agamemnon is

referring to his political power, his position authority, and is contrasting it with his description of Achilleus as 'very strong' (*karteros* 178). When later on Nestor tries to heal the divisions caused by the quarrel, he draws just the same distinction between the two (280–1).

194–5 Athene descended from the sky. The killing of Agamemnon by Achilleus is dramatically impossible, as he must survive the war to be murdered on his return home to Mykenai by his wife and her lover. So in part Athene's intervention to restrain Achilleus is a dramatic way of getting round a particular narrative problem; but, like all the scenes involving the gods, it would have been as real to Homer's audience as any scene amongst the humans. The scene is another example of divine motivation of the action (55–6n), rather than simply an indication that Achilleus has changed his mind.

202 Zeus of the aegis. Although the aegis belongs to Zeus, it is used by other gods too: Apollo grips in both hands 'the tempestuous terrible aegis, shaggy, conspicuous, that the bronze-smith Hephaistos had given Zeus to wear to the terror of mortals' (15. 308–10), and Athene threw across her shoulders 'the betasselled, terrible aegis, all about which Terror hangs like a garland, and Hatred is there, and Battle Strength, and heart-freezing Onslaught and thereon is set the head of the grim gigantic Gorgon' (5. 738–41).

214 by reason of this outrage. Athene's description of Agamemnon's behaviour as an 'outrage' (*hybris*) matches Achilleus' own reference to his 'outrageousness' (203); this is important in confirming his view of the events of the quarrel and the rightness of his stance.

218 If any man obeys the gods, they listen to him also. Achilleus defines the reciprocal relationship which Homeric man must establish with his gods if he is to benefit from them (cf. 40n). Athene acknowledged that he had the option not to do as she said—'but will you obey me?' (207)—and Achilleus' words here indicate that his decision not to kill Agamemnon is his own.

224 Atreides means 'son of Atreus', normally referring, as here, to Agamemnon; the plural form, Atreidai refers to Agamemnon and Menelaos.

225–30 You wine sack, with a dog's eyes, with a deer's heart. Agamemnon accused Achilleus of cowardice—'Run away by all means if your heart drives you' (173)—and Achilleus hurls back similar insults: 'wine sack' implies that only a person the worse for drink could act as Agamemnon has done; 'with a dog's eyes' associates him with the dog's tearing of human corpses (cf. 4n); and 'with a deer's heart' refers to the most frequent symbol of fear and cowardice in the poem. Achilleus accuses Agamemnon of stealing the spoil but doing none of the fighting: that is, he accuses him of having no standing authority in the army.

234–9   in the name of this sceptre. The sceptre is held by each man as he speaks in the assembly, when the kings administer Zeus' justice (238–9), and this is an indication of the gravity of Achilleus' oath. That the wood is now dead and will never bear leaf again may represent the finality of the oath, and its removal from the tree of which it was a part may be symbolic of Achilleus' withdrawal from the Achaian army (Easterling 1989).

240–4   some day longing for Achilleus will come to the sons of the Achaians. Achilleus' oath is a statement of the course of the poem up to the despatch of the embassy to him in Book 9, and it provides his reason for rejecting that embassy. His description of himself as **the best of the Achaians** consciously echoes his own sarcastic description of Agamemnon (cf. 86–91n).

247–52   Unlike Achilleus and Agamemnon, Nestor the fair-spoken is introduced in considerable detail: after the great display of power politics and heroic temper, Homer presents the contrasting qualities which Nestor brings to the scene and which give authority to his words—he is an excellent speaker and his long life of some seventy years has given him unrivalled diplomatic skill to deal with hot-headed heroes. His home is **Pylos** in Messenia, in southwest Peloponnese, where a major palace from the Mykenaian age has been uncovered.

259–74   Nestor recalls the battle in which he fought alongside the Lapiths and their king **Peirithoös** against the **beast men living within the mountains,** that is, the Centaurs, and he does so in the form of a ring composition (Introduction, 7(c)): the Centaurs were invited by Peirithoös to his wedding to Hippodameia, but battle broke out when they got drunk and attacked the Lapith women, a scene represented in the sculptures decorating the Parthenon in Athens. **Theseus** was Athens' greatest hero and the subject of many legends, but he plays no part in the saga of the Trojan War; in fact this is his only appearance in the poem. By means of this story Nestor tries to show that, despite his age, he is the equal of any of the present-day warriors, and so should be listened to, and that they should learn a lesson from the past.

275–84   In one breath Nestor urges Agamemnon not to take away Achilleus' prize and so seems to agree with Achilleus, but in the very next he supports the supreme authority of the king, because it is granted to him by Zeus and he carries the sceptre as token of it. Achilleus has just indicated clearly his view of that authority by hurling the sceptre to the ground (245). In calling Achilleus **stronger** (*karteros*) and Agamemnon **greater** (*pherteros*), Nestor uses just the same terms as Agamemnon (cf. 186n). Nestor makes his judgment, from an heroic standpoint, that Agamemnon is the greater because he has more troops at his command; Agamemnon too made this judgment when he dismissed Achilleus as 'king over the Myrmidons' (cf. 178–80n).

287–9   **here is a man who wishes to be above all others.** Agamemnon accuses Achilleus of trying to take over the position authority of commander: this may simply be Agamemnon exaggerating his opponent's claim during the quarrel, but it seems more likely that it reflects a more long-standing grievance in his relationship with Achilleus. His belief that Achilleus wants to **give them their orders** recalls his statement that Achilleus was ordering him to give Chryseis back to her father (134).

291   **they have not given him the right to speak abusively.** In fact abuse was precisely the weapon which Athene allowed to Achilleus when she restrained him from killing Agamemnon (211).

298–9   **I will not fight for the girl's sake.** Athene promised Achilleus that his restraint would be rewarded in the future by 'three times over such shining gifts' (213); the price of his restraint and his future reward is the surrender of his prize Briseis, and so, unlike Agamemnon earlier, he does not demand compensation for her loss. It is important to note that in the Greek **'you take her away who gave her'** refers to all the Achaians, not to Agamemnon alone.

307   **Patroklos** appears here for the first time, and he is named again at 337, but on neither occasion does he speak. He is Achilleus' only close companion at Troy and he withdraws from the battle along with him later in this book; in Book 16 he fights in Achilleus' armour and is killed by the Trojan champion Hektor. His introduction here seems deliberately understated as part of a carefully crafted characterization: it is only very gradually that the audience comes to know the man whose death will mark the turning point in Achilleus' anger.

311   crafty Odysseus. Throughout his own poem the *Odyssey*, he is famous for his intelligence and his cunning: he was responsible for the stratagem of the Trojan Horse, for example. As well as being entrusted here with the return of Chryseis to her father, he also takes on the difficult role of carrying Agamemnon's offer of compensation to Achilleus in Book 9.

313–14   The ritual purification of the Achaians from the pollution of Apollo's plague is a necessary preliminary to offering up sacrifice to him (Parker 1983).

321–5   Agamemnon sends two heralds to fetch Achilleus' girl. In fact he had threatened that he would come himself to Achilleus' shelter (185), so his despatch of the heralds either indicates his hatred of Achilleus or his fear.

341   there shall be need of me to beat back the shameful destruction. As in the case of his oath (cf. 240–4n), Achilleus here foreshadows (Introduction, 7(e)) the future development of the plot.

342   he makes sacrifice. This is a mistake in translation and should in fact read 'rages'.

348   the woman all unwilling went with them still reveals something of the feelings of Briseis, who is given no voice of her own to express them: her words later in the poem (19. 297–9) suggest that it is affection for Achilleus, rather than fear of Agamemnon, which she registers here.

350   beside the beach of the grey sea. Since his mother Thetis is a deity of the sea, it is appropriate that Achilleus should go to the shore to speak to her. However the scene also recalls the earlier occasion when the priest Chryses went to the sea-shore to speak with a god, Apollo, after he too was dishonoured by Agamemnon (cf. 35n); and when Achilleus is visited by Thetis after the death of Patroklos, he also walks along the sea-shore, in grief and in anger (19. 40).

352   you bore me to be a man with a short life. There was a tradition (Pindar *Isthmian Ode* 8) that the sea nymph Thetis was courted by both Zeus and his brother the sea god Poseidon, but that they heard that Thetis was fated to bear a son who would be greater than his father. Had Zeus married Thetis he would have been displaced as king of the gods by his son, just as he himself had deposed his own father Kronos. So Thetis was given instead to a mortal husband, Peleus, and their child Achilleus did indeed grow up to be greater than his father, or than any mortal. It is against this background that Achilleus' lament should be heard, because Zeus' continuing position as king of the gods was in fact predicated upon Achilleus' mortality (Slatkin 1986). Although Homer makes no direct reference to this legend, Achilleus' early death is a constantly recurring theme of the poem which always accompanies the appearance of his mother Thetis.

358   The **aged father** of Thetis is Nereus who with his wife Doris fathered fifty sea nymphs, the Nereids.

363   **Tell me, do not hide it in your mind** does not imply that Achilleus' divine mother does not already know his story; Thetis aims to ease his anger by having him share it.

366–9   **We went against Thebe, the sacred city of Eëtion.** Eëtion is the father of Andromache, wife of Hektor, and Thebe is her home. Unlike Homer's own account of recent events, Achilleus begins with the capture of Chryseis during the sack of Thebe, and so he is able to stress his own role in her capture and thus illustrate his main argument during the quarrel, that he does all the fighting but Agamemnon receives all the rewards (165–7).

380   **The old man went back again in anger.** When Chryses was dismissed by Agamemnon, the old man obeyed him 'in terror' (33), but in Achilleus' version he went back 'in anger', that is, Achilleus credits Chryses with the same reaction as his own.

390   'Lord' gives better sense than **king**, since it refers to Apollo; the gifts are the hecatomb sent as sacrifice to him by Agamemnon (309–10).

396–406   **many times in my father's halls I have heard you.** In fact the more usual version of the legend is that Thetis left the home of her husband Peleus, Achilleus' father, and returned to live with her own father beneath the sea. The story that Thetis summoned **the creature of the hundred hands**, Briareus, to defend Zeus against an attempted overthrow by the other gods may be an adaptation of the famous tale of the battle of the gods against the Titans told by Hesiod (*Theogony* 629–735): the gods were victorious in the battle, because of the help given by the three giants Briareus, Gyas and Kottos, and these three then guarded the Titans who were locked in their prison in Tartaros. The point of the tale here is to stress the role of Thetis in helping Zeus and so provide a good reason why he should return the favour and help her son. **Kronion** means the son of Kronos, that is, Zeus; by the same token Greek Aigaion probably means son of Aigaios, but it is not known who he was.

407–10   take his knees and remind him of these things. Supplication has its own ritual gestures which are necessary if it is to be successful: the suppliant grasps the knees and touches the chin of the person whose favour he is seeking (500–1). In the event Thetis reminds Zeus of none of the details, and in fact Homer achieves far greater pathos by having Achilleus tell the story, since the account of her saving the king of the gods himself only serves to highlight her helplessness when faced by her own son's fate. Achilleus' aim is not the restoration of Briseis but the humiliation of Agamemnon, and his wish to see his own side **back against the ships and the water, dying** to further his aim has led to accusations of selfish pride and lack of patriotism; but since every hero is acting for his own essentially personal motive and in pursuit of his own honour, such terms as patriotism and public duty have no relevance in this context.

412   madness in Greek is *ate*, sometimes translated 'delusion' by Lattimore. Agamemnon will give madness as the reason for his behaviour during the quarrel, just before he sends the embassy to Achilleus (9. 115–19); and during his reconciliation with Achilleus he will also place the blame for the quarrel upon Delusion (19. 91–2). *ate* is sent by heaven to mislead mortals, and at least partly excuses their behaviour; here of course Achilleus is condemning Agamemnon, and so he makes no mention of any interference by a god. Calling himself **the best of the Achaians** recalls the subject of the quarrel (cf. 86–91n).

417   your life must be brief and bitter. Achilleus is the only character who carries with him the certain knowledge that he will die at Troy (cf. 352n). His request here that the Achaians be defeated sets in motion events which will lead inevitably to his own early death.

423   Ocean was thought to be a river which flowed around the rim of the world. The delay of twelve days caused by Zeus' visit to the Aithiopians provides a period during which Achilleus is inactive and brooding on the injustice done to him. This period of inaction is paralleled at the end of the poem by the twelve days of truce given over to the burial of Hektor (24. 664–6); the effect is that the beginning and the end of the poem seem to mirror each other.

430–1   But Odysseus meanwhile drew near to Chryse. Thetis has left to arrange the destruction of the Achaians, which is to be punishment for Agamemnon's seizure of Achilleus' girl Briseis; at the same time, with the return of Chryeis to her father, Homer rounds off the tale of the previous destruction of the Achaians, which was also sent by a god as punishment of Agamemnon. At the very moment Agamemnon is offering amends for his previous error, he is repeating that error and bringing yet further catastrophe on his people.

449   washed their hands: the necessary preliminary ritual of purification before the sacrifice; **barley** represents the most ancient product of agriculture and is scattered as a bloodless offering over the beast to accompany the blood sacrifice.

451–3   Hear me, lord of the silver bow. Chryses' invocation of Apollo is the same as when he called on him to bring the plague down on the Achaian army (36–8). On that occasion he reminded the god of the offerings he had given, the temple he built and the sacrifices he made, because he was seeking a favour in return; but now he merely reminds Apollo of the earlier favour granted because he wishes to unsay it.

458–66   An almost identical description of the ritual of sacrifice is given at 2. 421–9, indicating that this is a traditional theme. The **meat from the thighs** was removed and the bones offered up to the god, and on these bones, wrapped in their layer of fat, were laid strips of flesh from the rest of the animal to represent the whole; along with the libation of wine, this was the god's portion of the communion feast. The wine was diluted with water in the **mixing bowls**: a libation of a few drops of wine was poured by each participant in the feast on to the ground as offering to the god and, as in the case of the meat, the rest was then consumed by the feasters.

488   But that other still sat in anger beside his swift ships. Just as the final image before the long and detailed description of Chryseis' return to her home was of Achilleus 'sorrowing in his heart for the sake of the fair-girdled woman' (429), so too the first image after the intervening scene is of him sitting in anger by his ships. Homer invites the conclusion that throughout this long day and night Achilleus has remained in the same dejected position, and the echoing of the swiftness of the ships in the swiftness of his feet serves to emphasize the immobility of this most active of warriors. This is his final appearance and it is this image which the audience retains of him until he reappears in Book 9.

500–1 By grasping Zeus' knees with her left hand and his chin with her right, Thetis adopts the proper position of the suppliant: by taking this position, the suppliant acknowledges her inferiority and demonstrates her self-abasement before the person she is supplicating.

505   give honour to my son short-lived beyond all other. Thetis seems almost to suggest that Zeus owes her son honour *because* he is to be short-lived (cf. 352n).

516   by how much I am the most dishonoured of all gods. Thetis associates herself totally with her son; his dishonour will be her own.

518–23   This is a disastrous matter is a strange reaction from one who is all-powerful and regarded as such by all the other gods. Zeus' fear is a dramatic device, for the next great scene in this book is to be his quarrel with Hera, which will be the divine equivalent of the quarrel of Achilleus and Agamemnon; so Homer must suggest at least the possibility of resistance from Hera, that she is not simply the meek wife who obeys her husband unquestioningly. There is a certain grim humour in Zeus' portrayal of himself as the hen-pecked husband who, when called upon to take the momentous decision about the fate of the Achaian army, is concerned only about his wife's likely reaction.

524   I will bend my head. This formal gesture marks a turning point in the narrative: Zeus' action sets in motion the dire events of the poem which will lead eventually to the deaths of Patroklos and of Hektor, and ultimately of Achilleus himself.

533–9   all the gods rose up. Zeus' return to his house introduces his quarrel with his wife Hera. This quarrel on Olympos balances the quarrel of Achilleus and Agamemnon, even to the extent of having Hephaistos act as peace-maker (cf. 571–83n) to parallel the role of Nestor. As in the human quarrel, at its heart lies the question of hierarchy and authority, and this is established at the outset as all the gods stand at the approach of Zeus. Zeus and Hera have all the appearance of a bickering mortal man and wife, with Zeus declaring his rights as head of the household and Hera fighting to promote her own interests. Hera speaks **revilingly** and does not hesitate to hurl the first insult, just as Achilleus did at Agamemnon (122).

544 The description of Zeus as **father of gods and men** is particularly fitting at this moment when his authority is challenged.

551 By the time the poem was composed the formula **the ox-eyed lady Hera** had lost its meaning, but it recalls a time when she was worshipped in the form of an animal.

571–83 The role of **Hephaistos** in this quarrel of the gods parallels that of Nestor in the human quarrel: so when he tells of the consequences of the quarrel for the rest of the gods, Hephaistos speaks very much as Nestor did when he predicted the suffering of the Achaians as a result of the quarrel of Achilleus and Agamemnon (254–8). However, there is an essential difference between the appeals made by the two peace-makers. Hephaistos can only appeal to Hera to respect Zeus as king and to give way before his power, because 'he is far too strong for any' (*phertatos*), and this echoes Nestor's word for Agamemnon, *pherteros* (cf. 275–84n). For his part, Nestor appealed to Achilleus to respect Agamemnon as king, but he also asked Agamemnon to respect Achilleus as heroic individual: so there were at least grounds for compromise for them to explore if they chose, but in the quarrel on Olympos nothing is offered to Hera, because Zeus is all-powerful, in all spheres.

590–4 **he caught me by the foot.** On a later occasion Zeus reminds Hera of the occasion he hung her on high, with two anvils attached to her feet and her hands fastened by an unbreakable chain of gold, and says that he threw down to earth any god who made a move to help her (15. 18–24); however there is no indication that Hephaistos here is referring to the same occasion. The **Sintian men** were the inhabitants of the island of Lemnos which was a centre for the worship of Hephaistos.

599–600 **uncontrollable laughter went up.** A potentially explosive situation, threatening real violence to one of the parties (567), has been resolved. The bustling Hephaistos attracts the ridicule of his peers and the community on Olympos benefits as a result; Homer leaves unstated the contrast with the display of heroic pride in the human quarrel and the catastrophe which results for the mortal community.

ILIAD 2

In this, and in succeeding books, Homer undertakes the long narrative task of introducing the background to the quarrel of Book 1, against which the anger of Achilleus will be acted out. In Book 2 his aim is to give an account of the Achaian forces assembled at Troy and those of the Trojans and their allies, an account which gives the book its popular title Catalogue of the Ships; he also describes the mood of the ordinary soldiers in the Achaian army, first by means of a test which Agamemnon sets them, and then through a scene in which one of their number, Thersites, denounces Agamemnon for his treatment of Achilleus.

It seems highly unlikely that the catalogues of this book, of the Achaian and Trojan forces, were Homer's own creations, if only because of the apparent accuracy of some of the description of the geography of Greece in the Late Bronze Age, some four or five centuries before the conventional date for the poet himself. One of the earliest, and most important, functions of oral poetry was to preserve such catalogues. The catalogue of the Achaian forces is a list of the Greek ships which left Aulis for Troy and of the commanders who sailed them; because the action of the poem is set in the tenth year of the war, Homer has no opportunity to describe the Achaians' embarkation, and so he has moved this traditional list to a position where it will serve his dramatic purpose. Full discussions of the contents of the catalogues themselves may be found in Kirk (1985), and Hope Simpson and Lazenby (1970).

3–4 **how he might bring honour to Achilleus,** in response, that is, to Thetis' request (1. 509–10).

12 **now he might take the wide-wayed city.** Zeus exploits the new situation created by the quarrel with considerable psychological insight: after the debacle of the quarrel, Agamemnon might well be tempted to go it alone and show everybody, and Achilleus in particular, that he can indeed manage without him.

20   in the likeness of Nestor. It was Nestor, the paradigm of wise old men, who gave his firm support to Agamemnon during his quarrel with Achilleus (cf. 1. 275–84n); so taking the form of Nestor is likely to make the dream even more convincing.

28–32   As instructed by Zeus, and entirely in keeping with the conventions of oral poetry, Dream repeats his words (11–15) exactly; and Agamemnon in turn repeats them to the assembled Achaian leaders (65–9).

37   he thought that on that very day he would take Priam's city. This is subtle characterization of Agamemnon: Dream has declared only that he might take Troy, but Agamemnon concludes that he will do so, and on this very day. That he should so believe, after nine long years of fruitless struggle and after the loss of his finest warrior, reveals the extent of his delusion.

46   The **sceptre of his fathers** is the symbol of Agamemnon's position authority as king, as Nestor declared during the quarrel (1. 279); it was handed down to him from Zeus himself (cf. 102–8).

72–5   let us see if we can arm the sons of the Achaians. This indicates that there is a doubt in Agamemnon's mind about his troops' loyalty, and this is borne out by their reaction to the test he now makes of them. The **trial** of the army he proposes played no part in Dream's message to him and is his own idea, to give the army the chance to demonstrate its loyalty to him by marching out to battle and to victory. Instead of asking for a vote of confidence, he invites the troops to abandon the expedition, and they respond by rushing headlong to the ships: the fact that Agamemnon can so badly miscalculate the reaction of his soldiers is an indication both of their morale in the aftermath of the quarrel and of his severe limitations as their commander.

80–3   Since Agamemnon has claimed that Dream appeared in his form, it would be difficult for Nestor to deny its reliability, but it is significant that he makes no mention of Agamemnon's scheme to test the army: it is clearly only the first of Agamemnon's proposals he has in mind in calling an end to the council of elders and moving on to the general assembly of the army. Unlike Achilleus, Nestor does not dispute Agamemnon's right to the title **best of the Achaians,** and a meaning 'declares' rather than **claims** may be nearer the mark.

87–90   Like the swarms of clustering bees. The word *ethnea*, 'swarms', is translated 'nations of men' at 91. The simile illustrates an important feature of the Achaians in this book: although they present the appearance of a united national force serving at Troy, in reality their army is the sum of its component parts, the various tribes from the far-flung borders of Greece and its islands, which are to be recounted later in this book. In addition the simile illustrates the discipline of the Achaian army for, in their organization into a working community, the bees surrender themselves to the discipline of the common cause.

103   **Argeïphontes** means 'the slayer of Argos', and refers to Hermes. According to legend, Zeus fell in love with Io a priestess of Hera; he turned her into a cow to protect her from the jealousy of Hera, though in another version it was Hera herself who did so. The hundred-eyed Argos was set to watch over Io, but Hermes lulled every one of the eyes to sleep, beheaded him, and set the eyes in the tail of the peacock.

105   **Pelops again gave it to Atreus.** The purpose of this description of the sceptre is to stress the unbroken continuity of royal power in Agamemnon's family which it symbolizes, and so it is no surprise that Homer does not mention one of the most notorious events in the family's history, when his father Atreus, son of Pelops, served his brother Thyestes with a dish of his own childrens' flesh (Apollodorus *Epitome* 2.13).

108   **lord of many islands and over all Argos.** It is unclear which are these many islands under Agamemnon's lordship; Argos here refers to the plain of Argos in northern Peloponnese, not to the city. According to the Achaian Catalogue, Agamemnon controls only the northern part of the plain (569–80n) and Diomedes governs the rest (559–68n): it is unclear which, if either, is the correct version of Agamemnon's kingdom.

111–15   **futility** translates *ate*, sometimes translated 'madness' by Lattimore and sometimes 'delusion' (cf. 1. 412n). There is unwitting irony in Agamemnon's fiction of Zeus' **vile deception,** for Zeus has indeed deceived him through the visit of Dream.

124   **cut faithful oaths of truce** is a standard formulation in Homer of oath-taking, and derives from the ritual of sacrifice which often accompanies it: first hairs are cut from the head of the sacrificial beast (3. 273), and this is followed by the cutting of its throat (1. 459).

127   **chose a man of Troy to pour wine for it.** By picturing the Trojans as wine stewards to the Achaians, Agamemnon boasts not just that the Achaians outnumber the Trojans by more than ten to one, but that they are their superiors too.

134–7   And now nine years of mighty Zeus have gone by. When the Achaians were assembled at Aulis for the expedition to Troy, they were given a prediction that Troy would be captured, but only after nine years had elapsed (301–29). Rather than trying to raise their hopes that the passing of nine years means that the moment of Troy's capture is now close, Agamemnon emphasizes the ruin those years have brought to their ships, and this serves only to increase the Achaians' despair and make their departure home even more urgent. Reminding the troops of **our own wives and our young children** at home is his ultimate miscalculation, and the resulting stampede to the ships bears ample testimony to the army's morale and its general's incompetence.

144–8   as on the sea the big waves in the main by Ikaria. The island of Ikaria was named after Ikaros, the son of Daidalos; he and his father fled from Minos of Krete by flying on wings built by Daidalos, but when Ikaros flew too high the wax of his wings melted and he fell into the sea. Both the simile of the sea and of the field of swaying grain convey the swaying feelings of the men, their susceptibility to persuasion.

155–6   a homecoming beyond fate might have been accomplished. This is not to be taken literally, since nothing can or does occur contrary to fate; rather it indicates how serious the situation has become, and the intervention of Hera and Athene in the following scene has the same effect.

157   Atrytone is Athene; for the **aegis** see 1. 202n.

175–81   Since Athene is passing on to Odysseus the instructions she herself received from Hera, she naturally repeats her words (158–65).

186   took from him the sceptre of his fathers. The sceptre is the symbol of Agamemnon's authority (cf. 46n), and it is on this he was leaning when he addressed the army, an address which has resulted in failure; so it is now the symbol of his lost authority, and while he watches helplessly the flight to the ships, it is left to Odysseus to take hold of it and demonstrate royal authority.

204–6   Lordship for many is no good thing. Let there be one ruler. Odysseus demands loyalty to the authority of the king, represented by the sceptre, but does not mention Agamemnon himself. When they halt their flight the soldiers show obedience to that authority, not to Agamemnon; their true feelings towards him are revealed in the next scene, through the person of Thersites.

212–19   **Thersites** is introduced to illustrate the feelings of the ordinary soldiers. He is given a far more significant role than any other ordinary soldier in the entire poem; his ugly appearance marks him as the very opposite of the heroes (Rose 1988). He has a reputation for insolence because he has taken on himself the role of scourge of the leadership; his aim is to raise a laugh and ingratiate himself with the soldiers, but their attitude towards him is one of contempt (272–7). According to later tradition he was killed by Achilleus for ridiculing him.

222–3   **The Achaians were furiously angry with him.** It is generally assumed that 'him' refers to Thersites and that the army disapproves of what he is saying; however it is equally possible that 'him' refers to Agamemnon, and that in this case Homer is describing the mood of the army in the wake of the devastating plague and the humiliation and withdrawal of Achilleus. The sense of the passage might then be 'The Achaians were furiously angry with [Agamemnon], their minds resentful. But he [Thersites, putting into words the anger and resentment which the others felt in their minds but did not dare speak] crying the words aloud, scolded Agamemnon'.

225–42   In Thersites' speech railing against Agamemnon there are close parallels to Achilleus' accusations during the quarrel (Postlethwaite 1988). The sentiment of **what thing further do you want** recalls Achilleus' accusation of greed (1. 122); **whom we Achaians give to you** recalls Achilleus' argument that Agamemnon receives the main portion of the spoil, but does nothing during the fighting to earn that portion (1. 166–7); **one that I, or some other Achaian, capture and bring in** appears to be no more than Thersites' general buffoonery in comparing himself to the great Achaian heroes, but his words clearly echo Achilleus' complaint that he does all the fighting (1. 165); **let us go back home in our ships** repeats Achilleus' threat to sail home and echoes his resentful 'I am minded no longer to stay here dishonoured and pile up your wealth and luxury' (1. 170–1). Thersites repeats the main points made by Achilleus during the quarrel; he offers the ordinary soldier's view of the dispute and the injury done to Achilleus, and that view condemns Agamemnon's role.

260   **Telemachos** is the only son of Odysseus by his wife Penelope. He was only a small child when Odysseus left for Troy, and will not see his father for a further ten years because of his prolonged journey back to Ithaka after the fall of Troy.

270   **Sorry though the men were.** Since it is clearly not Thersites' plight which causes the Achaians' sorrow, it must be their own: they feel sorrow, that is, because they have been prevented by Odysseus from returning home and because Agamemnon's proposal that they do so has proved to be a deception. Their laughter at the weeping and humiliated Thersites suggests no more than their pleasure at witnessing, at long last, the punishment of this unpopular braggart; there is no reason at all why they should not approve of Odysseus' action and at the same time approve of the words of Thersites, who has voiced the disappointment and disenchantment with Agamemnon's leadership felt by them all.

279   **grey-eyed Athene in the likeness of a herald.** Athene is the protectress of Odysseus in the *Odyssey*, but there is no particular need for her in this scene. As in the case of many divine interventions in human affairs in the poem, she is an explanation rather than agent: a hush falls on the crowd, and so a god must have caused it to happen (Willcock 1970.7).

284–8   **the Achaians are trying to make you into a thing of reproach.** Since Odysseus cannot escape the fact that it is Agamemnon's own extraordinary decision to test the army which caused its flight, he tries to conceal the fact by accusing the soldiers of disloyalty. His recollection that the Achaians promised **to go home only after you had sacked strong-walled Ilion** recalls Agamemnon's own words encouraging them to flee (140–1), and indirectly condemns his decision to test the army.

292   **Any man who stays away one month from his own wife.** Odysseus of course will have to suffer a further ten years away from home after the fall of Troy; it is longing for his wife and his home which drives him to overcome the many perils he encounters in the *Odyssey*.

303–20   It was from **Aulis** in Boeotia that the Achaian fleet set out for Troy; the poem ignores its more notorious association, that it was there that Agamemnon sacrificed his daughter Iphigeneia. The mention of the prodigy which took place at Aulis arises from the fact that Homer is about to recount the Catalogue of the Ships which sailed on the expedition. The prodigy of the **snake, his back blood-mottled** represents the Achaian forces, and they are similarly represented in another portent (12. 200–9); it is an association which Virgil employed to remarkable effect at *Aeneid* 2. 203–27. The bird and its eight young are taken to represent the nine fruitless years the Achaians have spent at Troy (326–8), but in his pathetic treatment of them Homer also prefigures the fate of the Trojan mothers and children when the city falls (Taplin 1992.87). Zeus strikes the snake to stone so it will stand as a monument to remind future generations of the expedition from Aulis and of its success.

336–41 **the Gerenian horseman, Nestor.** The meaning and origin of this formula for Nestor would have been obscure even to Homer. Like Odysseus before him (289), Nestor begins by comparing the army to children, and then goes on to condemn the troops for not keeping to their undertaking to fight to the end, as Odysseus did too (286). Nestor accuses the army of fickleness, which is the mark of children and which makes meaningless—'given to the flames'— oaths which were sworn with the pouring of wine.

346 **these one or two** recalls Thersites and Achilleus, who have both spoken in favour of a return home (225–42n): as in his judgment upon the quarrel (1. 275–84n), Nestor again declares his support for Agamemnon.

356 **to avenge Helen's longing to escape** suggests that she was taken by Paris from Sparta against her will: the more usual version of the story (*Odyssey* 4. 262–3) is that she was a willing partner in her abduction. Nestor uses whatever argument the troops are likely to accept, and if that entails a Helen who is lamenting and longing to escape, then he does not hesitate to picture her so.

362–4 **Set your men in order by tribes, by clans.** Homer has very skilfully crafted his narrative to include the Catalogue of the Ships: the testing of the army has illustrated the self-doubt of the commander, Agamemnon; the flight of the army has demonstrated its low morale; and the speech of Thersites has provided the explanation, that the army considers that Agamemnon has blundered in alienating Achilleus. So the narrative requires that Agamemnon now reassert his authority and that the troops regain their discipline

as an army, and this leads to the traditional theme of the Catalogue.
If you do it this way, and the Achaians obey you: not only does
Nestor suggest a strategy which really ought to have been obvious
to the commander, to organize the army, he also expresses a doubt
about whether the troops will obey Agamemnon—which would
perhaps be hardly surprising in the light of his recent actions and
words.

376–8 **who drives me into unprofitable abuse and quarrels.** Agamemnon places the blame for the quarrel on Zeus; on a later occasion
too he will try to shift responsibility, on to madness (*ate*) which is
also sent by Zeus (9. 115–19). At the same time, however, he admits
his own responsibility, that **'I was the first to be angry'**.

392 **to hang back by the curved ships.** This may be just a general
threat, but this is precisely what Achilleus is at present doing.

394–7 **as surf crashing against a sheer ness.** Along with the two
earlier similes (144–8n), this simile brackets the scene of
Agamemnon with his troops. By his comparison of the effect of
the wind on a field of grain, Homer demonstrated the low spirits
of the troops as they were swayed by Agamemnon urging them to
flee; now their excited response to the rallying speeches of Odysseus,
Nestor and Agamemnon is like the noise of the surf crashing against
a headland, and this illustrates their restored morale.

401 The **grind of Ares**, the god of war, means 'battle'.

405–6 This catalogue of the principal Achaians seems deliberately
designed to call attention to the one major hero who is missing,
Achilleus. The **two Aiantes** are the (unrelated) heroes named Aias
(cf. 1. 145n); the minor of the two is Aias the son of Oïleus, who
leads the contingent from Lokris (cf. 527–35n). **Diomedes,** son of
Tydeus, is a very important Achaian hero, leader of the forces from
Argos and Tiryns (cf. 559–68n).

412–18 **Zeus, exalted and mightiest.** Since Agamemnon fails to
mention any service he has given to Zeus, inevitably his prayer will
fail (cf. 1. 40n): by contrast, when Achilleus urged his mother Thetis
to ask Zeus for his help, he told her to remind him of her services
(1. 407–8).

421–31 The description of the sacrifice and the preparation of the
feast is a traditional theme; this closely parallels the description at
1. 458–68.

447 For the **aegis**, see 1.202n.

455–6   As obliterating fire lights up a vast forest. The Catalogue of the Ships is introduced by a dramatic cluster of six similes which are marked by the increasing detail which each provides (Leinieks 1986). The comparison of the glitter of the soldiers' armour to a forest fire illustrates their destructive force.

459–63   as the multitudinous nations of birds winged. As in the comparison of the Achaians to swarms (*ethnea*) of bees (cf. 87–90n), so now they are like nations (*ethnea*) of birds; in both cases Homer draws attention, not just to their vast numbers, but also to the diversity of the tribes which make up the army. The Kaÿstros river flows into the Mediterranean at Ephesos.

467–8   The river Skamandros, known to the gods as Xanthos (20. 74), is, with its tributary the Simoeis, the principal river of the Trojan plain. In Book 21 it takes a divine form and fights to protect Troy from Achilleus, and its defeat by the flames of Hephaistos in that battle is one of a number of symbols of Troy's imminent fall. **as leaves and flowers appear in their season** looks forward to the comparison which the Lykian warrior Glaukos, during his encounter on the battlefield with the Achaian Diomedes, makes between the passing generations of mankind and leaves scattered on the ground (6. 146–50). Here too the flowers and leaves grow 'in their season', and through this image Homer illustrates the impermanence of life and anticipates the eventual disaster which will overtake the army.

469–71   Like the multitudinous nations of swarming insects. Homer calls attention to the number of insects, but again he speaks of their nations (*ethnea*) and so illustrates the unified action of the disparate tribes of the Achaians. The courage and persistence of the insects suggest the same qualities in the Achaians, and the **milk pails** represent the riches of Troy for which they are striving.

474–5   as men who are goatherds. The simile of the goatherds illustrates the Achaian leaders' ready control of their contingents, but it also suggests their caring concern for their charges.

478–81   with eyes and head like Zeus. This physical description of Agamemnon, together with the simile **like some ox of the herd pre-eminent among the others,** is an impressive statement of his position authority. As he views the Achaian leaders from his position on the Trojan wall, the Trojan king Priam will describe Agamemnon as

> . . . there are others taller by a head than he is,

yet these eyes have never yet looked on a man so splendid
nor so lordly as this . . .'

(3. 168–70).

484–93 you Muses who have your homes on Olympos. To recount
the long Catalogue of the Achaian ships will require a great feat of
memory, and so Homer renews his invocation of the Muse (cf. 1.
1). **the multitude of them**: according to the Catalogue, the Achaian
fleet totals 1,186 vessels. It is unusual for the poet to include himself
as directly in the narrative as in **not if I had ten tongues and ten
mouths, not if I had a voice never to be broken and a heart of
bronze within me**. The poet's appeal to the Muse is a declaration
of the accuracy of the account he is about to provide.

493–760 The accuracy of description in the following account
suggests that it originated in the Mykenaian Late Bronze Age, with
additional material being included from subsequent centuries also.
Although he did not create it himself, there is no reason to believe
that Homer may not have been responsible for including the
Catalogue in the narrative. Five different regions of Greece and its
islands feature in the Catalogue of the Ships: (i) Central Greece,
including Boiotia (494–510), Orchomenos (511–16), Phokis (517–
26), Lokris (527–35), Euboia (536–45), and Athens (546–58); (ii)
Peloponnese, including Argos (559–68), Mykenai (569–80),
Lakedaimon (581–90), Pylos (591–602), Arkadia (603–14), and
Elis (615–24); (iii) Western Greece, including Doulichion (625–
30), Ithaka (631–7), and Aitolia (638–44); (iv) the Southern Islands,
including Krete (645–52), Rhodes (653–70), Syme and other small
islands (671–80); (v) Northern Greece (681–759). It might have
been more in keeping with the nature of the narrative to organize
the Catalogue according to the stature of the various leaders,
beginning with Agamemnon and Mykenai; the fact that it is
organized rather by region suggests that it originally stood quite
separate from the poem. For full discussion of the contents of the
Catalogue of the Ships, see Hope Simpson and Lazenby 1970; Kirk
1985.168f; Visser 1997.

494–510 The first geographical section, Central Greece, begins with
the **Boiotians**: the choice may be quite arbitrary, for if he is not to
lead off with Agamemnon and Mykenai, then the poet has to begin
somewhere. However, the region was important in Mykenaian

times, when major centres existed at Thebes, Orchomenos and Gla; in addition, Aulis, traditionally the point of embarkation of the Achaian fleet en route to Troy, was in Boiotia. The importance of the Boiotian entry is indicated by the fact that it contains more leaders and place-names, twenty-nine in total, than any other, and also that the number of troops in the contingent is given, fifty ships each carrying 120 men (509–10). Yet this apparent importance is at odds with the insignificance of the Boiotian leaders, none of whom plays a major role in the subsequent narrative. Tradition related that **Thebes** was destroyed by the expedition of the Epigonoi, the sons of the Seven against Thebes (4. 404–10), which took place before the expedition to Troy, and archaeology has confirmed this dating: so **lower Thebes** must refer to the area below the Mykenaian citadel which continued to be occupied after the destruction.

511–16   The **Minyai** took their name from their legendary king Minyas, who was ancestor of various of the Argonauts who sailed with Jason in search of the Golden Fleece. **Orchomenos** was said to have been founded by him, and was one of the most important cities of the Mykenaian world: during the Embassy in Book 9 Achilleus mentions its wealth alongside that of Egyptian Thebes (9. 381–2).

517–26   **Pytho** is a name for Delphi, the site of the most important oracle, of Apollo, in Greece. It gained its name from the dragon which once defended the site and which was killed by Apollo.

527–35   **Swift Aias son of Oïleus** is the lesser Aias, who is normally found in combination with his namesake, Telamonian Aias; his description **armoured in linen**, that is, light-armed, seems designed to contrast him with his namesake who is normally heavily armed with his great tower shield (7. 219–23). Similarly his followers are said not to carry shields and spears, but to fight with bows and slings, in contrast to the 'elaborate war gear' of the followers of Telamonian Aias (13. 714–20). Tradition related that, during the sack of Troy, he raped Kassandra on the altar of Athena; Homer (*Odyssey* 4. 499–511) tells that he was shipwrecked and drowned by Poseidon during his voyage home.

536–45   **their hair grown long at the back**. The rest of the Achaians wear their hair long except in time of grief; the Abantes wear it long at the back only, and seem otherwise to be short-cropped.

546–58 The birth of Athens' legendary king **Erechtheus** from the **grain-giving fields** represents the popular Athenian belief that they had always inhabited their land and had not migrated there. The Erechtheion was one of the most important buildings on the Athenian Akropolis. It is rather surprising that no mention is made of other locations in Attika, particularly Eleusis, the site of the shrine of Demeter, the goddess of grain, and of her important mystery cult, although the grain-giving fields may be an allusion to it. **Never on earth before had there been a man born like him**: in view of the fact that **Menestheus**, and the Athenians generally, play a relatively minor role in the poem, this description is rather extravagant. The absence of Athens' greatest hero Theseus, who traditionally belonged to an earlier heroic generation, lessens the impact of the Athenian contingent's description, and the praise of Menestheus is perhaps designed to compensate for this.

557–8 **Aias brought twelve ships**. This is Aias son of Telamon (cf. 527–35n). That a hero of such status as Telamonian Aias merits only two lines, compared to his namesake Oïlean Aias for example, is curious. However, it is the small island of Salamis and its small contingent—twelve ships, against the eighty of Diomedes in the next entry for example—which are being characterized, and their relative insignificance contrasts with the importance of their commander. There was a famous story that this brief entry was in fact a later addition by the Athenians, to support their claim to the island against the claim of their neighbour Megara.

559–68 The entry for **Argos and Tiryns** begins the second geographical section of the Catalogue, the Peloponnese. Together with the following entry for Mykenai itself, it covers the most important area of the Mykenaian world, the plain of Argos, or Argolid. Diomedes, whose role in the poem is to be Achilleus' substitute when he withdraws from the battle, is portrayed as king of all the southern part of this region, together with the adjoining island of Aegina. His fellow kings, Sthenelos and Euryalos, along with Diomedes himself, fought as Epigonoi, sons of the Seven against Thebes, who successfully attacked that city (cf. 494–510n).

569–80 The kingdom of **Agamemnon** covers the northern section of the Argolid, though little of the plain itself; it stretches through the hilly area north of Mykenai as far as, and including, Korinth, and then westward along the northern coast of Peloponnese. The **hundred ships** he brought is the largest contingent of all the Achaians, and it was on this basis that Nestor judged him greater than Achilleus (1. 281).

581–90   'With many ravines' (Willcock 1978.208) seems preferable to Lattimore's '**swarming**'. Menelaos' large kingdom of **Lakedaimon** stretches south from Sparta down the valley of the river Eurotas, to take in Southern Peloponnese except for Messenia, the kingdom of Nestor. **Helen's longing to escape and her lamentations** of course reflects Menelaos' own view point of her abduction/elopement.

591–602   The kingdom of the aged Nestor is based upon the city of **Pylos**. Excavation has revealed an imposing Mykenaian palace at the site of Ano Englianos in Messenia, with large quantities of palace records written in the Linear B script, and this is now generally accepted as Nestor's Pylos. The importance of Nestor is indicated by his contingent of ninety ships, which in size is second only to that of Agamemnon himself. The tale of **Thamyris** being robbed of his voice and memory by the Muses for trying to rival them recalls Homer's invocation of his Muse at the beginning of the Catalogue (484–92), in which he stressed his dependence on her.

603–14   Situated in the centre of the Peloponnese, **Arkadia** is the area of Greece furthest from the sea; for most other areas the sea provided the most convenient form of communication. In fact these men of Arkadia play no part in the narrative, nor does their leader **Agapenor**.

615–24   **Bouprasion and brilliant Elis** lie in the north-west of the Peloponnese, bounded by Achaia to the north, Arkadia to the east, and Messenia to the south.

625–30   The Catalogue now begins the third geographical section, Western Greece. Homer (*Odyssey* 16. 247–8) says that **Doulichion** was the home of 52 of the 108 suitors for the hand of Odysseus' wife, Penelope.

631–7   **Kephallenia** itself is the island named as Samos at 634; here it is used as a collective name for all the western islands under Odysseus' command, including his own home island of **Ithaka**. It is curious that Odysseus brings only twelve ships from all these very substantial islands, the same number as Aias from the single small island of Salamis (cf. 557–8n), and considerably less than the forty brought from Doulichion and its adjacent islands; and it cautions against placing much trust in the Catalogue as a true muster-list of the Achaian forces.

638–44   **Aitolia** is the region at the northern entrance to the Gulf of Korinth. It is a wild and mountainous area, and was the setting for the myth of the Kalydonian boar hunt. The story of **Meleagros** is told at 9. 529–99.

645–52   The fourth geographical section deals with the Southern Islands. Krete was the home in former times of the great Minoan civilization: fittingly for an island of such former importance, Krete is credited with sending eighty ships, the third-largest contingent after those of Agamemnon and Nestor. The Minoan civilization was based around palace sites at Knossos, Phaistos, Mallia and Zakros, but after its destruction there is clear evidence, in the form of clay tablets written in the Linear B script, of the presence of Mykenaians at Knossos. The leader of the Kretan contingent, **Idomeneus,** is said to be the grandson of Minos, the legendary ruler of Minoan Krete, and like his ancestor he rules the island from Knossos.

653   **Tlepolemos**, a son of Herakles, fights Sarpedon, a son of Zeus, at 5. 628–62, and is killed by him.

676–80   **Nisyros and Krapathos and Kasos** are islands to the west of Rhodes. The size of their contingent, thirty ships, is surprisingly large against, for example, the twelve Odysseus brought, but even more surprising is that no mention is made of the Cyclades, the large group of islands to the west.

681–94   **those who dwelt about Pelasgian Argos.** Homer introduces the fifth geographical section, Northern Greece. The Pelasgians were considered by the Greeks to have been the aboriginal pre-Greek inhabitants of their land: so this Argos, in Thessaly, was the precursor of the more famous city of that name in the Peloponnese. This entry for **Achilleus** and the **Myrmidons** is brief; there are only basic details given and there is no story from the past to distinguish it; instead Homer has adapted the normal entry pattern and so included recent events of the poem. He not only recalls the quarrel and the reason why this review of Agamemnon's army is now taking place, but he also takes the Catalogue from where it apparently belongs, at the embarkation from Aulis, and places it squarely at Troy in the tenth year of the war. **Hellas** and **Hellenes** are the names which the Greeks subsequently gave to their land and to themselves,

names which are used to the present day. Homer normally calls
them Achaia and Achaians, but here he is referring to tribal units
whose names later received much broader application.

695–710   **Phylake and Pyrasos** are in the area of south east Thessaly
on the gulf of Pagasai. **Protesilaos** is, with Philoktetes, one of two
men named as leaders of contingents even though they themselves
are no longer fighting at Troy. Protesilaos died, the first casualty of
the Achaians, at the very moment the fleet landed at Troy, as he
leapt first onto Trojan soil. His death represents the beginning of
the war and the terrible price exacted on both sides. The ship from
which he leapt is the first of the Achaian ships fired by Hektor at
the climax of the Trojan advance (15. 704–6).

711–15   **Iolkos**, in Thessaly, is home to the story of Jason and the
Argonauts, which traditionally predated the story of the expedition
to Troy by two generations. The leader of this contingent, **Eumelos**,
is the son of Alkestis, who was daughter of Pelias: it was Pelias,
king of Iolkos, who set Jason the challenge of fetching the golden
fleece from Colchis.

716–28   **They who lived about Thaumakia and Methone** are also
from the region of eastern Thessaly. Their leader, **Philoktetes**, was
left behind on Lemnos because of his infected wound. After the
death of Achilleus he was brought to Troy in line with a prophecy
that the Achaians would not take Troy without him. He slew
Achilleus' killer Paris with the bow and arrows which had belonged
to Herakles. He therefore represents the successful outcome of the
expedition.

729–33   The Catalogue now switches to the western side of Thessaly.
Asklepios was the Greek god of healing, whose most important
sanctuary was at Epidauros. Later tradition said that he was given
the blood of the Gorgon by Athene and used it to raise the dead;
when Hades protested at this, Zeus killed Asklepios with his
thunderbolt.

738–44   The **hairy beast men** are the Centaurs (cf. 1. 259–74n).
Peirithoös drove them from Mount Pelion in eastern Thessaly to
the Pindos mountains in the west.

750   **Dodona** in Epiros was home to the important oracle of Zeus. It
is **wintry** because it lies in a high mountainous area.

755   The **Styx** was one of the rivers of the Underworld; to swear by

its waters constituted the most important and binding oath-taking for the immortals (14. 271).

761–70   Tell me then, Muse, who of them all was the best and the bravest. The Achaian Catalogue ends as it began, with an invocation of the muse. Since the answer to the poet's enquiry is Aias, so long that is as **Achilleus stayed angry,** it seems clear that the invocation is designed to revert to Achilleus and to the narrative situation which has caused the Catalogue to be included.

771–9   The curved sea-wandering vessels highlight the inactivity of Achilleus, who is described as lying apart from the other Achaians, withdrawn even from the games with which his men while away the time. Achilleus brought fifty ships to Troy (685) and, if each held fifty men like the ships of Philoktetes (719), he is leading a force of 2,500 men: their idle competitions emphasize their restlessness and their longing for battle, and this in turn illustrates their frustration and that of their leader. The scene is a graphic illustration of the consequence of Achilleus' anger for his Myrmidons, in contrast to the sufferings and deaths which will befall the other Achaians before his return to battle.

780   as if all the earth with flame were eaten. This simile of destructive fire links with the first of the great cluster of similes (455–6), to bracket this long description of the Achaian forces.

782–3   Typhoeus was a monster destroyed by Zeus' thunderbolt and buried by him in Kilikia, **the land of the Arimoi,** where earthquakes were explained as his moving beneath the earth; the allusion serves to keep before the audience the figure of the god who is controlling the action of the poem.

788–93   These were holding assembly in front of the doors of Priam: for the first time the narrative moves away from the Achaian camp to the city of Troy. The **ancient burial mound of ancient Aisyetes** is an otherwise unknown landmark on the plain of Troy.

800   These look terribly like leaves, or the sands of the sea-shore illustrates the vast numbers of soldiers, but the leaves also evoke the idea of the soldiers' mortality (cf. 467–8n).

804   multitudinous is the speech of the scattered nations. The many foreign languages of the Trojan allies is a frequent motif in the poem, and is often associated with the noise the army is said to make; this in turn is made to represent their lack of cohesion and discipline, and is contrasted with the quiet steadfastness of the Achaians (cf. 3. 2–9).

813–14   There is no way of identifying this **Hill of the Thicket**, any more than the burial mound of Aisyetes, although there are many mounds around the Trojan plain and there is no particular reason why these names should not have been attached to them. At any rate the name, particularly when an alternative name is given by the gods, **the burial mound of dancing Myrina**, lends a certain authenticity to the description and so enhances the following Catalogue of the Trojans.

816–77   The Catalogue of the Trojan Allies, at a mere sixty-two lines, is very much shorter than that of the Achaians, and because there is no list of ships as in the case of the Achaians, there is no indication of the number of the forces involved. The Catalogue seems designed to match that of the Achaians, rather than be an authentic 'historical' roll-call of Trojan allies, and it too is divided into five sections: (i) Troy and its surrounding area (816–43); (ii) the western, European, side of the Hellespont (844–50); (iii) the eastern, Asian, side of the Hellespont and the southern shore of the Black Sea (851–7); (iv) inland Asia Minor (858–63); coastal Asia Minor (864–77). The Catalogue begins with their war leader **Hektor**, unlike the Achaian Catalogue which for no obvious reason begins with the contingent from Boiotia (493–760n). Hektor is the son of Priam, king of Troy.

819–21   For the pedigree of **Aineias**, cf. 20. 178–98n. His people, the **Dardanians**, lived below Ida, the mountain to the south east of Troy.

827   The importance of the bow of **Pandaros** is indicated by its being a gift from Apollo: it will play a significant role in the poem, for it is with this bow that Pandaros will break the truce by wounding Menelaos (4. 105–140).

828   The territory of **Adresteia** lies at the northern end of the Hellespont.

831–4   **who beyond all men knew the art of prophecy.** These lines are repeated when these two sons of Merops die at the hands of Diomedes and Odysseus (11. 329–32): there is pathos in the tale of the father who foresees his sons' death but is unable to prevent it.

835–9   **Perkote and Praktion** lie on the shores of the Hellespont.

Their leader **Asios** is an important figure whose death is used to introduce that of Hektor himself (cf. 13. 384n).

840   For **Pelasgians**, cf. 681–94n.

844–50   **Thrace**, like the territory of the **Kikonians** and the **Paionians**, lies on the western, European, side of the Hellespont. The attack on Ismaros, the city of the Kikonians, is the first of his adventures which Odysseus narrates at *Odyssey* 9. 39–61.

851–7   The **Paphlagones** are located on the southern shore of the Black Sea, as are the **Halizones**, who are even more remote beyond the river Halys.

858–77   The final five entries in the Trojan Catalogue—**Mysians, Phrygians, Maionians, Karians and Lykians**—cover the territory of western Asia Minor to the east and south of Troy.

860   **he went down under the hands of swift-running Aiakides in the river.** Aiakides is Achilleus, the grandson of Aiakos, himself the son of Zeus. Achilleus fights with the river Skamandros in Book 21, though in fact neither **Ennomos** nor **Nastes** (cf. 870–5) are amongst his victims there.

876   It is curious that **Sarpedon** and **Glaukos** merit only two lines at the very end of the Catalogue. They are two of the most important of the Trojan allies and are major characters in the narrative: their meeting at 12. 309–28 is one of the poem's most important scenes.

ILIAD 3

Having given details of the two armies in the previous book, Homer now introduces more of the poem's characters: so far only Achilleus and Agamemnon have been introduced in any great detail, and in this book Homer brings forward other major heroes on the Achaian side, and establishes the character and mood of their Trojan counterparts, in particular their king Priam and their military leader Hektor. At the same time he provides another important part of the backcloth to the anger of Achilleus, the two causes of the Trojan War, Helen and Paris. As well as introducing more of the characters, Homer's aim is to rehearse the theme of Troy's guilt. Paris' original crime against Menelaos is recalled in the formal duel between the two in this book, and the truce which is called to accommodate this duel is broken in Book 4 by the treacherous wounding of Menelaos by the arrow of the Trojan Pandaros: since the bow of Pandaros associates him with the Trojan renowned for his archery, Paris, his crime also serves an introductory purpose in restating the guilt of Troy.

The centrepiece of the book is the duel of Paris and Menelaos (Bergold 1977). This duel is not of itself particularly impressive, because it can have no decisive outcome and so is lacking in tension: the poetic tradition Homer inherited dictates that Paris must survive to shoot his fatal arrow at Achilleus, and that Menelaos must also survive to return with Helen to Sparta. Instead, the purpose of the duel is to introduce those elements listed above: the occasion of the duel brings Helen to the walls of Troy and from there she identifies some of the Achaian leaders for Priam; it brings the brothers Paris and Hektor face to face and helps to establish their characters and relationship; it brings Helen's two husbands face to face and so examines the cause of the war and Troy's guilt; and it introduces the object of the war, Helen herself.

2–9   as when the clamour of cranes goes high to the heavens. The
clamour of the cranes suggests the racket made by the Trojans, and
this illustrates the alien races and tongues making up their army,
and in particular its lack of discipline; the Achaians, in contrast,
are well disciplined and quietly determined **each in his heart to
stand by the others.** The theme of the cranes' attack on the Pygmies
was popular with later Greek artists but does not feature elsewhere
in Homer. The attack of the cranes is unprovoked, and so the
Trojans, to whom the cranes are compared, are presented as the
aggressors: so at the very outset Homer rehearses this book's theme,
the guilt of the Trojans.

16–20   Alexandros is the more common name in the poem for Paris.
He is hardly dressed for the part of Trojan champion, since he
wears no defensive armour and the leopard skin over his shoulders
seems more designed to enhance his handsome looks than his
military prowess: he has more the appearance of the archer he is
than the hand-to-hand spearman normal in Homeric combat.
However with bow, sword and two javelins he seems to have
overarmed himself against every conceivable eventuality: he is no
warrior, and his appearance is as empty a show as the challenge he
issues to the Achaians.

23–6   like a lion who comes on a mighty carcass. When Paris first
appeared he was wearing the skin of a wild animal, but now he is
compared to a carcass, the object of the wild beast's attentions;
this reversal of the image reflects the reversal of his role, from
proud aggressor to fearful victim.

33–5   As a man who has come on a snake in the mountain valley.
The snake is a frequent symbol of Achaian violence and aggression
(2. 303–20n). The shivers and green pallor of the man indicate
Paris' reaction to Menelaos' appearance, and this contrasts with
his earlier challenge. This simile and the previous one achieve a
striking contrast between the former and present husbands of Helen.

39–45   Evil Paris, beautiful, woman-crazy, cajoling. Hektor presents
his brother as the complete antithesis of a hero. His wish that his
brother were dead is matched by the wish of Paris' wife, Helen,
that she too had died (cf. 173). Hektor continually condemns Paris
for having no sense of shame (*aidos*).

46–52   Were you like this that time. Paris' abduction of Helen was
the original cause of the war, but Hektor's complaint seems to be,

not so much that he brought the war, but that he refuses to play his full role in it. Paris' indiscipline and frivolousness are contrary to everything Hektor represents—courage, loyalty and fidelity; and his abduction of another man's wife and the barrenness of his marriage to Helen contrast with Hektor's stable marriage to Andromache and their child Astyanax.

55–7   **when you rolled in the dust**. In Greek, *migeies*, translated 'rolled', has a primary meaning of 'have sexual intercourse': as Paris writhes in the dust, dying at the hand of Menelaos, his very act of dying, says Hektor, will be a parody of the sex act. The metaphor **you had worn a mantle of flying stones** refers to public execution by stoning, but in view of the emphasis in this scene on the physical appearance of Paris, there is an obviously ironical tone intended.

60   **your heart forever is weariless, like an axe-blade**: 'Paris' glowing flattery of Hektor seems deliberately ironical: 'Paris' praise is no praise—at least not in the mouth of one whose personality and chief virtues and values are totally different from the qualities he claims to approve . . . really he mocks Hektor' (Schein 1984.22).

66   **no man could have them for wanting them**. In fact Paris does have the gifts 'for wanting them': his sexual prowess, and Helen herself, were his rewards from Aphrodite for giving her the verdict in her contest with Hera and Athene.

71   **That one of us who wins and is proved stronger**. It seems clear that a duel between the former and present husbands of Helen to decide who should have her would make much better sense at the beginning of the war than in its tenth year; yet in fact Paris retains the right to refuse to return her even after he loses in this duel (cf. 7. 362).

97–8   **beyond all others this sorrow comes closest to my heart**: that is, Menelaos suffered more than anybody because of Helen's abduction and the war that followed, and this gives him the right of reply to Hektor's proposal.

107   **lest some man overstep Zeus' oaths, and make them be nothing.** Menelaos' refusal to deal with Priam's dishonest sons recalls how he was cheated before by Paris, and he now anticipates Paris' refusal to abide by the conditions of this duel and return Helen, and the breaking of the truce by Pandaros (4. 105–40).

125–8   **she was weaving a great web**. Helen presents a picture of domesticity in contrast to the figure of the woman who abandoned home, husband and child to follow her lover. She is recording her account of events at Troy, of the war fought on her behalf. Two other female characters are seen weaving in the Homeric poems: Andromache weaves as she awaits Hektor's return from his fatal encounter with Achilleus (22. 440–1), and Penelope puts off her suitors by weaving a shroud for Odysseus' father Laertes (*Odyssey* 2. 94–106). This may recall a time when royal females preserved in their tapestry work the traditional tales of their households, just as singers like Homer also preserved traditional stories by 'weaving' their songs. Helen continually expresses bitterness for what has happened to her and regret for what she has done, so the **struggles that they endured for her sake** reveal her preoccupation with her own sense of guilt

138 You shall be called beloved wife of the man who wins you. Helen offers no protest at being the object of a contest to determine her future, and it seems clear that this tale was once a marriage-suit legend, like the contest for Penelope's hand in the *Odyssey*. The result is that, like Briseis in Book 1, Helen appears here as little more than a possession of the heroes: she may be the most beautiful woman in the world, the daughter of Zeus himself, but she is still at the disposal of heroes.

139–40 sweet longing after her husband of time before, and her city and parents. This picture of Helen is in contrast to that of Paris as frivolous and irresponsible womanizer and confirms her self-image of remorseful and responsible wife.

144 Aithre, Pittheus' daughter was the mother of Theseus. The story was told, though not in Homer, that Helen was abducted by Theseus before ever she married Menelaos. She was rescued by her brothers Kastor and Polydeukes, who abducted Aithre in retaliation and gave her to Helen as handmaiden.

145 the Skaian gates are the main gates of Troy; throughout the poem they are important in marking the dividing line between the safety of the city, in which the women and old men are protected, and the plain of Troy on which the heroes fight and die (cf. 6. 237n).

146–244 Since antiquity the following scene has been known as the *Teichoskopia*, Viewing from the Walls, in which Helen identifies for Priam some of the leading Achaian heroes who are ranged before the walls of Troy—Agamemnon, Odysseus, Aias and Idomeneus. It is clearly incongruous that the Trojan king should need Helen to identify the enemy leaders for him even after nine years of sustained warfare: the scene rightly belongs in the first year of the war, but it is placed where it is for a good narrative reason, to enable leading figures on both sides to be characterized.

151–2   as cicadas who through the forest settle on trees. Through their incessant noise the cicadas illustrate the garrulity of old men, on the Skaian gates or in the modern taverna, whose days of action are behind them.

156   Surely there is no blame on Trojans. Homer does not himself describe the beauty of this most beautiful of women nor even its effect upon the old men, but has them voice their own feelings of both admiration and dread.

164   I am not blaming you: to me the gods are blameworthy. Although he has lost so many of his people and of his own family in the war, Priam is still able to express kindness towards Helen: again she is characterized through her effect upon others. The blame for what has happened lies rather with Aphrodite, and then with Hera and Athene, the three goddesses who took part in the Judgment of Paris: Helen is an unfortunate victim rather than herself to blame.

173–80   when I came hither following your son. It is clear that Helen followed Paris voluntarily but has long since come to regret doing so; the wish that she had died is a recurring theme of Helen's appearance in the poem (cf. 6. 345–8; 24. 764). **my grown child** is her only daughter by Menelaos, Hermione. Helen's description of Agamemnon, **a good king and a strong spearfighter,** makes no mention of his quarrel with Achilleus: like Priam's enquiry, she presents him rather as the idealization of kingly power. In her poignant cry almost of disbelief, **did this ever happen?** she contrasts her former life in Sparta with the present and leaves no doubt about which she considers the happier.

184–9   Phrygia, a region to the east of Troy, was named as an ally at 2. 862. The **Amazon women** are a race of female warriors who play an important role in the tale of Troy, though not in the *Iliad*. According to the lost epic *Aithiopis* they fought under the leadership of Penthesilea on the side of the Trojans following the death of

Hektor. Penthesilea herself was killed by Achilleus (Evelyn-White 1967.507).

196   like some ram, through the marshalled ranks of the fighters. The point of the simile is firstly to describe Odysseus' stocky build, but then the progress of the ram through the sheep flock illustrates the authority of Odysseus as he proceeds through the army; a similar effect was achieved by the comparison of Agamemnon to an ox standing pre-eminent amongst its herd (2. 480–1).

202   to know every manner of shiftiness and crafty counsels. This description of Odysseus' guile, and of his skill as a speaker in the account of Antenor which follows, reflects the traits for which he was famous, particularly in the *Odyssey*. The highlight of his role in the *Iliad* is to convey Agamemnon's offer of reparation to Achilleus and to persuade him to be reconciled in Book 9, and so his description here prepares for that scene.

205   Once in the days before now brilliant Odysseus came here. This visit of Odysseus and Menelaos to Troy before the outbreak of the war is recalled at 11. 140.

212–24   both of them spun their speech. The metaphor of spinning, or weaving, speech is designed to enhance the picture of Odysseus as a skilled and wily orator (cf. 202n). Antenor acutely observes how important eye contact and body gesture are in speech: but in the case of Odysseus, **eyes fixed on the ground beneath him, nor would he gesture with the staff,** his words alone were sufficient. In the simile of the **winter snows** it is the number of flakes which are emphasized, and hence the rapid flow of Odysseus' words.

226   Who then is this other Achaian of power and stature? In the absence of Achilleus, Aias is the best of the Achaians (cf. 2. 768–9), and this is indicated by his appearance, **towering above the Argives by head and broad shoulders.** Helen's description of him as **wall of the Achaians** reflects his role throughout the poem as the Achaians' greatest defensive warrior, in particular in his fight to save the Achaian ships (15. 674–746).

230–3   Helen's rapid transfer of attention to **Idomeneus** of Krete is a surprise, partly because Priam has not asked about him, but mainly because there are a number of more important Achaian warriors she could have identified, Menelaos, for example, or Nestor. Homer has already said that the announcement of the duel brought Helen fond thoughts of her former husband and family (139–40), and he gives an insight into her mind as her thoughts begin to wander away from the immediate and unhappy scene of battle which confronts her, to memories of happier times at Sparta as she recalls the frequent visits Idomeneus used to make.

237–42 **Kastor** and **Polydeukes** are presented as merely the mortal brothers of Helen: if he knew it, Homer chose to ignore as inappropriate the myth of Zeus' seduction of Leda in the form of a swan and the tradition that the lives of the two brothers alternated between Olympos and Hades (Pindar *Nemean Ode* 10. 55). Helen credits her brothers with her own emotions **of shame and all the reproach that is on me,** and in this way the poet continues his sympathetic portrait of her. It is of course unrealistic that Helen should not by now have heard of the fate of her brothers, but the point of the scene is to show how utterly isolated she is from her former background if she has remained ignorant of even the death of her own brothers, and the pathos of her isolation from **Lakedaimon** (Sparta) is heightened by the fact that her brothers are already buried there.

273–4 **the heralds thereafter passed these about to all the princes.** By accepting the hairs from the heads of the sacrificial victims, each of the princes of the Achaians and the Trojans accepted the oaths sworn: so when Trojan Pandaros breaks the oath in the next book, by firing an arrow at Menelaos, all the Trojans are incriminated.

278–80 **you who under the earth take vengeance** are the Erinues, the Furies; the sense is that, even in death, those who break the oath shall not be free from punishment. By witnessing the oath, the various powers become guarantors of it.

281–91 **If it should be that Alexandros slays Menelaos.** The terms of the duel indicate that it can have no conclusive outcome, because the oral tradition dictates that Menelaos will only regain Helen as a result of Troy's fall. However the terms do emphasize the formality of the duel and hence the crime of Paris when he fails to hand over Helen following his defeat, and so they confirm the duel's purpose within the narrative, to rehearse the guilt of the Trojans.

286 **and pay also a price to the Argives which will be fitting.** Agamemnon's demand for compensation if Menelaos wins shows that, as far as he is concerned, the duel is about more than just possession of Helen. **price** translates Greek *time* (Introduction, 8), with the suggestion that the compensation paid by the Trojans will comprise the heroic honour won by the Achaians. Some indication of how much will be **fitting** comes later in the poem, when Agamemnon himself is forced to hand back a woman, Achilleus' girl Briseis, and he offers a vast range of compensation (9. 120–57).

301 **let their wives be the spoil of others.** This is the fate that Hektor envisages for his wife Andromache after his death, dragged off into slavery by one of the enemy (6. 455). Edwards (1987.194) compares the role of the mass of the soldiers here (cf. 7. 178–80; 17. 414–24) to that of the chorus in tragedy, commenting on the drama unfolding before them.

321 **whichever man has made what has happened happen** does not indicate that there is doubt in anyone's mind, on either side, about who is the guilty party (cf. 451–4); rather it shows the feelings of the ordinary soldiers, their desperate longing that somebody win the duel and bring an end to their sufferings.

328–38 The description of Paris as **lord of lovely-haired Helen** highlights the purpose of the duel at the very moment he stands to face her former husband. This is the first of four arming scenes in the poem, the others being the arming of Agamemnon (11. 17–46), of Patroklos (16. 131–44), and of Achilleus (19. 369–91). The description in all four cases is very similar and this indicates that the motif is a traditional theme of oral poetry, which is employed at times of important combat, when the combat leads, or appears that it will lead, to a turning point in the story (Armstrong 1958). The arming of Paris recalls that, when first he appeared, he was wearing a leopard skin instead of body armour (cf. 16–20n), and the fact that he has to borrow a corselet from **Lykaon his brother** shows that he is an archer accustomed to fight at long range.

354 **doing evil to a kindly host, who has given him friendship.** The Trojan War, and now this duel, are being fought because Paris the guest abused the hospitality of Menelaos the host by abducting his wife. So Menelaos calls upon Zeus, as god of hospitality, in the expectation that he will support him. In fact it is Paris who receives divine support when he is rescued by Aphrodite.

375–6 **She broke the chinstrap.** Like Athene's intervention to prevent Achilleus killing Agamemnon (cf. 1. 194–5n), Aphrodite's action is to be taken literally: Paris is saved from certain death, so it must be that a god has saved him.

381   wrapped him in a thick mist. Aphrodite saves Paris a second time by, in effect, making him invisible, just as Athene covers Odysseus in a mist in *Odyssey* 6 and enables him to walk through the city of the Phaiakians unseen. The assistance Aphrodite gives to Paris repeats the assistance she gave when he originally cheated Menelaos by seducing his wife, and it leads naturally to the following scene in which she forces Helen to join Paris in the bedroom in a repetition of the original seduction.

386   likening herself to an aged woman. Aphrodite's disguise as an old woman with special call on Helen's affections increases the sense of deception pervading this whole scene; but as well as being the goddess who controls the scene, she is the expression too of Helen's own sexuality

390–4   Aphrodite's description of Paris seems consciously to recall his description at the beginning of this book: **shining in his raiment** recalls the leopard-skin he was wearing (17); **his own beauty** recalls Hektor's description of him as beautiful (39) and handsome (45); and her declaration that **you would think he was going rather to a dance** recalls Hektor's jibe that his lyre would not help him in combat with Menelaos (54). The goddess flaunts before Helen what Hektor had so roundly condemned.

399–412   Why are you still so stubborn to beguile me? The coming scene between Helen and Paris recalls her original seduction by him, and her accusation here is that her seduction was the result of Aphrodite's deception. Her questions to Aphrodite are bitterly ironical as she envisages her fate as the goddess' plaything, to be given at her whim to any mortal she wishes. Helen vents her feelings to the goddess in a way she was not permitted to do when first she was told about the duel (cf. 138n).

418   Helen daughter of Zeus was frightened. Helen's argument with Aphrodite may represent her own inner debate, between her sense of honour and her sexual desire (Farron 1979), but when she gives way to Aphrodite, she does so out of fear, not for sexual gratification, and she has to be **led by the goddess**: in this re-enactment of Helen's original seduction and marriage to Paris, Aphrodite's action represents the escorting of the bride to the chamber of her new husband. Bespaloff (1947.62) concluded that

'Aphrodite rules her despotically; the goddess commands and Helen bows, whatever her private repugnance. Pleasure is extorted from her; this merely makes her humiliation the more cruel. Her only resource is to turn against herself a wrath too weak to spite the gods'.

433–4   I advise you rather to let it be. It can hardly be, as is sometimes suggested, that Helen's anxiety for Paris here is genuine; rather she is being bitterly sarcastic and really does wish that he had lost. Paris' reply to her tirade does not suggest that he has heard genuine anxiety in her words.

439   Menelaos with Athene's help has beaten me. Since Paris owes his life to Aphrodite's intervention, there is considerable irony in this.

441–6   let us go to bed and turn to love-making. By being spirited away from the duel Paris has for a second time cheated Menelaos and, as in the case of the original seduction, intercourse with Helen will consummate the act; so Homer has Paris draw the clear parallel with the earlier occasion. Helen's innocence, both now and in the original abduction, has been established because she is compelled by Aphrodite; Paris has broken the terms of the truce, and so his guilt, and the guilt of Troy, is established.

448   So these two were laid in the carven bed. Inside Troy's walls there is a world of women and old men, of passive spectators of the war, who await its outcome and their own fate; and within this world there is just one man of fighting age who is not fighting, Paris, who now lies in bed with the wife of the enemy. The overtly erotic presentation of Paris in this book has been carefully devised, for in Book 6 Hektor, who in all respects is the opposite of his brother, will enter this world of women and old men and he will encounter the three women in his life, his mother Hekabe, Helen and his wife Andromache, and they, in their different ways, will try to lure him away from the world of men and to persuade him to stay in the world of women. At the end of that book Hektor will turn his back on his family and will leave his city for the last time. Paris in Book 3 has been presented as the model of the man within the world of women, the role which Hektor will refuse to adopt (Arthur 1981.23).

449   ranged like a wild beast up and down the host. The image of the wild beast recalls the beginning of the Paris-Menelaos episode,

when Menelaos was compared to a lion which has come upon the
carcass of a horned stag or a wild goat (3. 23–6); in the earlier
simile the joy felt by the lion reflected Menelaos' anticipation of
revenge, but now he feels only frustration, that once again he has
been cheated.

454   he was hated among them all. The Trojans hate Paris because
his actions brought the war, but now their hatred is even greater
because by his disappearance he has cheated them of the promise
of an end to the war.

ILIAD 4

In Book 3 Homer rehearsed the cause of the Trojan War, Paris' abduction of Helen, by means of the duel of Paris and Menelaos. However, the duel introduced into the narrative the serious anomaly that the struggle for Helen was not decided in this way within the oral tradition, and so Homer employed divine intervention, the rescue of Paris by Aphrodite, to solve the narrative difficulty. This in turn has now produced a further problem: Zeus promised Thetis that the Trojans would achieve such a victory in the absence of Achilleus that the Achaians would come to realize their dependence upon him, but very obviously Menelaos has won the duel, even if he is unable to point to Paris' corpse to prove it. So far events in the poem have gone quite counter to Zeus' declared intentions. This is the result of the introductory purpose which these early books serve, of painting the full backcloth to the anger of Achilleus and its development. In this book Homer presents two further details of this backcloth. First, continuing the theme of the previous book, he portrays the guilt of the Trojans through the treacherous wounding of Menelaos by Pandaros. Second, he continues the presentation of the Achaian forces at Troy, and in particular of a number of their leaders, which he began in the Catalogue of the Ships in Book 2 and the Teichoskopia in Book 3: he achieves this through Agamemnon's review of his troops in the Tour of Inspection (Epipolesis), which provides a picture of heroes such as Diomedes and also a clearer insight into the character of Agamemnon himself.

2 **the goddess Hebe,** the daughter of Zeus and Hera, is the goddess of youth; when the hero Herakles was made immortal, she was given to him as his bride. Wine-pourer to the gods is a task more usually associated with Ganymedes, the handsome Trojan youth whose beauty so captivated Zeus that he abducted him (cf. 20. 232–5).

12   Even now she has rescued him. Zeus taunts his wife Hera with the knowledge that Aphrodite has just been able to rescue her favourite Paris from the jaws of death. Hera's hatred of Paris, and of Troy, arose from the fact that he spurned her when he judged her competition with Aphrodite and Athene.

18   the city of lord Priam might still be a place men dwell in. This accords with the terms of the duel which Paris declared (3. 73–5) but, in view of Hera's declared hatred of Troy, Zeus' words are clearly designed to provoke her (cf. 5–6).

26–9   the sweat that I have sweated in toil. There is a certain grim humour in Hera's reply and this is an indication of Zeus' success in provoking her; but what emerges most of all is the gods' callous disregard for the sufferings of mortals, even of their favourites.

31–6   Dear lady, what can be all the great evils done to you. Zeus' question is heavily ironical, because he is well aware that the reason for Hera's hatred of Troy is the Judgment of Paris. Hera's wish to **eat Priam and the sons of Priam raw** (O'Brien 1991.106) is echoed by Hekabe's longing to eat the liver of Achilleus, the killer of her son Hektor (24. 212–13).

43–9   I was willing to grant you this with my heart unwilling. Although Zeus promised Thetis in Book 1 that the Trojans would have short-term success, he knows that in the end Troy is doomed, even though **never yet has my altar gone without fair sacrifice**: 'This scene . . . is a nightmare picture for men. Punctilious service of the gods, even divine affection, is no defence; the will of another god overrules any human claim' (Griffin 1978.17).

52   Hera's agreement to the future destruction of **Argos and Sparta and Mykenai** is generally taken to refer to the widespread destructions which occurred at the end of the Bronze Age in Greece and the Aegean region (Introduction, 3).

59   I am first of the daughters of devious-devising Kronos. Hera is the sister of Zeus as well as his wife.

66   make it so that the Trojans are first offenders. This is the main purpose of this book, to reaffirm the guilt of Paris, and of Troy and the Trojans.

75–9   As when the son of devious-devising Kronos casts down a star. The shooting star is the point of comparison in the simile, but then Athene seems almost to be transformed into it, because it appears to the soldiers who are amazed by the sight.

88–9 **godlike Pandaros** was described in the Achaian Catalogue as 'the shining son of Lykaon, Pandaros, with the bow that was actual gift of Apollo' (2. 826–7), drawing attention to his great skill as an archer which was god-given. In view of the role he is about to play in breaking the truce and in restarting the war, much has been made of Homer's description of him as **a man blameless**. Another, more notorious, example of this epithet being misused is Aigisthos, the lover of the adulterous Klytaimestra and with her the murderer of her husband Agamemnon, who is called blameless at *Odyssey* 1. 29. These are typical of the occasional lapses of the oral composer, who from time to time uses the traditional formulaic diction inappropriately, though in the present case it may be that Homer is suggesting that Pandaros is the innocent instrument of the gods' intention that Troy be destroyed.

95 **win you glory and gratitude in the sight of all Trojans.** Although Athene presents the wounding of Menelaos to Pandaros as an act to win heroic glory, it is not the act of a true hero who fights in face-to-face combat. The bow is particularly associated with Paris (cf. 3. 18): so Homer is connecting Pandaros' action here with Paris who, having just been roundly defeated in proper heroic combat by Menelaos, now succeeds in wounding him by proxy with a treacherous arrow.

105–26 The importance of the **bow** of Pandaros, the weapon with which the peace treaty is broken, is illustrated by the wealth of detail in its description. When Pandaros killed the goat he was concealed in a covert, and this matches his wounding of Menelaos with the bow made from the goat's horn, for again he is concealed (Atchity 1978.13). **his brave friends held their shields in front of him**: their actions have the effect of involving them too in Pandaros' guilt. Like the detail of the bow itself, the careful account of Pandaros stringing it, drawing it back, releasing the arrow, and of the arrow's flight, enhances both the drama and the significance of the moment.

128 **Zeus' daughter** is Athene, who now acts to preserve Menelaos, having persuaded Pandaros to fire the arrow at him in the first place. So the whole scene is very carefully contrived: the wounding of any of the Achaians would have been enough to restart the war, but only the wounding of Menelaos will serve Homer's artistic purpose of recapitulating Paris' crime. Athene is **the spoiler** because of her role in bringing warfare, which itself brings spoils to the combatants.

130–1   as lightly as when a mother brushes a fly away from her child. The purpose of the simile is to illustrate Athene's protective concern for Menelaos, but the effect of his comparison to a child is to diminish his status as a warrior.

141–7   As when some Maionian woman. The initial point of comparison in the simile is the colour of the dye and the colour of Menelaos' blood, but then **it is laid up to be a king's treasure** illustrates the great value and beauty of the ivory which is dyed, and so the nobility of the hero who is bloodied. The poet's direct address to Menelaos is called *apostrophe*; its effect is to personalize the event and so enhance its pathos.

155–82   Agamemnon's speech is a very carefully crafted piece of characterization. His concern for his wounded brother and his remorse for exposing him to danger present a vivid picture of a caring brother and a responsible commander; but then he thinks of the effect on his own reputation if he returns home with the expedition a failure, and self-doubt and self-pity soon replace anxiety and remorse. Agamemnon's threat that the Trojans will pay **with their own heads, and with their women, and with their children** echoes the wish of both Achaians and Trojans that whoever broke the terms of the truce should be punished (cf. 3. 300–1). **the tomb of great Menelaos**: Agamemnon has in mind the kind of mounded tomb the Achaians construct over their dead (7. 435), and which Achilleus devises for himself and for Patroklos (23. 125).

184   Do not fear, nor yet make afraid the Achaian people. Even though he is lying injured, Menelaos can see that, as in the case of Agamemnon's earlier outburst when he doubted the success of the expedition (cf. 2. 119–22), such self-doubt in the commander will undermine the army's morale.

194   For **Asklepios**, see 2. 729–33n.

219   Cheiron is the Centaur who educated Achilleus: this tradition is largely suppressed in the poem (cf. 11. 831n).

223   Then you would not have seen brilliant Agamemnon asleep. The sudden change in the presentation of Agamemnon from that of his speech a moment ago (155–82n) is designed to introduce his *Epipolesis*, or Tour of Inspection.

231–421   ranged through translates Greek *epepoleito*, which gives the following episode its title *Epipolesis*, Agamemnon's Tour of Inspection. The episode continues the introduction of the Achaian leaders and, in particular, it defines the qualities of the outstanding hero in advance of the first true display of heroic military prowess, by Diomedes in Book 5. Agamemnon encounters in turn Idomeneus, the two Aiantes, Nestor, Odysseus and Diomedes; in each case the characters are revealed through their own words rather than, as in the *Teichoskopia*, through description.

242–5   **arrow-fighters** is an accusation of cowardice, of shirking the front line; it recalls the action of Pandaros in firing his arrow from a distance under the cover of his companions' shields (95n). **like young deer** associates them with the faintheartedness of the Trojans who are often compared to deer. Agamemnon offers no explanation for the Achaians' bewilderment, but it is most likely their reaction to the sudden disappearance of Paris after the duel and the wounding of Menelaos.

254   **Meriones** is the closest companion of Idomeneus (cf. 2. 650–1).

262   **still your cup stands filled forever** means that Idomeneus is honoured by his companions (cf. 12. 310–11), but Agamemnon doesn't say why this great honour is paid to Idomeneus in particular. It is in contrast to the insult he hurls at Odysseus, that he is always the first to hear about a feast and is happy enough to drink the wine, but is backward when it comes to fighting (cf. 345n).

267   **as first I promised you**: that is, when he swore along with the other Achaians to come to Troy and not return home until they had captured it (cf. 2. 286–8).

273–9   For the **Aiantes**, see 2. 405–6n. The metaphor of the **cloud of foot-soldiers** presents a picture of close-compacted soldiers (281); but it also suggests other metaphors, the 'cloud of war' (17. 243) and the 'cloud of death' (16. 350), and through these associations it may itself become a metaphor for death (Moulton 1979.290). The cloud of the metaphor is taken up in the simile, in **a goatherd watches a cloud move on its way over the sea,** and the cloud in the simile, as it piles the storm before it, suggests the aggression of the soldiers as they prepare for their first battle encounter in the poem. The focal point of the simile is the goatherd through whose eyes the approaching cloud is viewed, and he in turn highlights the two figures of the Aiantes.

301–9   First he gave orders to the drivers of horses. The normal use
of chariots in the poem is to transport warriors to the centre of the
battle, where they dismount to fight; so Nestor's advice here on
the tactics of chariot warfare is out of place, and it may look back
to a previous era, as he himself implies (308). Like all the advice
Nestor offers in the poem, it also reflects the character of this most
long-winded and self-important of heroes.

315   age weakens you. For Nestor's great age, see 1. 250–2.

319   Nestor recalls his defeat of **Ereuthalion** later when he attempts
to shame the leading Achaians into accepting a challenge from
Hektor. There he claims that Ereuthalion, the champion of the
Arkadians, was the tallest and strongest man he ever killed, while
he himself at that time was the youngest man in the Pylian army (7.
136–56).

327–48   Menestheus appears in the Achaian Catalogue as leader of
the Athenians (2. 552). Homer makes it clear that he and Odysseus
are not hanging back through cowardice, but Agamemnon misreads
the situation and launches into a tirade against them. His first insult,
you with your mind forever on profit, recalls the insult he himself
received from Achilleus (1. 149), and **your ways of treachery** recalls
Odysseus' distinguishing quality, his cunning; and he goes on to
accuse them of not making their proper contribution in battle, again
much as Achilleus accused him (1. 226). Agamemnon tries to assert
his position authority by treating his companions as he was himself
treated earlier.

345   There it is your pleasure to eat the roast flesh. In the later literary
tradition Odysseus became notorious for his gluttony (Stanford
1954). In return for leading his people a hero receives their honour,
the pride of place at the feast, the best cuts of meat, and the best
piece of land (cf. 12. 310–14): so Agamemnon's charge is that
Menestheus and Odysseus are not behaving like heroes, because
they accept the honours without carrying out their responsibilities.

353–5   if it concerns you. Odysseus implies that Agamemnon is a
coward and so will not be at the front to see him fighting; by calling
himself **the very father of Telemachos,** he is proudly declaring his
pedigree as a hero, against Agamemnon's charge of behaving as a
coward.

365–7   high-spirited Diomedes is presented as the paradigm of the
hero in the poem, and in the next book he will be a worthy substitute

for Achilleus. He is the **son of Tydeus**, who was a member of the great heroic expedition of the previous generation, the Seven against Thebes. His companion **Sthenelos** is also a son of one of the Seven, Kapaneus. The insults Diomedes receives here from Agamemnon are like those Achilleus received, but his calm reaction to them is very different from that of Achilleus.

376–81 Once on a time he came, but not in war, to Mykenai. The occasion is the journey made by **Polyneikes** around the major centres of Greece to enlist support in a war against his brother Eteokles. They were the sons of Oidipous, and they agreed to share the kingship of Thebes between them; but when Eteokles refused to hand over his share, Polyneikes raised the expedition of the Seven to besiege the city. According to the tradition, Mykenai played no part in the expedition, so Agamemnon explains his city's absence by speaking rather vaguely of **portents** sent by Zeus.

385 The Thebans are called **Kadmeians** after their ancestor Kadmos.

399–402 he was a father to a son worse than himself at fighting, better in conclave. As in the case of Odysseus, the charge is that Diomedes is an unworthy hero, better at words than deeds; but unlike Odysseus, Diomedes remains silent **in awe** of the authority of Agamemnon. This is very different from Achilleus' declaration to Agamemnon 'tell other men to do these things, but give me no more commands, since I for my part have no intention to obey you' (1. 295–6).

405 we are better men by far than our fathers. Sthenelos answers Agamemnon's charge head on. The expedition of the Seven against Thebes failed, but their sons, known as the Epigonoi, who included Diomedes and Sthenelos, succeeded in capturing Thebes. So not only is Agamemnon's accusation that Diomedes is inferior to his father tactless and unjustified, events show that it is also untrue.

415 this will be his glory to come. Diomedes defines the responsibilities of kingship of which he is in awe (cf. 399–402n), and he presents a picture of the hero's acceptance of his position within the hierarchy of heroic society: Diomedes accepts his, Achilleus in Book 1 did not. So the actions of Diomedes, here and in following books, provide the yard-stick of the heroes' conduct in general, and of Achilleus' in particular.

422–6 As when along the thundering beach the surf of the sea strikes. This simile describing the Achaians' advance marks the end of the

Epipolesis. It recalls two other similes which described the rallying of the Achaians after their headlong flight to the ships: they were like surf washing upon a beach (2. 209–10), and they were like surf crashing against a cliff (2. 394). The continuation of the imagery in the present simile recalls the spirit of the Achaians as it was before Homer broke off to narrate the long digression of the *Teichoskopia*, the duel of Paris and Menelaos, and now the *Epipolesis*: the surge of the sea is relentless and irresistible, reflecting the intensity of the Achaians' advance.

433–8   **as sheep in a man of possessions' steading.** The sheep are docile, waiting helplessly to be milked, and in the background the voice of their lambs recalls the families of the Trojans helpless within their walls. The contrast with the previous simile is marked: there Homer pictures the Achaians' strength and resolution, here the Trojans' fear for themselves and their families; in the one there is quiet determination, in the other babbling indiscipline, because **there was no speech nor language common to all of them.**

452–5   **As when rivers in winter spate running down from the mountains.** The noise of the two rivers meeting echoes the thundering surf at 422, and the force of the rushing water recalls the surging waves crashing against the rocks. The simile captures the enormity of the clash of the two armies, for **the winter spate** and **the great springs** suggest an image of almost infinite numbers of soldiers. **far away in the mountains the shepherd hears their thunder** recalls the simile of the approaching cloud observed by the goatherd, who shivers at its approach and drives his herd into a cave (273–9n). In both cases the poet is concerned not just with a natural force but with an individual's response to it: in both cases he places that individual in a remote location, and so points up more effectively man's helplessness in face of such natural forces; and the very remoteness of the shepherd recalls another remote figure, Achilleus, who hears the clash of the two armies from the distance of his shelter.

457–544   In the description of general fighting which now follows through to the end of this book the slaughter is evenly divided between Achaians and Trojans; but in the description of the Achaian advance which begins the next book, as far as 5. 83, it is only Trojans who are killed. A crude device it may be, but it effectively establishes the course of the battle, while at the same time offering some variation through its account of the carnage.

473–89 **Telamonian Aias struck down the son of Anthemion Simoeisios.** Simoeisios takes his name from the river Simoeis which with the Skamandros is Troy's principal river, and his death may prefigure the end of Troy itself. He is compared to a poplar **with branches growing at the uttermost tree-top** and this suggests a picture of a young man reaching heroic maturity and laid low in his prime. There is a fine symmetry in the felled poplar lying by the banks of a river, representing the end of the young man's life, and his birth by the banks of the Simoeis. That the poplar has been felled to make an instrument of war, a chariot wheel, pathetically prefigures the deaths of other young men beyond Simoeisios himself (Schein 1984.73).

508 **high Pergamos** is the citadel of Troy.

513 **beside the ship mulls his heartsore anger.** Apollo's words are a timely reminder, as this first battle takes shape, of the absence of Achilleus, and so of Zeus' intention to bring defeat to the Achaians.

515 Just as the Trojans are urged on by Apollo, so the Achaians are driven forward by **Tritogeneia,** that is, Athene; and this matching of god with god confirms the evenness of the battle (cf. 457–544n).

ILIAD 5

In this book Homer continues his introduction of the backcloth to Achilleus' wrath by presenting the ideal hero, Diomedes. His exploits in this book mark him as the greatest of heroes and a substitute for the absent Achilleus. In the previous book his controlled reaction to extreme provocation from Agamemnon contrasted with the reaction of Achilleus in Book 1 to a similar situation (cf. 4. 415n), and he presented a yardstick against which the words and actions of Achilleus were to be measured. His exploits culminate in an encounter with, and wounding of, Aphrodite and Ares, just as Achilleus himself, when he returns to the battle, will encounter and fight the river god Xanthos in Book 21. Diomedes' spectacular advance highlights Achilleus' inaction. In addition this book continues the theme of Troy's guilt from the previous book: there the guilt of the Trojans was established through the wounding of Menelaos by the arrow of Pandaros, and in this book the punishment of Troy and the Trojans is prefigured by the death of Pandaros at the hands of Diomedes. See further, Andersen 1978.

2 **that he might be conspicuous.** Diomedes' exploits will mark him out in this book as the best (*aristos*), and so his advance is called his *aristeia*; his is the first of a number of such *aristeiai* by a number of individual heroes at different times in the poem.

4–6 **She made weariless fire blaze from his shield and helmet.** Similarly when Achilleus makes his move to return to the battle after the death of Patroklos, Athene places a golden cloud around his head and kindles a flame from it (18. 205–6): both the imagery and the goddess' actions indicate the association between the two scenes. **that star of the waning summer** is Sirius, Orion's Dog; towards the end of the poem as Achilleus advances to kill Hektor, he is seen by Priam as like this same star, and this establishes the association of Diomedes and Achilleus even further. In each case the star heralds the destruction which Diomedes and Achilleus are bringing to the Trojans.

9   **Dares** appears nowhere elsewhere in the poem, but the name later became attached to a Latin epic poem, supposedly by a survivor of the war, which told the tale of Troy from the Trojan side.

24   **that the aged man might not be left altogether desolate.** There is pathos in Hephaistos thinking of the blameless old man and preserving one of his sons as reward.

37–83   **the Danaans bent the Trojans back** introduces a catalogue of Achaians killing Trojans, as a result of Athene leading Ares, the protector of the Trojans, out of the battle (cf. 4. 457–544n).

50   **Skamandrios** bears the name of one of Troy's rivers, Skamandros, just as Simoeisios bore the name of the other, Simoeis (cf. 4. 473–89n), but nothing is made of this in the narrative.

62–8   **He it was who had built for Alexandros the balanced ships.** This associates Phereklos directly with Paris' crime of abducting Helen, and so his death prefigures the punishment of all Trojans for that crime.

76   **Hypsenor** is son of the priest of the river god Skamandros (cf. 50n).

87–92   **like a winter-swollen river in spate.** Although the simile paints a vivid picture separate from the main narrative, it is continually drawn back to it: the description of the blossoming vineyards and the lovely works of the young men, and the devastating effect which the flood has on them, calls the image back from the world of nature to the world of the battle and portrays the effect of Diomedes' attack on Troy and the Trojans. The simile looks back to the earlier comparison of the meeting of the two armies to the meeting of two rivers in winter spate (cf. 4. 452–5n); it also looks forward to Diomedes' retreat in face of Hektor, when he is compared to a man standing helplessly at the side of a rushing river which bars his progress (597–9).

98   **hit him as he charged forward, in the right shoulder.** The wounding and retreat of Diomedes so soon after the start of his *aristeia* is strange, but the clue lies in the warrior who wounds him. Diomedes is the second person to be wounded by Pandaros, who shot Menelaos in the previous book and broke the truce by doing so. His action restated Troy's guilt, and in time the whole of Troy

will be made to pay for it, but for now it is Pandaros himself who will be punished and Diomedes will be the instrument; so Homer here prepares for their fatal encounter.

107   drew back again to his chariot and horses. The normal use of chariots in the poem is to transport heroes into battle and then, as here, to wait nearby to carry them out again.

116   if ever before in kindliness you stood by my father. It is normal to pray to a god for help by reminding him either of an offering made to him (cf. 1. 40n), or, as here, of an earlier benefit rendered by him.

125–8   I have put inside your chest the strength of your father. In part this is Athene's response to Diomedes' request for the same support she gave his father; but she is also confirming his heroic status, by declaring him to be his father's equal, and so she is refuting Agamemnon's charge that he falls short of Tydeus' greatness (4. 370–400). **you may well recognize the god and the mortal:** telling gods and mortals apart is a common theme in the poem: Aineias says he is unsure whether Diomedes is a god (177), and Pandaros too is uncertain in his reply to Aineias (183). Athene's help will be important, for during his *aristeia* Diomedes will encounter not just Aphrodite, but Apollo and Ares too.

136–42   as of a lion. The simile begins by describing the rage of Diomedes, but the focus very quickly shifts to the effect of the lion's rage on the flock, and so to the effect of Diomedes' *aristeia*; so the simile's function is the same as the earlier comparison of Diomedes to a winter-swollen river (87–92n).

144–65   Diomedes now kills four pairs of warriors, of whom all but the first are brothers: this gives the poet scope for pathos and irony, but it also increases the status of Diomedes. There is pathos in Homer's observation that the **dream-interpreter Eurydamas** did not answer the dreams of his sons, that is, he was unable to foretell their death at Troy. The **two sons of Phainops** fare less well than the two sons of Dares, of whom Hephaistos spared the one so that their father might not be left altogether desolate (24n). The effect of these brief anecdotes is to personalize each death and each brutal scene, so that a sense of deep humanity is imparted to what might otherwise appear a limitless catalogue of slayings.

161–2   As among cattle a lion leaps. The episode of the killing of the pairs of warriors is bracketed by this lion simile and the lion simile at 136–42: perhaps this is one and the same lion, and the beast which was wounded in the first simile is continuing to wreak its revenge. There is pathos in the fact that the ox or heifer which are the lion's victims are pictured grazing, and so are killed at a moment when they least expect attack, when they are at their most defenceless.

166 **Aineias** appears in the poem for the first time outside the Trojan Catalogue. Although he is destined to continue the Trojan line after the death of Hektor and the fall of the city (20. 307–8), his role in the poem is very much secondary to that of Hektor. His ancestry is given at 20. 215–41.

169 For Pandaros, the **blameless son of Lykaon,** cf. 4. 88–9n.

188–91 **I have shot my shaft already, and hit him in the shoulder.** Pandaros is going to be killed by Diomedes, but he is an archer and so he is never likely to be close enough to be killed by him or anybody else. So Homer has him renounce his bow and arrows and move to close-quarters fighting, through frustration at having hit Diomedes and Menelaos already without killing them. It is now clear that the apparently pointless wounding of Diomedes by Pandaros earlier (cf. 98n) was designed to lead to the present scene. **Aidoneus** is the god of the Underworld.

204 **So I left them and made my way on foot to Ilion.** Pandaros was not prepared to commit the best of his armoury to the Trojan cause, which characterizes well this temporary champion and the cause he is fighting for.

230 **Keep yourself, Aineias, the reins and your horses.** One hero must control the horses while the other fights Diomedes (cf. 107n): and since the horses know Aineias best, it is Pandaros who will face Diomedes. This fine attention to detail ensures that what might otherwise be an unconvincing transformation of Pandaros, from archer to front-line warrior, is achieved in a completely natural fashion.

245–8 **one of them well skilled in the bow's work.** Pandaros' skill with the bow links him to Paris, and his death at Diomedes' hands enacts the punishment owed to Paris. In addition his treachery in breaking the truce in Book 4 represents the crime of all Troy, and so his death represents the punishment of all Trojans. This episode both recalls the cause of the war, Troy's crime, and anticipates its end, Troy's fall. Like Achilleus, Aineias has a mortal father and a

goddess mother: his father Anchises was seduced by Aphrodite as
he tended his herds on Mount Ida, and she bore him Aineias.

265–73   **These are of that strain.** The great value of Aineias' horses
is shown by their pedigree, and so their capture will bring great
honour to Diomedes: the honour of winning Aineias' horses
contrasts with the dishonour of mounting his own horses in flight
(255). Ganymedes was abducted by Zeus to be wine-pourer to the
gods, and this was one of the causes of Hera's hatred of Troy and
her wish to destroy it.

290–6   **shore all the way through the tongue's base.** There is a certain
grim irony in this very brutal description of Pandaros losing his
tongue, for he has been quick to boast about his triumphs, and to
break the Trojans' oaths.

302–4   **a stone, a huge thing which no two men could carry** is just
the type of superhuman feat which sets the major heroes apart,
whilst at the same time stressing that they are humans not gods.

314   Aphrodite's attempt to rescue **her beloved son**, Aineias, is
frustrated by Diomedes, and it needs Apollo to achieve it (445).
Aphrodite had rather less difficulty rescuing Paris (3. 374–82), but
here the purpose of the scene is quite different, to enhance the
status of Diomedes by his wounding of the goddess.

330–3   The **lady of Kypros** is Aphrodite, whose name means 'foam-
born': when Kronos castrated his own father Ouranos, he hurled
his genitals into the sea, and Aphrodite was born in the foam which
was caused; she was brought first to the island of Kythera, and
from there she came to Kypros (Cyprus). Diomedes is able to attack
Aphrodite because Athene has allowed him to tell gods and mortals
apart (125–8n) and gave him permission to attack her (131–2).
Enyo is the goddess of war.

340   The gods eat immortal ambrosia and drink nectar (1. 598), and
so naturally they have special blood, **ichor**, in their veins; this makes
them immortal but does not prevent them feeling pain (361).

348–9   **It is not then enough that you lead astray women** is little
short of a claim that Aphrodite has been wounded for her part in
Helen's abduction.

359   **rescue me and give me your horses.** Just as a warrior in battle
has a chariot nearby to enable him to make a quick departure (107n),
so too does a goddess, when she takes on the role of fighter.

371–4   The figure of **Dione**, mother of Aphrodite, contrasts with the myth of Aphrodite's birth (330–3n); her words **as if you were caught doing something wicked** seem to recognize, like those of Diomedes, Aphrodite's responsibility (cf. 348–9n).

375   The incongruous description of Aphrodite as **sweetly laughing,** when she is in fact feeling pain as well as anger, arises from the composer's use of a traditional formula (Introduction, 5).

385–404   Dione tells her daughter three stories of other gods wounded by mortals; none of these stories is told elsewhere. According to *Odyssey* 11. 305–20, **Ephialtes and Otos** were the sons of Iphimedeia and Poseidon; by nine years of age they measured 9 cubits (13½ ft) broad and 9 fathoms (54 ft) tall; they tried to scale heaven by heaping Mount Ossa, Mount Pelion and Mount Olympos on top of each other; they were destroyed by Apollo before they reached maturity. Clearly Dione is rather carried away by the moment, when she suggests the impossible, that Ares, an immortal, might have died. **the strong son of Amphitryon** is Herakles. **Paiëon** is the god of healing; he also tends the war god Ares when he is wounded by Diomedes (899–901).

407–15   **that man who fights the immortals lives for no long time.** In fact Diomedes, **Tydeus' son,** will not be punished for his attack, because Athene has given him permission; but the lesson is clear enough, and looks forward to the moment when Patroklos makes his fatal attack on Apollo (16. 788–9). Dione's description of Diomedes as **very strong** (*karteros*) associates him even closer with Achilleus, since this was the term used by Nestor to describe Achilleus during the quarrel (1. 275–84n): this is further indication that Diomedes is the yardstick against which the conduct of Achilleus is to be measured. **Aigialeia,** wife of Diomedes, is daughter of Adrastos king of Argos.

422–3   **moving some woman of Achaia to follow after those Trojans.** Athene's words intentionally recall Aphrodite's infatuation of Helen which caused her to follow Paris from Sparta many years ago; the reason for Athene's, and for Hera's, gloating is that at last Aphrodite is being made to pay for the war and the suffering it has brought, and for her victory over them in the Judgment of Paris. Aphrodite is immortal and so cannot be killed, but she can be wounded and taught a lesson.

436–42   Diomedes' charge against Apollo, **three times, furious to cut him down,** anticipates the three-fold attack of Patroklos, also on Apollo (16. 784–5). When Diomedes charges a fourth time, he is warned by Apollo and backs off: because Diomedes learns the limitations of his heroic status, he survives his encounter with Apollo; Patroklos on the other hand does not learn that lesson, and he perishes. The description **like more than a man** is also echoed in Patroklos' attack, when he is described as 'like something greater than human' (16. 786–7).

447   **Artemis** is Apollo's sister, **Leto** is their mother.

471   **Sarpedon** is a figure of major significance in the poem. His friendship with Glaukos mirrors, on the Trojan side, that of Achilleus and Patroklos on the Achaian. Both friendships will be terminated by violence, the one when Patroklos kills Sarpedon, the other when Hektor kills Patroklos: so Sarpedon's death will present Patroklos with his greatest glory, but it will also lead directly to his death. It is perhaps no accident that Sarpedon makes his appearance during the Diomedes episode, for in the next book Diomedes will encounter his close friend Glaukos on the battlefield in one of the poem's most memorable scenes (6. 119–236).

472–92   Sarpedon's speech, **in abuse**, to Hektor contains some similar thoughts to Achilleus' during the quarrel (1. 152–60): both speakers declare that they are not fighting for themselves, but for the cause of another; that the enemy has done no harm to their possessions, nor will do; that they are far from home where they would rather be; and that they both fight while their commanders do nothing. However there are differences: Sarpedon speaks of his wife and baby son left at home and this contrasts with the solitary Achilleus, and associates him rather with Hektor whose wife and child will feature in the next book; and Sarpedon says that, despite all the reasons why he would prefer to be at home, he stays and fights bravely, whereas Achilleus uses the arguments to support his decision to abandon the Achaians. So the speech of Sarpedon both echoes, and comments upon, the Achaian hero's alienation.

499–502   **As when along the hallowed threshing floors the wind scatters chaff.** The point of the simile is straightforward, to compare the dust thrown up by the horses and whitening the soldiers' faces to the chaff which the wind scatters; but its effect is to lend a different perspective, by contrasting the harshness of battle with a scene from the peaceful world, the world as it was at Troy before the coming of the Achaians. **Demeter** is the goddess of corn.

522–6 The steadiness of the Achaian leaders is portrayed by two similes in one: the **clouds** which are motionless show their determined resistance, but then the **tempests high screaming** provide a contrast, to represent the noise and violence of the battle which rages all around them.

533–710 There is now a long description of general fighting which may appear formless and monotonous, but which in fact has a carefully designed structure. At first the evenness of the battle is indicated by alternating deaths: Trojan Deïkoön, Achaian Orsilochos and Krethon, Trojan Pylaimenes and Mydon, Achaian Anchialos and Menesthes, Trojan Amphios, and Achaian Tlepolemos (533–667). The Achaians then gain the advantage and this is represented by Odysseus slaying all before him—Koiranos, Chromios, Alastor, Halios, Alkandros, Prytanis, and Noemon (668–78); but then the battle swings round again as Ares intervenes and aids Hektor in the slaughter of the Achaians—Teuthras, Orestes, Trechos, Oinomaos, Helenos and Oresbios (689–710). By the end eleven Achaians and eleven Trojans lie dead.

554–8 **as two young lions in the high places of the mountains.** Diomedes was earlier compared to a lion which, though wounded, still is strong enough to drive off a shepherd and devastate his flock (136–42n). Now the two lions represent the defeated Achaians. The two similes bracket the intervening narrative and highlight the change from Diomedes' success to that of the Trojans.

565 **Antilochos**, Nestor's son, is an important figure in the epic tradition. In the lost epic *Aithiopis*, a part of the Epic Cycle (Evelyn-White 1967), he rescued his aged father, much as he rescues Menelaos here, but was killed doing so. His action here is a fine example of heroic loyalty and comradeship, and offers a contrast to the alienated figure of Achilleus.

597–600 **like a man in his helplessness.** Earlier Diomedes was like a torrent in full winter spate destroying the dikes and blossoming vineyards (cf. 87–92n), but now he is himself the victim helplessly retreating before the torrent which bars his way: the reversal of the imagery reflects the reversal Diomedes has suffered. His retreat marks the temporary victory of the Trojans; the same effect is achieved when Aias too is forced to give ground before the Trojans' numbers (626).

628–9 Although **Tlepolemos** is the grandson of Zeus and **Sarpedon**

is his son, they are enemies. Tlepolemos is leader of the Achaian contingent from the island of Rhodes (2. 653–4), and Sarpedon commands the Trojan allies from Lykia on the mainland of Asia Minor facing the island.

640–2   he came here on a time for the sake of Laomedon's horses. In a previous war at Troy Herakles took vengeance upon the Trojan king, Laomedon, by killing him and sacking the city. Herakles had landed at Troy on the way back from performing his ninth labour, which was to bring back the girdle of Hippolyte, the queen of the Amazons; at that time Troy was in the grip of a sea beast sent by Poseidon and Apollo, whom Laomedon had refused to reward for building the walls of Troy. Laomedon promised Herakles the gift of his famous horses if he would save his daughter Hesione who was due to be offered up to the creature, but when Herakles was successful Laomedon reneged on the deal. The story is a further example of the Trojans as untrustworthy breakers of promises and oaths, and just as Herakles destroyed their city in punishment of their perjury, so too will the Achaians in the present generation.

684–91   Son of Priam, do not leave me lying. Sarpedon's plea in the name of his wife, soon to be widowed, and their baby, soon to be orphaned, anticipates the events of the following book, the scene in Troy between Hektor and his wife Andromache, soon to be widowed, and their baby Astyanax, soon to be orphaned. At the end of that scene Hektor will ignore the appeal of his wife and will return to the battle, just as here he ignores Sarpedon's appeal. Hektor's headlong pursuit of glory recalls Sarpedon's earlier accusation that in his actions he showed no gratitude towards his allies (476–92).

703   Who then was the first and who the last that they slaughtered. Although the Muse is not mentioned, the question is nonetheless directed to her, and she gives authority to the following catalogue of victims.

722–32   Hera and Athene unite in an approach to Zeus to seek permission to attack Ares. Each goddess is introduced by the description of an object particularly associated with her: in the case of Hera, the magnificence of the description of her **chariot—** all gold, silver, iron and bronze—emphasizes the picture of the goddess herself, who is **furious for hate and battle.**

734–47   Athene's actions are highly symbolic as she **slipped off her**

elaborate dress and puts on Zeus' armour and, with it, a warrior role. Her dressing matches, on the divine level, the traditional theme of a warrior's arming (cf. 3. 328–38n). It is unclear how the **aegis** is to be visualized: Athene throws it across her shoulders, whereas Apollo (15. 308) is said to grip it in his hands. The aegis has the force of the different personifications decorating it, Terror, Hatred, Battle Strength, and Onslaught, and like Hera's chariot, it increases the stature of the goddess. The **Gorgon** is Medusa, whose stare turned to stone anyone who met it; she was decapitated by Perseus who viewed only her reflection in his shield.

749   The goddesses proceed from the sky to Olympos. Like two heroes emerging from the city in a chariot (cf. 7. 1), Hera and Athene are visualized as passing through the gates, which in reality are the clouds, guarded by the Horai, or Seasons.

760   **Kypris** is Aphrodite (cf. 330–3n).

778–9   **walked forward in little steps like shivering doves.** Some see this as humorous: 'strutting or waddling—hardly a dignified motion' (Kirk 1990.139); but it is the eagerness of the goddesses Homer is describing, and so a rapid, scuttling movement seems more likely.

785   **Stentor** has given English the adjective stentorian, to describe any loud-voiced sound.

800–8   **Tydeus got him a son who is little enough like him** recalls the very similar criticism which Agamemnon made of Diomedes (4. 372); Athene also tells of the same escapade of his father Tydeus in Thebes which Agamemnon spoke of (4. 385–400).

818–24   **you would not let me fight in the face of the blessed immortals.** By recalling Athene's warning, Diomedes is reinforcing the moral of this book, that a hero must be aware of the limitations placed on his heroic prowess and achievement unless a god is fighting beside him.

832–3   **promising that he would fight against the Trojans.** Athene persuaded Ares to withdraw from the battle (29–35), but he made no such promise as Athene now claims.

842–5   **Ares was in the act of stripping gigantic Periphas.** No other god is ever shown performing this action which is typically that of the hero. In effect Ares has taken on the role of hero, and when Diomedes now faces him he is confronting the greatest possible challenge, a duel with a hero who is himself a god. By making Athene invisible to Ares, the **helm of Death** places Diomedes before

Ares in a one-against-one fight, and his wounding of this god/hero is the climax of his *aristeia* and the measure of his heroic status, since he will now have fought and wounded two gods, Aphrodite and Ares.

859–61   **Ares the brazen bellowed.** The gods may be immortal but this does not protect them from pain; Ares' bellow may be compared to Aphrodite's shriek (343) when she too was wounded by Diomedes. It is paradoxical that Ares' bellow should be compared to the noise of attacking soldiers, at the very moment the war god is beating retreat.

875   **you brought forth this maniac daughter** implies the tradition that Athene was born from the head of Zeus and had no mother, although this tale is not actually recounted in Homer.

898   **you would have been dropped beneath the gods of the bright sky** is a reference to the Titans who were imprisoned in Tartaros, 'where the uttermost depth of the pit lies under earth' (8. 14–5); Zeus' threat is that Ares would have been imprisoned with them.

909   **after they stopped the murderous work of manslaughtering Ares.** This book, through the *aristeia* of Diomedes, has shown that the Achaians are the natural winning side in the war: they may suffer a reversal when an enemy god intervenes, but their own supporting gods quickly put matters to right. The natural order is Achaian attack and Trojan defence; individual Achaian heroes are naturally superior to Trojan and under normal circumstances will be victorious. However the circumstances of the poem are not normal, for Zeus has promised Achaian defeat. So this book has shown the war as it is, or as it would be if Achilleus, for whom Diomedes stands substitute, were himself present.

ILIAD 6

In Book 6 Homer introduces one more element of the background to the anger of Achilleus, his Trojan counterpart and adversary, Hektor; and through Hektor and his family he illustrates the human tragedy which the fall of Troy will represent. For the most part, the book is set in Troy and is concerned with events and characters within the walls; and so it complements Book 3 which introduced Helen, Paris, and Priam; but whereas Book 3 presented the reason, and the justification, for the Achaians' attack, Book 6 arouses the pity of the audience for the doomed people of the city. There is little description of the physical results of the siege, the suffering and the starvation, for Homer is seeking to illustrate the mood of Troy's inhabitants rather than their surroundings. The book portrays the character of Hektor and his reasons for fighting, through scenes in which he meets first his mother Hekabe, then his sister-in-law Helen, and finally his wife Andromache; each of the three women in his life tries to restrain him from returning to the battlefield, but each fails. As the book opens, the battle has swung decisively in favour of the Achaians: Ares has retired, injured and humiliated by Diomedes, and has abandoned the Trojans to their own devices, and the divine supporters of the Achaians, Hera and Athene, have felt able to leave the field to mortals, having achieved their object, the rout of the war god (5. 907–9). The result is that the actions of this book are those of humans, without interference from the gods: the natural trend of events, as indicated by Diomedes' aristeia, is inevitably Achaian ascendancy (5. 909n). On the Hektor and Andromache episode, see Schadewaldt 1959; de Romilly 1996.

4   **Xanthos and Simoeis** are the two rivers of Troy; Xanthos is the name by which the gods know Skamandros (20. 74) and is the river against which Achilleus fights at 21. 211f.

5–36   Achaian victory is represented by the death of no fewer than
fifteen Trojans, without a single casualty among the Achaians. Defeat
of the Trojans on this scale is directly contrary to Zeus' promise of
Trojan victory in Book 1, and this indicates that Homer has not yet
returned to the central theme of the poem, the anger of Achilleus.
The Trojan deaths are presented almost in the form of a catalogue,
whose purpose is to establish such conditions of defeat and
demoralization of the Trojans that Hektor will return to Troy to
consult the elders and to order sacrifices.

13–17   **a friend to all humanity**. Brief details such as this of victims'
lives are often added to the description of their death in order to
add pathos, here by contrasting the victim's hospitality with the
failure of any of his guests to save him.

37–65   **Adrestos** falls into the hands of Menelaos who is inclined to
spare him, but he is killed by Agamemnon. The episode makes the
character of Menelaos clearer: 'neither an outstanding warrior . . .
nor a good counsellor . . . he has more zeal than true valour . . .
[he] has a soft streak' (Parry 1972.16). For **catching him by the
knees** as the proper ritual of supplication, cf. the visit of Thetis to
Zeus (1. 500–1n). This is the first example of a common theme in
the poem, the plea of a defeated warrior for his life (Thornton
1984): in fact none of the pleas is successful.

58–9   **the young man child that the mother carries still in her body**
represents the generations of Trojan warriors yet unborn:
Agamemnon threatens the total eradication of the Trojan people,
and his ruthless desire for revenge on the enemy contrasts with the
friendly words and feelings of Diomedes towards the enemy in the
following scene (119–236).

62   **since he urged justice** may be one of the rare occasions when
Homer passes his own comment, but it is more likely that he is
presenting the viewpoint of Menelaos, that his heart is bent because
he believes that his brother is urging justice.

75   **Helenos** is one of the many sons of Priam (cf. 244–6), and as
seer he plays the same role as Kalchas on the Achaian side. It was
Helenos who prophesied that Troy would be captured when
Philoktetes was brought to Troy from Lemnos (Sophocles
Philoktetes 604–13).

81–2   **before they tumble into their women's arms.** An important
theme of this book is the separation of the world of women and

old men within the walls of Troy from the world of fighting men outside (cf. 3. 448n): the separation is represented by the Skaian Gate (237n). Helenos here anticipates the most dramatic, and the most persuasive, appeal Hektor will encounter during his visit to the city, from his wife Andromache, who will try to persuade him to stay in this world of women and direct his army from the security of Troy's rampart (431–4).

86   **but you, Hektor, go back again to the city.** At this time of peril for the Trojan army, Hektor's place is clearly at the head of his army, not visiting the women and old men in the city: Homer's introductory purpose, of bringing Hektor into Troy to meet his wife Andromache and others, proves to be more important than such fine details of logic.

88   **at the temple of grey-eyed Athene high on the citadel.** Along with Hera, Athene was the loser in the Judgment of Paris, when the Trojan prince was persuaded to award the prize to Aphrodite, and so she is in fact one of Troy's enemies in the poem. The reason that she nevertheless has a temple on Troy's citadel is that she is protector of citadels generally. Later tradition told of an image of Pallas Athene, the Palladion, which guaranteed the city's safety, and which was stolen by Odysseus and Diomedes (Virgil *Aeneid* 2. 164); tradition also related that it was brought by Aineias to Rome where it played the same protective role.

99   **For never did we so fear Achilleus even** is one of a number of passages which remind the audience of Achilleus despite his absence from the scene since Book 1: previously Hektor pictured him beside the ships (4. 512), and Hera pointed out that when he was still fighting the Trojans were afraid to venture beyond the city's gates (5. 788–90).

113–15   **to make their prayer to the immortals.** The conventions of oral composition would normally require Hektor to repeat what Helenos said to him just a few lines earlier (86–95), but there is good reason why he doesn't: his purpose is to rally the Trojans to stout resistance while he is away from the battle, and he is hardly likely to achieve this by communicating to them the state of near-panic which led to Helenos' proposal.

117   **against his ankles as against his neck clashed the dark ox-hide.** This seems to be an example of the Mykenaian body-shield, either oblong or figure-of-eight in shape, of which representations are

found dating to the early part of the Late Bronze Age (Lorimer 1950.132). The shield would be slung over the warrior's back when not in use, held at the neck by a strap, and covering his entire body right to the ankles. Such objects are an important indication of the great age of the oral tradition, but otherwise little detail of the Mykenaian period of Greek history survives in the poems.

119–236 During Hektor's absence in Troy the meeting of **Glaukos** and the **son of Tydeus**, Diomedes, takes place. The episode has three parts: Diomedes declares that he is unwilling to fight against a god, if such Glaukos is, and tells the story of Lykourgos to justify his decision (119–43); Glaukos replies by giving his genealogy and telling the story of his ancestor Bellerophontes (144–211); and the two then recognize their ancestral guest-friendship, and exchange gifts (212–36).

128–43 **I will not fight against any god of the heaven** runs counter to Diomedes' actions in Book 5 when he fought both Aphrodite and Ares, but on that occasion he was given permission by Athene: Diomedes has a natural instinct for restraint and self-discipline. The story of **Lykourgos**, king of Thrace, who opposed the god Dionysos and drove his nymphs from his sacred mountain Nysa, and even forced the god himself to take refuge with Thetis beneath the sea's waves, may be rationalized as an attempt to drive the worship of Dionysos, or Bacchos, from Thrace. Lykourgos was punished by being struck blind and died soon afterwards, and so Diomedes illustrates the need for restraint when humans deal with the gods: the man who shows restraint remains safe from their anger.

146 **As is the generation of leaves, so is that of humanity** The comparison of men to leaves also occurred in a simile which introduced the Catalogue of the Ships (2. 467–8n), presenting a picture of the mortality of the soldiers, as well as of their vast numbers. The leaf which grows in spring must die in the autumn fall, but it is replaced in season; so man too must die in his autumn, but he is replaced and gains significance from his position, as the offspring of his ancestors and as the ancestor of his own descendants. The theme of man's mortality is an important aspect of Achilleus' response to Agamemnon's ambassadors in Book 9, when he declares that, if death awaits both brave man and coward alike, then he will no longer risk his life in battle but will return home.

152–5 Glaukos begins a long account of his genealogy, in particular the tale of his ancestor **Bellerophontes**. **Ephyre** is the city of Korinth, to the north of the plain of **horse-pasturing Argos**. Bellerophontes is the grandfather of Glaukos (196–206), and is himself the grandson of **Sisyphos**, whose punishment in the Underworld is pictured at *Odyssey* 11. 593: he is forced for ever to roll a boulder up a hill only to have it for ever roll down again. In legend Sisyphos was the archetypal trickster: for example, the tale was told that when Autolykos, the grandfather of Odysseus, stole some cattle, Sisyphos ensured their discovery by fastening tablets to their hooves inscribed 'stolen by Autolykos'. So Sisyphos is described here as **sharpest of all men**; his father **Aiolos** was the ancestor of the Aiolian race of Greeks.

156–66 **To Bellerophontes the gods granted beauty**. Bellerophontes is presented as hero *par excellence*, blameless, handsome and valiant, and so able to overome every hazard in his path. **Proitos** is king of Argos: the tale of his queen **Anteia** who, when her passion for the younger man is unrequited, tells her husband that the man has tried to seduce her, is a traditional story which finds its parallel in the tale of Phaidra and Hippolytos.

168 **murderous symbols** may well be a distant memory of the Mykenaian script, preserved at various Bronze Age sites in the Linear B tablets but unknown to Homer and his audience, except as a barely understood formula in the oral tradition.

179–93 The tasks which Bellerophontes is set by the king of Lykia, and the king's daughter who is his reward, indicate that this is a traditional marriage-task legend. The **Chimaira** was a creature with the heads of a lion, a goat and a snake; the **Solymoi** were the original inhabitants of Lykia; for the female warrior **Amazons**, see 3. 184–9n: their name, meaning 'breastless', was supposed to derive from their practice of cutting off their right breasts to enable them to draw their bows. The **portents of the immortals** are left deliberately vague, to emphasize Bellerophontes' ready obedience to divine will.

194 **the men of Lykia cut out a piece of land.** The gift of the finest piece of land is an important sign of the hero's status; cf. Sarpedon's words to Glaukos at 12.31–4.

200 **But after Bellerophontes was hated by all the immortals.** Bellerophontes had the help of the winged horse Pegasos in his attack on the Chimaira, and afterwards he rode on its back up to heaven to spy on the gods: as punishment, Zeus forced him to wander alone about the **plain of Aleios,** in Kilikia. Glaukos makes no mention of this tale, precisely because it gives a reason for Bellerophontes' fall: such a scheme of crime and punishment is at odds with the pessimistic message that he has given, that man is at the mercy of the gods' whims (Scodel 1992). Diomedes' tale of Lykourgos, on the other hand, is a tale of human crime and punishment by the gods, and from it he concludes that, if man does not antagonize the gods, he will remain unharmed (cf. 128–43n).

208   **to be always among the bravest.** Hippolochos' advice to his son on being a hero is exactly the same as that given by Peleus to Achilleus (11. 783), although Lattimore chooses to translate differently.

215–25   Diomedes declares that Glaukos is his ancestral **guest-friend.** The exchange of gifts between Diomedes' grandfather **Oineus** and Glaukos' grandfather Bellerophontes created a bond of guest-friendship between them which now binds their descendants (Herman 1987.2). Gift-exchange is the external expression of the guest-host relationship (*xenia*), which underpins the relations between heroes. Paris broke the rules of this relationship when he stole his host Menelaos' wife and possessions; so the Diomedes–Glaukos episode provides the measure of Paris' actions which were the cause of the war. **I was little when he left me:** Diomedes' father Tydeus helped Polyneikes recruit for the expedition of the Seven against Thebes (cf. 4. 376–81n), and died on that campaign.

234–6   **Zeus the son of Kronos stole away the wits of Glaukos.** At least two reasons may be given for Glaukos handing over armour very much more valuable than he receives. Firstly, that he acts from fear: he fears for his life, and so when Diomedes proposes a non-aggression pact, sealed by an exchange of armour, he can scarcely believe his good fortune and quickly accepts, even though he loses out on the exchange. Secondly, that he acts from pride: he presses the gift of the golden armour on Diomedes, in a display of his superior wealth and so of his heroic stature. The second is the likelier, because it is developed in Book 9 when Agamemnon tries to assert his superiority over Achilleus by a great show of wealth. Recent discussion of the question in Calder 1984, Traill 1989, Donlan 1989. Others feel that the emphasis on the value of the two suits of armour detracts from the chivalry of the act, and lends humour to the scene.

237 The **Skaian gates** play a very important role in the poem: it is above this gate that Hektor meets his wife and son and where they part for the last time (393f); it is below this gate that Hektor stands as his mother and father plead with him to come within the walls, and where he resolves to face Achilleus and death (22. 6f); and it is at this same gate that Achilleus himself will die at the hands of Paris and Apollo (23. 359–60). The gate stands as the boundary between the city and the surrounding land, between Trojans and Achaians, between the city at peace and the city at war, between civilization and barbarism. Behind it Hektor stays as Patroklos storms the city (16. 712), and beyond it he dared not venture when Achilleus was still fighting (9. 354). It is presented as the symbol of the world of women and old men: upon it the ineffectual old men, like cicadas (3. 149), discuss the progress of the war, and from it Helen identifies for the aged Priam the greatest of the Achaian fighting men (3. 171–242). For detail see Arthur 1981, Scully 1990.42. The **oak tree** is also mentioned with the Skaian gates at 9. 354 and 11. 170; oak trees were sacred to Zeus, and so this tree is probably a symbol of the city's defence.

238 **all the wives of the Trojans and their daughters.** From the outset it is the role of men and women within the context of the family which is stressed in this episode, for it is in this role that Hektor is to be observed shortly.

244 **fifty sleeping chambers.** The interconnecting bedchambers for Priam's sons and daughters and their spouses present a picture of marital harmony and family unity, which typify Troy before the war came; but Homer is also drawing a contrast between this picture of Priam's palace and that of Paris which he will describe shortly (314n). Priam declares himself a polygamist at 24. 497.

251–85 During his visit to the city, Hektor meets the three important women in his life: each makes an appeal and tries to delay his return to battle, and each is unsuccessful. The first appeal is by **his bountiful mother** Hekabe, who fears that he is worn out with fighting and urges him to take a refreshing cup of wine. Hektor refuses from fear that the wine will sap his strength.

266–8 Hektor is quite right that he cannot pour a libation or pray to Zeus **with hands unwashed**, without first performing the full ritual of purification (1. 449n); but his insistence on remaining **with blood and muck all spattered** has an artistic purpose too, in setting the tone of his visit to Troy, his urgency to return to the battle.

281–2   How I wish at this moment the earth might open beneath him recalls Hektor's damning criticism of his brother Paris at 3. 39–57. After his rescue from his duel with Menelaos, Paris was deposited in his bedroom with Helen, and he has been there ever since (cf. 3. 448): it is Paris' crime in starting the war, and then his cowardice before Menelaos that Hektor condemns, and his mother Hekabe has no words with which to defend her son.

289–92   the work of Sidonian women. Paris captured these women of Sidon, a city of Phoenicia, on the same journey on which he abducted Helen from Sparta. So the robes made by them are associated with his crime, and it is no surprise that Athene denies the appeal of the Trojan women who come bearing one of them.

297–310   **The scene of the offering of the robe to Athene echoes the ceremony during the Panathenaic festival in Athens in which a robe (*peplos*) was borne in procession as offering to the statue of Athene, a scene which was among the representations on the Parthenon. **Kisseus is king of Thrace. **Antenor** is one of the most important of the Trojan elders. For **our city's defender,** cf. 88n.

**313–68   **Hektor now moves on to the house of Paris, where he meets both his brother and Helen. The scene is a continuation of Book 3, where Homer described the same triangle of relations: there Paris was presented as the man within the world of women (cf. 3. 448n), the man who, when he ventured onto the battlefield, had to be rescued from it by the goddess of love, the man who represents everything which Hektor is not.

314   a splendid place he had built himself. Although he is a son of Priam, Paris does not live with Priam's other children in his palace. Paris' house is the best that money can buy, and indicates the same love of luxury as the exotic leopard-skin he wore at his first appearance (3. 17). It is situated in a prime position on the peak of the citadel which associates him with the leaders Hektor and Priam, even though he himself contributes nothing to Troy but anguish and death.

319   the eleven-cubit-long spear is a very impressive object, some 16 ft in length; later, the hero Aias fights with a pike 22 cubits, or

32 ft, in length (15. 678). What to the modern reader may seem incredibly unwieldy objects are handled with ease by heroes, and such feats generally indicate the gap between heroes and ordinary mortals. However, this spear is hardly a practical object to be carrying indoors and clearly Hektor does so for an artistic reason: the spear emphasizes his recent departure from the battlefield and his urgency to return to it (cf. 266–8n).

322 **turning in his hands the curved bow**. There is a neat correspondence in the scene which meets Hektor's eyes, Paris on the one side, Helen on the other, both busily occupied, and this suggests a correspondence between the tasks on which they are engaged, so that Paris' handling of his weapons becomes closely associated with the handiwork of Helen and her female attendants. Homer draws a contrast between the almost erotic attention Paris pays to the corselet, shield, and bow, and the heroic dimensions of the spear which Hektor carries, and in this way he presents the picture of Paris as the man in the world of women. Although the poem has advanced by three books, this is still the same day as the duel of Paris and Menelaos: it was to Paris' chamber that Aphrodite ordered Helen (3. 391), and so Homer conveys the impression that they have been occupied in his bedchamber ever since his rescue by Aphrodite.

336–7 Paris' wish **to give myself over to sorrow** may be the result of his defeat by Menelaos in the duel in Book 3, or it may be remorse for all that he has brought on his people. In the light of his reception by Helen after his rescue from the duel (3. 428–36), it is clear that Paris' recollection of her **soft words** is flawed, as though he has not been defeated, as though he totally ignores the duel and the ignominy of his defeat, as though he believes he still retains his wife's affections. Yet it seems that her words have made some impression upon him, and that the sorrow he feels is a manifestation of it.

343–58 Like Hekabe, **Helen** tries to persuade Hektor to stay with her for a time; her condemnation of herself is a continuation of the earlier picture of her when she also wished for death (3. 173–80n). Helen has been judged harshly by some critics: 'nothing but a flirt and professional charmer', and 'wanton, self-centred, deceitful, bewitching and beguiling' (Ryan 1965.117); Edwards (1987.89) speaks of 'Helen, thinking as usual of herself'. In fact none of the characters in the poem condemns her as she condemns herself, and for this reason she retains a unique dignity. Her anxiety that Hektor rest from the fighting is a measure of the guilt she feels for the Trojans' suffering, and her affection for her brother-in-law contrasts with her loathing for her husband. **I wish I had been the wife of a better man** draws the contrast between her marriage to Paris and that of Hektor to Andromache which will feature in the following scene. Her marriage is adulterous, the result of her abduction, and it is childless; in contrast, the marriage of Hektor and Andromache is marked by their deep love, and it is fulfilled in their small child Astyanax. See further, Ebbott 1999.

365–8   I do not know if ever again I shall come back this way. Hektor is struck with foreboding and a sudden need to see his wife and child. Homer intends this scene to be Andromache's farewell to Hektor before his death, even though his death will not take place until Book 22: were he to make the farewell scene the stated purpose of Hektor's journey to Troy, rather than an apparent afterthought, he would certainly achieve even greater emotional impact, but he would also arouse in his audience an expectation of Hektor's immediate death. So he keeps the introduction of the scene deliberately subdued, incidental almost, and so overcomes the difficulty of the husband and wife saying farewell some sixteen books before the drama makes it strictly necessary.

373   taken her place on the tower in lamentation. Andromache's lamentation establishes at the outset the air of foreboding which pervades the Hektor–Andromache episode.

388–9   like a woman gone mad The Greek *mainomenei eikuia* evokes the frenzy with which the followers of Dionysos, the maenads, are totally overcome (Seaford 1994.330); the same image occurs later in the poem when Andromache, hearing the sound of the Trojans mourning the death of her husband, runs out of the house 'like a raving woman' (*mainadi ise*, 22. 460). This association of imagery in the two scenes clearly marks the present scene as anticipating the later: her anxiety now 'because she heard that the Trojans were losing' foreshadows her fear that 'great Achilleus might have cut off bold Hektor, alone, away from the city' (22. 455–6); and so by anticipating Hektor's death, Homer transforms the meeting of Hektor and Andromache into their farewell.

393   Locating the Hektor–Andromache scene at the **Skaian gates**

(cf. 237n) will provide great pathos later in the poem: as Hektor waits beneath this same gate for Achilleus to attack and contemplates appealing to him, his meeting with Andromache is recalled, when he compares himself to some love-struck youth (22. 125–8). The apparent incongruity of comparing himself and Achilleus to two young lovers is explained by the recollection that it was here that he parted from his wife.

397   Achilleus' destruction of **Thebe below Plakos,** the city below Mount Ida ruled by Andromache's father Eëtion, plays a prominent part in the poem (Taplin 1986). Achilleus himself spoke of it to his mother Thetis (1. 366–9), and later it emerged that it was on this same expedition that he took Briseis prisoner (2. 690–1). After Patroklos' death, Briseis laments over his body that she saw her husband and her three brothers killed by Achilleus (19. 292–6); and now Andromache recalls how Achilleus slew her father Eëtion and her seven brothers (414–24). In this way Homer connects the experiences of Briseis and Andromache, both deprived of their loved ones by Achilleus on the same expedition. For Briseis the consequence was that she was driven into the arms of their killer, with whom she lived as wife until she was removed on Agamemnon's orders; for Andromache the consequence is absolute dependence upon her husband Hektor (cf. 429–30).

402   Hektor's name for his son, **Skamandrios,** associates him with the river Skamandros (cf. 4n), which with its tributary the Simoeis acts as the great natural protection of Troy and against which Achilleus battles in Book 21. For all others, his name Astyanax marks him as the *anax* of the *asty*, the lord of the city.

418   **burned the body in all its elaborate war-gear.** This is the only time a hero buries his enemy rather than trying to strip the body and abuse it. Homer makes Achilleus' treatment of the body of Andromache's father the exception and so highlights his later treatment of her husband Hektor, his corpse dragged behind his chariot. By stripping the armour from the body and taking possession of it, Achilleus would have added to his own honour; by not doing so, he effectively gives honour to the dead king. So his honourable treatment of Eëtion's body shows him as motivated by more than an heroic quest for honour, and Andromache interprets it as respect (*sebas*).

425   **and when he had led my mother.** The fate of Andromache's

city, Thebe, is connected to that of Troy: just as Thebe was sacked, its king Eëtion killed, and its queen, Andromache's mother, led off to slavery, so Troy itself will be destroyed, its king Priam will be killed, and its queen Hekabe and her daughter-in-law Andromache will be taken as slaves (cf. 455); and as she laments over her dead husband, Andromache herself will allude to the similar fates of Thebe and Troy (22. 477–9).

431–4   Please take pity upon me. Andromache will not be present when Hektor stands beneath the walls of Troy awaiting Achilleus' attack in Book 22, and so Homer has her make her appeal now: the appeal will be echoed in those of his parents, Priam and Hekabe, in the later book. Her words **stay here on the rampart** mark the climax of a scene which has been carefully prepared, both in Book 3 and now in Book 6 (cf. 81–2n): she is urging him to remain within the world of women, and from there direct his troops who are in the world of men. Andromache's words are not battle tactics, except in the most general sense, but they are a final desperate appeal to her husband to forsake the world of war and men and remain in the world of women, to take on, that is, the role which has been illustrated through the figure of Paris.

441–2   I would feel deep shame before the Trojans. The background to Hektor's statement is Helen's words to him on the subject of Paris 'I wish I had been the wife of... one who knew modesty and all things of shame that men say' (cf. 343–58n). This quality of shame (*aidos*) (Cairns 1993) in the face of public opinion is the difference between Hektor and his brother (cf. 3. 39–45n); it is just this quality which will lead to Hektor's death for, as he contemplates fleeing inside the walls of Troy before Achilleus' attack, he will also conclude that 'I feel shame before the Trojans and the Trojan women with trailing robes' (22. 105–6).

444   I have learned to be valiant reveals the depths of Hektor's dilemma: he knows the risk to his family if he fights, but as a hero he must fight in front of his people to win honour, and this role must, and does, override his role as husband, son and father; yet his words here perhaps hint that this is not his natural role nor one which comes easily to him, but rather is one he has had to learn and from which he might wish to escape were it not for his people's expectations. It is in order to highlight Hektor's mental conflict that such emphasis is placed throughout this book, and again in

Book 22, on his family attachments. On Hektor's quest for *kleos*, see further Mackie 1996.85ff.

456–7   in Argos you must work at the loom of another recalls the fate Agamemnon threatened for Chryseis when he refused her father's pleas (1. 31). Since **Messeis** and **Hypereia** were probably in Thessaly, **Argos** does not refer to the city or the plain of Argos, but must stand for Greece as a whole.

463–5   to be widowed of such a man who could fight off the day of your slavery. Although he feels pity for Andromache's fate, Hektor seems at least as concerned about how her fate will reflect on himself: he claims that he could indeed fight off the day of her slavery, but he is not prepared to forego his role as hero to do so.

468   frightened at the aspect of his own father. At the beginning of this scene Andromache was called the wife of 'Hektor of the bronze helm' (398), and this presented the twin aspects of Hektor, his role as husband and his role as warrior. In this scene with his son his helmet is again the symbol of the two aspects: when he wears it he appears an enemy figure, an object of terror, to his son, but when he lays it on the ground his son is happy to be tossed in his arms.

476–81   Hektor's prayer that his son may be as I am, pre-eminent among the Trojans runs counter to his declaration that in his heart he knows that Troy will perish (447–9): it is a prayer for a kind of immortality, that his son may carry on his life and its works, but it is an impossible request. In fact Astyanax will not long survive his father and, as Andromache laments over her husband's body, she will give an accurate prediction of their son's fate (24. 734–6).

490   take up your own work recalls the scene which Hektor encountered when he entered Paris' house, where Helen was directing the work of her handmaidens (324): Hektor is no more seduced by the world of women now than he was then, but turns his back on it, on his family and on his city, for ever.

494–8   So glorious Hektor spoke and again took up the helmet. This is a deeply symbolic moment as Hektor again puts on the helmet which so terrified his son, and so resumes his heroic role. So too his description as **Hektor the slayer of men** points up the choice he has just made, to forego his role as husband and father in favour of his role as hero, and adds to the poignancy of the parting.

500   So they mourned in his house over Hektor while he was living. Having described Hektor's decision, Homer now anticipates its tragic consequence. This final scene of the Hektor–Andromache episode neatly balances the first, for the reluctance with which the women see him return to the world of men contrasts with the eagerness with which they welcomed him into the world of women (cf. 238).

506–11   As when some stalled horse. In this fine simile the beauty of the horse recalls the picture of Paris which has been painted earlier in this book and in Book 3, his handsome looks and his almost narcissistic awareness of them. However, beautiful though the horse is, the point of the simile lies in the speed with which it gallops from its stall to the river, with its mane floating and its quick knees, and in its keenness to be loose and to join the other horses at pasture, so that it breaks its tethering rope. So the simile describes Paris' zest for the battle, and anticipates Hektor's final accusation that he has been hanging back from the battle of his own accord (523).

513–15   shining in all his armour of war as the sun shines. When Hektor first saw Paris in his house, he was sitting polishing this same armour (cf. 322n), so a contrast is drawn between Hektor, still bemired by the day's toil in battle (268), and Paris, sleek and shining in his unused armour. Paris' charge to the battle-field, **laughing aloud**, is almost childlike in its enthusiasm and recalls the earlier occasion when, dressed in a leopard skin, he leapt forward and challenged the Achaian champions (3. 15–20). That Hektor, who chivvied his brother to enter the battle being fought on his behalf (328), should be caught by him **where he yet lingered** is ironic, but it also presents one final pathetic image of the Hektor–Andromache scene, as the husband looks fondly after his retreating wife and child.

518   Brother, I fear that I have held back your haste. There is irony, if not gentle sarcasm, in Paris' gushing apology, although Hektor himself seems to take it at face value.

523–5   But of your own accord you hang back, unwilling. Hektor points up the contrast between his brother and himself. His decision to turn from his wife and child, and to face the enemy and death, and the shame which he feels and which in time will force him to face Achilleus' attack, are highlighted by his brother's reluctance to engage the enemy and his indifference to the comments of his people.

ILIAD 7

Homer has now completed his introduction of the backcloth to the poem's theme, the anger of Achilleus. The advantage of plunging into the middle of the action, the quarrel in Book 1, and of then reviewing background details of character and occasion, is that the reader retains the initial impact of the quarrel scene throughout, and despite, the volume of detail which fills the intervening Books 2 to 6. In this book Homer returns the narrative to the theme of Book 1 by describing the consequences for the Achaian army of the alienation of Achilleus, who will not himself reappear until Book 9. He does so in two ways: in the first place, a duel is fought between Hektor and the Achaian hero who is acknowledged to be their best after Achilleus himself, Aias; and then, as a result of the duel, a truce is called to allow for the collection and disposal of the dead on both sides, and during this the Achaians take the opportunity to build a defensive wall around their ships. These two events are closely connected, since Aias is himself carefully characterized in the poem as the Achaians' supreme defensive warrior. So this book represents the shift which takes place in the fortunes of the Achaians as a result of Achilleus' withdrawal from the battle, and it portrays the new defensiveness in their actions.

4–6 **And as to men of the sea in their supplication.** The simile illustrates the physical hardships of the Trojans and their weariness, and so recalls their situation before Hektor left them to go on his mission into Troy in Book 6. Their defeat has clearly continued, and he has returned none too soon: so the purpose of the simile is to present a dramatic improvement in the Trojans' morale, when they see the approach of the men for whom they have been longing, and a real shift in their fortunes.

111

8–9 Areïthoös is called **of the war club** because he carried into battle 'a great bar clubbed of iron' (141); his home **Arne** is in Boiotia.

15   as he leapt up behind his fast horses shows that the Achaian Iphinoös is in hasty retreat when he is struck, and this heightens the impression conveyed by the successes of Paris, Hektor and Glaukos.

22   For the **oak tree**, cf. 6. 237n.

38   Let us rouse up the strong heart in Hektor. Since it is the Achaians who are being defeated, it is hardly surprising that their protectress Athene should wish to halt the fighting; Apollo on the other hand is a supporter of the Trojans and is well aware that Achilleus' absence gives Hektor his best chance of defeating any Achaian champion, so his motive in calling for a duel is quite disingenuous.

44–5   For **Helenos**, cf. 6. 75n. This is a variation on the normal way of motivating human behaviour, which is that a god puts an idea into a mortal's head or pays him a visit (cf. 1. 55–6n); Helenos, excellent soothsayer that he is, is able to divine for himself the gods' intentions.

51   to fight man to man against you. A second duel so soon after the duel of Paris and Menelaos in Book 3 may seem strange, but its purpose is very different: this will be a true contest of prowess between the champions of the Trojans and the Achaians, whereas the earlier duel was part of Homer's introductory purpose, designed to recall the cause of the Trojan War.

59–61   assuming the likenesses of birds, of vultures. Birds of prey are an appropriate disguise for Athene and Apollo as they view the coming duel. **taking their ease** points the stark contrast between the gods who watch humans at their leisure and humans who suffer at the gods' whim (Griffin 1978). In a similar scene the goddess Sleep takes the form of a singing bird in a pine tree to help Hera in her seduction of Zeus (14. 290).

63–4   scatters across the water conveys the ripple effect of the wind on the sea's surface, and hence the similar effect in the plain as the soldiers settle and jostle each other.

69–70   would not bring to fulfilment our oaths. Since Menelaos was the clear winner in the earlier duel and yet Helen was not then returned to the Achaians, and since the Trojans then broke the truce when Pandaros wounded Menelaos with his arrow, the non-fulfilment of oaths was in fact entirely on the Trojans' part and

Hektor is less than honest in blaming everything on Zeus.

73–86   Seeing now that among you are the bravest of all the Achaians.
The duel of Paris and Menelaos was proposed as a means of
resolving the dispute between them and so of bringing the war to
an end; hence the terms, when announced by Agamemnon (3. 381–
7), declared that Helen was the object of the contest and would,
along with her possessions, be awarded to the victor. In the present
case it is a contest of prowess which is proposed, between Hektor
and a champion of the Achaians, so there is to be no prize for the
victor other than the armour stripped as in battle from the corpse
of his victim.   **the broad passage of Helle:** Helle was the daughter
of Athamas, king of Boiotia, and Nephele. Threatened with being
sacrificed by her father, she was rescued by Nephele, and she and
her brother Phrixos were carried off on the back of a golden-fleeced
ram. As they passed over the Dardanelles, between Europe and
Asia, Helle fell into the sea, which was ever since known as the Sea
of Helle, or Hellespont. Phrixos sacrificed the ram to Zeus and
hung the golden fleece in the grove of Ares.

89–91   glorious Hektor killed him. The striking feature of this epitaph
is that the man buried within the mound remains nameless, whilst
his killer Hektor is memorialized by being named. Homer presents
a picture of Hektor as hero in pursuit of heroic glory (*kleos*) and
this contrasts with the picture of him as father and husband in
Book 6, torn between his responsibility to his family and his
ambition as hero. So his duel with Aias in this book is designed to
establish his role as Trojan champion.

94–102   at long last Menelaos stood forth. Homer has Menelaos
respond to Hektor's challenge, just as he did to Paris' (3. 21–3),
and this illustrates the contrast between the two occasions: when
the contest was for Helen, Menelaos was the only possible choice,
but in a contest of prowess he is far too weak. Since it was believed
that humans were made of water and earth, Menelaos' wish **may
all of you turn to water and earth** means that he wishes them all
dead—which is just how they are behaving **with no life in you.**

**113–14   It is an obvious exaggeration to claim that even Achilleus
trembles to meet this man** and it is quite at odds with the
presentation of Achilleus and Hektor in the poem, but it does lend
weight to Agamemnon's argument; it also of course offers further
insult to Achilleus.

125–8   Surely he would groan aloud, Peleus, the aged horseman.
The mention of Peleus naturally calls to mind his son, Achilleus,
who would be the obvious opponent for Hektor at this moment.
Nestor speaks of the occasion at 11. 768–9, when he and Odysseus
visited the palace of Peleus during their campaign to recruit for the
Achaian expedition to Troy.

132–60   If only, o father Zeus. Nestor recalls an exploit earlier in
his long life in order to justify his intervention here (cf. 1. 260–
73); as usual, his tale is told in the form of ring composition
(Introduction, 7(c)). Like all his tales, it is recounted at great length,
but the bare facts are that as a young warrior of Pylos he fought
against the Arkadians and defeated their champion, Ereuthalion,
who was wearing armour handed on to him by Lykourgos, king of
Arkadia, who had himself stripped it from the body of Areïthoös
when he had killed him. Although Nestor's purpose is to highlight
the present cowardice of the Achaians, he nevertheless takes the
opportunity to point out that his opponent was the tallest and
strongest man he ever killed, and by association this emphasizes
also the stature of Hektor on this occasion.

179–80   The choice of three favoured candidates of the Achaians is
significant: at 11. 200–5 Hektor receives advice from Zeus to avoid
Agamemnon; at 11. 349 he is defeated by **Diomedes**; and in the
present duel he is, in effect, beaten by **Aias.** So the Achaians can be
confident of their chances, whichever champion is selected.

197   since no man by force will beat me backward unwilling. Aias is
ranked second only to Achilleus by the Achaian troops; throughout
the poem he is the model of the strong defensive fighter who, even
against the heaviest odds, will never panic, whose retreat will always
be strategic and resistance stubborn. He fights to protect Odysseus
(11. 464–86) and Menestheus (12. 370–7), he fights at the forefront
of the defence of the Achaian ships during Hektor's rampage (15.
674), and he defends the body of Patroklos (17. 132–7). So the
choice of Aias here as Achaian champion indicates the new defensive
attitude of the Achaians following Achilleus' withdrawal.

211   the wall of the Achaians This description of Aias is echoed in
the description of his great tower shield as 'like a wall' (219), and
in the defensive wall which the Achaians construct around their
ships (436–41): each emphasizes the defensive qualities of Aias as
hero.

219–23 **carrying like a wall his shield.** Aias does not receive a full arming scene as Paris, Agamemnon, Patroklos and Achilleus do (cf. 3. 328–38n): instead Homer describes the armour most closely associated with him, his shield. This is generally taken to be a Mykenaian body shield, half-cylindrical in shape and of a size to protect the entire body (6. 117n). This type of shield was very probably obsolete by the time of the Trojan War, and its description by Homer is to be explained by oral transmission over the intervening centuries. More than anything else, this shield suggests Aias' role as defensive warrior (cf. 11. 485; 17. 128): a huge and heavy piece of armour, its use in battle is described in detail at 8. 266–72, where he protects the archer Teukros beneath its shelter. **Tychios** is not known otherwise but his name means, appropriately enough, Maker.

226–32 **what the bravest men are like among the Danaans even after Achilleus.** Before the duel come the boasts of the two combatants: Aias boasts that he is a fitting replacement for the Achaian champion, but the effect is to draw attention to Achilleus' absence and so to the defensive mentality of the Achaians.

237–41 Hektor's outburst has been provoked by Aias' suggestion that Hektor have first shot with the javelin, a suggestion designed to assert his inferiority. Hektor's reply is highly rhetorical, with its five-fold repetition of the Greek *oida*, **I know.** Hektor employs a striking metaphor from dancing: **I know how to tread my measures on the grim floor of the war god.** Normally dance is presented in the poem as the antithesis of battle: for example Paris, straight from his battlefield duel with Menelaos, is said by Aphrodite to be like one fresh from the dance (3. 394). Although Hektor is clearly laying claim to military skill for his forthcoming duel, there is irony in this contrast with his brother's earlier duel.

244–72 There is a careful balance between the actions of the two fighters: each throws a spear, each then thrusts with a spear, and finally each hurls a rock, but in every case it is made clear that Aias is the more effective. The duel itself paints a picture of Aias as defensive force, as twice Hektor strikes a blow at the great tower shield, and twice it provides an impenetrable defence: on the second occasion Hektor's spearhead is actually bent back by the shield's strength. For his part, although he draws blood and succeeds in knocking Hektor down, Aias is unable to finish him off. The duel is altogether less one-sided than the earlier duel of Paris and Menelaos, and it is only the approach of nightfall that brings a proposal of a truce.

279–82 In effect the herald declares a draw. **Night darkens now** seems a rather artificial reason for ending the duel, and it may be that it is used to avoid the other possibility, divine intervention, which is how the duel of Paris and Menelaos ended.

287–302 **with the spear you surpass the other Achaians.** Hektor only agrees to the truce by declaring that he has fought against the greatest of the Achaians, and although he clearly declares his own prowess too, there is a certain chivalry about his words. **joined with each other in close friendship, before they were parted**: in these imagined words of the Achaians and Trojans, and in the gifts which Aias and Hektor exchange, Homer seems to be consciously echoing the chivalrous conclusion of the Glaukos–Diomedes scene (6. 224–31).

309 **escaping the strength and unconquerable hands of Aias.** Hektor has fought the greatest of the Achaians and survived; but Aias is not Achilleus, and as long as he who is truly the greatest is not fighting, the Achaians will not win. So this duel marks an important shift: the Achaians are no longer the natural attackers and the natural victors, and the possibility of at least partial Trojan victory has been established.

331–5 **we should set a pause to the fighting.** The proposal to collect and bury the dead masks a clear artistic purpose, since from the mound which will be heaped over the dead will be built a defensive wall around the ships, complete with gates and ditch, a further indication, that is, of the new defence-mindedness of the Achaians. **so that each whose duty it is may carry the bones back**: it is difficult to see quite what Nestor intends, for if the bones are to be collected and buried beneath a communal mound, it will hardly be possible to transport home the bones of each individual after the war's end. Some suggest that this passage is a much later addition to the poem, since the practice of transporting the bones of warriors for burial at home dated to fifth-century Attika. By the same token, it is also difficult to establish the precise relationship between the heaping up of the mound and the construction of the wall.

337 **build fast upon it towered ramparts, to be a defence of ourselves and our vessels.** The building of a defensive wall and ditch by the

Achaians has long been a cause for criticism, not least because it is built apparently without any resistance from the Trojans. The main objection has been that, if the Achaians had built such a wall, it would have been at the time of their arrival at Troy, not in the tenth year, and in fact Thucydides (1.11.1) says that this is just what they did. However it seems clear that Homer's purpose is to represent the shift in the Achaians' fortunes in Achilleus' absence, and to prepare the way for their promised defeat. The tide is turning in the Trojans' favour, and a sequence of events is begun which will culminate in the firing of the Achaian ships and ultimately the death of Patroklos: the besieged will become the attackers, the attackers will become the besieged, and to represent this reversal of roles Homer provides the Achaians with their own defensive wall.

345–53　The scene of the **assembly of Trojans high on the city of Ilion** constitutes a review of the Trojans' role in the war. **Antenor** is the Trojan elder who argued for the return of Helen to Menelaos (3. 159); he does so again now, and he declares Troy's guilt by referring back to the duel of Paris and Menelaos. The conditions of that duel were very precise, that Helen was to go to the victor (3. 281–7): **our true pledges made into lies** recalls Paris' resounding defeat in the duel and subsequent re-enactment of his seduction of Helen.

363　Paris' willingness to give back **the possessions I carried away**, but not Helen herself, reveals just the same selfishness and irresponsibility as his original crime of which they are a re-enactment, and removes Troy's last chance.

373–4　**giving the word of Alexandros.** If it lies within Priam's power to order Paris to surrender Helen, his failure to do so is damning. His appeasement of his son associates him and his city with Paris' guilt, and seals their fate.

390–3　Idaios' wish that Paris **had perished before then,** together with his view that Helen is **the very wedded wife of glorious Menelaos** and his declaration that the Trojans generally want Helen to be returned, reveal the deep disagreement about Troy's conduct which Homer described at the outset as an assembly 'fiercely shaken to tumult' (346).

402　Diomedes' belief that **by this time the terms of death hang over the Trojans** is a reminder that the Trojans will ultimately be punished, and that the coming Achaian defeat will only be the fulfilment of Zeus' promise in Book 1 and not the ultimate outcome of the Trojan War.

412   The **sceptre** had been handed down through Agamemnon's ancestors from Zeus himself (cf. 2. 101–8).

421–33   the sun of a new day struck on the ploughlands. This description of the new day indicates the importance of the occasion, as the truce takes effect; the dawn at 433 is presumably that of the following day. The disciplined silence of the grieving Trojans is in marked contrast to their usual characterization as noisy and ill-disciplined (3. 2–9n).

446–63   There follows a scene between the divine brothers, Poseidon and Zeus, which is designed to account for the fact that in historical times there remained no trace of the wall the Achaians have built— that is, the gods destroyed it. Poseidon and Apollo built the walls of Troy for Laomedon, but were then cheated of payment by him and so sent a sea monster to terrorize Troy; Herakles killed this monster but he in turn was cheated of payment by Laomedon (see 21. 441–57). **After once more the flowing-haired Achaians are gone back with their ships** is another reminder that the coming Achaian defeat is a temporary one, for Zeus' promise to Poseidon envisages a time when the Achaians will have gone, when Troy will have fallen. The wall's destruction after the departure of the Achaians is described at 12. 15–33.

468–9   The story was told that the Argonauts on their journey to Colchis came to the island of Lemnos where the women had slain the men. They stayed for a year and mated with the women, and **Jason** had two sons by **Hypsipyle** the ruler of the island (cf. Pindar *Pythian Ode* 4. 251; Apollonius *Argonautica* 1. 774).

478   all night long Zeus of the counsels was threatening evil. The book ends with a final reference to Zeus' promise, as the Achaian defeat for which Achilleus prayed in Book 1 is imminent.

ILIAD 8

In Book 7 the building of a defensive wall around the Achaian ships and the important role taken by the defensive warrior Aias indicate the change which has taken place as a result of Achilleus' withdrawal from battle. In this way Homer has prepared the ground for the Achaian defeat which, in accordance with the promise Zeus made to Thetis, will demonstrate their need for Achilleus and will show him to be 'best of the Achaians'. The promised defeat will itself be described at very great length and will not reach its climax until Book 15, when Hektor reaches the Achaian ships and calls for fire to destroy them. Book 8 begins that long description, but its main purpose is more immediate, to motivate the sending of an embassy to Achilleus to seek his help. The book's function, of describing a particular reversal for a particular purpose, within the broader context of the more general, and much more serious, Achaian defeat, does much to explain its generally unsatisfactory nature. By the end of the book the impression is given of a Trojan victory in spite of Achaian superiority, that although the Trojans have been successful and are camped in the plain to prove it, their victory is far from complete because of the frequent Achaian successes along the way. The major Achaian defeat is to be so great as to cause Achilleus to relent in Book 16, to the extent of allowing Patroklos to fight in his place, and to die at Hektor's hands. In comparison the defeat of Book 8 is to be minor, just sufficient to panic the Achaian leadership into seeking Achilleus' help; so the shortcomings of this Trojan victory are designed to ensure that it in no way lessens the impact of the Achaian defeat from Book 11 onwards. The result is that Book 8 consists of Achaian initiatives, or the initiatives of their divine supporters Hera and Athene, being denied by the Trojans or their supporting deity Zeus, rather than of initiatives made by the Trojans themselves.

3   **upon the highest peak of rugged Olympos.** Zeus summons the
assembly of the gods on the same peak he was occupying when
Thetis visited him to put to him Achilleus' request for an Achaian
defeat (cf. 1. 499), and this indicates that he is now putting into
effect his promise to her.

7–16   **let no female deity, nor male god either.** Zeus' assertion of his
will contrasts with his anxiety about Hera's likely reaction when
Thetis put to him her request (1. 518–23). **against the gods' will** is
better translated 'apart from the gods'. Although there are occasions
when it is broken, Zeus' instruction to the gods and goddesses will
remain in force until he formally withdraws it at 20. 23–5; Zeus
grants himself sole control of the war and so is able to bring about
the promised defeat of the Achaians. The Underworld is called the
house of Hades, the god who rules it; **Tartaros** is the deep pit
beneath it, a sunless place where Zeus imprisoned his father Kronos
and the Titans after he overthrew them.

19–27   **Let down out of the sky a cord of gold.** Zeus challenges all
the other gods and goddesses to compete with him in a curious tug
of war, to prove his superiority to them all combined. He seems to
claim to be able to haul them all, and the earth and the sea as well,
upwards with a golden rope, which he will then tie around the
peak of Olympos, leaving all dangling in mid air: however, since
Olympos is itself firmly rooted in the earth it is perhaps better not
to press the details too closely, but to accept the scene as merely an
exaggerated boast of his total supremacy.

39–40   **I say this not in outright anger.** Since Zeus intends to restrain
all the gods, by violent means if necessary, this seems to be a
contradiction, but he may mean no more than that the final outcome
of the war remains unchanged and that the Trojans' approaching
triumph will be temporary. He makes the same declaration, also to
Athene, at 22. 183–4.

48   **Gargaron** is the highest peak of the Ida range.

57   **caught in necessity, for their wives and children.** The result of
this book is that the role of the Trojans will be reversed and they
will become the besiegers instead of the besieged, so at the outset
they are pictured as the defenders, of their wives and children.

69   The result of this battle has already been promised by Zeus, and
so it is clear that the metaphor of Zeus' **golden scales** is a dramatic
representation of his own decision: from this point he is in charge,

the scales obey his will, and the fate of the Achaians is settled. Similarly when Homer employs the same passage at 22. 209–10 to picture Zeus weighing the fates of Achilleus and Hektor, he does not suggest that there is any doubt about the outcome of their encounter, rather he marks the moment of Hektor's death with a gesture of dramatic solemnity.

78   The retreat of such substantial Achaian leaders as **Idomeneus, Agamemnon** and the **Aiantes**—and Nestor is himself only prevented from retreating by the loss of his horse—indicates the significance of Zeus' weighing the two portions of death (69–70).

97   **Odysseus gave no attention.** The meaning of the verb *esakouse* is more ambiguous than Lattimore's 'gave no attention', for it can mean both 'did not listen to' and 'did not hear': the former would suggest an act of cowardice, and so it is more likely that Diomedes' words were drowned by the general din of battle. Homer is highlighting the courage of Diomedes who, even though he is deserted by the other Achaian heroes, single-handedly goes to the rescue of Nestor, and so a scene which began as an Achaian retreat now illustrates the heroism of the Achaian Diomedes: in this way Homer is able to present a Trojan victory without detracting substantially from the Achaians.

99   **The son of Tydeus, alone as he was.** The single-handed rescue of Nestor appears elsewhere in the story of the Trojan War: Pindar (*Pythian Ode* 6. 28–42) tells how, having been cut off when one of his horses is shot by Paris, he is rescued by his son Antilochos, although on this occasion it is Memnon, the leader of the Aithiopians, who threatens the old man. This story appeared also in the lost epic *Aithiopis* (Evelyn-White 1967.507), which also told of the death of Antilochos at the hands of Memnon. The similarities between the two accounts of Nestor's rescue, by Diomedes and by Antilochos, suggest that they are variations of the same theme. However the critical school of Neoanalysts (Kullmann 1984) argues that the account in the *Iliad* imitates that in the *Aithiopis*.

108   **horses I took away from Aineias.** Diomedes captured the horses at 5. 323, after he defeated Aineias in combat, only for him then to be rescued by Aphrodite.

118   **as he raged straight forward the son of Tydeus threw at him.** At 88 Hektor was approaching Nestor at speed and threatening imminent death; by 115 Diomedes has noticed the danger, failed

to rally Odysseus, made a speech to Nestor and taken him on board his chariot, and now he is racing towards Hektor; yet Hektor's chariot has still not brought him to Nestor. Homer has transformed an essentially rearguard action, in defence of Nestor, into a triumphant charge by Diomedes, who comes close to hitting Hektor himself and in fact kills his charioteer; so, in a brief scene which began with even the Aiantes fleeing in panic before Zeus' thunder and lightning (79), the initiative now lies with Diomedes.

128   **Archeptolemos,** who replaces Eniopeus as Hektor's charioteer, is himself killed at 312 by Teukros' arrow; on this later occasion also Hektor comes very close to death, and only the intervention of Apollo saves him. These two narrow scrapes illustrate Hektor's courage in fighting so far forward, but they also enhance the presentation of the Achaians who, even in the midst of defeat, come close to killing the Trojan war-leader. A third charioteer of Hektor's, Kebriones, is killed by Patroklos during his combat with Hektor (16. 738).

133   **He thundered horribly and let loose the shimmering lightning** presents a vivid picture of Zeus' support for the Trojans, but again the impression is of an empty Trojan victory, that, without the intervention of Zeus, Diomedes and the Achaians would have won the day against Trojans who are compared to sheep (131). Zeus signalled his opposition to the Achaians with his thunder and lightning (75–6); he thunders his support for the Trojans at 170–1; and he threatens the interfering goddesses Athene and Hera with the stroke of his lightning at 405.

148   **some day Hektor will say openly before the Trojans.** Diomedes displays a typically heroic sense of *aidos*, a proper regard for how others might view his actions (cf. 6. 441–2n).

162   **pride of place, the choice meats and the filled wine-cups.** The fullest account of the honour shown to the hero by his followers is in Sarpedon's speech to Glaukos (12. 310–28), where there is also emphasis upon the choice cuts of meat and the filled wine cups. In return for these privileges the hero was expected always to fight at the forefront of his people (Introduction, 8).

175–81   **the son of Kronos has bowed his head and assented to my high glory.** Hektor claims the glory for himself, and this recalls his decision in Book 6 to leave his family behind and to pursue heroic glory: now he sees the day's victory in terms of that glory, rather than as a salvation for his city and his people. His triumphant words **so that I can set their ships on fire** anticipate the climax of the Trojan onslaught at 15. 718 when he calls for fire to destroy the Achaian ships.

185–90   Hektor is paying honour to the horses which have carried him to a victory which has tilted the balance of the war, permanently for all he knows; he is exhilarated, and his words reflect his euphoria. Since wine is the drink of heroes, it follows that Andromache gives **mixed wine** to his horses.

192–7   The **shield of Nestor** and Diomedes' **corselet that Hephaistos wrought** are presented as items of major significance and yet neither appears elsewhere in the poem, and so are probably invented to illustrate Hektor's excitement: his claim that the capture of these two objects might cause the Achaians to flee on this very night is simply exaggeration.

201–11   **far-powerful shaker of the earth** is Poseidon the sea god, the brother of Zeus, who is also god of earthquakes. **Helike** and **Aigai** are shrines of the god in Achaia. Although Hera has no success in persuading Poseidon to join her in defying Zeus, the scene does establish a sense of resistance to Zeus and looks forward to the scene where she succeeds in persuading Athene (350).

221   Homer does not make clear the purpose of this **great coloured mantle**, though it is probably a kind of standard, a rallying point for the army; however, there is no other example of such a standard in the poem.

231–2   As in Hektor's scornful words to Diomedes (cf. 162n), the **abundant meat** and **great bowls filled to the brim with wine** implies that the Achaian champions are not performing their heroic duties in return for their privileges.

236–7   **is it one of our too strong kings you have stricken in this disaster now** is more accurately translated by E.V. Rieu (1966): 'Father Zeus, was a great king ever fooled by you like this, and robbed of all his glory?' Agamemnon is complaining that he has been cheated by Zeus, even though he has offered him proper sacrifice, and he is probably also recalling the false dream sent by Zeus to tell him that Achaian victory was at hand (2. 6–34). **stricken** translates *ate* (cf. 1. 412n), the delusion sent by Zeus to rob a man of his wits: Agamemnon is awakening to the realization that his own behaviour, caused by Zeus, may be the reason for the Achaians' predicament.

245–52   Zeus' decision to spare the Achaians is at odds with the recent scene in which his scales favoured the Trojans (cf. 69n), and again serves to limit the Trojan victory. In the dramatic omen, the eagle represents the strength of the Achaians, and the fawn, as so often in the poem, represents the Trojans (cf. 22. 1n).

266–8   **Teukros, bending into position the curved bow.** Teukros is a half-brother of Telamonian Aias (283), but he is a minor hero because he fights with a bow. He kills a total of ten Trojans during his *aristeia*, a major feat, but his method of fighting, from beneath the shelter of Aias' shield, detracts from it. So Teukros' *aristeia* gives a picture of brief Achaian victory, but without the impression of a rout.

306–8   **as a garden poppy bends.** The simile calls to mind the death of another young Trojan, Simoeisios (cf. 4. 473–89n), which was also marked by a simile taken from nature, the felling of a tall poplar tree. The seeds of the poppy-head which, along with the raindrops, cause it to bend, suggest an image of fertility which lends pathos to the picture of the young Gorgythion killed in his prime; the image of pastoral beauty presents the countryside at peace and contrasts with the present horror taking place, and this recalls the beauty which was Troy before the Achaians came.

329–40   **the bow fell from his hands** marks the end of the Achaian rally; Teukros' actions have been just sufficient to remove a sense of total Achaian calamity. The simile of the **hunting hound** has the same effect, for the **wild boar or a lion** on the run represents the retreating Achaians, but it still has much greater strength than the hound and might at any time turn and savage its pursuer.

348   The head of the **Gorgon** featured as one of the motifs on Zeus' aegis (cf. 5. 734–47n), and the 'blank-eyed face of the Gorgon with her stare of horror' decorates the shield of Agamemnon (11. 36). In each case the creature is a symbol of terror, but in the *Iliad* its power to turn those who look at it to stone is not made explicit.

363–9   Homer nowhere specifies that there were twelve labours imposed on **Herakles** by **Eurystheus** king of Mykenai (cf. 15. 639). The only labour he names is the present one, to bring back **the hound of the grisly death god**, the three-headed dog Kerberos, the guardian of Hades. The **Stygian water** is the Styx, a river of the Underworld across which Charon ferried the souls of the dead; the river was also called upon by the gods to witness their most solemn oaths (14. 271).

371   **who kissed his knees and stroked his chin in her hand** recalls Thetis' supplication of Zeus in Book 1, at the very time Zeus has begun to execute his plan. Thetis clasped the knees of Zeus (1. 557–8), but Athene pictures her kissing them and exaggerates the intimacy she thinks took place, and so she reveals the jealousy she feels (cf. 373).

385–91   **slipped off her elaborate dress** (cf. 5. 733–52). The symbolism of the description is manifest, as Athene lays aside her female clothes and puts on the war tunic of Zeus in preparation for her entry into the male world of war. Athene's description **she of the mighty father** is also found in her other arming scene (5. 747): it is highly appropriate as she now prepares to make her stand against the power of her father. In fact the scene leads nowhere because Zeus intervenes, but yet again there is an impression of Achaian aggression and initiative at the very moment they are penned by their ships.

393   **the gates of the sky** are the clouds, guarded by the Horai, the Seasons (cf. 5. 749n).

415–24   As usual, Iris' report to Hera and Athene is identical to Zeus' original declaration, but she also adds two lines of her own (421–2). The tone of **bold brazen wench** contrasts with her usually mild and placid tone and highlights the goddesses' outrageous behaviour in disobeying the king of the gods.

447–56   **Why then are you two sorrowful.** Zeus gloats over his humiliation of Hera and Athene, remembering perhaps how they themselves gloated over the wounding of Aphrodite (5. 421–5). The scene closes with Zeus asserting his authority, **such is my strength and my hand so invincible,** just as it opened with his declaration of his powers (5–27), and his two speeches effectively bracket the goddesses' fruitless challenge to his will.

476   **in the narrow place of necessity over fallen Patroklos.** Originally Zeus' promise to Thetis was that the Achaians would suffer a defeat sufficient to make them aware of their need for Achilleus and so to honour him as the best of the Achaians (1. 509–10). Zeus' prediction here of Patroklos' death as part of that defeat is an important

development: 'while it is part of the story of the *Iliad* and therefore of the fatality of the poem as known to Zeus, Patroclus' death is a consequence, not of the success of the Plan of Zeus, but rather of its failure' (Redfield 1975.141).

479–83   It was to the 'murk of **Tartaros**' (cf. 7–16n) that Zeus threatened to consign any god who opposed him. **Iapetos** is the father of Prometheus, **Kronos** is Zeus' own father, and together they represent the race of the Titans, the previous rulers of the world whom Zeus overthrew and replaced. The thought that the wandering Hera might come to that sunless place in her sulking echoes Zeus' earlier threat to send her there.

485–6   **the shining light of the sun was dipped in the Ocean trailing black night across the grain-giving land** is an impressive description, which marks the dramatic significance of this nightfall, for during the course of this night the Achaians will decide to send an embassy to Achilleus.

489–96   **taking them aside from the ships**. This assembly of the Trojans in the plain, far from their protective walls, indicates their new-found confidence. The **eleven-cubit-long spear** stands in place of the sceptre on which a hero normally leans to address the assembly and symbolizes Hektor's new martial stance and that of his Trojans. This is the same spear he carried on his recent visit to Troy, when it symbolized his determination not to be seduced by the world of the city but to return to the battlefield in pursuit of heroic glory (6. 319n).

500–11   **the darkness came too soon** is another indication of Trojan success, for in his duel with Aias the darkness of night intervened to save Hektor when he was having the worst of it (7. 282), but now he is able to claim that only the coming of darkness has saved the Achaians and their ships from destruction at his hands. The **many fires** are to prevent the Achaians fleeing from Troy under cover of darkness, and they too indicate the confidence victory has produced in Hektor: the flight of the Achaians would bring an end to the suffering of the Trojans, but Hektor wants more than this.

532–3   **if the son of Tydeus, strong Diomedes, will force me back**. Diomedes' *aristeia* in Book 5 established him as a substitute Achaian champion for Achilleus, and as Hektor has already fought Aias, Achilleus' other substitute, in Book 7, Diomedes is the obvious opponent for Hektor to contemplate facing.

538–41   **if I only could be as this in all my days immortal and ageless.**
Hektor declares his absolute certainty that the following day will
bring evil to the Achaians, and he does so by contrasting it to the
obvious impossibility that he will himself be immortal and ageless:
so the passage is not really a wish for immortality, but an expression
of his confidence and the excitement of this heady moment, a
moment he wishes to last forever.

551   The gods' rejection of the Trojans' sacrifice because **so hateful
to them was sacred Ilion** is clearly at odds with the recent support
given by Athene and Hera.

555–9   **As when in the sky the stars.** This impressive simile illustrates
the vast number of the fires, but it also reflects the emotional state
of the Trojans. The shepherd's joy comes from his situation, as he
observes the stars from his place amongst his flocks in the plain; so
too it is the joy of the Trojans that Homer portrays, the joy of
liberation from the confines of their long-besieged city. The finely
understated picture of their horses, quietly champing the barley
and oats whilst awaiting the dawn with no awareness of the triumph
it promises, points up the excitement and anticipation of their Trojan
masters. The shepherd's joy is an entirely appropriate image with
which to end a book which has charted the transformation of the
Trojans from besieged to besiegers, in which their elation is matched
by the despair of the Achaians, who now set in motion the poem's
next episode, the Embassy to Achilleus.

ILIAD 9

Book 9 constitutes the restatement of the theme of the poem, the Anger of Achilleus. It is without equal in the poem for its sustained rhetorical power, as Achilleus hears three very different types of appeal, from Odysseus, Phoinix and Aias, each of whom tries to persuade him to renounce his anger and return to the battle. Achilleus rejects all three appeals, but his responses to them display a very marked shift, from his first declaration that he intends to sail for home the next day, to a statement that he will put off until the next day a decision on returning home, to a final assertion that he will not rejoin the battle until it reaches his own ships, which in effect acknowledges that he no longer intends to return home. Achilleus explains his presence at Troy through the choice of destinies which he says his goddess mother declared to him: a short but glorious life, culminating in death at Troy, or a long life of anonymity at home (410–16). His presence at Troy indicates the choice he has made, and the shift in his responses to the ambassadors is his restatement of that choice. So Book 9 examines the ethical code which binds all heroes, and Achilleus especially, in their pursuit of heroic glory, and it offers Achilleus' view of how that ethical code was breached by Agamemnon during the quarrel in Book 1. By his refusal to accept the vast array of gifts which the ambassadors offer in Agamemnon's name, Achilleus sets in train a tragic sequence of events which culminate in Book 16 in the death of his companion Patroklos. See further, Griffin 1995.

4–7 **As two winds rise to shake the sea.** The violent imagery of this simile describing the Achaians' emotions contrasts with the peaceful night sky and the joy of the shepherd as he views it, in the simile characterizing the Trojans (cf. 8. 555–9n).

14–15 **like a spring dark-running.** This simile appears also when Patroklos approaches Achilleus with news of the Achaian defeat and seeks permission to return to the battle (16. 3–4). The two contexts are very similar, for in both cases the Achaians have just suffered a defeat, and in both cases there follows an appeal to Achilleus; but Homer draws the contrast between the abject despair and self-pity in Agamemnon's tears here and the sympathy Patroklos shows for the Achaians' plight on the later occasion.

17–28 **Futility** translates *ate* (cf. 1. 412n): Agamemnon used this term in the previous book to complain of his treatment by Zeus (8. 236–7n), and it is a theme which will be taken up later in this book when he declares that his behaviour during the quarrel in Book 1 was the result of *ate* sent by Zeus (9. 115). **let us run away with our ships** is not the first time Agamemnon has proposed retreat: in Book 2 he tested the morale of the army in words which are echoed here (18–28 = 2. 111–18, 139–41). On that earlier occasion the result was to present him as an incompetent commander (2. 134–7n), who chose precisely the wrong moment to test his army and who was rewarded with a forceful demonstration that he had lost the confidence of his troops, but where earlier he proposed retreat only as a test of morale, now his purpose is serious.

34–9 **I was the first of the Danaans whose valour you slighted** recalls Agamemnon's accusation (4. 365–410) that Diomedes was hanging back from the battle. Diomedes' reaction now is very different to his earlier one, when he not only remained silent in the face of Agamemnon's insults but reprimanded his companion Sthenelos when he answered Agamemnon in kind: on that occasion he respected Agamemnon's status as commander, now in effect he accuses him of cowardice. Diomedes is portrayed as the foil for Achilleus, as he bides his time and gains his revenge: it was precisely Achilleus' inability to swallow his anger for the moment which allowed the quarrel to get out of control. For Agamemnon's **sceptre** as the gift of Zeus, see 2. 100–8; the sceptre is the symbol of his kingship and Diomedes' accusation is that Agamemnon is not acting in accordance with it.

42 **if in truth your own heart is so set upon going** echoes Agamemnon's own invitation to Achilleus at the height of the quarrel to take his ships and flee (1. 173). Diomedes' sarcastic **so many of them!** recalls that Agamemnon brought the largest number of ships to Troy, a hundred in total (2. 576), and so is the most powerful leader.

49   **it was with God that we made our way hither.** The gods are
divided in their support for both sides in the war, so this may be no
more than a statement of general belief, as of all armies, that God
is on their side; but it is more likely that Diomedes is speaking of
the support of Zeus, as protector of hosts and guests, and so
reminding Agamemnon of their purpose in coming to Troy, to regain
Helen.

52   **Nestor** the peace-maker intervenes to defuse this quarrel between
Diomedes and Agamemnon, just as he had also tried to calm the
passions of Achilleus and Agamemnon (1. 247–84).

63–4   Nestor's description of the fighting as **among his own people**
seems to indicate the trouble which Agamemnon has brought on
the Achaians as a result of the quarrel; so in assigning blame to
Agamemnon, he is paving the way for his proposal that Agamemnon
acknowledge his responsibility for the quarrel and send an embassy
to him.

70–1   The communal **feast** creates an important bond between the
heroes, confirming the leadership of Agamemnon and the loyalty
of his companions (89–90). In fact, Nestor says **your** [not our]
shelters are filled with wine; there is a criticism implied in Nestor's
words, that Agamemnon is falling down on his responsibilities as
leader, by failing to foster the comradeship of the heroes by
providing hospitality for them.

98–9   **Zeus has given into your hand the sceptre.** Nestor deliberately
recalls Diomedes' reference to the sceptre (34–9n), in order to assure
Agamemnon that, unlike during the quarrel, there is no challenge
on this occasion to his leadership.

108–10   Nestor's version of the removal of Briseis from Achilleus is
different from events in Book 1: he says that Agamemnon acted
against the will of the rest of us, but none of the heroes actually
spoke against it; and he says that **I for my part urged you strongly
not to**, but omits to say that he did so in the course of publicly
asserting Agamemnon's superiority (1. 275–81). From Achilleus'
own viewpoint of the quarrel, he stood alone against Agamemnon
and not one of his companions was prepared to support him; but
Nestor makes no mention of this and so places the blame for the
Achaians' troubles squarely on Agamemnon's shoulders. **a great
man** (*pheriston*) is more accurately translated 'greatest'; it is a form
of the word *pherteros*, the term Nestor used for Agamemnon when

he acknowledged that Achilleus was 'the stronger man' (*karteros*) but Agamemnon was 'the greater', on the grounds that he was leader of more men (cf. 1. 275–84n): so Nestor now seems to have revised his original judgment and declares Achilleus the greatest.

113 Nestor urges that full amends be made to Achilleus for what has happened, and the offer is to be two-fold, both gifts of friendship and words described by Nestor as *meilichioisi*, translated **of supplication**, but rather meaning 'soft' or 'gentle'.

115 this was no lie when you spoke of my madness. Nestor blamed Agamemnon's anger, Agamemnon blames **madness** (*ate*, cf. 17–28n) sent by Zeus. It is a principle throughout the poem that human behaviour may result from 'double motivation' (Taplin 1992.99), from a combination of a human's own responsibility for his actions and of divine prompting: so by introducing the idea of *ate*, Agamemnon attempts to explain, and to excuse, his behaviour as caused by a Zeus-sent blindness, which diminishes, without removing, his own direct responsibility. Agamemnon's admission here is in part a fulfilment of Achilleus' request to Thetis, that Zeus give the Trojans victory so that Agamemnon might recognise his *ate* (1. 409–12).

120–1 Agamemnon's willingness **to make all good** means a willingness to **give back gifts in abundance**: significantly missing are the gentle words which Nestor also proposed, to the extent that Agamemnon fails even to name Achilleus during this entire speech. The prizes awarded to a hero are an indication of his honour (*time*, cf. 1. 99n), and so the removal of Achilleus' prize (*geras*) Briseis in Book 1 amounted to the removal of his *time*. Agamemnon now offers Achilleus **gifts in their splendour**, and so infinitely greater *time* than he forcibly took from him. However, Agamemnon's offer is also an assertion of his authority, because he is showing that he has many more possessions, and is seeking to make Achilleus indebted to him by his generosity.

122–56 The list of gifts offered by Agamemnon. **seven women of Lesbos**: Taplin (1986.16) observes that women predominate in the gifts offered and concludes that 'there is the largely suppressed taunt that Achilleus should be happy as long as he has plenty of women: and that is to miss the whole point of why he took offence at his deprivation of Briseis in book 1'. **load it deep as he pleases** answers Achilleus' charge during the quarrel that, after the sack of a citadel, Agamemnon always helps himself to the far larger share of the spoils (1. 166–7). Agamemnon's offer **he may be my son-in-law** is an honour, but one involving a subsidiary, if not dependent, position for Achilleus; in the later tragedians Agamemnon's daughters are the more famous Elektra and Iphigeneia. The **seven citadels** he offers are **at the bottom of sandy Pylos**, that is, in Messenia and so subject to Nestor; Agamemnon is offering cities which are not even his to dispose of and about which he seems to have had no consultation with Nestor.

157–61 **All this I will bring to pass for him** contains a tone of condescension and seems to be an assertion of Agamemnon's authority, within whose power it lies to distribute such bounty to others (cf. 120–1n). His demand in return for this bounty is stronger than the translation **Let him give way**, for the Greek *damnasthai* indicates breaking an animal beneath the yoke, and the subjection which accompanies defeat in battle: far from using 'gentle words' (113n), he is demanding Achilleus' subjection to him, and it remains his intention from Book 1 to tame the recalcitrant warrior and subject him to his command. Through disdain or through fear, he does not convey his own message but employs ambassadors; but even in this act of reconciliation he rehearses the theme of hierarchy and asserts his authority over his rival, **let him yield place to me, inasmuch as I am the kinglier**. Although the Greek will certainly give the meaning **born the elder**, it seems more likely that Agamemnon is here claiming that his ancestry is superior (Hainsworth 1993.80).

168–70 This is no random selection by Nestor, since each member will make his own, quite individual, appeal to Achilleus: **Phoinix**, to whom the youthful Achilleus was entrusted by Peleus when he sent him on the expedition to Troy (438), will appeal to him in terms of family loyalty and heroic precedent; **Aias** will appeal in terms of heroic companionship; and **Odysseus** will recount Agamemnon's offer of gifts and will attempt to persuade Achilleus that Agamemnon has changed his ways. The two heralds alongside the three ambassadors recall the two heralds who came to Achilleus' shelter to remove the girl Briseis (1. 320–1), and Eurybates is common to both visits.

180–1 Although Nestor named Phoinix as leader of the embassy, it is to Odysseus he gives closest instruction, presumably to indicate that he is to undertake the delicate task of conveying Agamemnon's offer, and so of recalling the hated figure once more to Achilleus. There may be a recollection of this in the curious scene at 223. **Peleion** is Achilleus, son of Peleus.

182–4   The identity of **these two** is one of the most notorious problems in the entire poem. Homer employs the Greek dual number, which specifically denotes two of anything; he states that two men made their way to the shelter of Achilleus, despite the fact that only fourteen lines earlier three ambassadors were named: and the problem is heightened when all three named ambassadors appear shortly in Achilleus' shelter, and all three are heard to make their appeal to him. Many explanations have been offered, usually arguing that the two are Odysseus and Aias: that Phoinix is of a lower social ranking and so is not entitled to proceed to Achilleus' shelter in their company (Tsagarakis 1979); that Phoinix goes ahead of the two others to prepare, from his position as trusted companion of Achilleus, the way for them (Ailshie 1965); that Phoinix was introduced at a later date to an embassy which originally consisted of only Odysseus and Aias (Page 1959.297); that the dual does not refer to the ambassadors at all, but to the two heralds who accompany them (Segal 1968). Perhaps this last is the most likely, that Homer recalls the first mission of the heralds, to remove Briseis from Achilleus, at the very moment the girl is being offered back to him. **Aiakides** is Achilleus, grandson of Aiakos.

186   **delighting his heart in a lyre.** Achilleus cuts an almost gentle figure as he sits, playing his lyre and singing, with the silent Patroklos facing him; this is a very different figure from the one who confronted the heralds, sitting sullenly by his shelter and his ship, and inspired terror and awe in them (1. 331). The lyre on which Achilleus accompanies his song was part of his spoils from the sack of Thebe, Eëtion's city (cf. 6. 425n). Skill with the lyre was one of the insults which Hektor hurled at his brother Paris when he accused him of shirking the battle (3. 54): Achilleus the warrior has become the man of inaction, who now only recalls 'men's fame' (*klea andron*), the stories of heroes which have been handed down through the oral tradition (Ford 1992.60).

197   **greatly I need you.** As translated by Lattimore, the need is Achilleus', that after his long isolation he is in need of some friendly company; but the Greek may also mean that the need is that of the

Achaians for his services, and in this case the words represent a sense of satisfaction in Achilleus that his absence from the Achaian ranks has led to their defeat and to this approach to him.

205–21 For sacrifice and the feast, see 1. 458–66n. The rather exaggerated size of the feast Achilleus offers them and its conviviality contrasts with Nestor's implied criticism of Agamemnon for not holding a feast for the leaders; it contrasts too with Achilleus' later refusal to rejoin his community at the feast (cf. 70–1n).

223 **Aias nodded to Phoinix, and brilliant Odysseus saw it.** Owen (1946.94) commends this 'charming little touch of humorous imagination, Ajax very willing to pass on the task to Phoenix, Odysseus confident that in any other hands than his own the thing will be bungled'. There is nothing to suggest what Aias' nod implies, but most likely it is to indicate that Odysseus has been designated to take the lead in accordance with Nestor's instructions (cf. 180–1n).

225–306 The Speech of Odysseus. It is appropriate that Odysseus takes the lead, for every ounce of his guile will be required to persuade Achilleus even to listen to the message from the hated Agamemnon. His opening words are better translated **we** [not you] **have no lack of equal portion**, that is, a polite statement of appreciation of Achilleus' generous hospitality, even in comparison to that provided by Agamemnon: Odysseus begins with words of appeasement in comparing Achilleus favourably to Agamemnon.

231–8 The metaphor in **put on your war strength** derives from putting on war armour: Odysseus maintains his flattering tone by acknowledging that only Achilleus can protect them. His repeated mention of **Zeus, son of Kronos** unwittingly confirms to Achilleus that Zeus is now granting the Trojan victory that he asked his mother Thetis to request (1. 408).

249 **It will be an affliction to you hereafter.** Affliction is Greek *achos*, a word found in Achilleus' own name, which may derive from Greek *achos/laos*, 'affliction of the people' (Nagy 1979.69). The affliction Odysseus fears is the remorse Achilleus will feel when the Achaians are destroyed, but in reality it will be his grief and remorse at the death of Patroklos.

253–8 **hold fast in your bosom the anger of the proud heart.** Nestor recalls this same visit he and Odysseus made to the home of Achilleus' father Peleus when they were recruiting support for the expedition to Troy (11. 783); on that occasion Peleus' advice to Achilleus was 'to be always best in battle and pre-eminent beyond all others'.

264–99 The first part of Odysseus' speech consisted very much of his own words and thoughts, carefully designed to appeal to Achilleus as warrior. The second half now reports the offer of Agamemnon, an offer also designed to persuade Achilleus the hero, with its magnificent array of gifts representing heroic *time*, and he does so by repeating Agamemnon's words at 122–57.

300–6 Odysseus omits the last four lines of Agamemnon's speech and so suppresses his demand that Achilleus acknowledge his superiority (157–61). It has been suggested (Wyatt 1985.401) that there is nothing sinister in this, on the grounds that they were not part of the statement which the commander wished to be reported to Achilleus, but this is very unlikely because in fact they constitute his demand in return for the gifts. Odysseus realizes that, despite the apparent generosity of his gifts, in the hierarchical dispute nothing has changed in Agamemnon's mind, and that to reveal that fact to Achilleus will hardly help persuade him to return to the Achaian fold. Odysseus replaces Agamemnon's demand with a further appeal to Achilleus as hero, the possibility of being honoured like a god.

308–429 The Speech of Achilleus in reply to Odysseus. **that man, who hides one thing in the depths of his heart, and speaks forth another** seems almost to offer an apology for what he is about to say, but he is also voicing his suspicion that Odysseus has been less than frank in relaying Agamemnon's message, and he is declaring his distrust of Agamemnon even when he is offering compensation.

316 **gratitude** (*charis*) is precisely what binds together the heroes in a spirit of fellowship; each of the heroes provides his services to the cause of Agamemnon, and expects a proper return from him of honour and prizes.

318–20 The sense of each of the following lines is complete at its end, which is marked by a stop; the effect is to convey the precisely ordered sentiments of this early part of the speech, and to present a picture of Achilleus very deliberately mastering his emotions the better to marshal his arguments, which are voiced almost like epigrams. **Fate** (*moira*) also means 'share', and so in this apparently general statement about fate there is also a particularized complaint, that the man who holds back, Agamemnon, receives the same share as the man who fights hard, Achilleus. The same idea is conveyed in **We are all held in a single honour,** that all receive the same share of *time*, represented by the distribution of the spoils. So Achilleus rehearses the same dispute as in Book 1, that the authority of Agamemnon entitles him to the same, or greater, share of honour as himself, even though he bears most of the fighting and the risk-taking. **A man dies still if he has done nothing, as one who has done much**: later in this speech Achilleus will say that his mother Thetis has told him of his choice of destinies, of a short but glorious life or a long life without glory, and so for the first time he visualizes a life without risk-taking and without glory. He has examined his own humiliation by Agamemnon in the light of heroic life in general, and he voices his disillusionment born of his experience, that the conventions of heroic comradeship may be breached, with apparent impunity, by one, to the obvious injury of another (Gill 1996.136).

323–4 **as to her unwinged young ones the mother bird brings back morsels.** Odysseus appealed to Achilleus to honour his father's advice to keep his hot temper under control (253–8n), and he replies by declaring himself the parent who has fed all his brood. The simile puts into Achilleus' mouth the parent/child motif which characterizes his association with Patroklos (see, for example, 16. 6–10).

336–41 By describing Briseis as **the bride of my heart,** Achilleus is able to argue that, at the very moment he is doing more than any of the Achaians to recover the stolen wife of Menelaos, his own wife has been stolen by the brother of Menelaos, and so his sense of injustice is heightened. **Let him lie beside her and be happy** addresses Agamemnon's oath that he has not slept with Briseis (274–5): in effect he says he is a liar, and credits him with a sexual motive in contrast to his own feelings for her as her husband. There is an unintentional irony in his question **Are the sons of Atreus alone among mortal men the ones who love their wives,** for even as he speaks Agamemnon's wife Klytaimestra is unfaithful to her husband with Aigisthos.

348 **there has been much hard work done even without me** has a tone of heavy sarcasm, but it reflects the defensive strategy the Achaians have adopted in Achilleus' absence, for without him the

Achaians shelter behind their wall and ditch, where formerly it
was the Trojans who would not venture beyond their wall.

356-63   now I am unwilling to fight against brilliant Hektor.
Achilleus counters Odysseus' final argument that he has the chance
to encounter Hektor and win the greatest honour (304). In the
final analysis Hektor, not Helen, is the reason Achilleus is at Troy:
though she may be the cause of the war, his objective is the honour
which the killing of the Trojan champion and the sacking of his
city will bring. So his declaration that he is unwilling to face Hektor
indicates the disenchantment which Agamemnon's words and
actions have caused him. **my ships in the dawn at sea:** Achilleus
will not in fact carry out his threat to sail for home, but will modify
it in reply to Phoinix (618-9) and Aias (650-3).

379-82   Not if he gave me ten times as much. Since he declares that
no amount of gifts will win him over, it must be that he will only
be satisfied when Agamemnon has suffered humiliation as he has,
and that he considers that to accept the gifts will be to accept
subjection. Mueller (1984.47) however, suggests that 'the words
cannot be taken as referring to some inadequacy in Agamemnon's
offer. Rather, they show that there is no conceivable settlement
that Achilles would accept'. **Orchomenos** was the principal city of
Boiotia in the Late Bronze Age, following the destruction of Thebes;
its legendary king was Minyas. It seems likely that the naming of
Thebes alongside Orchomenos referred originally to Boiotian
Thebes, and that Egyptian Thebes became attached later in an
attempt to lend an air of greater wealth and power (Willcock
1976.102).

392   kinglier than I am. Achilleus appears to echo the final words of
Agamemnon's speech to Odysseus 'and let him yield place to me,
inasmuch as I am the kinglier' (160); although these words were
never reported to him by Odysseus, he nevertheless assumes that
such an insistence on his superiority lies behind Agamemnon's
apparent generosity, and this causes him to see through Odysseus'
speech and to reject the offer it contains.

395   Hellas and Phthia are both areas of Achilleus' homeland of
Thessaly.

400-5   not worth the value of my life are all the possessions. The
significance of this lies in Sarpedon's declaration of the heroic ethos

to Glaukos (12. 322–8) that, since death awaits all men, it is better to meet it in the pursuit of glory. Heroes are not in pursuit of possessions as such, but of the honour which the possessions represent; but if the prizes of honour are divorced from generosity of spirit in the giver, then both the prizes and the honour itself are debased, and are not worth the risk involved. Indeed of what worth are the prizes now being offered by Agamemnon, if they too can be taken away just as quickly as they are offered? For **Pytho**, i.e. Delphi, cf. 2. 517–26n.

410–16   I carry two sorts of destiny. The choice of destinies which Achilleus claims his mother offered him is in a sense the choice which all heroes must make, to risk early death in order to achieve glory. Except for his later denial that he ever received any prophecy from his mother (16. 36–51), no further mention is made of this tale. Throughout the poem there is an acceptance that Achilleus is to be short-lived, a theme which is continually emphasized by the appearance of his mother (cf. 1. 352n). **return home** (*nostos*) is what differentiates Achilleus from the hero of the *Odyssey*, to whom he is talking at the moment; Odysseus will employ every daring stratagem to achieve his return to Ithaka and his wife and child. **my glory shall be everlasting**: everlasting glory (*kleos aphthiton*) is what all heroes aspire to; it is the celebration of their heroic deeds in song, which grants to them immortality in the memory of mankind (Nagy 1974). So the *Iliad* comprises the *kleos aphthiton* of Achilleus for, despite his stated wish to turn his back on it, he does not of course leave Troy but dies an early death.

434–605   The Speech of Phoinix is by far the longest of the three appeals to Achilleus. Phoinix' task is to make the personal appeal as life-long family friend, by harking back to Achilleus' childhood when he had been as a father to him. In truth he seems almost to regard him as a child still (437, 440, 444), and Achilleus addresses him later as his surrogate father (607). It contains three clearly defined sections: he establishes his credentials with Achilleus by recounting an episode from his own past when he was well received and treated by Peleus (447–95); he recounts the Allegory of the Prayers (*Litai*), which tells of the punishment of those who refuse to respond to supplication (502–12); and he tells the story of Meleagros, whose experiences closely parallel those of Achilleus

(529–99). For close analysis of the speech, see Rosner (1976), Scodel (1982), Wilson (1996.25–9).

447 **as I was that time when I first left Hellas.** There are similarities between the tale that Phoinix tells about his past and the recent experiences of Achilleus: Phoinix tells that he and his father were in dispute over a concubine, just as Achilleus and Agamemnon quarrelled over the concubine Briseis in Book 1; Phoinix was entreated by his kinsmen not to leave, just as Achilleus is being entreated by his best friends amongst the Achaians; and Phoinix contemplated killing his father but was restrained by an immortal, just as Athene held Achilleus back from killing Agamemnon (1. 193–8).

454–7 For the **furies** (Erinues), see 3. 278–80n. **Zeus of the underworld** is Plouton; **Persephone** was abducted by Plouton from her mother Demeter and forced to spend six months of each year with him in the Underworld. His father's curse **that I might never have any son** introduces Phoinix' role as Achilleus' adopted father, which establishes his right to offer him advice.

464–84 Phoinix was besieged in his own bedroom by his relatives **with supplications repeated**: it might have been expected that he would lock himself in his room to escape his father's anger, but in fact he says he was locked in by his relatives, with a guard close mounted, out of their affection for him and in an attempt to stop him fleeing. So Phoinix tries to picture himself and his fellow ambassadors now as like his own kinsmen years ago, desperate to prevent Achilleus leaving. By speaking of **lord Peleus, who accepted me with a good will**, Phoinix is trying to suggest to Achilleus the kindness and riches which Agamemnon is apparently offering; but the lessons offered by Phoinix' tale are clearly not appropriate to Achilleus' position and he seems quite deliberately to be fostering in Achilleus' mind a false picture of Agamemnon's attitude.

488–91 **until I had set you on my knees.** This extraordinarily vivid portrait of Achilleus as young child reverses his own picture of himself as mother bird bringing food for its fledglings (323–4n).

497–501 The **sacrifices and offerings for endearment** to the gods are the equivalent of the gifts offered to Achilleus by Agamemnon: if the gods receive gifts they pardon those who give them and, Phoinix suggests, Achilleus should follow their example. When the gods accept these offerings, they do so because mortals are offering them **in supplication,** and, Phoinix implies, Achilleus similarly is receiving supplication; but in fact Agamemnon has neither come in person nor told the ambassadors to adopt the posture of suppliants, but rather he has demanded Achilleus' submission.

502–12 The second part of Phoinix' speech is the allegory of **the spirits of Prayer** (*Litai*). It was suggested by Leaf (1900.408) that this allegory is a description of Agamemnon the penitent suppliant: **lame of their feet** because he is reluctant to ask Achilleus' pardon, **wrinkled** with the mental struggle of humbling himself, and **cast their eyes sidelong** because he is unable to look in the face the man he has wronged; but this is hardly plausible, since Agamemnon has made it clear that he is neither penitent nor suppliant.

504 **the spirit of Ruin** translates Greek *ate*, the madness which leads men to commit foolish acts, which Agamemnon blamed for leading him astray during the quarrel (115n). The lesson of the allegory is that where Ruin has led a person astray, the Prayers come to heal the damage caused. Phoinix intends Achilleus to believe that, as Agamemnon said (though not in Achilleus' presence), *ate* was the source of the trouble; that Agamemnon, having recognized his delusion, is now sending prayers, or apologies, to Achilleus; and that, if Achilleus now refuses to accept these, *ate* will follow once more to create yet more havoc. However, the spirit, as well as the words, of Agamemnon's message force the conclusion that at no point did Agamemnon offer an apology, and that Phoinix is misrepresenting Agamemnon's true attitude. Nevertheless Phoinix' persuasiveness was sufficient to convince Grote (1884 ii.180), who drew the extraordinary conclusion that 'the main event of the ninth book [is] the outpouring of profound humiliation by the Greeks, and from Agamemnon especially, before Achilleus'.

520 **he has sent the best men to you to supplicate you, choosing them.** In fact it was Nestor who chose the ambassadors and who furthermore urged Agamemnon to offer words of supplication and gifts of friendship (112–3); when Phoinix claims that Agamemnon sent these best men to supplicate Achilleus, he is very clearly misrepresenting Agamemnon's intention.

529–99 The third part of Phoinix' speech is his long account of the story of Meleagros, and his attempt to persuade Achilleus that Meleagros' experiences should serve as an example to him. An

alternative version of the story of Meleagros is told by Bacchylides
(v. 94) and Ovid (*Metamorphoses* 8. 270): that his mother Althaia
had been told that, when a brand on the fire had burned through,
her son would die, and so she put out the brand and preserved it in
a box; that Meleagros killed his uncles, the brothers of Althaia,
during a quarrel which followed the hunt for the Kalydonian boar;
that his mother in revenge threw the brand on the fire and, when it
had burned through, Meleagros died; and that his mother and his
wife Kleopatra subsequently hanged themselves. Phoinix' aim is to
present the tale in a way which most closely relates to Achilleus'
own situation; for discussion of this episode, see March (1987.34).

529–49 **The Kouretes and the steadfast Aitolians** both lived in
Aitolia, at the entrance to the Gulf of Korinth. The hunt for the
Kalydonian **wild boar** is included to provide the occasion of
Meleagros' tale. Meleagros recruited large numbers of men to hunt
and kill the boar, but their success was followed by rivalry for its
head and hide, and then by battle. Later tradition told that the
expedition included Jason, Theseus, Phoinix, Telamon, Peleus,
Nestor, Laertes and the heroine Atalanta who drew first blood. It
was Meleagros' gift of the spoils of the hunt to Atalanta which
resulted in the subsequent quarrel.

556–62 **Kleopatra** was renamed **Alkyone** by her parents because
her mother Marpessa's weeping had been like the cry of the *alkuon*,
translated by Lattimore 'sea-bird', but more accurately 'kingfisher'.

565 **with this Kleopatra he lay mulling his heart-sore anger** suggests
a close parallel between the stories of Meleagros and Achilleus.
Meleagros lay apart with his wife Kleopatra mulling his anger, and
Achilleus is in his shelter with his companion Patroklos: it is not
too fanciful to suggest that the audience would hear the name Kleopatra as the reversal of Patro-klos.

574–96 **the Aitolian elders supplicated him.** By telling of the repeated
supplications which were made to Meleagros, Phoinix is trying to
persuade Achilleus that the representations made by the three
ambassadors also constitute supplication; for discussion, see
Muellner (1996.147). The priests sent by the Aitolian elders equate
to Odysseus sent by Agamemnon, and the gift of **a piece of land,
an entirely good one** is every bit as heroic a gift as those offered to
Achilleus. The supplication by Meleagros' father **Oineus** and by
his mother and sisters equates to the appeal of Phoinix himself,

who has carefully presented himself as Achilleus' surrogate father (485–95). The supplication by Meleagros' friends, **the most honoured and dearest of all,** anticipates the appeal of Aias who claims that he and the other ambassadors 'desire beyond all others to have your honour and love' (641–2). The final appeal to Meleagros, which is successful, is that of **his wife, the fair-girdled bride,** Kleopatra; and in Achilleus' case the fourth and final appeal, which will also prove successful, occurs at 16. 21–45 and is that of Patroklos.

598–605   **yet these would no longer make good their many and gracious gifts.** By returning late to the battle, Meleagros was deprived of the promised gifts, and so, Phoinix concludes, his honour was diminished. By recounting the actions of Meleagros, Phoinix unwittingly provides Achilleus with the model of his own future actions, for he will indeed resolve to withhold from the battle until the very last moment, until the Achaians confront total defeat. Like Meleagros, Achilleus will return to battle, not for prizes, but in the knowledge that he alone can ward off disaster.

607–19   The Speech of Achilleus in reply to Phoinix. Achilleus' assertion **such honour is a thing I need not. I think I am honoured already in Zeus' ordinance** recalls his request to Thetis in Book 1. He asked her to persuade Zeus to send a defeat on the Achaians, and she responded by asking Zeus to grant honour to Achilleus (1. 505); Achilleus now observes that Zeus has done so. Achilleus' words are often taken to represent him as an outsider, as one who has questioned and rejected the values of the heroic community: Whitman (1958.193), for example, believes that he has progressed 'from the simple assumptions of the other princely heroes onto the path where heroism means the search for the dignity and meaning of the self'. In fact, however, it is Agamemnon whose words and actions have placed him as the outsider, whilst Achilleus himself remains firmly in tune with the ethical beliefs of his community voicing his judgment on the behaviour of his antagonist; for discussion, see Gill 1996.

618   **we shall decide tomorrow** is a significant shift in Achilleus' position, since he declared in response to Odysseus that he would sail for home the following day (360).

624–42   The Speech of Aias is much the shortest of the appeals to Achilleus. After Achilleus, Aias is the greatest of the heroes (cf. 7.

197n), and so his terse remarks also reflect the heroic standpoint. He too stresses the compensation on offer, but his message is one of heroic friendship betrayed by Achilleus.

632–6   yet a man takes from his brother's slayer the blood price. The passage looks forward to one of the scenes depicted by Hephaistos on the great shield he fashions for Achilleus (18. 497–508), in which a lawsuit is conducted about the payment of the blood price to the relatives of a murder victim. Aias draws an unfavourable comparison between Achilleus' refusal to accept compensation from Agamemnon and the attitude of a murdered man's relatives who do accept payment, rather than seeking revenge through the death of the murderer. Of course Achilleus is refusing to accept payment, not for the murder of a relative, but for the stealing of the woman he considers his wife, and so the comparison is not a true one; in fact a much closer comparison is the abduction of Helen, as Achilleus argued (cf. 336–41n), but Aias chooses to ignore it.

638   Yet now we offer you seven, surpassingly lovely. Aias makes just the same mistake as Agamemnon in believing that at issue is a question of possessions, rather than one of honour and respect (cf. 122–56n).

644–55   The Speech of Achilleus in reply to Aias shows a further shift in his stance, and he no longer speaks of leaving for home. So for all his anger and for all his refusal to accept Agamemnon's gifts, he shows that he remains sensitive to the ties of loyalty to the heroic community which Aias has voiced. **darken with fire our vessels** anticipates Achilleus' fateful decision in Book 16 to send Patroklos into battle in his place: he will do so, at Patroklos' request, in response to the firing of the first Achaian ship, but he will be prevented by his declaration here from fighting himself, because the fire will not have reached his own ship (cf. 16. 61–3).

663–8   Achilleus slept in the inward corner. The details of the sleeping arrangements in Achilleus' shelter continue the comparison with the story of Meleagros in Phoinix' speech: Achilleus continues to sleep alongside his companion Patroklos, whereas Meleagros left his wife Kleopatra in order to save his people (596). **Skyros** is the island where Achilleus was hidden by his mother to avoid joining the expedition to Troy, and where his son Neoptolemos lives (cf. 19. 331–2)

683–9   he will drag down his strong-benched, oarswept ships to the water. Odysseus gives no indication that Achilleus has twice shifted his stance and reports only his original threat to leave Troy, and Whitman (1958.190) suggests that Odysseus, of all people, may have failed to notice the shifts. It is far more likely that he fails to report Achilleus' final decision, that he will do nothing until in effect all the ships are destroyed and with them any chance of returning home, because he fears its effect on Achaian morale. His appeal to **Aias, and the two heralds** purports to guarantee the truth of what he is saying, and their silence indicates their connivance.

698   I wish you had not supplicated. Diomedes chooses to ignore Agamemnon's demand for Achilleus' subjection (158–61), and regards his offer of gifts as supplication which he considers Achilleus has been wrong to reject. Many modern critics have followed Diomedes and have argued for Achilleus' responsibility: 'the recovery and repentance of Agamemnon remove what excuse [Achilleus] had before, and now he alone is to blame for the dire punishment of the Achaians . . . By the death of Patroklos Achilles is punished' (Bowra 1930.19). Yet repentance is hardly a fitting way to describe Agamemnon's stance in this book, and Achilleus' stance hardly makes him blameworthy or a suitable case for punishment.

ILIAD 10

Because of the central role which the Trojan Dolon plays in this book,
it is referred to as the Doloneia. *The book is usually thought to be a*
later addition to the poem, and the grounds for suspicion include: that
no reference is made in the main body of the poem to the events of this
book, and so it could be removed entirely without affecting the story;
that the composer seems unduly fond of pseudo-archaisms, and that
this suggests a later author trying to imitate the distinctive Homeric
diction; and that the composer seems to cultivate literary mannerisms,
particularly antithesis. See further, Danek 1988.

After the momentous events of Book 9, the next great turning point
in the narrative is to be the death of Patroklos in Book 16: Achilleus
has reaffirmed his anger and Homer now works towards the tragic
outcome of that reaffirmation. At the moment Patroklos, like all of
Achilleus' Myrmidons, is absent from the battle, and so the following
books are to contain a description of an Achaian defeat which will
cause his return. However the Achaians are already in a state of defeat
as a result of events at the end of Book 8, a defeat which was designed
to cause the sending of the embassy to Achilleus. So the purpose of
Book 10 is to establish a position for the Achaians from which they
can suffer another defeat. This book will provide the Achaians with a
limited victory, but Homer employs neither the usual pitched battle
nor an heroic aristeia, *but a unique night raid on the Trojan camp by*
Odysseus and Diomedes during which they encounter the Trojan Dolon,
who happens to be on an identical night raid on the Achaian camp.
This encounter has a very contrived air, and indeed it takes no less
than 331 lines actually to get the two Achaians and the Trojan on their
way. The episode is unique in that the events occur at night, and this
itself characterizes the actions of the warriors since deeds performed

under cover of night or in disguise are less heroic. The episode is unique too in the emphasis placed upon the wearing of animal skins: on the Achaian side, Agamemnon wears a lion skin (23), Menelaos a leopard skin (29), Nestor a fleece (134), and Diomedes a lion skin (177), while on the Trojan side Dolon wears a wolf-pelt (334); Odysseus is not wearing an animal skin but he does have a unique helmet made of boars' tusks (264), Dolon wears a marten's hide cap (335), and Diomedes wears a bull's hide helmet (257) and is said to be lying on an ox hide (155). It is an extraordinary collection and may be designed to prefigure the bestiality of the book's events.

5–8   **As when the lord of Hera the lovely-haired flashes his lightning.** The comparison of Agamemnon's turmoil to Zeus' lightning is very far from vivid, and is not improved by the catalogue of other disturbances in nature, of rain, hail and snow; the transfer to Zeus as bringer of battle is particularly harsh, an 'instance of the pretentious usage of traditional language characteristic of the book' (Hainsworth 1993.157).

11–13   **Now he would gaze across the plain to the Trojan camp.** The object is to recall, through the image of the Trojan camp-fires in the plain (cf. 8. 554–63), and through the light-hearted sound of their flutes and pipes piercing the night, the superiority enjoyed by the Trojans and their confidence at the end of Book 8.

19   **work out a plan that would not fail.** Nestor was the author of the plan in Book 9 which did fail, to send the embassy to Achilleus, though it is unlikely that any reference to that is intended here.

38   **to go and spy on the Trojans** introduces, very abruptly, the theme of this book, the joint spying mission of Odysseus and Diomedes on the Trojan camp. The scheme for a night raid runs quite counter to Diomedes' proposal at the end of the previous book, that they get a good night's sleep and then draw up for battle (9. 705–9), a proposal which won support from the whole leadership.

47–50   **so much evil as Hektor, beloved of Zeus, has wrought on the sons of the Achaians** is a considerable exaggeration of Hektor's success the previous day, when it was in fact the Achaian archer Teukros whose exploits were highlighted. The exaggeration indicates Agamemnon's panic, but it also prepares the ground for the improvement in the Achaians' fortunes in the present book.

56–7   Seven sentries were placed on guard, each commanding one hundred men (9. 80–6), so the very grand periphrasis **sacred duty of the guards** is designed to recall the great size of the guard posted and hence the siege mentality which now grips the Achaian side. Nestor's **own son** is Thrasymedes, who was named as commander of the guard at 9. 81.

69 **Give each man due respect.** Agamemnon displays uncharacteristic tact, quite at odds with his behaviour elsewhere, particularly during his Tour of Inspection in Book 4, and this shows the effect the failure of the embassy has had on him.

79 **he gave no ground to sorrowful old age.** Although it is true that Nestor does his share of the fighting, he often laments that old age prevents him fighting as he did when he was young (7. 132–3).

88–95 **whom beyond others Zeus has involved in hard work** continues Agamemnon's earlier complaint that he and his brother Menelaos were born to shoulder the 'burden of evil' (71). His description of his symptoms is exaggerated, and the composer's portrait of Agamemnon's panic in this opening section is itself excessive (cf. 47–50n).

101 The possibility of spying under cover of night was suggested by Menelaos (38), and now Agamemnon wonders whether the Trojans **might not be pondering an attack on us in the darkness**; night-time military activity appears only in this book.

110 **Aias the swift-footed** is Aias son of Oïleus, the lesser Aias. The **powerful son of Phyleus** is Meges, though he hardly belongs alongside such major heroes as Diomedes, Odysseus and Aias: it may be the naming of Odysseus that calls him to mind, because Meges is leader of the forces from Doulichion and was named in the Catalogue of the Ships immediately before Odysseus (2. 625–30).

116–21 **he sleeps and has given to you alone all the hard work.** Nestor's criticism of Menelaos is no more justified than Agamemnon's **often he hangs back and is not willing to work hard**: Menelaos did after all fight Paris in a duel (3. 21), and he was also the only Achaian champion to volunteer to answer Hektor's challenge (7. 94).

137–50 Nestor first approaches **Odysseus**, and then **Diomedes**, the two heroes, that is, who will undertake the night raid later in the book. The stated reason why Agamemnon and Nestor are wandering around the camp in the dark was to ensure that the guards were awake (97), but Nestor is rousing his companions to **deliberate the question of running away or of fighting.**

163–7   Aged sir, you are a hard man. The humorous tone of Diomedes' reply reflects the easy familiarity which all the heroes feel towards the aged Nestor. Diomedes has more cause than most to resent being woken, since it was his suggestion, approved by all the kings, that they get a good night's sleep before being rallied by Agamemnon in the morning (9. 705–9); so his tone also registers that he finds the sudden change of plan disconcerting.

188–9   they were turning always toward the plain. The looks of the Achaians towards the plain characterize their nervousness, just as the noise characterizes the Trojans' excitement at the prospect of the new day.

194–201   Having completed his inspection of the guard, Nestor now moves on to assemble the leaders, but remarkably he does so outside the Achaian defences in **a space not cumbered with corpses.** It may be that this spot is chosen because it is out of hearing of the troops, but more likely it is designed to point a parallel with the Trojan encampment in the plain, and to set the mood of the assembly: 'what was straightforward has become eerie, atmospheric' (Griffin 1980a.13).

203–10   Once again it is **Nestor** who initiates the Achaian action, just as in the case of the embassy in the previous book, but the reasoning behind the proposed strategy is, at best, strained. The object of this book is the meeting of Odysseus and Diomedes with Dolon and their capture of the horses of the Thracian Rhesos: so the proposed spying expedition is simply a transparent attempt by the composer to provide them with a motive for going to the Trojan camp.

215   The gift of a **black sheep, female, with a lamb beneath** presents one of this book's many antitheses, in that the prize offered to the Achaians contrasts with the prize which the Trojan Dolon demands, and Hektor promises, the horses and chariot of Achilleus himself (322).

227–32   many were willing to go with Diomedes. The eagerness of the Achaian heroes to join Diomedes contrasts with their reluctance to meet Hektor in combat at 7. 92, and highlights the book's purpose of bringing the Achaians a limited victory. For **Nestor's son,** cf. 56–7n.

240   **was frightened for Menelaos.** Agamemnon's concern that his brother might be selected by Diomedes matches his concern at 7. 109, when he had to restrain him from accepting Hektor's challenge to a duel which would have meant certain death.

245   **Pallas Athene loves him.** It is in the *Odyssey* rather than in the *Iliad* that Athene's love for Odysseus is apparent; in his own poem she is Odysseus' protective deity, of both him and his family.

261–70   **the white teeth of a tusk-shining boar.** It is generally acknowledged that this is the description of a Mykenaian object: archaeology has produced from Late Bronze Age contexts examples both of the tusks themselves, with holes bored for sewing them to the inner cap, and of representations of the helmets in both paintings and ivory carvings (Lorimer 1950.212). The helmet is given a detailed pedigree to increase its importance. **Autolykos** was the grandfather of Odysseus and was arch-thief and trickster (see *Odyssey* 19. 395): so the helmet takes on these associations and this contributes to the episode's atmosphere of theft (of the horses of Rhesos) and deception. **Amyntor** is the father of Phoinix, and **Eleon** is a town in Boiotia; **Skandeia** is a town in Kythera, an island off Southern Peloponnese. For a **gift of guest-friendship**, cf. 6. 215–25n.

285–90   Agamemnon spoke of the exploits of **Tydeus** when he accused Diomedes of being inferior to his father (4. 391–400). Tydeus killed all but one of the group set to ambush him on his way back from Thebes, an exploit which anticipates Diomedes' own massacre of the Thracians in this book. **Asopos** is a river of Boiotia; the Thebans are called **Kadmeians** after their ancestor Kadmos.

299–313   There is a carefully contrived balance between the wakefulness of Hektor and that of Agamemnon (3–4); between the summoning of a Trojan assembly and that of the Achaians (195–7); and between the musings of Hektor and those of Nestor (204–17). There is the same transparency about motivating Dolon's trip into the night, as there was in the case of the two Achaians (cf. 203–10n): in fact Hektor needs only to wait for dawn to discover the effect on the Achaians of their recent defeat, so the identity of motive on the two sides is very contrived. The Trojans are **stricken to silence**, just as the Achaians were by Nestor's suggestion (218).

314–17   The physical description of **Dolon**, like that of Thersites (2.

216–19), indicates that he is unsuitable for an heroic role, although his swift-footedness will be put to the test during this episode. Willcock (1976.119) wonders whether the detail that he was a single son with five sisters suggests he was probably encouraged to overestimate his own importance and prowess.

322 It is another of this book's contrived antitheses that Dolon should ask for **the horses and the chariot** of Achilleus as his reward, and that it is the horses of Rhesos which become the spoils taken during the raid by Odysseus and Diomedes. Dolon's request is presumptuous and arrogant, given his unheroic status.

343 In contrast to Dolon's arrogant self-regard is Odysseus' suspicion that he may be out **to strip some one of the perished corpses**: stripping the armour from a defeated opponent is an essential part of combat (cf. 7. 77–83), but here the implication is that Dolon is skulking under cover of night on a mission almost of body-snatching.

355 **He thought in his heart** may also be translated 'he hoped in his heart': through both meanings the composer characterizes Dolon's fearful reaction to his lonely excursion, and this complements the comparison of him to the fearful prey, a deer or a hare, of the hounds. **as when two rip-fanged hounds** characterizes both the speed of Odysseus and Diomedes in pursuing their quarry and the violent end Dolon meets (456–7).

383–400 **let no thought of death be upon you.** Odysseus' calm assurance is designed to put Dolon at his ease; similarly **Odysseus the resourceful smiled** represents a deliberate deception of an enemy which is quite at odds with normal heroic practice, and so Dolon's killing is all the more shocking as a result.

402 **Aiakides** is Achilleus, grandson of Aiakos; his **horses** are named Xanthos and Balios, and are divine horses born of Podarge and the West Wind (16. 149–51).

415 **godlike Ilos** was the founder of Ilion, Troy; he was the grandfather of Priam.

420–2 **their far-assembled companions in battle are sleeping.** The Trojans themselves mount the guard because it is their own wives and children who are threatened by the Achaians; their allies have no such concern as their wives and children are at home, and so they sleep soundly. Dolon's reasoning is hardly convincing and is transparently designed to lead into his assertion that the sleeping allies, particularly Rhesos and his Thracians, are vulnerable.

427–31 I will accurately recite all these things to you. Dolon gives
no answer to Odysseus' question (409) about the Trojans' plans,
which was the stated reason for the mission, but instead gives details
of the disposition of the allies. The list of the allies is not quite the
same as in Book 2: the **Leleges** and the **Kaukonians** were not
included there.

435–8 his are the finest horses I ever saw. There is irony in Dolon,
who set out with the intention of winning Achilleus' splendid horses
and chariot, now praising those of **Rhesos** in the hope that Odysseus
will be distracted by their magnificence from killing him. This vivid
description marks an important moment in the book's narrative,
for Odysseus and Diomedes now abandon all pretence of spying
out the Trojans' intentions and concentrate entirely on stealing
Rhesos' horses. Whitman (1958.176) suggests that the tale may
have originated in the story of the theft, also by Odysseus and
Diomedes, of the Palladion, the sacred image of Athena, Troy's
talisman.

454–9 the man was trying to reach his chin with his strong hand;
cf. 1. 407–10n. Like all supplications on the battlefield, Dolon's is
unsuccessful, but the detail of his **head still speaking dropped in
the dust** is not in keeping with even the most violent deaths in the
poem: 'a bizarre and gruesome thought, typical enough of this poet'
(Hainsworth 1993.198). Dolon's death is followed by a parody of
the heroic practice of stripping body armour from a victim, when
they remove the marten's hide cap and wolf's pelt from his corpse.

483–93 he began to kill them one after another. The systematic
slaughter of sleeping warriors which follows is quite out of keeping
with the rest of the poem; and even by the grim standards of this
book, the observation that Odysseus drags the corpses to the side
so that the horses will not be disturbed by treading on them seems
particularly unattractive.

494–7 But when the son of Tydeus came to the king. Homer makes
no direct reference to the tradition of a prophecy that if Rhesos,
newly arrived at Troy, were to survive his first night there and if his
horses were to drink the water of Troy's river Xanthos, then the
city would never be taken, a story which Virgil makes central to his
treatment of Rhesos (*Aeneid* 1. 469–73). **Oineus' son** means
Diomedes, who is in fact grandson of Oineus.

544–53 how did you win these horses? What began as a spying mission has ended as a successful booty raid: Nestor was the one who laid out the aims of the mission (204–10), but now he has no question about it beyond enquiring about the horses. The purpose of the scene has been to present a limited Achaian triumph and so to indicate a change in their fortunes after their recent disaster: the progression from a limited defensive strategy, under the protective cover of darkness, to a full-scale massacre of the Thracians is an indication of the change in morale which now affects the Achaians.

558   **These horses, aged sir, that you ask about are newcomers from Thrace**: cf. 494–7n.

566   The **rejoicing** of the Achaians is in contrast to the panic which gripped them at the beginning of Book 9 as a result of their defeat. The impression has been created that they are now on the crest of a wave, and so the scene is set for the great defeat which will bring Patroklos back into the battle and to his death.

ILIAD 11

In this book Homer begins to establish the circumstances in which Patroklos can approach Achilleus to seek his permission to return to the battle. Serious defeat caused the Achaians to send the embassy to Achilleus in Book 9 in the hope of persuading him to return; now a second serious defeat is required to motivate Patroklos' appeal in Book 16. The intervening Book 10, though not describing an Achaian victory, has described an incident, the night raid on the Trojan camp by Odysseus and Diomedes, which has helped to lessen the sense of defeat and demoralization which characterized the Achaians both before and after the embassy to Achilleus. The impression of Achaian superiority has once more been established, and this impression is heightened at the beginning of this book by the arming of Agamemnon and the description of his subsequent exploits; but as the book progresses the major Achaian warriors are wounded and withdraw, and the Trojans once more have the upper hand.

1   **Dawn** is the goddess Eos, who fell in love with **Tithonos,** the son of Laomedon and the brother of Priam (cf. 20. 237). She begged Zeus to grant Tithonos immortality, but failed to ask him also for the gift of eternal youth for her lover. Tithonos fathered Memnon, king of the Aithiopians, who was killed at Troy by Achilleus. None of this tale features in the *Iliad*'s version of events. 'noble' is a better translation than **haughty.**

4   There is no indication what this **portent of battle** may be, but Zeus' aegis, carried by Athene, is called the 'portent of Zeus' and features **Hate** amongst its decorations (5. 738–40).

13   **And now battle became sweeter to them.** These lines also described the recovery of the Achaians' spirits after the debacle of

their flight to the ships caused by Agamemnon's testing of the army (2. 453–4); here too they describe the new-found, though temporary, confidence which the night raid has given the Achaians.

16–44   he himself put the shining bronze upon him. The arming of Agamemnon is the second of four appearances of the traditional arming motif; in each case the description is the same, but the amount of embellishment varies (cf. 3. 328–38n). **Kinyras** is the king of Cyprus (**Kypros**); for **guest present,** cf. 6. 215–25n. The lavish detail of Agamemnon's **corselet** enhances the importance of its wearer: the snake motif is associated in portents with the Achaians as aggressors (cf. 2. 303–20n), and so its appearance on Agamemnon's corselet and on the **strap of the shield** illustrates the change in the Achaians' fortunes, since Agamemnon was recently urging flight. In spite of his splendid armour, Agamemnon will be the first of the Achaian leaders to be wounded in the coming encounter, so its description ironically points up his, and the Achaians', new-found confidence at the moment their defeat is about to begin. For the **Gorgon** on the aegis of Zeus, cf. 5. 734–47n.

47–9   Although Nestor gave a rather garbled account of tactics for fighting from chariots (4. 301–9n), in fact this is the normal method of employing them in the poem: warriors dismount to fight, and charioteers wait in the wings to transport them from the field when battle is over.

52–5   The image of the **dews dripping blood from the sky** sent by Zeus is similar to the tears of blood which Zeus weeps when his son Sarpedon dies (16. 459). **to hurl down a multitude of strong heads to the house of Hades** recalls the first image of the poem (1. 3–4).

57   **Poulydamas** acts almost as an *alter ego* of Hektor; he continually offers sound advice which contrasts with the reckless instincts of Hektor, and which is normally ignored by him.

67–72   like two lines of reapers. Like a number of other similes, and like some of the scenes on the shield made for Achilleus by Hephaistos in Book 18, this offers a picture of the normality of peace-time and the harvesting of Troy's plain before the arrival of the Achaians, in contrast to the full horror of the war which is soon to be described. The metaphor **the pressure held their heads on a line** seems to be of an invisible line between the two armies, which neither side can cross either in advance or in retreat: 'the pressure of combat locked them head-to-head' (Fagles 1991) is clearer.

73–5   The gods observe the prohibition imposed by Zeus (8. 5–12). **Hate, the Lady of Sorrow** is a personification rather than a god, and she is acting at Zeus' instruction (cf. 2–12).

86–9   at that time when the woodcutter makes ready his supper is another illustration of the battle from the world of peaceful nature (cf. 67–72n), and calls attention to the Achaians' heightened aggression, for they increase their efforts at the time the woodcutter relaxes from his.

91–147   Agamemnon now kills six named victims, and this is made more impressive by the fact that they confront him in pairs (92–3, 101, 122).

104–5   Before this Achilleus had caught these two. This theme is developed in greater detail in the story of Lykaon, also a son of Priam, whom Achilleus spared and ransomed, only to capture him on a subsequent occasion and kill him (21. 34–135); so there is a contrast between the unremitting savagery of Agamemnon and the mercy Achilleus showed in former times. **at the knees of Ida** means in the foothills of Ida.

113–19   as a lion seizes the innocent young of the running deer. Unusually this lion simile focuses on the violence of the beast rather than its courage, and so the fearfulness of the doe draws the reader's sympathy to Agamemnon's victims. The lion image for Agamemnon continues at 129 and 173. The deer is a frequent symbol of the Trojans (cf. 22. 1n).

140   The visit of **Menelaos, who came as envoy with godlike Odysseus** to Troy was recalled by Antenor to Helen at 3. 205–24, but there was no mention on that occasion of Antimachos' proposal that the two Achaian ambassadors be put to death; here it fills out the tale that Antimachos was bribed by Paris to oppose the return of Helen to the ambassadors (124).

155–7   As when obliterating fire comes down. There is a combination of images in this simile: the fire represents the destructiveness of Agamemnon's rampage, and the tumbling uprooted bushes represent the flight of the Trojans in face of him.

163   Zeus drew Hektor out from under the dust and the missiles. No reason is given, but when next Hektor appears he is 'standing among the compacted chariots and by the horses' (198), and he is advised to stay out of the fighting until he sees Agamemnon wounded; so Zeus' purpose here must be to avoid the possibility of Agamemnon being wounded by Hektor.

166–70   For the **barrow of ancient Ilos,** see 10. 415n; for **the Skaian gates and the oak tree,** see 6. 237n.

172–6   **like cattle when a lion, coming upon them in the dim night.** The association of Agamemnon with lion imagery continues (cf. 113–19n): as in the earlier simile, it is the isolation of the victim which is emphasized, as the poet offers almost a bird's-eye view of the general state of panic of the amorphous stampeding herd, before, like the lion, singling out the victim; together the similes provide a powerful illustration of the ferocity of the attacker and the defencelessness of the victims.

191–4   **But when, either struck with a spear or hit by a flying arrow.** The *aristeia* of Agamemnon is marked out as the acme of Achaian fortunes, and his wounding is to be the turning point; but there is also a clear statement of the limitations placed on Hektor, that he will be successful only **until the sun goes down.**

218   **Tell me now, you Muses.** The address to the Muses draws attention to the wounding of Agamemnon: this is the beginning of the rout of the Achaians which will eventually lead to Patroklos' appeal to Achilleus in Book 16, and so Homer is careful to mark the moment.

221–45   The story of **Iphidamas** is told at considerable length: he is the son of Antenor and Theano, herself the daughter of Kisseus king of Thrace; he was brought up by Kisseus and given as husband by him to one of his daughters, that is, to his aunt. Having given **a hundred oxen** for his bride, he is a man of wealth and stature, and so a worthy victim for Agamemnon. Pathos is leant to his early death by the fact that **he had known no delight** from his bride, and also by the metaphor of his **brazen slumber.**

248–63   Hektor remains in the background as Zeus advised, and Agamemnon is wounded by the relatively insignificant **Koön,** the brother of Iphidamas. It appears that, at this moment of Achaian defeat, Homer is not prepared to portray Hektor as superior to his Achaian opponents, particularly when two other major Achaians, Diomedes and Odysseus, are wounded, but neither by Hektor.

269–71   **As the sharp sorrow of pain descends on a woman in labour.** The simile contributes to the characterization of Agamemnon: his wound below the elbow is hardly mortal but, having 'shuddered with fear' (254), he reacts as though to pain no man can know; the significance of the great king, wounded by a comparative nonentity, being compared to a woman, is marked. **Hera** is the goddess of marriage and her **daughters** are the Eileithuiai, the spirits of childbirth.

286 **Trojans, Lykians and Dardanians** are led, respectively, by Hektor, Sarpedon and Aineias, and, like their leaders, they represent the foremost on the Trojan side.

292–3 **against some savage beast, wild boar or lion.** The change in the battle is indicated by the fact that the lion which was associated with Agamemnon's unbridled savagery (cf. 172–6n) is now itself the object of attack.

305–8 **as when the west wind strikes in the deepening whirlstorm.** The comparison of Hektor to a whirlstorm and the Achaians to the battered clouds and waves intensifies the previous comparison of Hektor to 'a high-blown storm-cloud' and the Achaians to 'the blue sea-water' (297–8).

312–19 The combined exploits of **Odysseus** and **Diomedes** recall the night raid they made in the previous book, and so when they are wounded and withdraw from the battle this destroys the effect on Achaian morale which the raid had. The episode parallels the earlier one, when Diomedes summoned Odysseus to defend Nestor but he either did not hear or else he paid no heed (cf. 8. 97n). On the present occasion the roles are reversed, but Diomedes does not hesitate to stand by Odysseus.

324–5 **as when two wild boars hurl themselves.** This reverses the action of the earlier simile (292–3n) and so illustrates the temporary triumph of Odysseus and Diomedes and the relief it brings to the Achaians. The image of the boar is continued at 414–18.

329–32 There is pathos in the tale of the father, **Merops of Perkote,** who could foretell the death of his sons but was unable to prevent them going to war: the theme appeared also at 5. 149–51, but the most pathetic example, which pervades the poem, is Thetis' foreknowledge of her son Achilleus' early death, but powerlessness to do anything to prevent it.

354–70 Hektor is wounded and retreats from the battle, and the leading Achaians, Odysseus and Diomedes, are themselves subsequently wounded; the result is that, despite the Achaian defeat, the stature of the Trojan leader is not improved by it (cf. 248–63n), particularly as his immediate replacement is the brother he continually derides for his cowardice, Paris.

375–8   Diomedes is wounded by Paris' arrow in **the flat of the right foot**; he was also wounded by an arrow, fired by Pandaros, in the shoulder (5. 98). Diomedes' wounding here parallels the death of Achilleus himself, shot in the ankle by Paris' arrow, as described in the lost epic *Aithiopis* (Evelyn-White 1967.509).

385–95   **lovely in your locks, eyer of young girls.** Diomedes' emphasis on Paris' looks and womanizing recalls Hektor's condemnation of him (3. 39). In its portrayal of the widow **with cheeks torn in lamentation** and her orphaned children, Diomedes' speech is like one of the brief sketches which accompany many of the descriptions of the deaths of minor fighters. **there are more birds than women swarming about him** recalls the poem's opening image of bodies left as carrion for the dogs and birds, but it is a particularly appropriate adaptation which echoes Paris' reputation for womanizing.

404–10   Odysseus debates whether he should stand and fight or flee, and draws the heroic conclusion that he must fight **if one is to win honour in battle.** When Hektor stands to face Achilleus, he too contemplates flight but concludes that it would be shameful (22. 99–110): for a hero, his sense of shame effectively removes the choice.

445   **Hades of the horses** is so called because it was believed that he transported the dead to his underworld kingdom in his chariot.

453–4   **the tearing birds will get you.** Odysseus taunts the dying Sokos with the same fate promised to Paris by Diomedes (395).

474–81   The simile is complicated by the joining of two separate images: the scattering of the **bloody scavengers** represents the fleeing Trojans, but then the lion eats the stag, whereas Aias in fact rescues Odysseus. When first they surrounded Odysseus the Trojans were compared to 'the hounds and lusty young men' of the hunt (414), but now they are like scavengers: 'the degeneration from hounds to cowardly jackals implies that an inferior band of men has wounded a worthy warrior' (Lonsdale 1990.79).

485–95   For **Aias, carrying like a wall his shield**, see 7. 219–23n. As **when a swollen river hurls its water**: Aias is like the swollen river, the fleeing Trojans he kills are like the trees felled by the river's

force. Such offensive action contrasts with Aias' more usual role as
the Achaians' defender (cf. 548–61n).

506   **Machaon,** a son of Asklepios, is the Achaian army physician
(cf. 4. 193–4), so his wounding by Paris, along with the wounding
of many major warriors, is another severe blow to the Achaians.

521   Hektor summoned his brother **Kebriones** to be his charioteer
(8. 318) after Archeptolemos had been killed. Kebriones will himself
in turn be killed by Patroklos (16. 737–43).

544   Aias' action, **swung the sevenfold ox-hide shield behind him,** is
hardly a practical form of defence but serves rather as a symbolic
representation of the change in his stance from offensive to
defensive.

548–61   Although Aias displays the courage and strength of **a tawny
lion,** it is the **donkey, stubborn and hard to move** which comes
away satisfied; so Aias' stubborn resilience is even more important
to his successful retreat than his lion's strength. The famous simile
of the donkey dominates the presentation of Aias in the poem, just
as much as the great tower shield which is associated with him. He
is the supreme defensive warrior of the Achaians who, like the
donkey which only departs when it has eaten its fill, will continue
obstinately to resist against even insuperable odds.

593   **Aias came back to join them.** The withdrawal of Aias from the
battlefield ends the description of this engagement. Numerically
the Achaians have had much the better of the battle, as many minor
Trojans have fallen before them; but in the space of 300 lines the
Achaians have lost Agamemnon, Diomedes and Odysseus through
injury, and Aias through retreat, and these, in the continuing absence
of Achilleus, represent the very heart torn from the Achaian forces.

597–600   **Machaon** received a shoulder wound from Paris' arrow
(505–7). His wounding is the first in a chain of events which will
lead eventually to the death of Patroklos, so it is important enough
for Achilleus himself to take note. Achilleus' position, **standing on
the stern of his huge-hollowed vessel,** is significant: when he last
appeared, he was sitting in his shelter, singing of men's fame and
paying no heed to events on the battlefield (9. 185–91); recent
events have rekindled his interest in the battle.

603   **and this was the beginning of his evil.** It is Achilleus' wish to
learn the identity of the injured man and his summoning of Patroklos
which brings the beginning of the evil, for which Achilleus will in

time hold himself responsible. From this point Patroklos increasingly takes on the role of Achilleus, and eventually he will arm himself in Achilleus' armour, and go out to his death.

608–9   now I think the Achaians will come to my knees and stay there in supplication. Many have considered it inconceivable that the same poet who created the Embassy to Achilleus in Book 9 could also have placed these words in the mouth of Achilleus here, since they apparently contradict the supplication he received and the gifts he was offered. However, it is clear that the preference he expressed for honour 'in Zeus' ordinance' (9. 608) required the presence of the Achaians at his knees in supplication, and that this passage, in showing what he does want, also indicates what he feels he did not receive in Book 9. In sending Patroklos to enquire about the wounded Machaon, Achilleus is providing the Achaians with the opportunity, in their despair after their defeat and the wounding of their leaders, to do what they failed to do during the embassy. Achilleus is gloating over the **need past endurance** which the Achaians are suffering rather than sympathizing with it.

616   went on the run. The urgency with which Patroklos undertakes his mission looks forward to the following scene in which his return to Achilleus is delayed by Nestor and he is subjected to the old man's persuasive words.

**629–39   As refreshment for warriors returning from the battle, this meal of bread and honey, washed down with wine and with onion accompaniment, makes a striking contrast to the usual Homeric feast wholly centred upon meat. The purpose of the onion is probably to offset the sweetness of the wine and honey; however the potion (*kukeon*) which Hekamede prepares seems to have magical qualities as well as the medicinal required in the present context, since it was the drink given to the initiates at the Eleusinian Mysteries, and it was also the potion with which Kirke captivated Odysseus' followers (*Odyssey* 10. 234–5); so it may well be that the food here also has magical connotations. In this scene Patroklos takes his first step to rejoining the community of heroes, and so the ritualized description and the magical properties of the food and drink may themselves be part of that process.

632–6   a beautifully wrought cup which the old man brought with him. The cup bears some resemblance to one found in Shaft Grave IV at Mykenai and, although it is quite certain that Homer is not here describing that particular object, there is a possibility that this, like the helmet fashioned from boars' tusks (10. 261–70n), is a reminiscence of a Bronze Age object. Great heroes generally are associated with outstanding pieces of armour—Achilleus' spear, Agamemnon's breastplate, Aias' shield, Hektor's helmet; the old man Nestor holds the symbol of the feast, which is itself symbolic of the community of heroes, in anticipation of the scene in which Patroklos is persuaded to return to the heroic community.

647–53 Cf. 616n. There is subtle characterization in Patroklos' speech: of Achilleus, whose strength of personality inspires respect, or even fear, in Patroklos; of Nestor, whose garrulity will cause him, given half a chance, to recount his life's story; and of Patroklos himself, conscious of his responsibility to Achilleus and tactfully trying to exercise it in face of Nestor. In particular, Patroklos' description of Achilleus, **a dangerous man; he might even be angry with one who is guiltless** gives a first indication of Patroklos' growing disenchantment with his companion's stance, which will culminate in his accusation of pitilessness (16. 29–35) and his request that he be permitted to fight in his place (16. 38–45).

655–65 **Now why is Achilleus being so sorry for the sons of the Achaians.** Achilleus betrayed no hint of the sympathy with which Nestor credits him, but was concerned only with the supplication which he hoped he would now receive (cf. 608–9n). **Is he going to wait then till the running ships by the water are burned:** this is just what Achilleus declared he intended to do, when he replied to the appeal of Aias (9. 650), but this was not reported to the Achaians by Odysseus, who told only of Achilleus' first response to himself, that he intended to sail for home in the morning (9. 682–3). So there is bitterness and unintentional irony in both of Nestor's questions.

670–760 Nestor tells a long tale of his exploits in a cattle war fought by his city Pylos against neighbouring Elis. This is the longest of Nestor's tales in the poem, and some have considered it to be inappropriate at a time when Patroklos is looking to hurry back to Achilleus; it is also objected that the tale seems to have little relevance to the present situation. As in the case of his other tales, it establishes Nestor's heroic status, despite his advanced years, and so it validates the advice he is giving and seeks to inspire others to emulate him.

681–701   Neleian Pylos. Neleus is the father of Nestor; Pylos is the site in Messenia, in south west Peloponnese, where the Palace of Nestor has been excavated, dating to the Late Bronze Age. The attack of **Herakles** on Pylos was mentioned by Dione (5. 392) when she spoke of his wounding of Hera and Hades. **Augeias** was the king of Elis: the cleaning of the Augeian Stables was one of Herakles' Labours.

716–17   Neleus would not let me be armed. Nestor has already told that he is the only surviving son of Neleus (691–2) and this explains his father's attempt to restrain him. It is a theme repeated in Priam's unwillingness to allow his youngest and dearest son Polydoros to fight (20. 407).

727   Alpheios is the sacred river of Pylos; for the offering of bulls to a river god, cf. 21. 131.

749–50   the young Moliones, scions of Aktor feature in another of Nestor's tales (23. 638–42), where he says that they defeated him in a chariot race; there was a tradition that they were Siamese twins. In fact their real father was Poseidon **who shakes the earth in his wide strength,** not Aktor.

755–7   For Bouprasion, the Olenian rock, and **the hill of Alesios,** cf. 2. 615–17.

761–3   if it ever happened. This idiom appears occasionally in the poem when a character recalls an experience so fondly that he seems almost to doubt that it ever occurred: for example, when Helen recalled her early life with Menelaos in Sparta, she seemed to question whether it had really happened that way (3. 180). **he will weep much, too late, when his people are perished from him** predicts that many more deaths will result from Achilleus' intransigence, but in particular it foreshadows the death of Patroklos himself. Odysseus made this same point to Achilleus during the embassy, when he spoke of the affliction which would come upon him if he did not relent and aid the Achaians (9. 249n).

764   Menoitios, the father of Patroklos, took him as a child to the palace of Peleus in Phthia after he had killed another boy during a game of dice (23. 85–88), and so he was brought up there alongside Achilleus. Nestor is recalling the occasion he and Odysseus came to Phthia during their journey to raise an expedition against Troy, and his words seem deliberately to echo Odysseus' words to Achilleus (9. 252–3), when he recalled this same visit.

782–8   Peleus' advice to his son Achilleus, **to be always best in battle and pre-eminent beyond all others,** recalls the advice Glaukos was given by his father Hippolochos 'to be always among the bravest, and hold my head above others' (6. 208). Menoitios' advice to his son Patroklos was **speak solid words to him, and give him good counsel.** The advice Achilleus and Patroklos received from their fathers describes their relationship, Achilleus the headstrong warrior, Patroklos the older man of good counsel. There is irony in **If he listens to you it will be for his own good,** for having failed to persuade Achilleus to fight he will convince him that he should himself fight in his place, and this will be very far from being for his own good.

793–6   **But if he is drawing back from some prophecy** may perhaps refer to Achilleus' declaration during the embassy that his mother had told him of the choice he must make, between a short life with glory and a long life without (9. 410–16); but it is more likely that Nestor is suggesting an easy way out for Achilleus, a reason for not fighting himself while allowing Patroklos to do so. **you may be a light given to the Danaans** is an image frequently associated with Achilleus' return to battle: he himself declares 'I was no light of safety to Patroklos' (18. 102).

797–8   **let him give you his splendid armour to wear.** Achilleus' armour becomes the symbol of Patroklos' attempt to take his friend's heroic place, and Achilleus' agreement forces him to carry the burden of responsibility for his death. In fact Nestor's plan is a failure, as only Sarpedon so much as hints that there might be some doubt about the identity of the person in Achilleus' armour (16. 423–5).

808   **Eurypylos, who had been wounded in the thigh with an arrow.** Homer now combines a number of themes which he has begun, apparently without consequence, in the course of this book: the wounding of the healer Machaon (506), the wounding of Eurypylos (582–3) as he brought help to Aias, and the sending of Patroklos to Nestor's tent (610) to discover the identity of the wounded warrior; in the absence of the wounded healer Machaon, the wounded Eurypylos appeals to the passing Patroklos to treat his wound.

815   **Poor wretches.** In the wounded Eurypylos Patroklos recognizes the suffering of all the Achaians, and his compassion for them contrasts with Achilleus' disregard which Nestor has just condemned

(664). His concern is sufficient to overcome his anxiety to return to Achilleus which he tried to impress upon Nestor (647–53), and it will prove to be his undoing.

831   **Cheiron, most righteous of the Centaurs.** The tradition that Achilleus was raised as a child by the Centaur Cheiron is for the most part ignored in the *Iliad*. The poem generally plays down the mythic aspect of Achilleus, and in this case the story is excluded in order to elevate the role of the mortal Phoinix as Achilleus' surrogate father (cf. 9. 434–605n).

837–40   **But even so I will not leave you in your affliction.** Homer portrays Patroklos as a gentle and compassionate man, deeply troubled by the plight of the Achaians and the consequence of Achilleus' inaction; in order to give aid to a wounded companion, he disobeys Achilleus for the first time and displays independence of action which will bring about his death.

ILIAD 12

The events of Book 12 centre upon the defensive wall which the Achaians built around their ships at 7. 437–41, and so in antiquity it was given the title Teichomachia, Battle at the Wall. *The Achaian wall is as much a fiction as the poem in which it is described, and so no trace of it is to be found at the modern site of Troy. The poem provides the reason why it was built when it was, in the tenth year of the war rather than when the Achaians first landed at Troy (cf. 7. 337n). The effect of the withdrawal of Achilleus from the battle is to be the complete reversal of Achaian fortunes: Homer has described the Achaians' defeat in the previous book through the wounding and withdrawal of their major heroes, and from this book onwards he will show their reversal by presenting the besiegers as the besieged. It was with this in mind that he described the building of the wall as an extension of the mound heaped over the funeral pyre of the dead Achaians, and for the Achaians this wall now becomes the equivalent of the great wall of Troy. The book ends with Hektor breaking down the gate of the wall and the Achaians scattering amongst their ships.*

1   The return of the **son of Menoitios,** Patroklos, to Achilleus' shelter is suspended at this point; the narrative returns to him at 15. 390, where he is still tending the injured Eurypylos.

6–9   **had not given to the gods grand sacrifices.** Poseidon gave two reasons for objecting to the building of the wall, that the Achaians did not offer grand sacrifice and that it would detract from the wall around Troy which he and Apollo had previously built for Laomedon (cf. 7. 446–63n). **therefore it was not to stand firm for a long time** explains why there was no trace of the Achaian wall in later times: it continues, and explains away, the poetic fiction of the building of the wall.

17–23   Poseidon and Apollo took counsel to wreck the wall. This is in accordance with Zeus' promise (7. 459–63) that he would allow the Achaians' wall to be destroyed after they had left Troy. The rivers **Rhesos, Heptaporos, Karesos, Rhodios** and **Grenikos** do not appear elsewhere; the **Aisepos** flowed near Zeleia (2. 824–5); for the **Skamandros** and the **Simoeis**, see 2. 467–8n. The description of the heroes as **the race of the half-god mortals** is unique and is at odds with the poem's view of them as humans, but of superior strength and courage. The concept of heroes as intermediate between humans and gods is associated rather with Hesiod (cf. *Works and Days* 160–1).

29–30   logs and stones the toiling Achaians had set in position. The contrast is drawn between the hard labour of the Achaians in building the wall and the ease with which the god is able to demolish it. The description of the future destruction of the wall by Poseidon and Apollo serves the narrative purpose of showing that the wall will outlast the present Trojan attack on it: that is, whatever short-term triumph the Trojans are about to enjoy, the Achaians will have eventual victory. For the **passage of Helle**, that is, the Hellespont, see 7. 73–86n.

41   As when among a pack of hounds and huntsmen assembled. The wild boar recalls the comparison of Odysseus and Diomedes to boars (11. 324–5n), and Odysseus alone to a boar (11. 414); in those similes, as in this, the courage and determination of the hunted boar is emphasized as it rounds on its attackers. The description of the men **closing themselves into a wall** parallels the situation of the Achaians behind their defensive wall. **it is his own courage that kills him** parallels the actions of Hektor in the following scenes, as his self-confidence overcomes the restraint his companion Poulydamas tries to exercise over him; Andromache too declared that Hektor's great strength would be his death (6. 407).

50–80   the fast-footed horses balked at the edge of the lip. The contrast is drawn between the fear the Achaian defences cause in the horses drawing the Trojan chariots and the reaction of the soldiers when dismounted, **strong in their effort**. This elaborate contrast is designed to introduce the strategy of an attack on foot proposed by Poulydamas (75–9), and this **counsel of safety** is designed to characterize Poulydamas as thoughtful and circumspect, in contrast to Hektor. **Poulydamas** was born on the same night as

Hektor (cf. 18. 251) and appears as his *alter ego* (Redfield 1975.143). Throughout the poem he presents the voice of sanity and urges restraint on the more headstrong Hektor, advice which is usually resented by him and generally ignored: 'alone of them [he] looked before and behind him. He was companion to Hektor . . . but he was better in words, the other with the spear far better' (18. 250–2).

88–104   The division of the Trojan army into five battalions, each with three leaders, allows a catalogue of Trojan heroes and this illustrates the scale of their coming victory. The list of Trojans organizing themselves for battle calls to mind the list of major Achaian warriors who were injured and withdrew in Book 11, and this highlights the contrasting fortunes of the two sides. Beside the major Trojan heroes are a number of less prominent fighters: **Kebriones** is a brother of Hektor who took over as his charioteer (8. 318–19); **Alkathoös** is the brother-in-law of Aineias, having married his sister Hippodameia (13. 428–33); **Agenor** is the son of Antenor, who fights Achilleus and is rescued by Apollo (21. 545–98); **Helenos**, 'best by far of the augurs' (6. 75), and **Deïphobos** are the most prominent sons of Priam, after Hektor and Paris; **Archelochos** and **Akamas** were named with Aineias as leaders of the Dardanians (2. 819–23); **Asteropaios**, leader of the Paionians, fights Achilleus and is killed by him (21. 154–83).

110–17   **Asios, Hyrtakos' son**, joint leader of the third battalion, was marked out from the others in the mini-catalogue by a brief anecdote (96–7), and now he is the only one of the Trojans not to follow Poulydamas' advice to dismount. The role of Asios is intended to illustrate the reliability of any advice that Poulydamas gives, and the usually fatal result of not following it; and this is shown by the poet's direct comment on him, **poor fool**. Asios' misplaced self-confidence and ignoring of Poulydamas is matched by Hektor, and they both share the same fate. Asios dies at the hands of **Idomeneus, proud son of Deukalion** at 13. 384–93; Idomeneus is leader of the Kretan contingent and a grandson of the legendary ruler of Krete, Minos.

128–36   The **high-hearted sons of the spear-fighting Lapithai** are the first generation after the Lapithai who fought against the Centaurs (cf. 1. 259–74n). The Lapithai are one of the tribes of Thessaly. The simile develops, from describing their stature like

two oaks on a mountain crest, to describing their resilience as they await Asios' approach like trees whose **great roots reach far and are gripped in the ground.**

146–50   in the likeness of two wild boars. This second simile describing the Lapithai also shows a development, illustrating first the firmness of the Lapithai in face of the rabble which confronts them, and then the noise of the spears grating against their breastplates.

162–3   beat on both thighs with his hands. Throughout the poem this curious gesture heralds the death of the person who performs it or of somebody close to him. It is performed by Patroklos when he sees the plight of the Achaians and decides to ask Achilleus to be allowed to return to the battle (15. 397), and by Achilleus in turn when he sends Patroklos into battle, in effect to his death (16. 125); for detail, see Lowenstam 1981.

167–70   as wasps quick-bending in the middle. The simile shows the insects as defenders of their homes and their young ones against the attack of those who have come to destroy them; so the image illustrates the new role the Achaians are forced to adopt in this book, of people besieged inside the city formed by their defensive wall.

200–9   carrying in its talons a gigantic snake. The snake appeared in a portent, devouring the young of a sparrow (2. 303–20n); it also featured as a motif on Agamemnon's breastplate and his shield strap (11. 16–44n). It serves as a symbol of the Achaians' aggression who here, although apparently overcome by the Trojans, still have enough strength to inflict a severe wound.

211–29   somehow in assembly you move ever against me. Poulydamas hints at a continuing struggle between Hektor and himself, between his authority as the Trojans' best counsellor and Hektor's authority as army commander. **could not finish carrying it back to give to his children** is Poulydamas' own addition to the description of the portent, and it allows him to draw his own interpretation of it, that the Achaians will cut down many of the Trojans by the ships.

235–40   you who are telling me to forget the counsels of thunderous Zeus. Zeus sent Iris (11. 186–94) to tell Hektor to avoid Agamemnon during his *aristeia*, but he also guaranteed him the power 'to kill men, till he makes his way to the strong-backed vessels, until the sun goes down and the blessed darkness comes over'. Hektor remembers the guarantee he was given, but forgets the limitation put on his victory, and he compounds his error by arrogantly dismissing Poulydamas' interpretation of the portent, **I care nothing for these, I think nothing of them**. This helps to establish the theme of Hektor's rash self-confidence.

256   in the confidence of the portents shown. In fact Hektor did not offer an interpretation of the portent, but the Trojans accept Hektor's rejection of Poulydamas' interpretation as one itself, and it is their confidence in this, and the sudden duststorm, they now display.

263   fencing the battlements with the hides of oxen. That is, the Achaians formed a fence along the top of their wall with their shields and hurled their weapons from behind it.

269–70   The two Aiantes describe the horizontal divisions of society, and this looks forward to Sarpedon's account later in this book of the heroic ethos (310–28). The top stratum comprises the heroes, the men who do most of the killing and about whom Sarpedon speaks; those of middle estate are the men who are killed by the heroes and so qualify to be named and often to have a brief story told about them before they die; those of low account are the nameless masses who form the backcloth to the exploits of the heroes.

278–86   as storms of snow descend to the ground incessant. This simile develops the earlier one describing the Lapithai defending the Achaian wall with stones which 'dropped to the ground like snowflakes' (156–7). In both cases the Achaians are trying to repel a Trojan attack on their wall, but the detail of this second simile is much richer and this indicates that this second attack is the more serious. In the first simile the snow was blown by the winds' blast into drifts, but here Zeus has stilled the wind and so the snow covers everything evenly: the whole land is buried beneath the snowfall and this illustrates the powerlessness of man in face of nature; even the sea's surf is stilled by the fall, and the silence everywhere contrasts with the violent din of battle in the narrative.

299–307   like some hill-kept lion. This simile looks back to the introduction of Sarpedon as 'like a lion among horn-curved cattle' (293), but the richer detail here, of the hunger of the lion, and then its proud heart and courage, in turn illustrates Sarpedon's hunger

for heroic glory and pride in his heroic prowess. So the simile is a
fine introduction to the hero who will now define the heroic ethos.

309–28   Sarpedon is already closely associated with **Glaukos, son of
Hippolochos** (cf. 2. 876–7), and his speech to him here should be
heard against the background of Glaukos' own exchange with the
Achaian Diomedes (6. 119–236). The speech of Sarpedon is a
companion piece to that of his friend, and serves to define those
heroic values about which Achilleus spoke in Book 9. The Speech
of Sarpedon has three parts: he first defines the meaning of heroic
status in terms of the privileges the hero receives (310–14); he
then recounts the duties of the hero in return for these privileges
(315–21); and finally he defines the heroic ethos (322–8).

310–21   **the choice meats and the filled wine cups in Lykia.** Sarpedon
is speaking of the reciprocal relationship between chieftain and
people: 'the granting of material goods, land, service, and privilege
by the group to the leaders, as something "due" them, by virtue of
their rank' (Donlan 1981.160). The emphasis Sarpedon places on
the rewards due to the hero during the feast is important, because
it looks forward to Achilleus' steadfast refusal to join the feast with
the other heroes (cf. 19. 209–14). In return for these rewards it is
the duty of the chieftain to fight in the forefront and lead by
example, and to do the lion's share of the fighting.

322–8   **Man, supposing you and I, escaping this battle.** It is normal
to read Sarpedon's speech in terms of *noblesse oblige*, that their
very status imposes on Glaukos and Sarpedon the duty to fight on
behalf of their people. The gifts and privileges they are awarded
represent their noble status and impose on them their obligation;
if death could be avoided, Sarpedon says, they would not fight, but
since they are denied immortality, they seek the nearest thing to it,
undying renown won in death (*kleos*). *Kleos* is preserved and
celebrated in heroic song, and so the *Iliad* is a remembrance of the
heroes' immortal renown: Achilleus was himself singing 'of men's
fame' (*klea andron*, 9. 189) when the ambassadors came to appeal
to him. The hero seeks to transform his mortal *time* into immortal
kleos, a transformation achieved in death, and so death is a necessary
part of the elevation of the hero: 'the logic of heroism demands
the rejection of human life: the hero dies in order to live forever in
glory; he loses his life in order to save it' (Rubino 1979.13).

331–4   **Menestheus,** the leader of the Athenians, was accused, with

Odysseus, by Agamemnon of hanging back from the battle though willingly accepting all the privileges of heroic status (4. 338–48), that is, of being the very antithesis of the heroic picture Sarpedon has just painted. His behaviour now confirms Agamemnon's judgment and contrasts with that of Sarpedon.

335–6   saw the two Aiantes, insatiate of battle, standing on the wall introduces a long description of battle which will end in Hektor breaking through the gates in the Achaian wall (453–62). The object of this passage is to divert the mighty Aias to that part of the wall defended by Menestheus, for in the absence of Aias, Hektor is then able to make his advance.

350   Although he is an archer, **Teukros** is a warrior of considerable standing, mainly because he is Aias' half-brother and is frequently associated with him (cf. 8. 266–72).

383   of men such as men are now. Homer often draws this distinction between heroes and ordinary men of his own day: like Aias here, Hektor will attack the Achaian gates with a stone that no two men could lift, 'of men such as men are now' (445–9).

387–8   Teukros with an arrow struck the strong son of Hippolochos, Glaukos. Homer is planning his narrative ahead: when Sarpedon is killed by Patroklos, he will call with his dying breath on Glaukos to defend him, and it is the wound he sustains here which will prevent Glaukos doing so (16. 508–26).

402–3   Zeus brushed the death spirits from his son. Zeus easily saves his son Sarpedon on this occasion, but when he contemplates doing so again he will be dissuaded by Hera, and Sarpedon will be doomed (16. 433–8).

421–3   as two men with measuring ropes in their hands. The comparison is between the distance separating the two sides and the lengths of rope held by the two quarrelling men: that is, they are within arm's length of each other across the battlements.

433–5   as the scales which a careful widow holds. As in the previous simile, Homer recalls the world of peace while describing the most frenzied fighting, and contrasts the productive work of the widow, who ekes out a living, with the destructive force of war. The widow and her orphaned children lend pathos, but they also recall a theme particularly associated with Hektor's wife Andromache (cf. 6. 432; 22. 484–507), at the very moment he himself is making the decisive breakthrough.

450   Hektor's feat of heroic strength in lifting the stone matches Aias' (383n), except that **the son of devious-devising Kronos made it light for him,** and this marks him as of lesser heroic status than the Achaian champion.

451–2   **As when a shepherd easily carries the fleece of a wether.** Again a simile from peaceful nature illustrates an intense moment of battle; the fleece the shepherd is carrying recalls the wool which the widow weighs (433–5n).

463–4   **with dark face like sudden night.** When Apollo came down from Olympos to bring his plague of arrows on the Achaians, he too came like night; for the possible meaning, cf. 1. 47n. Here the contrast is drawn with **the ghastly glitter of bronze that girded his skin.**

465–6   **No one could have stood up against him, and stopped him, except the gods.** This is the climax of Hektor's attack, and he seems almost the equal of a god, just as he had earlier wished (8. 538–41); and his appearance, **eyes flashed like fire,** is like the fire which he has just called for to hurl against the ships (441). In fact, however, **except the gods** is anticipating the opposition of Poseidon to him and the Trojans in the following book.

ILIAD 13

In this book Homer introduces a major reversal of his narrative: having described the Trojans' successful attack on the Achaian wall at the end of Book 12, with the leading Achaians removed from battle and their ships at the mercy of the Trojans, he now declares that Zeus relaxes his control over the battle's progress, with the result that the Achaians are able to reassert themselves for the next two books. The Trojan successes in Books 11 and 12 are the fulfilment of Zeus' promise to Thetis in Book 1 to grant the Trojans such a victory that the Achaians would realize their need for Achilleus and would honour him as the best of the Achaians. In his reply to the embassy in Book 9, Achilleus said that he would not think of joining the battle again until Hektor brought fire to his own ships (9. 650–3), and at the end of Book 12 Hektor called on the Trojans to 'wreck the ramparts of the Argives, and let loose the inhuman fire on their vessels' (12. 440–1). It is a poet supremely confident in his own narrative skills who can at this point choose to deny his audience's expectations and defer for another two thousand lines the moment when Hektor will take hold of the Achaian ships.

The events in this book are part of a much larger whole, for besides continuing the battle of Books 11 and 12 it also forms a unit with Books 14 and 15, in which Poseidon inspires a rally of the Achaians when Zeus is distracted by the seductive charms of his wife Hera. The aristeia of Idomeneus in this book, and the Deception of Zeus (Dios apate) in Book 14, are devices to delay the response of Achilleus to the Achaians' plight; at the same time they provide filling action while Patroklos returns from Nestor's shelter to that of Achilleus; and they provide a background of Trojan defeat against which to present their Zeus-inspired success in Book 15, and so make the impact of Patroklos' appeal to Achilleus in Book 16 even more dramatic.

3–9 Zeus' gaze wanders away from the plain of Troy: the **Thracians** are to the west, on the opposite side of the Hellespont from Troy, and the **Mysians** are to the north; the name of the **Hippomolgoi** means 'horse-milkers', and they and the **Abioi** (meaning 'the non-violent ones') are also northern tribes. Zeus does not believe that any of the gods **would come down to stand by either Danaans or Trojans,** because he expressly forbade them to do so (8. 7–12).

10 **the powerful shaker of the earth** is Poseidon, god of earthquakes, and a supporter of the Achaians throughout. He sits on the summit of the mountainous island of Samothrake, which at over 5,000 ft affords a view over the intervening island of Imbros to the plain of Troy itself some 80 km. away. There is a neat poetic balance between the two divine brothers and their actions: from his position on Ida Zeus allows his gaze to wander ever further from Troy to the northern territories, while opposite on the summit of Samothrake Poseidon pays ever closer attention to Troy and to the sufferings there of the Achaians.

17–38 **he came down from the craggy mountain.** Poseidon's descent from the mountain matches the descent of Apollo from Olympos (1. 44–7): just as the first half of the poem began with a god's descent from a mountain top, so now Homer repeats the image at the beginning of the second half. Four giant steps take the god from Samothrake to Aigai, and from there his chariot carries him in stately progress to his cave between Tenedos and Imbros. Why not simply four giant strides directly to Troy? Because his journey marks an important, though temporary, turning point in the story, and so the drama of it is prolonged.

39 **The Trojans, gathered into a pack, like flame, like a stormcloud** describes the position at the end of Book 12, with the Trojans streaming through the Achaian wall. The image of the flame describes the speed of their advance, the stormcloud their clamour (cf. 3. 2–9n).

53–4 **that berserk flamelike** repeats the flame image; berserk (Greek *lussodes*) suggests that battle fever has so overtaken Hektor that he has become like a rabid dog: this image is often associated with Hektor (Redfield 1975.201), and he is even pictured as foaming at the mouth in his battle madness (15. 607). Hektor's reported claim that **he must be son of Zeus** is not to be taken literally, for he is the son of the mortal Priam and never claims to be anything else: Poseidon exaggerates to spur the Aiantes on.

59 **Poseidon circles the earth** as god of the sea and **shakes it** as god of earthquakes.

62–72 **like a hawk with quick wings** describes the speed of Poseidon's departure, and does not imply that he has changed into a bird. So when Aias says that he recognizes him as a god by **the form of his feet, the legs' form from behind him,** this is just an ornate expression to say that he knows a god when he sees one, not that Poseidon has taken the shape of a hawk; Aias is registering the inspirational effect of the god's visit.

84 **were cooling the heat of the inward heart** means 'were reviving their spirits'. The idea is that the body revives as it cools down, and so too does the heart, the seat of feeling and emotions.

95–124 **save our ships from destruction** is a recurring theme of Poseidon's speech (cf. 101, 107, 110, 123), as is the idea that the Achaians are hanging back from the battle (97, 108–9, 114, 118, 121). Poseidon is speaking in the guise of Kalchas, the Achaian seer (cf. 45). Kalchas was the principal witness to the quarrel of Achilleus and Agamemnon, and is better qualified than anybody to pass judgment on it, on its causes and its consequences: so it is no mere incidental detail that Poseidon takes his form. He places the blame for the Achaians' present position unequivocally on **the weakness of our leader,** Agamemnon: Leaf (1902.11) suggests 'incompetent' as a translation of *kakoteti*, and Janko (1992.57) points out that the word can also mean cowardice. **our people who have made their quarrel with him**: at no point have the Achaians displayed this anger with Agamemnon, but Poseidon is crediting them with emotions which support his argument. **sooner let us heal it** refers to 'the hanging back of our people', and is urging the Achaians to swallow their resentment.

137–43 **like a great rolling stone from a rock face.** The image of the rolling stone, gathering momentum as it careers downwards, out of control and crushing everything in its path, fits well with the general portrait of Hektor as an uncontrollable and reckless force. In the present context his attack appears irresistible, but just like the stone when it reaches level ground, he too is finally halted.

152 **they are building themselves into a bastion against me.** In fact the Achaians are now concentrating on attack (cf. 135), but Hektor thinks of them as a bastion, *purgedon*, a word which recalls the fortification they have built around their ships. Hektor sees the close formation of the Achaians as continuing their defensive strategy of recent times, but this is a misjudgment and the battle now turns against him and his Trojans in the form of the *aristeia* of Idomeneus. **I am driven by the greatest of gods**: Hektor was told of Zeus' support for him by Iris (11. 200–9), but again he is deluded, because Zeus is now looking elsewhere (3–4).

156–68   The recovery of the Achaians begins with an *aristeia*, of Idomeneus, and it is introduced by the seemingly pointless encounter of his companion **Meriones** and the Trojan **Deïphobos**. Meriones hurls his spear but without success as the shaft snaps on Deïphobos' shield, and the engagement is immediately broken off as Meriones returns to the Achaian camp to collect another spear; the result is a sense of anticlimax. The explanation of this curious little episode is very soon evident when Idomeneus, on his way into battle, encounters Meriones on his way out of it to collect his fresh spear (240–7): it is in order to introduce this encounter, and their conversation, that Homer has Meriones clash with Deiphobos here.

178–80   he dropped like an ash tree. The tree's prominent position on the mountain's crest enhances Imbrios' warrior status, and its **delicate leafage** scattered on the earth recalls the leaves on the ground to which Glaukos compared the generations of mortals (cf. 6. 146n).

185–205   There is a short passage of battle before Idomeneus' *aristeia*, at the end of which advantage is seen to lie with the Achaians, as first Hektor is driven back from the bodies by Aias, and then the corpses of both Achaian and Trojan are dragged from the field by the Achaians; finally Oïlean Aias hacks off Imbrios' head and hurls it at the feet of Hektor.

206–20   Poseidon is angry about **his grandson's slaying**, that is, Amphimachos (185), and so rouses Idomeneus to battle. For **Idomeneus**, see 2. 645–52n. On this occasion Poseidon adopts the guise of **Thoas** 'a man stubborn in battle' (228), an important leader who brought forty ships on the expedition to Troy (2. 638–44).

241   drew his splendid armour over his body. Although Homer has explained why Idomeneus is absent from the fighting—he has been attending to a wounded colleague (211)—he makes no attempt to explain the more surprising fact that he is not even armed for battle. The context provides the explanation: he is unarmed because he must go to his shelter and there meet Meriones, just as Meriones hurled and lost his one spear because he too must go to his shelter (cf. 156–68n).

249–94 The Conversation of Idomeneus and Meriones. This is a long passage of great charm and humour, and with well-observed characterization. Neither of these friends is where a hero might be expected to be found, at the front line, and both appear acutely conscious of the fact: 'Why, Meriones, what are you doing here— are you wounded? *I'm* on my way to the front'—'I have come for a fresh spear to replace the one I lost fighting at the front'—'Take one of mine: I have lots I have taken in battle, and lots of other armour too, because my way is to fight hand to hand'—'So have I; still, my tent is further away than yours. Don't think I'm not keen for battle'—'Of course not, there's no need to tell *me* about your courage.' Each tries to cover his embarrassment by defending his position, and to assure himself of the respect of the other.

275–94 Idomeneus' almost uncontrolled babbling at this point is sure indication of his intense embarrassment, and is a rare moment of true humour. His claim that **a hidden position** [is where a] **man's courage is best decided** recalls one of the insults Achilleus hurled at Agamemnon during the quarrel, that he did not have the courage to 'go into ambuscade with the best of the Achaians' (1. 227); it is a claim that will be borne out by the Achaians' greatest ambush, the Trojan Horse.

298–303 The comparison of a hero to the war god **Ares** is common throughout the poem (e.g. 328), so his son, personified **Terror** (Phobos), is a suitable companion. The **Ephyroi** and the **Phlegyes** live in Thessaly.

307 **Deukalides**, the son of Deukalion, is Idomeneus: this Deukalion is the son of Minos, the legendary ruler of Krete, and is not to be confused with Deukalion, the son of Prometheus, whose deeds made him the Greek equivalent of Noah.

334 **as when under the screaming winds the whirlstorms bluster.** The simile describes the speed with which the two armies clash and the mêlée which results, but it becomes almost a part of the battle itself, in the dust of the plain which the battle stirs up.

347–55 **Zeus willed the victory for the Trojans and Hektor** contradicts the picture of Zeus' inattention at the beginning of this book, but in fact introduces a restatement of his promise to Thetis. **Zeus was the elder born**: both Poseidon and Zeus, along with Hestia, Demeter, Hera and Hades were born to Kronos and his sister Rhea. Kronos swallowed all of his children except Zeus, whom Rhea saved by substituting a stone for him, but the children Kronos swallowed remained as infants within him, while Zeus grew to maturity. Kronos was forced to vomit up his brothers and sisters, and so Zeus became the eldest, even though he had been the last born.

358–9 a crossing cable of strong discord. The metaphor is of an encircling cable whose two ends are pulled tight to constrict all caught within it, and so it illustrates the inescapability of the battle.

361–82 Idomeneus, greying though he was is an important detail of Idomeneus' description, for his *aristeia*, which now begins, will not last long and it will be physical tiredness that ends it. **Othryoneus** had offered to drive the Achaians from Troy in return for the hand in marriage of Kassandra, daughter of Priam: it is presumptuous of so inconspicuous a warrior to hope to marry into the royal family of Troy, and his description **he came onward with high stride** indicates his self-confidence, but in his story there is also the pathos of youthful love and ambition destroyed. **Kassandra** has a very limited role in the poem, and there is no mention of the later tradition that Apollo granted her the gift of prophecy, but then cursed her with the fate of never being believed. Idomeneus' sarcastic boast, **we would give you the loveliest of Atreides' daughters,** echoes the offer Agamemnon made to Achilleus in his attempt to persuade him to return to battle (9. 142–7): only a hero of Achilleus' stature may presume to marry a king's daughter.

384 Asios is the most significant of Idomeneus' victims; he was named as one of the Trojan commanders in the Trojan catalogue (2. 837–9), and his death was forecast (12. 116–17) when he alone ignored Poulydamas' advice to dismount from his chariot and attack the Achaian wall on foot. The death of Asios is intended to illustrate an important aspect of the death of Hektor, in that both die as a consequence of ignoring advice given by Poulydamas (cf. 12. 110–17n).

389 He fell, as when an oak goes down or a white poplar recalls the simile of the felled ash tree (178–80n) describing the death of

Imbrios at the hands of Teukros, and also the simile of the fallen poplar which characterized the death of Simoeisios (4. 473–89n). In the Simoeisios simile the poplar is bent 'into a wheel for a fine-wrought chariot', and here the tree is intended to make a ship's timber: in each case the tree has been felled to provide material for man's crafts, and this constructive purpose within the simile contrasts with the destruction of human life in the narrative.

402 Deïphobos in sorrow for Asios now came close. Deïphobos' fight with Meriones was ended when the latter's spear broke on his shield (159–62), and it will be rejoined at 528; in the meantime Homer brings him back into the battle temporarily.

427–44 Alkathoös is married to Hippodameia, daughter of Anchises, and so is a brother-in-law of Aineias: for a brief moment he is brought from obscurity by the poet and his death is given significance and pathos by the portrait of his wife now widowed by the action of Idomeneus. The intervention of Poseidon, who strikes Alkathoös so that he stands motionless **like a statue or a tree**, matches that of Apollo on behalf of Hektor (16. 788–805), and of Athene on behalf of Achilleus (22. 214–47).

450–3 Cf. 307n. **Minos,** the king of Knossos in Krete, was the son of Europa, daughter of Phoinix king of Tyre, and of Zeus, who took the form of a bull and swam with her on his back from Tyre to Krete (cf. 14. 321–2).

460 he was forever angry with brilliant Priam. There has been no previous mention of this anger felt by Aineias towards the Trojan king, though the passage suggests that it is long-standing and that it reflects a rivalry between two branches of the ruling dynasty: this is supported by Achilleus' words to Aineias when they meet on the battlefield, when he mocks him that Priam will not reward him with the Trojan leadership even after he has dared to face Achilleus, because he has sons of his own to receive that honour (20. 180–3). The scene recalls Meleagros who withdrew from battle through anger with his mother (9. 553–65), and above all the theme of the *Iliad* itself, the wrath of Achilleus, who has refused to fight through anger with Agamemnon. So it may be that the very mention of the fact that Aineias is not engaged at the front is enough to suggest the traditional theme of the hero who hangs back through anger.

471–5 he stood his ground like a mountain wild boar. The simile signals the end of Idomeneus' *aristeia*, because the boar, for all the

confidence of his strength, adopts a defensive stance, and so too
Idomeneus now summons the protection of his companions.

484–515   the flower of youth is his. Homer introduced the idea of
Idomeneus' advancing years at the beginning of his *aristeia* (361–
82n); when he first encountered Aineias he behaved 'as if he were
a stripling' (470), now he stresses that he is older than his opponent,
and finally, having killed Oinomaos, he has neither the strength to
strip the body nor the speed to make a hasty withdrawal. Homer
presents the picture of the superior warrior, whom not even Aineias
can defeat, beaten by age. So the *aristeia* ends on a low note, but it
has served its purpose in putting a check on the Trojan onslaught.
as when the sheep follow the lead-ram: the focus of the simile
shifts, as at first Aineias is like the ram leading the sheep to water,
but then he is like the shepherd who is gladdened by the sight.

519–672   There follows a long passage of apparently formless and
inconclusive battle: three deaths on the Achaian side (Askalaphos
519, Aphareus 541, Deïpyros 576) are evenly matched by three on
the Trojan side (Thoön 546, Adamas 568, Peisandros 615), but the
withdrawal of the wounded Deïphobos (529) and Helenos (593)
indicates that the advantage lies slightly with the Achaians. Two
more deaths, Harpalion (654) and Euchenor (671), further illustrate
the evenness of the battle, but the Trojan Harpalion is killed by
Meriones while retreating, and the ignominy of his death is
heightened by his comparison to a worm (654).

525   the immortal gods were sitting still, in restraint from the battle
is a reminder that present events are merely an interruption in Zeus'
strategy to give victory to the Trojans.

528–39   The *aristeia* of Idomeneus was introduced by his
conversation with his companion Meriones (249–94). To bring
about that conversation, the combat between Meriones and the
Trojan Deïphobos was broken off while Meriones returned to the
Achaian camp to fetch a spear: the end of the *aristeia* is marked
now by the renewal of that combat, in which Meriones wounds
the Trojan with the spear he has fetched.

588–92   As along a great threshing floor. Once more a simile from
the peaceful world illustrates by contrast the world of battle. The
repetition of the rebounding arrow from 587 effectively echoes
the bouncing beans in the simile.

617   both eyes dropped, bloody, and lay in the dust at his feet before

him is, if anything, even more bizarre than the spear shaken by the beating heart (442–4), yet not so bizarre that the poet can't repeat it (cf. 16. 741).

625 the guest's god is Zeus. By his abduction of Helen when he was a guest in Menelaos' home, Paris broke the bonds of the host–guest relationship which were protected by Zeus *xeinios*. Menelaos' words recall the prayer he addressed to Zeus during his duel with Paris (3. 351–4).

636–9 Since there is satiety in all things. Just as many of the poem's similes point up the horror of the war by contrasting the world of peace or of nature, so here Menelaos illustrates the unnaturalness of the Trojans' insatiable appetite for war by contrasting the natural desires of men: sleep, lovemaking, singing and dance. His bitterness emphasizes the reader's knowledge that Zeus is prepared to put all the Achaians at risk in order to give honour to Achilleus.

653–9 sitting among the arms of his beloved companions adds pathos to Harpalion's death, as does the picture of his weeping father Pylaimenes walking beside the chariot which bears his son's body. Homer overlooks the fact that Pylaimenes was killed by Menelaos (5. 576–9), but such trivial contradictions are to be expected in orally improvised verse.

661 he was his guest friend among many Paphlagonians. It is a fine irony that Paris should be roused to action by the death of a guest-friend, as it was his breaking of the bonds of guest-friendship that Menelaos condemned a moment ago (625n).

663–72 Euchenor joined the Achaian expedition to Troy partly to avoid paying the penalty for not joining: similarly Agamemnon was given a mare by Echepolos to avoid joining the expedition (23. 296–9). But Euchenor was also given a choice between a painful death at home or death in battle at Troy, a choice similar to the one Achilleus was offered by his mother (9. 410–16). Euchenor's decision was the same as Achilleus', to die at Troy, though for very different reasons; but his death points up the closeness of the parallel with Achilleus, for he too dies at the hands of Paris, struck in the heel by his arrow.

673–8 The scene now shifts to the centre of the battle where Hektor was seen earlier breaking through the gate (12. 445–71). The description of the fight as **in the likeness of blazing fire**, and later of Hektor as 'flame-like' (688), pictures the fire that will mark the climax of the Trojans' assault on the Achaian ships. 'With his own strength' gives better sense than Lattimore's **and his own strength**.

681–4   **Protesilaos** was the first Achaian casualty of the war, killed as he leapt ashore first of all the Achaians; so his ship was beached furthest up the shore. Homer here anticipates the climax of the Trojan attack, for Protesilaos' ship will be the first to be fired by Hektor (15. 704–8). Homer gives no indication of why **the wall they had built lay lowest** at this point: the reason is simply that this is where the battle is about to take place.

685   There follows a short catalogue of the Achaians fighting in the centre of the battle. For the **Boiotians**, see 2. 494–510n. The **Ionians with their trailing tunics** is the only reference to Ionians in the poem; they are in fact the same as the **Athenian men**. The **Lokrians** appear in the main Achaian Catalogue at 2. 527–35; the **Phthians** are from Achilleus' homeland (2. 683–5); the **Epeians** appear at 2. 615–24.

701–18   The two Aiantes, though unrelated, often act in close association: the greater of the two, **Telamonian Aias**, leads the contingent from Salamis (2. 557), and his namesake, **Aias the son of Oïleus**, is commander of the Lokrians (2. 527). There is a marked difference between their respective contingents: the followers of Oïlean Aias are light-armed soldiers, who fight with arrows and slings, those of Telamonian Aias are front-line fighters who appear more like the contemporary heavy-armed hoplites; despite this difference, the two heroes form an unbreakable partnership described in the simile of the two yoked oxen, in which **only the width of the polished yoke keeps a space between them** illustrates the single purpose with which they fight. For the **great shield** of Telamonian Aias, see 7. 219–23n.

724–47   Homer has prepared for the introduction of **Poulydamas** here through the death of Asios (cf. 384n), which illustrated his wisdom and the dangers of ignoring his advice. Poulydamas' wisdom contrasts with the fighting strength of Hektor, and in his speech here he draws that contrast. Poulydamas spoke out against fighting by the Achaian ships but his advice was angrily rejected by Hektor (12. 216–50), and he now points out the consequences of Hektor's headstrong actions. The additional contrast, between the warrior and **one to be a dancer, to another the lyre and the singing**, recalls the contrast Hektor drew between himself as warrior and Paris as lyre-player (3. 54). **beside their ships lurks a man insatiate of fighting** is important in calling attention to Achilleus, even when he takes no part in the narrative.

754   **like a snowy mountain** illustrates the stature of the Trojan hero, because the mountain is conspicuous above all around it.

769   **Evil Paris, beautiful, woman-crazy, cajoling.** Hektor hurled this same insult at Paris when he tried to avoid a duel with Menelaos (3. 39). He contrasts Paris' accomplishments as a seducer of women with the actions of the true hero, though the words are much less appropriate to the present context, as Paris has just been seen urging his companions into battle.

795–9   **as out of the racking winds the stormblast.** There is an intensification of imagery in this simile: the speed of the Trojan advance is like the rush of the wind, then the simile highlights the noise of their advance, and finally the waves of Trojans attacking the beached Achaian ships are as relentless as the sea's waves sweeping towards the beach.

813–14   **your heart is hopeful utterly to break up our ships.** The word translated **break up**, *exalapaxein*, is only used elsewhere in the poem of sacking a city (Taplin 1992.95). Aias sees the Achaian ships as their own city behind their own defensive wall, in contrast to the defensive wall of Troy (816): it is appropriate that it should be the great defensive warrior Aias who speaks thus.

825   **If I could only be called son to Zeus of the aegis.** Hektor's declaration recalls the euphoria of his earlier triumph, and he employs the same curious idiom as on that earlier occasion (cf. 8. 538–41n). It is the certainty that the day will bring evil to the Achaians that Hektor declares, by contrasting it with the impossibility that he might be called the son of Zeus and Hera and honoured on a par with Apollo and Athene. Earlier in this book, Poseidon said that Hektor laid claim to being a son of Zeus (cf. 53–4n).

ILIAD 14

In the previous book the Trojan advance was halted, and the final scene pictured a Trojan surge led by Hektor but withstood by the Achaians (13. 836). The support of Poseidon was important in achieving this, and the god continues to promote the Achaian cause in this book also. In the previous book he was able to intervene because Zeus had turned his gaze away from the battlefield (13. 3), and in this book Zeus is removed completely from the action, seduced and lulled into a deep sleep by his wife Hera. Since antiquity the title Deception of Zeus (Dios apate) has been assigned to this book, and by common consent it contains one of the most delightful episodes in the entire poem. Like so many of the scenes amongst the gods, this scene is characterized by light-heartedness, and is in contrast to the serious business of the battlefield and human affairs; Hera's attempt to defy Zeus and to alter the course of events results in a scene of humour and mild eroticism.

3 **Machaon,** the son of Asklepios, was wounded by Paris' arrow (11. 505–7). He was brought by Nestor to his tent, and Achilleus sent Patroklos to enquire after him (11. 610–16): his wounding was the first in the series of events which in time will result in Patroklos' death (cf. 11. 597–600n).

6–7 **until Hekamede the lovely-haired makes ready a hot bath for you.** The fact that Machaon is still waiting for treatment to his wound does not indicate that Nestor has been falling down on his duty, but is an example of the convention that in Homer simultaneous actions are always told successively (Introduction 7(d)): when the scene shifted from Nestor's shelter at the end of Book 11, the roles of Nestor and Machaon were suspended while the poet narrated the simultaneous action of Poseidon's intervention in Book 13. Homer now turns his attention back to Nestor's shelter, and their situation is just as it was left at the end of Book 11: so they are still drinking wine and Machaon has still not had the **filth of the bloodstains** washed away.

11 Thrasymedes carried the shield of his father points up the fact that his father, Nestor, is not himself fighting in the battle; as a result Nestor is more closely associated with Diomedes, Odysseus and Agamemnon, all of whom are out of action wounded, and who visit him in the next scene.

16–19 As when the open sea is deeply stirred to the ground-swell. The simile describes Nestor's indecision and contrasts with the similar one at the end of Book 13, when the determination of the advancing Trojans was like the 'numerous boiling waves' driven by Zeus' stormblast (cf. 13. 795–9n).

27–40 Now there came toward Nestor the kings under God's hand. Diomedes, Odysseus and Agamemnon are **each leaning on his spear**, because they were wounded at 11. 252, 376 and 437 respectively. Their wounding represented the Achaians' lowest point, and Homer recalls it in order to highlight the temporary improvement in their fortunes during this book. In the previous book the Achaians were rescued from disaster by Poseidon's intervention, and in this book there will be a second divine intervention, by Hera, which will also inspire an Achaian rally. The two interventions, and the two rallies, are simultaneous but are narrated in sequence: so here the Achaians are once again portrayed as gripped by despair, as though the events of Book 13 had not taken place.

44–7 I am afraid huge Hektor may accomplish that word against me. Agamemnon's words recall the hope Hektor spoke of to the Trojans, that he might be allowed to fire the Achaian ships (8. 180–3): that is, the poet credits Agamemnon with knowledge which, strictly, he does not have.

49–51 the other strong-greaved Achaians are storing anger against me. The anger may be the Achaians' pent-up frustration after ten years of fruitless warfare, but Agamemnon's addition of **as Achilleus did** suggests that he fears their feelings are now closer to those of Thersites (2. 225–42), that he has dishonoured Achilleus, that this is the root of their troubles, and that they would be better off under the leadership of Achilleus. His words of self-doubt, or even self-pity, are spoken even before he has received a report from Nestor, and so are a sure indication of his state of mind.

54   There is irony in Nestor's assertion **nor in any other way could even Zeus who thunders on high accomplish it,** since it is precisely Zeus' promise to Thetis which has caused their problem.

74–81   **let us take all those ships.** Agamemnon's reaction to Nestor's report, his strategy of launching and anchoring their ships with a view to flight, and the sentiment that the **man does better who runs from disaster,** is entirely in character. He proposed that the Achaians flee at 2. 139–41, but the quick wits of Odysseus halted them, and again at 9. 26–8, when Diomedes opposed the proposal. In fact the strategy Agamemnon proposes here, to give up the expedition and launch the ships under the cover of night, is just the feigned strategy which will succeed in capturing Troy, by deceiving the Trojans into thinking that the Achaians have sailed for home leaving behind the Trojan Horse as an offering.

83–95   **I wish you directed some other unworthy army.** The result of Agamemnon's speech is precisely that anger, or contempt, which he has just said he fears the Achaians feel towards him (49–51), and it is voiced by Odysseus. When Odysseus opposed Agamemnon's earlier proposal that they flee (cf. 74–81n), he declared:

> Lordship for many is no good thing. Let there be one ruler,
> one king, to whom the son of devious-devising Kronos
> gives the sceptre and right of judgment, to watch over his people
>   (2. 204–6)

Those words supported Agamemnon's position, but his speech now stands in marked contrast, and he declares **now I utterly despise your heart,** for Agamemnon by his speech has shown himself unworthy of his position as **sceptred king.**

99   The metaphor in **headlong destruction swing our way** is of weighing the fates of the two sides in the balance.

109–27   **Diomedes** was insulted during the *Epipolesis* (4. 365–400) by Agamemnon, who accused him of being unworthy of his ancestors; and then, when Diomedes opposed Agamemnon's proposal to flee home, Nestor patronized his youth (9. 31–62). So there is considerable irony in Diomedes' voice when he now says **by birth I am the youngest among you,** and then goes on to give a lengthy account of his ancestry, concluding that **you could not,**

saying that I was base and unwarlike by birth, dishonour any word
that I speak. The scene is designed to recall that of Agamemnon
and Diomedes in Book 4, and so to provide further commentary
on the quality of Agamemnon's leadership. Diomedes' father,
Tydeus, fought as one of the Seven against Thebes (4. 376–8) and
died on the expedition.

133   they listened well to him, and obeyed him. This long scene,
between Agamemnon, Nestor, Odysseus and Diomedes, ends as
they move off to battle. It has served well to characterize much of
the Achaian leadership, by drawing the contrast in their reactions
to the crisis: panic on Agamemnon's part, firm judgment on the
part of his subordinates.

136–46   in the likeness of an old man. This is Poseidon's third
disguise, having already appeared as Kalchas (13.45) and Thoas
(13.216). His message is the opposite of Odysseus' a moment ago.
He puts the blame unequivocally on Achilleus, and so says precisely
the words Agamemnon would wish to hear, and he encourages
him to ignore the blame Odysseus and the army heap on him. The
victory Poseidon promises Agamemnon, when the Trojans **take flight
for their city,** may refer to the short-term success in this book, or,
with heavy irony, to the return of Achilleus which will bring victory
to the Achaians, but which will also show Agamemnon's folly in
dishonouring the best of the Achaians.

153–351   Hera, she of the golden throne. Hera's seduction of her
husband Zeus continues Poseidon's rallying of the Achaians. Her
purpose is to remove Zeus' control of the war and so to achieve a
Trojan defeat, including the wounding of Hektor. Within the poem's
story, this serves as a preliminary to the great Trojan victory in
Book 15 which will bring Patroklos back into the battle to his death.
The Trojan defeat is brief and Zeus easily restores the situation in
the following book, and this strongly suggests that Homer has
included the Deception of Zeus (*Dios apate*) for its own sake.

166–85   Hera is cold-blooded in her careful preparations for the
seduction of her husband, and an atmosphere of deception is
established at the beginning by the **secret door-bar,** which provides
the absolute privacy in which she makes herself ready. The details
of her preparation seem to echo the theme of the arming warrior,
and the whole scene takes on the air of a military campaign (Golden
1989). Her **zone** is a belt or girdle. Hera's hatred of Zeus and her

deception of him are a betrayal of her own marriage and of marriage itself, of which she is patron goddess, as she cynically exploits her sexuality. The clothes and ornaments she puts on enhance not merely her beauty but also her feigned chastity; her final item of dress is her **sweet fresh veil** (*kredemnon*), which is a common symbol of female chastity in the poem.

188   Hera's deception is directed at no fewer than three gods: it starts here with **Aphrodite**, then Sleep (231), and finally Zeus himself (292).

198   Hera asks for **loveliness and desirability,** which she hardly needs when she has made herself so sexually attractive; what she really wants is the *zone*, the girdle which is the representation of sexual attractiveness and which endows its wearer with all the qualities figured on it (214–17). Only with this girdle can success against Zeus be assured, and Griffin (1980a.66) remarks that 'the whole scene shows perfect mastery of the arts of indirectness and of a psychology far from transparent'.

201–4   **Okeanos, whence the gods have risen, and Tethys our mother.** The more usual version of the gods' origin is as children of Ouranos (Heaven) and Gaia (Earth). For **Zeus of the wide brows drove Kronos underneath the earth,** cf. 8. 479–83n.

205–10   **resolve their division of discord.** There is considerable irony in this fiction of their parents' marital problems being used by Hera to conceal her own deceptions.

213   **you, who lie in the arms of Zeus, since he is our greatest** is ironical, since to lie in the arms of the greatest of the gods is precisely the object of Hera's request. Clearly the moral authority of a pantheon is flawed, in which the queen of the gods, the protectress of marriage, will so easily lie to the goddess of sexual love, the better to seduce the king of the gods and so give free rein to her hatred of the mortal Trojans.

225–30   Hera does not take the direct route but travels along the coast, from the gods' home on **Olympos** in the region of **Pieria** in Thessaly, northwards via **Emathia** in Macedonia, through Thrace to **Athos** the easternmost of Chalkidike's three promontories, and from there across the sea to the island of **Lemnos**, half-way to Troy.

231   **Sleep, the brother of Death.** The two brothers appear later, to

transport the body of Sarpedon, killed by Patroklos, to his home in Lykia (16. 682–3).

233–4   if ever before now you listened to word of mine. A more usual way for Hera to put her request would be to remind Sleep of a past service rendered, and so of a favour owed (cf. 1. 40n). It is a large part of the humour of this scene that the theme is reversed, so that Hera recalls to Hypnos the occasion when he did indeed listen to her, and very nearly paid a severe penalty for doing so (249–61).

236–41   Put to sleep the shining eyes of Zeus. Hera is unable to conceal the fact that the object of her scheming is Zeus, but she is careful not to reveal her reason for asking for Sleep's help and instead concentrates on the reward she is offering. It soon emerges that the throne and footstool are merely an opening gambit to arouse his interest and she does not hesitate to improve her offer, in the form of one of the Graces for whom Sleep has long been pining (267–9).

245–6   Okeanos, the sea, is thought of as a river which completely surrounds the land; on the shield Hephaistos makes for Achilleus, this river is fashioned on the outer rim to surround all the other illustrations on the shield (18. 606–7).

249–61   Before now, it was a favour to you that taught me wisdom. Zeus expands this story (15. 18–33) when he reprimands Hera for her actions and recalls his severe punishment of her behaviour on this previous occasion. For the occasion when Herakles **had utterly sacked the city of the Trojans,** see 5. 640–2n.

271–4   Swear it to me on Styx' ineluctable water. When Zeus awakes after his seduction and discovers Hera's deception, she swears her innocence with equal facility by 'the dripping water of the Styx' (15. 37). According to Hesiod (*Theogony* 793–806), any god who breaks an oath sworn by Styx, the river of the Underworld, is condemned to lie for a year without breath or voice, and is then excluded from the company of the gods, from their banquets and their councils, for nine more years. The **undergods** are the Titans (cf. 279), whose rule Zeus overthrew and who were then consigned to Tartaros (8. 7–16n; 8. 479–83n).

281   For Lemnos, see 225–30n; **Imbros** is an island between Lemnos and Troy.

287   went up aloft a towering pine tree. An important feature of
Hera's deception in this scene is that, when urged by Zeus to make
love, she will feign modesty and fear that they may be observed by
one of the other gods (331–6), when all the time Sleep is above in
this pine tree watching them.

296   their dear parents knew nothing of it. The relationship of Zeus
and Hera is incestuous as they are brother and sister.

309–11   for your sake so you will not be angry with me. Hera feigns
a wifely subservience quite alien to her portrait throughout the
poem, and this coupled to her enhanced sexuality proves irresistible
to Zeus. The contrast between her words here and her attack on
Zeus during their quarrel (1. 540–3) shows the extent of her
deception and her disguising of her true feelings for him.

314–28   The seduction of Zeus is a scene of great charm and humour,
not the least of which is that he sees himself in the role of seducer.
So overwhelmed is he by his wife's sexuality that he declares that
he has never been so aroused by a goddess or a woman. This
declaration establishes a link between this and another erotic scene
in the poem, the seduction of Helen by Paris (3. 441–6), who also
declared that he had never experienced such passion before, not
even at their first love-making. With stunning tactlessness, Zeus
catalogues some of his former sexual triumphs, and, not content
with listing the females whose eroticism was no match for that of
Hera, he also names the children he sired upon them. Zeus'
behaviour explains Hera's hatred of him, and is more than a match
for the immorality of her actions, but there is no moralizing in the
scene; instead Homer exploits the full humour of the situation, as
Zeus' passion causes him tactlessly to recount his own cheating
while all the time he is cheated himself.

317–28   The **wife of Ixion** was Dia. Probably in retaliation for Zeus'
seduction of Dia, Ixion attempted to rape Zeus' own wife, Hera;
his punishment was to be bound to a wheel of fire which revolves
eternally through the heavens. **Akrisios** was king of Argos; he
received an oracle that his daughter **Danaë** would bear a child who
would overthrow him, and so he confined her in an underground
chamber of bronze. Zeus entered the chamber as a shower of gold
and fathered Perseus upon her. When Akrisios discovered the child,
he placed him and Danaë in a chest which he let loose on the sea;
but mother and child were saved on the island of Seriphos. For

Europa, cf. 13. 450–3n. **Semele** was the daughter of Kadmos king of Thebes; when she was pregnant by Zeus, Hera caused her to be consumed by his thunderbolt, but Zeus saved the unborn child, Dionysos, from the ashes by sewing him into his own thigh, and from there he was born in due course. **Alkmene** was the wife of Amphitruo; she vowed to remain a virgin until her husband avenged the murder of her brothers, but while he was away fighting, she was seduced by Zeus who took the form of her husband. To Zeus she bore Herakles, and to Amphitruo she bore Iphikles who was younger by one night.   The offspring of Zeus' union with **Demeter** was Persephone, and of his union with **Leto** were Apollo and Artemis.

333–8   **if some one of the gods everlasting saw us sleeping.** The humour of the scene is increased by Hera's feigned modesty, because her delaying stratagem only inflames Zeus further. In fact it is not modesty but the need to get Zeus into her own bed-chamber that leads her on, the **chamber, which my beloved son Hephaistos has built for me, and closed the leaves in the door-posts snugly.** Hera of course does not mention the 'secret door-bar, and no other of the gods could open it' (168), because it is her intention that this door-bar will trap Zeus and so allow a much larger-scale reversal of his plans than has occurred so far; but she has overplayed her hand and her scheme is frustrated by his insistence on satisfying his passion immediately.

344–9   **Not even Helios can look at us through it.** The seduction of Zeus by Hera is matched in Book 8 of the *Odyssey* when the bard Demodokos sings of the adulterous affair of Ares and Aphrodite. The lovers are caught in a net constructed around the bed by Aphrodite's husband Hephaistos, and they are visited by the other gods who ridicule their embarrassing situation: this of course is the situation Hera says she fears, and Zeus replies that even the sun (**Helios**) will be unable to see them. In the *Odyssey* the story is used to contrast Aphrodite's infidelity with the steadfast chastity of Odysseus' wife Penelope; in the *Iliad* the scene, like so many scenes involving the gods, contrasts their carefree existence with the grim reality of humans' lot. The contrast is also illustrated by the scene's imagery as the earth itself celebrates the union by producing new life, and this in turn points up the human carnage which will result from this scene.

366-7   now Achilleus in the anger of his heart stays still among the hollow ships. With Zeus now asleep and his grip on events completely relaxed, Poseidon is in a position to restore Achaian fortunes by reversing his plans, and so it is an appropriate moment to recall the figure of the absent Achilleus.

370-7   let us take those shields. Poseidon proposes that the Achaians swap armour, with the best fighters taking the best armour, and the worst fighters the worst armour. To do such a thing at the height of the battle is hardly realistic, but the scene is designed to illustrate the revitalized spirit of the Achaians, and their new and more positive stance.

384-93   Poseidon the shaker of the earth led them. Now it is Poseidon who is at the head of the Achaians in place of the wounded and ineffectual Agamemnon (cf. 134), and this is an indication of the dramatic reversal of events which have taken place: in confirmation of this, **the breaking of the sea washed up to the ships and the shelters of the Argives,** the whole land is inundated by Poseidon's own element, the sea.

**394-9   **The intensity of the sound of the battle is heightened by three brief, but carefully matched, similes from nature—roaring sea, bellowing fire, crying wind.

402-32   glorious Hektor made a cast with his spear at Aias. This combat of Aias and Hektor continues their earlier meeting (13. 809f), when they made all the usual threats and boasts, but then the fight itself came to nothing, and the book merely ended with the observation that the Trojans raised an 'unearthly clamour' and the Achaians did not 'forget their warcraft' (13. 834-6). Now the two warriors hurl their spears without any word of introduction: the account of their fight was suspended while the poet recounted the Deception of Zeus, and now it is resumed.

434   whirling Xanthos, whose father was Zeus the immortal is the river Skamandros, called Xanthos by the gods (cf. 20. 74). It is against this river/god that Achilleus fights in Book 21.

440-522   they saw Hektor withdrawing from them. The wounding of Hektor by Aias and his retreat heralds a rout of the Trojans: at first the battle is even, with two warriors on each side killed, but then the death of the Trojan Ilioneus (489) introduces a catalogue of no fewer than nine Trojans killed, as well as the many victims of Oïlean Aias (520).

449   For **Poulydamas**, see 12. 50–80n: the fact that, in Hektor's
absence, the Trojans' resistance is centred on his *alter ego*,
Poulydamas, means that their defeat is inevitable, because he is
inferior as a warrior, though better in counsel. **I think he has got it
for a stick to lean on as he trudges down into Death's house:** Janko
(1992.218) remarks that 'Poulydamas' vaunt is brilliantly sarcastic',
and it may be that its dark humour deliberately recalls the picture
of the wounded Achaian leaders leaning on their spears for support
(cf. 27–40n).

470–4   **Think over this, Poulydamas, and answer me truly.** Aias' boast
answers that of Poulydamas; similarly the boast of Trojan Akamas
(479–85) is matched by Achaian Peneleos (501–5), and these
parallels indicate the evenness of the struggle at this point.

492–500   The description of the death of **Ilioneus** at the hands of
Peneleos is one of the most detailed and gruesome in the poem,
with the head severed and held aloft and the eyeball stuck on a
spear's point. The image is made all the more shocking by the
comparison to **the head of a poppy**, which seems to contain an
intentional echo of the simile comparing the dying Gorgythion to
a drooping poppy (cf. 8. 306–8n).

508   **Tell me now, you Muses who have your homes on Olympos.**
Homer's appeal to the Muses highlights the importance of the
moment and gives his assurance that the following catalogue of
Trojan dead is accurate (cf. 11. 218n).

ILIAD 15

The position Homer established in the course of two books, 11 and 12, has now been totally reversed, also in the space of two books, 13 and 14. At the end of Book 12 the Achaian defences were breached, Trojan victory appeared inevitable, and Hektor was euphoric; by the end of Book 14 the Achaians are once more victorious, the Trojans are being massacred, and Hektor lies wounded. Such are the results of the intervention of Poseidon in Book 13 and of Hera in the Deception of Zeus in Book 14. Homer's ultimate goal is an Achaian defeat great enough to cause Patroklos to return to the battle, to his death at the hands of Hektor, and so it is clear that the divine interventions of the two previous books form a major interruption in the forward movement of the narrative: the purpose of this book, therefore, is to restore the narrative to the position at the end of Book 12. The book comprises two sections: first a scene amongst the gods (1–262) continues the drama of the Deception of Zeus and serves to reassert Zeus' authority; and then the remainder of the book describes the consequence of this for mortals, as the restoration of Trojan fortunes culminates in Hektor calling for fire to hurl on the Achaian ships.

1   **But after they had crossed back over the ditch.** The climax of Trojan success, before divine intervention allowed the Achaian recovery, was marked by Hektor smashing through the defensive gate at the Achaian ships and the Trojans swarming over their defensive wall (12. 459–71). The Achaian success of the last two books is now indicated as the Trojans stream back across the ditch.
11   **not the weakest Achaian had hit him.** Hektor was hit by Aias with a stone (14. 409–13); although he recovered partially, his condition remains much as it was: 'lay back on the ground again, while over both eyes dark night misted' (14. 438–9).

14 Hopeless one is better translated 'uncontrollable' (Fagles 1990.388).

18–30 Do you not remember that time. The occasion was the earlier sacking of Troy by Herakles, son of Zeus, who on his return journey was blown off course by Hera after she had enlisted the help of Sleep to dispose of Zeus. When Zeus awoke, Sleep managed to get away, but Hera was subjected to the punishment described here. This is the occasion Sleep spoke of (14. 247–62), although he did not specify the punishment Hera received. Zeus' tone and threat of violence serve both to reassert his authority and to recall his quarrel with Hera (1. 536–67). Zeus does not say what he hung Hera from, but probably it was a beam or a hook: with her hands bound together, the weight of the anvils was designed to make the torture even more painful. The punishment with which Zeus threatened the gods, to be cast down to earth from heaven, recalls the way he punished Hephaistos when he brought help to Hera (1. 590–3).

35–46 The humour of the previous book is continued in Hera's solemn oath and in her denial of complicity between herself and Poseidon, for she speaks something less than the truth, and yet in neither case does she actually lie. For Hera's oath by **the dripping water of the Styx**, see 14. 271–4n. For the goddess of marriage to swear an oath by **the bed of marriage between us**, in which, though she has not betrayed her husband, she has certainly deceived him, may be hypocritical, but Zeus has consistently betrayed her and at the height of his passion actually boasted of his sexual conquests (cf. 14. 317–28n). Her protestation that **it is not through my will** that Poseidon acted is specious: when Sleep reported to Poseidon that Hera had lulled Zeus to sleep, it is clear he was acting in line with her wishes (14. 352–60).

47–53 the father of gods and men smiled on her. His smile and his words show that Zeus believes Poseidon took his lead from Hera: so the resolution of the Deception of Zeus contains the same spirit of deception as the episode itself, as Hera's half-truths are half accepted by her husband.

59–77 Zeus reveals the future course of events to Hera, and shows that in the long term his plans for the outcome of the war correspond to her own ambitions for the Achaians. From the very beginning Zeus' plan has been to bring the Achaians to their knees and so cause them to acknowledge Achilleus' greatness, but now he spells out the consequence of this, the inexorable succession of deaths which are to be the tragic result of Achilleus' request to Thetis in Book 1: Sarpedon, Patroklos and Hektor. Foreshadowing of this sort is common in the poem (Introduction 7(e); Duckworth 1966), but this particular passage has been criticized on the grounds that Zeus removes all suspense from the story. Yet for the oral audience the effect was probably quite the opposite, in providing fixed reference points in the coming battles; the foreshadowing here also lends pathos to the moment, for Zeus predicts the death of Hektor even as he anticipates the imminent success of the Trojans against the Achaian fleet.

71   **capture headlong Ilion through the designs of Athene** refers to the Trojan Horse, which was devised by Odysseus at the instigation of Athene (cf. *Odyssey* 8. 493).

74   Zeus has just foretold the death of Patroklos at Hektor's hands (65) as part of a chain of deaths, and his death is now linked directly by that chain to **the thing asked by the son of Peleus;** in this way Homer establishes a direct causal relationship between Achilleus' wish for an Achaian defeat and the death of his companion, and it is Achilleus' realization of this that will transform the nature of his anger in the final books of the poem.

80–2   **As the thought flashes in the mind of a man.** The comparison of the speed of Hera's departure to the speed of thought is a highly unusual simile; its closest parallel is a simile comparing Achilleus' pursuit of Hektor to the experiences of a dream (22. 199–200).

87   **Themis** is a daughter of Ouranos (Heaven) and Gaia (Earth), that is, she is one of the Titans; she sided with Zeus in his battle with her brother Kronos and the other Titans. By Zeus she is the mother of the Horai (Seasons) and the Moirai (Fates). Her name is a personification of righteousness and justice.

93–112   From her first words to Themis Hera is bent on trouble-making: she makes two speeches, separated only by a forced smile (101), each carefully designed to lead her audience on to wish to hear more and to provoke maximum hostility towards her husband. **one now still feasts at his pleasure:** by breaking off without naming the unfortunate god—actually Ares—Hera effectively intensifies the shock, and so the provocation, to him (110). Her provocation of Ares serves as a paradigm of Homer's forward planning: **Askalaphos** was killed by Deïphobos (13. 519), and Homer commented that his father Ares had not heard of his death but was sitting on Olympos, 'held fast by command of Zeus'. Homer stressed that Ares was subject to Zeus' will, and so prepared the ground for his anger and frustration now.

113–14   Ares struck against both his big thighs with the flats of his hands. Cf. 12. 162–3n.

119   Fear and Terror, along with Hate, were pictured beside Ares and Athene driving the two sides into battle (4. 439–40).

136   come back to batter us on Olympos. Athene's fear of Zeus' violence echoes his own story of how he treated his wife (18–30n), and so the gods are left in no doubt that Zeus' prohibition on their interference is still in force; and the listener is left in no doubt that Zeus' plan for Achilleus has been reinstated, and that the defeat of the Achaians will begin again.

165–6   I am far greater than he is in strength. Zeus calls himself greater (*ph: *pherteros*) than his brother, the same term Agamemnon used during the quarrel to claim he was superior to Achilleus (1. 186; and cf. 1. 275–84n). Zeus also calls himself **elder born,** just as Agamemnon did when he told the ambassadors to demand Achilleus' subjection (9. 160–1). So this scene recalls the dispute over leadership authority in Book 1 which drove Achilleus apart from his heroic society. The other gods may resent it, but Zeus' status is beyond challenge, and this demonstration of his absolute power enhances the significance of his support for Achilleus' own challenge to Agamemnon.

186–93   who am his equal in rank. In claiming to be Zeus' equal, Poseidon is disputing his brother's claim to supreme authority on the grounds of being the elder: for Zeus' claim, despite being the last born of Kronos, cf. 13. 347–55n. The division between the three brothers took place after the overthrow of Kronos and the Titans (cf. 8. 479–83n). The distribution was random, by lot, and this indicates that the brothers ostensibly have equal power, but Poseidon does not address Zeus' claim to privileged power on the grounds of age. The **earth and high Olympos,** home of mortals and of the gods, were not allocated to any one brother because these are the two areas in which the gods act out their conflicts.

204   For the **Furies** (Erinues), cf. 3. 278–80n.

210   **Endowed with destiny like his** is better translated 'endowed with an equal share (of authority)'.

218–19   **went, merging in the sea, and the fighting Achaians longed for him.** The drama of the gods' reversal of the course of the war began with the sudden inattention of Zeus and the descent of Poseidon from the heights of Samothrake in Book 13, and it continued through the seduction of Zeus by his wife in Book 14; in contrast its end is recounted in just two lines with Poseidon's departure beneath the waves.

220   **After this Zeus who gathers the clouds spoke to Apollo.** At 154 both Iris and Apollo 'came into the presence of Zeus the cloud-gatherer', and Zeus gave Iris 'first of the two' (157) her instructions to take his message to Poseidon. With that scene completed, Zeus now turns to Apollo with his instructions; this is one more example of the convention of narrating simultaneous actions successively (Introduction 7(d)).

225   The gods **who gather to Kronos beneath us** are the Titans (cf. 8. 479–83n); Zeus' meaning is that the battle with Poseidon would have been heard even in the Underworld; but he also implies that the outcome for Poseidon would have been just as dire as was the outcome for the Titans of their battle with him.

233   For **the crossing of Helle**, see 7. 73–86n.

237–8   **in the likeness of a rapid hawk** describes the speed of Apollo's descent, just like the simile at the beginning of the poem when he was compared to night; both similes describe the speed with which death comes to the Achaians (cf. 1. 47n).

263–8   **As when some stalled horse.** The simile was used earlier (6. 506–11) to describe Paris' entry into battle. Within an oral tradition, there is no case for assigning priority between the two examples; rather the simile serves to recall the context of the earlier occasion—Paris' high spirits and disregard for danger, as he dashed from bedroom to battlefield—and points the contrast with Hektor, recovered from his injury, confidence restored by Apollo, and exhilarated by the prospect of final triumph.

271–6   This second simile describes the effect of Hektor's return on the Achaians: the **horned stag or a wild goat** represents the Trojans; the **men who live in the wilds**, hunters who have chased the beast but have lost its track, are the Achaians; and the **great bearded**

lion, a symbol of strength and courage, which turns the hunters to flight, is Hektor.

281–99 For **Thoas**, cf. 13. 206–20n. Thoas' proposal is in line with Zeus' prediction (232–3): he suggests that the Achaians retreat, with the principal Achaians providing protection. Thoas' strategy serves the important artistic purpose of immediately establishing the Achaians as the defenders once more, penned in and besieged by their ships.

306–89 The following battle is of great significance because it will cause Achilleus to send Patroklos into battle in Book 16; but Homer is careful to limit the scale of the Trojan victory, because it must not after all be so great that it brings Achilleus himself back into battle. However this early part presents unmitigated disaster for the Achaians, as no fewer than eight of their number, though none of major importance, are killed without a single loss for the Trojans.

308–10   **the tempestuous terrible aegis, shaggy, conspicuous.** When Athene put the aegis on (cf. 5. 734–47n), it was described as

> . . . the betasselled, terrible
> aegis, all about which Terror hangs like a garland,
> and Hatred is there, and Battle Strength, and heart-freezing Onslaught
> and thereon is set the head of the grim, gigantic Gorgon,
> a thing of fear and horror, portent of Zeus of the aegis.

and Athene was said to throw it across her shoulders. Here Apollo is gripping it in both hands (cf. 229–30).

313–14   **the arrows from the bowstrings jumping.** Janko (1992.261) refers to the Trojans' 'animated weaponry', their arrows seeming almost to reach their targets of their own accord, and it is the role of Apollo which is featured rather than that of the Trojan fighters themselves (320–7): the effect seems deliberately to downplay the Trojan achievement.

323–5 The simile links with the earlier one (271–6): now the Achaians are like **a herd of cattle or big flock of sheep**; the **two wild beasts** that scatter them represent Hektor now fighting with Apollo in support, and the absence of any herdsman for the cattle or sheep indicates the absence of Achilleus' protection for the Achaians. The transformation of the Achaians, from hunters in the previous simile to hunted in this, intensifies the picture of their fear and disarray.

347–51   let the bloody spoils be. Similarly Nestor warned the
Achaians against hanging back to strip the corpses (6. 68–71).
Hektor's threat that **the dogs shall tear him to pieces** recalls the
beginning of the poem (1. 4–5n): it is a common enough threat but
not, as here, against fighters on one's own side.

362–6   The Achaian wall is described as **much hard work and painful
done by the Argives,** and this recalls both the effort of its
construction and the deaths and wounds suffered in its defence. In
the simile on the other hand, both the building and the destruction
of the sand-castles are described as **innocent play:** the indifference
of the boy as he destroys his own handiwork illustrates the same
wantonness of the god, but it also points the contrast, that it is the
efforts of others that the god destroys.

381–3   as when the big waves on the sea wide-wandering. The
relentless Trojan attack is illustrated by the sea waves washing over
the ship's sides, an appropriate image since, following the breaching
of the Achaian rampart and the destruction of their wall, the attack
is now on the ships themselves. The ship image is continued in a
third simile (cf. 410–12n).

390–8   The account of the battle at the Achaian ships is interrupted
briefly by a description of **Patroklos'** reaction to it. Patroklos had
been on his way from Nestor's tent taking news of Machaon's
injury to Achilleus when he met the wounded Eurypylos (11. 804f),
and since then he has been tending his wound; now, seeing the
Achaian defeat, he rouses himself to leave. It is hardly realistic that
Patroklos should have failed until now to notice the Achaian
disasters, including the destruction of their wall: in fact, in line
with the convention of describing events consecutively, Patroklos'
role has been held in suspense until the Trojans are within reach of
the Achaian ships. For the gesture of striking **both thighs with the
flats of his hands,** see 12. 162–3n: by means of it Homer indicates
that this is the beginning of the end for Patroklos.

401–2   I go in haste to Achilleus, to stir him into the fighting. Nestor
urged Patroklos to use his friendship with Achilleus to force him
either to come himself to the rescue of the Achaians or to allow
Patroklos to do so (11. 789–802); now Patroklos mentions only
the former. Having just indicated that Patroklos' death is
approaching, Homer immediately associates it with Achilleus'
refusal to help the Achaians himself (cf. 74n).

410–12   as a chalkline straightens the cutting of a ship's timber.
This simile introduces the second half of the battle at the Achaian
ships, and the image of the chalkline guiding the carpenter's saw
indicates that this second half is to be a much more even affair.
Although the battle will result in Trojan victory with Hektor taking
hold of one of the Achaian ships and calling for fire, in fact the
victory involves the death of six Trojans against only four for the
Achaians.

415   Hektor made straight for glorious Aias. Hektor and Aias are
natural opponents, since Aias is the best of the Achaians, after
Achilleus, and Hektor is his Trojan counterpart; they fought a formal
duel in Book 7. However Aias is renowned as a defensive warrior,
and this indicates the Trojans' present superiority.

430–2   he had killed a man in sacred Kythera. As so often, the death
of an inconspicuous victim is individualized by brief details of his
life. Exile as a result of murder is a common motif, for example,
the case of Patroklos (11. 764n). The island of Kythera, to the
south of the Peloponnese, was **sacred** to Aphrodite.

461–2   Zeus, who was guarding Hektor is an important reminder
that this battle is the climax of Zeus' promise to Thetis in Book 1
to give victory to Hektor and the Trojans. **Telamonian Teukros** is
the illegitimate son of Telamon, and so half-brother of Telamonian
Aias.

**486–99   After their single combat, Hektor and Aias each make a
speech to rally their troops, and there is a fine symmetry between
them, in length, content and effect (500 = 514). In claiming that
Zeus is granting the Trojans glory and **diminishes the strength of
the Argives**, Hektor fails to recall all of the promise made to him
by Iris,

> . . . Zeus guarantees power to you
> to kill men, till you make your way to the strong-benched vessels,
> until the sun goes down and the blessed darkness comes over.
>
> (11. 207–9)

Zeus is indeed granting the Trojans his favour, but it is limited, and
that limit has almost been reached (cf. 11. 191–4n). **the Achaians
must go away with their ships to the beloved land of their fathers:**
Hektor's battle-cry contrasts with his actions at the end of this

book when he tries to destroy the Achaian fleet with fire and so prevent the Achaians returning home.

502–13   if our ships fall to helm-shining Hektor. In his speech rallying the Achaians, Aias identifies the ships as their last line of defence, because the wall behind which they have been besieged has been destroyed and its place has been taken by the ships (cf. 381–3n): so after their brief respite during the Deception of Zeus, the Achaians are once more under siege. **He is not inviting you to come to a dance**: the poem presents dance as the standard antithesis of war; for example, when Aphrodite urged Helen to join Paris in bed after he was rescued from his duel with Menelaos, she said that he looked as though he was on his way to a dance (3. 393).

532   A guest and friend had given him it. For guest-friendship and the practice of gift-exchange, cf. 6. 215–25n.

568   Antilochos is the son of Nestor: his youthfulness, speed of foot and his fighting strength are just the qualities of which old age has robbed his father. He is a particular companion of Menelaos, and risked his own life in his defence (cf. 5. 565n).

579–88   Two similes describe the actions of Antilochos. In the first he is the aggressor, **as a hound rushes against a stricken fawn,** but immediately he becomes the quarry, **like a wild beast who has done some bad thing,** and this illustrates further the Achaians' combination of aggression and defence.

593–9   were bringing to accomplishment Zeus' orders is a reminder that this is the climax of Zeus' plan to give victory to Hektor and the Trojans (cf. 461–2n); but Hektor's victory is merely a part of a much greater divine strategy whose true purpose is to give the glory to Achilleus (612–14). Lattimore's **the prayer of Thetis** omits its description as *exaision*, 'disastrous' (Fagles 1990).

605–30   Hektor's attack is marked by a variety of images: he is like **fire or spear-shaking Ares; a slaver came out around his mouth,** which suggests the appearance of a rabid dog (cf. 13. 53–4n); he is **lit about with flame on all sides,** he is like a **battering wave,** and he is like **a murderous lion.** Yet for all the violence of the imagery, and for all that Zeus **honoured this one man,** he succeeds in killing only one man, the unfortunate Periphetes of Mykenai.

618–28   they closed into a wall. The Achaians' metaphorical wall replaces their wall which has been destroyed: the metaphor recalls the description of Aias, their greatest defensive warrior, as 'wall of the Achaians' (cf. 13. 152n). The collapse of Achaian morale in the face of Hektor's attack is presented through two similes in which his force is like that of the sea: at first they withstand him **like some towering huge sea-cliff** which withstands wind and sea, but then they are like sailors whose **ship goes utterly hidden under the foam,** and their courage turns to fear.

638–48   **Periphetes of Mykenai** trips on the rim of his shield in his eagerness to retreat; this is most likely a tower shield of the type illustrated on objects from the Mykenaian Bronze Age, and most closely associated in the poem with Aias (cf. 7. 219–23n). Periphetes is the only named member of the contingent from Mykenai, other than its leader of course. His father had been intermediary between the earlier king of Mykenai, **Eurystheus**, and the hero on whom he had imposed his twelve labours, **Herakles**. This heightens Periphetes' status as Hektor's opponent, but his clumsiness leading to his death, as well as his comparison to an ox (636), detracts from Hektor's achievement.

662–3   Nestor's appeal to each Achaian to **remember his children and his wife, his property and his parents** recalls Hektor's appeal to the Trojans (496–8), and vividly portrays the Achaian ships and camp as their home-city to be defended at all costs.

668–9   **from their eyes Athene pushed the darkness immortal of mist.** There has been no previous mention of this mist covering the Achaians; it is included here precisely so that Athene may dispel it and allow the Achaians to recognize Hektor and the other Trojans, and so demonstrate her support for them. In a similar scene Zeus scatters the mist and darkness which surrounds the Achaians, in response to Aias' appeal (17. 648–50).

674–8   Throughout the poem Aias is the epitome of brave defensive resistance, and now he stands alone to confront the attacking Trojans. On this occasion his equipment is not his usual defensive tower shield but **a great pike for sea fighting**, which at 22 cubits— some 32 ft—denotes aggression as well as defence. Hektor carried a spear 11 cubits long when he visited Troy (cf. 6. 319n).

679–84   **as a man who is an expert rider of horses** illustrates the speed and agility of Aias. The horse rider's purpose in leaping from the back of one mount to another seems to be to share the burden between the four of them. The result is that people on the road turn to admire his feat, and this matches the admiration of the Achaians for Aias as he leaps from ship to ship in their defence.

694–5   from behind Zeus was pushing him onward hard with his big hand is a particularly expressive example of the metaphor of the hand of God. Hektor is on the point of achieving the climax of the Trojan attack promised by Zeus, the firing of an Achaian ship, and Homer is careful to mark the god's role at this point.

704–6   The ship is distinguished by its description, **a grand, fast-running, seafaring ship**, because it is the ship of a great hero, **Protesilaos**: he had been killed as he leapt, first of all the Achaians, onto Trojan soil (2. 698–702). Since the first day of the war this ship has been without its commander, and this detracts from Hektor's achievement in laying hands on it; but as the ship which brought the first Achaian, it is a fitting symbol of Hektor's attack on the invaders.

719–25   Zeus has given us a day worth all the rest of them. In his euphoria Hektor declares that the triumph has been granted by Zeus, but again he fails to remember that this victory represents the climax, and the end, of Trojan success (cf. 486–99n). **our counsellors' cowardice** recalls his clashes with his counsellor Poulydamas who continually attempts to restrain his excesses (cf. 13. 724–47n), and ironically calls to mind those very qualities which will shortly bring about his death.

736   Have we some stronger wall that can rescue men from perdition. Hektor has just spoken of the Achaian ships as the symbol of their aggression (720), but Aias recognizes them as the Achaians' final defence, the equivalent of their city wall, to be defended at all cost (cf. 502–13n).

741   Salvation's light is in our hands' work, not the mercy of battle. Aias' meaning is that their safety will only be gained through courage, not through hanging back, in battle.

ILIAD 16

In antiquity this book was given the title Patrokleia, *because it tells of the* aristeia *and subsequent death of Patroklos at the hands of Hektor; it constitutes the denouement of the theme of Achilleus' anger, as it demonstrates his role in the death of his friend. After the events of this book, Achilleus' anger towards Agamemnon is relegated to the background and is replaced by a consuming passion for vengeance upon Hektor, as he attempts to assuage his own sense of responsibility for the death of Patroklos. When he rejected the embassy in Book 9, having first declared his intention to sail for home the very next day (9. 357–63), Achilleus finally vowed that he would only fight again when the Trojan attack reached his own ships and threatened them with fire (9. 650–3). The fact that the Trojans' fire has reached the Achaian ships, but not yet as far as his own, prevents him from entering the battle himself, but he gives way to Patroklos' demand that he be allowed to fight in his place. In this way the resulting death of Patroklos is linked to the continuing intransigence of his friend.*

For all the intensity of their relationship, and despite the importance of that relationship to the poem's narrative, the exchange between Achilleus and Patroklos at the beginning of this book is their only direct conversation in the entire poem, a fact which can only lend pathos to a scene in which Achilleus reveals the depth of his feeling for his friend. The basis of their relationship is described later in the poem by Patroklos' ghost when he implores his friend to give him burial (23. 69–92). He tells how as a child he killed a companion and was brought by his father Menoitios to seek sanctuary with Achilleus' father Peleus, and such was the friendship that resulted that Patroklos' ghost asks that his ashes should be held in the same urn as those of Achilleus when he dies. The relationship of the two companions was represented as overtly homosexual by a number of later writers (Clarke 1978; Halperin

1990.85); it is also suggested that Patroklos is in some way the 'second-self' (Van Nortwick 1996.49), or the alter ego *of Achilleus (Sinos 1980.55). Homer refers to Patroklos as Achilleus'* therapon, *a word variously translated by Lattimore 'henchman' (243) and 'companion' (17. 271). His battle with Hektor is by rights Achilleus', and his death both anticipates and represents the death of Achilleus himself: 'one has the feeling that Patroklos was created to serve dramatic ends: to help define Achilles and for nothing more' (Beye 1968.86). See further, Collins 1998.15ff.*

2   The formula **shepherd of the people** is also used to describe Menelaos and Agamemnon, but this is the only time it attaches to Achilleus; the metaphor serves to enhance the sympathetic stance he takes (5). Patroklos left Achilleus' shelter at 11. 616 to go to Nestor, and he finally left the wounded Eurypylos to return to Achilleus at 15. 405.

3–4   **like a spring dark-running.** This simile was also used to describe the weeping Agamemnon (9. 14–15), and it associates Patroklos' panic and despair with that of Agamemnon then. On the earlier occasion Agamemnon sent Odysseus, Phoinix and Aias on the embassy to Achilleus, and in the present case Patroklos tells him of Nestor's suggestion that he be allowed to return to the battle: the repeated simile may suggest that Patroklos' appeal continues the appeals of Book 9.

6–10   **Why then are you crying like some poor little girl.** Achilleus' relationship with Patroklos is reflected in his tone of gentle mockery. During the Embassy Achilleus compared his role as provider for the Achaian army to that of a mother bird with her thankless task of bringing morsels of food to her brood (9. 323–6). Although Patroklos is the elder, Achilleus presents himself as the parental figure and, by stressing Patroklos' dependence on him, he introduces the theme of his own failure to protect his companion. The tears, the comparison to a little girl, and the gentle mockery all illustrate Patroklos' vulnerability and inadequacy for the role he takes on in this book, of Achilleus' replacement.

19   **Tell me, do not hide it in your mind, and so we shall both know.** These are the same words Achilleus spoke to his mother Thetis (1. 363), and in their intimacy and compassion they identify his role as parent (cf. 6–10n) and the obligations he feels towards Patroklos.

20   **Patroklos the rider.** Homer's heroes travel in chariots, rather
      than on horseback. The title is one of honour, like English 'knight'.
23–9 **are lying among the ships with arrow or spear wounds.**
      Diomedes was wounded at 11. 252, Odysseus at 11. 376,
      Agamemnon at 11. 437, and Eurypylos at 11. 582. Homer also
      represented the desperate situation of the Achaians by listing these
      same wounded (minus Eurypylos) at 14. 28–9. **the healers skilled
      in medicine** recalls Patroklos' own role as healer immediately before
      his return to Achilleus' shelter (11. 843–7), and his care there for
      the wounded Eurypylos, in constrast to Achilleus' neglect.
36–7 **if you are drawing back from some prophecy.** There is a veiled
      suggestion of cowardice in the idea that Achilleus may be holding
      back from the battle because of information given by his mother, a
      suggestion Nestor made to Patroklos (cf. 11. 793–6n). Achilleus
      told Odysseus during the Embassy (9. 410–16) of the choice offered
      to him by his mother, of a short but glorious life and early death at
      Troy, or a long life free from care but with no glory won. It may be
      that Patroklos is recalling that incident here, and that this indicates
      Nestor's success in isolating him from Achilleus.
40–5 **Give me your armour to wear on my shoulders.** The suggestion
      that Patroklos wear Achilleus' armour to deceive the Trojans was
      first made by Nestor (36–45 = 11. 794–803). The plan soon proves
      a failure: although at 281–2 the Trojans generally appear to think
      that Achilleus has returned to the battle, at 423–4 Sarpedon makes
      it quite clear that he at least is not fooled. In part Homer is preparing
      the ground for the narrative of Book 18, when Hephaistos will
      forge new armour for Achilleus: before new armour can be made,
      his old armour must be lost when Patroklos is killed by Hektor.
      But Patroklos' donning of the armour has an important symbolic
      significance, of his attempt to take on Achilleus' warrior role. **with
      a mere cry** foreshadows the moment when Achilleus makes his
      return to the battle, and from the Achaian ditch lets out a cry to
      terrify the Trojans (18. 217–18).
50   **I have not any prophecy in mind** contradicts Achilleus' words at
      9. 410 and is his defence against the suggestion of cowardice; it
      shows the success of Nestor's appeal to Patroklos (cf. 36–7n).
60–3 **we will let all this be a thing of the past.** Achilleus relents but
      not to the extent of returning to battle himself; he is moved
      sufficiently by Patroklos' appeal to feel sympathy for the Achaians,

but not to forego his hatred of Agamemnon. So just as his stance shifted in response to each of the three ambassadors, so now also he makes one more, fatal, adjustment, and agrees to Nestor's plan.

71–3   **cram full of dead men the water-courses** foreshadows the actual result of Achilleus' return to battle, when he does cram the river Skamandros with Trojan dead (cf. 21. 15–16). **if powerful Agamemnon treated me kindly** has been seized upon by those trying to disprove the poem's unity of authorship: Leaf (1902.153), for example, believed that the words entirely contradict 'the ample, and indeed abject, humiliation of Agamemnon in [book 9]'. In fact, however, what Achilleus says he wishes would happen reveals what he believes did not happen during the Embassy (cf. 11. 608–9n), for a gentle or kindly attitude was quite the opposite of Agamemnon's motive in sending the embassy: he required, and he said that he required, the submission of Achilleus to his will (cf. 9. 157–61n), and so there is no contradiction in Achilleus' wish that Agamemnon would treat him kndly.

84–6   **great honour and glory in the sight of all the Danaans.** Here too it is claimed that there is an inconsistency best explained by postulating more than one author, and that the Embassy to Achilleus was a later addition to the poem: for how can Achilleus express the hope that he will receive both the girl Briseis and shining gifts in addition, when he has so recently rejected Agamemnon's offer of precisely those things? Yet it seems clear that what he rejected were the gifts of Agamemnon, because they represented the assertion of his authority, and that what he now wishes for are the gifts of the Danaans, because they will represent great honour and glory bestowed by them. His alienation from Agamemnon remains, but if the other Achaians will approach him, not in the name of Agamemnon as the embassy did, but acknowledging his status by means of their gifts, he will relent.

87–90   **So you will diminish my honour.** By fighting in his place Patroklos will win *time* for Achilleus as well as for himself, by showing how much the Achaians are missing their best warrior, but if he alone routs the Trojans, he will detract from Achilleus' *time* because the Achaians will not then be made aware of their dependence upon him; and so he encourages Patroklos to a limited victory only. At the same time Achilleus' words reveal his gnawing anxiety for Patroklos' safety.

95   **You must turn back** is the fourth time Achilleus urges Patroklos
not to advance (cf. 87, 89, 91): this anticipates the moment of
Patroklos' death, when three times he will surge forward to attack
and on the fourth he will encounter Apollo and be struck down
(784–8n), and highlights Achilleus' inability to halt the inexorable
catastrophe. The **light of salvation** takes up Patroklos' own
suggestion (cf. 39), and echoes Aias' declaration 'salvation's light is
in our hands' work' (15. 741).

97–100   Remarkably, many have chosen to take literally Achilleus'
prayer, **if only not one of all the Trojans could escape destruction,
not one of the Argives**, as his ultimate betrayal of his comrades and
their cause in his selfish pursuit of vengeance: rather it is a fanciful,
and eloquent, expression of his frustration with his self-imposed
exile, and of his love and fear for Patroklos as he goes out to fight
alone, and it is also full of pathos, because neither Patroklos nor he
will survive to see Troy's fall.

102–5   The scene on the battlefield is recalled as it was at the end of
Book 15, where Hektor was calling for fire and Aias was retreating
in the face of mounting pressure (102–3 = 15. 727–8); but whereas
earlier the emphasis was on Aias' pike and so on his aggressive
stance (cf. 15. 674–8n), now it is on his defensive armour, his helmet
and his shield. **The will of Zeus beat him back**: in the absence of
Achilleus, Aias is the best of the Achaians, and so his retreat is
marked as the fulfilment of Zeus' promise to Thetis and the climax
of the Trojan advance. **the shower of strokes** raining down on Aias
recalls the simile of the donkey, on which the sticks of the young
boys rain down (cf. 11. 548–61n).

123–5   **the fast ship** is the ship of Protesilaos, which Hektor first
took hold of (cf. 15. 704–6n): it is appropriate that this move to
cut off the Achaians from their means of returning home should be
played out on the vessel which brought the very first Achaian to
land at Troy (cf. 2. 698–702). The firing of the ship marks the
beginning of the denouement of Patroklos' tragedy, and the moment
is marked by Achilleus' gesture **struck his hands against both his
thighs**; Patroklos himself made this same gesture (cf. 15. 390–8n).

130–42   The Arming of Patroklos is the third such arming scene,
following those of Paris (cf. 3. 328–38n) and Agamemnon (cf. 11.
16–44n); a fourth will be the arming of Achilleus himself (19. 369–
91). The order in which the pieces of armour are put on is the

same in each case, because this is a traditional theme of oral poetry, but Homer varies the details, and so the **two powerful spears that fitted his hand's grip** draw attention to the great spear of Achilleus which Patroklos does not take. In this way Homer illustrates Patroklos' inadequacy for his role as replacement for Achilleus.

143   Later tradition told that **Cheiron** who, like Zeus, was a son of Kronos, was the Centaur who educated Achilleus (cf. 11. 831n), as well as Asklepios and Jason. He was particularly associated with the art of medicine.

149–54   **Xanthos and Balios** are immortal horses, which were a wedding gift to Peleus (381); by contrast, **Pedasos** was part of Achilleus' spoils from the sack of Thebe, the home of Andromache before her marriage to Hektor, and of her father, king **Eëtion**, who was killed during its sack (cf. 6. 397n). Other spoils taken from the city were Chryseis, the girl awarded as *geras* to Agamemnon (1. 366–9), the lyre which Achilleus was playing when the ambassadors approached (9. 186–9), and a valuable lump of iron which is offered as a prize by Achilleus during the funeral games for Patroklos (23. 826–9). So the horse represents one of Achilleus' great triumphs of the past, but its yoking alongside the divine horses is symbolic of Patroklos' mortality.

156–63   **as wolves who tear flesh raw**. It might be thought that the wolves' bloatedness in this simile presents an image of torpor rather than tirelessness and bravery, and that the Myrmidons' hunger for battle would more obviously be associated with ravening hunger in wild beasts; nevertheless, Odysseus offers his view that an army fights better on a full stomach (19. 167–70).

168–97   **Fifty were the fast-running ships** (cf. 2. 681–5), each with fifty men at the rowing benches, which Achilleus brought to Troy, compared to the one hundred ships Agamemnon brought (2. 569–76), and this is the basis of Agamemnon's right to command the expedition (cf. 1. 281). The Myrmidons are divided by Achilleus into five battalions, each presumably of 500 men, an arrangement which matches the ordering of the Trojan forces by Hektor and Poulydamas (12. 86–104). No further mention is made of these troop divisions on either side, and it seems clear that Homer provides this detailed account of the forces in order to heighten the significance of the occasion, the entry of Achilleus' forces into battle for the first time in the poem. As the daughter of Peleus, though not of Thetis since Achilleus was their only child, **Polydore** is half-sister to Achilleus. For **Hermes Argeïphontes,** cf 2. 103n. **The fourth battalion was led by Phoinix,** who is now with the Myrmidon army because he stayed behind in Achilleus' shelter after the failure of the embassy (cf. 9. 658–62).

203–6   **We should go back home again.** By saying that his men wish to abandon the expedition and sail home, Achilleus recalls his own threat during the embassy (9. 360), but he credits them with a different motive: he acted from anger at his treatment by Agamemnon, but they act out of frustration at being kept from the fight by him.

212–13   **as a man builds solid a wall** recalls the wall the Achaians have built around the ships; and so the simile confirms the Achaians' defensive mentality and the limited strategy Achilleus urges on them (246–8).

220–30   The **tunics and mantles** and the **fleecy blankets** are symbols of his mother's concern for Achilleus, and they heighten the pathos that Thetis is unable to save her son. The **wrought goblet,** with which the greatest of mortals celebrates his communion with the greatest of gods, marks the significance of the moment, of this final parting of Achilleus and Patroklos; the scene is full of pathos, as Zeus has already announced Patroklos' imminent death (15. 65), and of irony, for as Achilleus vainly prays for Patroklos' deliverance, in reality he is hastening his friend's death, and with it his own. The ritual cleansing of the goblet is intended to ensure the success of the invocation of Zeus, and its failure to do so emphasizes the fact that the death of Patroklos is itself part of Zeus' plan.

233   For **Dodona,** cf. 2. 750n; for **Pelasgian,** cf. 2. 681–94n.

236–8   **As one time before when I prayed to you** recalls Achilleus' request that Zeus 'pin the Achaians back against the ships and the water, dying' (1. 409–10), so that they would come to see the folly of Agamemnon's treatment of him. Zeus has granted that request in full, and Achilleus is now trying to withdraw it and is requesting instead victory for Patroklos and honour for himself. Zeus' refusal to grant this second request makes it clear that the death of Patroklos is a part of, indeed the climax of, the Trojan victory for which Achilleus prayed.

259–65   **like wasps at the wayside.** Once they are roused to anger by the boys, the wasps are indiscriminate in their attack, and so too the Myrmidons, having been roused to anger like their leader by Agamemnon's conduct, direct their anger indiscriminately against those they encounter. The wasps are said to **live in their house by the roadside** and to **fight for their children**, and their human aspect is even more pronounced in their emotions, for they are **angry** and **in heart of fury**.

269–74   Agamemnon may recognize his madness. Patroklos echoes Achilleus' request to Thetis (1. 411–12), and this is further indication that his *aristeia* to win honour for Achilleus, and his death which results, are directly linked to that request. He makes no mention of Achilleus' order that he go no further than beating the Trojans back from the ships, and this anticipates his disregard for Achilleus' orders in the heat of battle.

284–350   Patroklos begins the rout of the Trojans with two killings, and these are followed by a further eight Trojan deaths without the loss of a single Achaian.

297–300   as when from the towering height of a great mountain. That it is Zeus who causes the clearing of the air again indicates that Patroklos' actions are the culmination of Zeus' plan. The simile recalls an earlier one describing the sight of the Trojans' camp fires as they spent the night in the plain (cf. 8. 555–9n), and the recollection of their confidence then casts into relief their present defeat and illustrates the effect of Patroklos' return to the battle.

329   The Chimaira is 'a thing of immortal make, not human, lion-fronted and snake behind, a goat in the middle, and snorting out the breath of the terrible flame of bright fire' (6. 180–2).

352–5   as wolves make havoc among lambs recalls the earlier simile of the wolves bloated with the flesh of a stag, which described the eagerness of the Myrmidons' return to battle (cf. 156–63n), and balances it by characterizing the result of their attack. The two similes mark off the intervening description of increasingly bloody carnage. The thoughtlessness of the shepherd indicates Hektor's neglect in turning to flight in the face of the Achaian attack.

364–76   As when a cloud goes deep into the sky from Olympos. The simile recalls the comparison of the hard-pressed Achaians relieved by Patroklos to the scattering by Zeus of the clouds from a high peak (cf. 297–300n). The image has been intensified, and whereas earlier Zeus merely stirred the cloud from the peak, now Patroklos is like a **hurricane** in driving the Trojans before him; and the image is then continued in the dust-storm thrown up by the retreating Trojans. Hektor **abandoned the people of the Trojans,** coming immediately after the assertion that he 'stood his ground to save his steadfast companions' (363), serves to enhance the effect of Patroklos' *aristeia*.

384–92   The image of the **hurricane** is a continuation of the previous simile. Three references to wrongdoing in the space of just two lines—**they pass decrees that are crooked, and drive righteousness from among them and care nothing for what the gods think**— suggest that this simile is intended to show that the tribulations of the Trojans at Patroklos' hands are punishment from Zeus (Janko 1992.365); and so the destruction of the **works of men** in the flood may prefigure the destruction of the Trojans' city.

406–8   **as a fisherman who sits out on the jut of a rock** contains a rare reference to angling in Homer. Scylla's seizure of Odysseus' men (*Odyssey* 12. 251) offers another such simile.

418   Some of the irony has been lost in translation. No fewer than twelve named Trojans are felled by Patroklos to the earth, described as *pouluboteire*, **bountiful** in Lattimore's translation, but more literally translated 'much-nourishing' or 'many-nourishing'.

419–507   The death of **Sarpedon** at the hands of Patroklos is the first death of a major figure, and is the first of three deaths which will dominate the remainder of the poem—Sarpedon, Patroklos and Hektor: each of these leads inexorably to the next and, beyond the limits of the poem, to the death of Achilleus himself. The appearance of Sarpedon recalls his meeting with Glaukos, where he was presented as the paradigm hero and, in his words to his companion, acknowledged that his quest for *kleos* might end in death, indeed that death is an essential part of winning it (cf. 12. 322–8n).

423–4   **so I may find out who this is.** Clearly Sarpedon is not taken in by the disguise of Achilleus' armour (cf. 40–5n).

433–43   **The heart in my breast is balanced between two ways.** Neither Zeus nor Hera appear to be in any doubt that he can alter Sarpedon's destiny if he wishes, and in time he will also contemplate saving Hektor (22. 174–6), though he will decline to do so. It may appear that Zeus has the power to act contrary to fate, but in reality he does not do so.

445–57   **if you bring Sarpedon back to his home.** Hera uses two arguments: that if Zeus saves his son other gods will wish to do the same, and that to deny Sarpedon death will be to deny him his heroic *kleos*. It is the second that persuades him, and he grants Sarpedon the accolade that his body will be returned home in honour by Death and Sleep. The granting to Sarpedon of **due burial with tomb and gravestone** by his countrymen reflects a contemporary ritual of hero-cult (Nagy 1983.204).

459   **he wept tears of blood.** Zeus also 'cast down dews dripping blood from the sky' (11. 54) in anticipation of the deaths to come.

467–9   **the spear fixed in the right shoulder of Pedasos.** The mortal horse Pedasos serves as a symbol of Patroklos' mortality (cf. 149–54n), so its death at the beginning of his fight with Sarpedon prefigures his own imminent death.

482–4   **as when an oak goes down.** The same simile described Asios' death (cf. 13. 389n): in both cases the tree is felled for a constructive purpose, the making of a ship's timber, and this contrasts with the destruction in the narrative.

486–9   The death of the **blazing and haughty bull** in the midst of its herd represents the loss of leadership the Trojans now suffer. **haughty** (*megathumos*) is better translated 'great-hearted', and this identifies the dying bull more closely with the dying hero.

492–501   Sarpedon calls on his companion **Glaukos** to rescue his body, and his words call to mind his conversation with him (12. 310–28), as he now urges him to fulfil his responsibilities as hero.

510–26   Glaukos was wounded in **his arm** by an arrow from Teukros' bow (12. 387–91). His prayer displays little distress at his companion's death, but speaks instead of his heroic duty to protect the body; his emphasis on the seriousness of his wound excuses his failure to save his companion, at the same time as asking Apollo to help. The wound itself is quickly healed once it has served its purpose (528). **who will not stand by his children** recalls Sarpedon's own speech to Hektor, when he pointed out that in order to come to Troy he had left at home his defenceless wife and baby son (cf. 5. 472–92n).

567   Earlier Athene dispelled the mist in order to assist the Achaians (cf. 15. 668–9n); now **Zeus swept ghastly night far over the strong encounter** in order to hinder them.

571–6   The brief story of **Epeigeus the brilliant** is significant, for in fleeing his homeland and coming as suppliant to the home of Peleus, his career is like that of Patroklos. His death prefigures Patroklos', and in the sorrow which now takes hold of Patroklos may be heard the sorrow which takes hold of Achilleus when Patroklos himself dies.

608–10   Aineias threw his bronze spear at Meriones. The clash between Aineias and Meriones closely parallels Aineias' encounter with Idomeneus who, just like Meriones here, swerved to avoid his spear (cf. 13. 502–5). Idomeneus is of course the companion of Meriones.

617   though you are a dancer. For dance as the standard antithesis of fighting, cf. 15. 502–13n.

629–30   Warfare's finality lies in the work of hands, that of words in counsel. Patroklos' words to Meriones show the change of roles which has occurred in this book: Achilleus has taken on a passive role in his tent, now merely giving advice to Patroklos (cf. 80–95), while Patroklos has cast aside his role of counsellor to Achilleus and has become the man of deeds rather than words.

633–4   As the tumult goes up from men who are cutting timber recalls the frequent comparison of the young warrior killed to a tree hewn by a carpenter, which was used earlier of Sarpedon's death (cf. 482–4n). **the sound is heard from far off** suggests the distant figure of Achilleus (cf. 4. 452–5n).

641–3   as flies through a sheepfold thunder about the pails. The simile becomes almost a part of the narrative itself, with the suggestion of flies swarming around the rotting corpse of Sarpedon; the life-giving milk splashing about in the buckets contrasts with the blood which makes Sarpedon's body unrecognizable.

644–7   nor did Zeus ever turn the glaring of his eyes from the strong encounter. As events move to their climax, Zeus' role in them is again stressed (cf. 102–5n; 236–8n; 297–300n), in order to show that Patroklos' death is the final act in the working out of his plan.

658   For Zeus' sacred balance, cf. 8. 69n.

667–75   Go if you will, beloved Phoibos, and rescue Sarpedon. Because Sarpedon has been presented as the custodian of heroic values, he is honoured in death both by Zeus' tears of blood (459–61) and by Apollo's rescue of his body. This 'lovely, idealized picture of funeral rites' (Edwards 1987.263) contrasts with the harsh treatment meted out to the corpse of the other great Trojan casualty, Hektor. **anoint him in ambrosia:** similarly Thetis will distil ambrosia and nectar through the nostrils of the dead Patroklos to protect his body until its burial (19. 38–9).

685–7   **in a huge blind fury**. Patroklos falls victim to *ate* (cf. 1. 412n). It was an important part of the argument Phoinix put to Achilleus during the embassy that, if he did not respect the Prayers (*litai*) the ambassadors brought, then *ate* would be visited upon him (cf. 9. 504n): Achilleus of course did not respect the Prayers, and now *ate* is visited upon Patroklos. **the command of Peleiades** is Achilleus' command that Patroklos should be content with driving the Trojans back from the ships and should not attack Troy itself (cf. 95n).

693   **Patroklos, as the gods called you to your death?** The pathos of this prediction of Patroklos' imminent death is heightened by the poet's direct address to him (apostrophe).

702–4   **Three times Patroklos tried to mount the angle of the towering wall**. The fall of Troy is not recounted in the *Iliad*, and in fact this is the only time the war reaches the wall of Troy itself (though Andromache told of an occasion the Achaians tried to storm it, 6. 435). So this is a significant moment, and is a symbol of Patroklos' limitations: he may reach Troy's wall but he may proceed no further. **the immortal hands beating back the bright shield**: the hand of god, of Zeus, was also important in Hektor's earlier advance (cf. 15. 694–5n).

707–9   **Give way, illustrious Patroklos**. Apollo's words recall his orders to the charging Diomedes (cf. 5. 436–42n). Like Patroklos here, Diomedes was making his fourth charge against the god, and like Diomedes then, Patroklos now gives way before Apollo's warning: so he preserves his life temporarily, but this serves only to highlight his failure to heed at 784–92, when his death results immediately.

712   The **Skaian gates** represent the separation of the world of the city and safety from the world of the plain and war (cf. 6. 237n): so Hektor's position inside them, and his subsequent decision to leave it, persuaded by Apollo, represents a crucial moment. Having dissuaded Patroklos from attacking the wall, Apollo now persuades Hektor not to defend it.

717–19   **Asios, who was uncle to Hektor** makes no other appearance and was probably invented for his role here, but there is another Asios who plays a much more important role in the poem: he was killed by Idomeneus, and his death prefigured that of Hektor (cf.

13. 384n). So it is significant that, at the moment Hektor makes his crucial decision to remain outside the wall, it should be a namesake of Asios whose form Apollo takes to advise him.

727   **Kebriones**, a half-brother of Hektor, has been serving as his charioteer since the death of Archeptolemos (8. 315), who had himself been a replacement for Eniopeus (8. 123). His death in the following scene means he is the last named victim of Patroklos: because Patroklos cannot climax his career by killing Hektor, who will be killed by Achilleus, he is shown instead killing his half-brother and charioteer, and this is one more indication of the limitations of Patroklos (cf. 702–4n).

742–50   The simile **like a diver**, unusually, is then continued and expanded by Patroklos himself in his image of the man **diving for oysters**. In Patroklos' sarcasm there is an echo of Aineias, who mocked Meriones by complimenting him on his agility, like that of a dancer (cf. 617n).

752–3   **his own courage destroys him.** The simile anticipates Patroklos' death which, like that of the lion, results from his own actions, taken against the direct advice of Achilleus. Similarly Andromache warned Hektor that 'your own great strength will be your death' (6. 407).

756–69   **like lions who in the high places of a mountain.** This second simile develops the previous one, as both Patroklos and Hektor are now compared to lions; and its setting, high on a mountain, is then taken up in a third, comparing them to two winds in the mountain valleys.

776   **mightily in his might, his horsemanship all forgotten.** The death of the insignificant Kebriones attracts this, the most striking epitaph in the entire poem, because he is the last person to die at Patroklos' hands. The line is partly repeated to describe Achilleus writhing in the dust after he has heard of Patroklos' death (cf. 18. 26–7).

784–8   **Three times he charged in with the force of the running war god.** Earlier Patroklos attacked three times and was beaten back on the fourth (cf. 702–4n); now also he charges in three times, but on the fourth he is struck by Apollo. On his fourth and fatal charge he is **like something greater than human** (*daimoni isos*), like a daimon, as his disregard for Achilleus' orders brings him before Apollo. For the poet's direct address to Patroklos, cf. 693n. **Phoibos came against you there:** Patroklos does not die in single combat at the hands of Hektor, but as the victim of no less than three attackers, the god Apollo, Euphorbos and finally Hektor himself, and this fact detracts markedly from Hektor's *time*.

792–804   The first assault on Patroklos is by Apollo who knocks the armour from his body. The most likely explanation of this is that originally Achilleus' armour, which Patroklos is wearing, was invulnerable, and so has to be removed: there was a traditional tale that Achilleus was himself invulnerable, except for the ankle by which Thetis had held him when she dipped him in the river Styx to give him protection. **the helmet four-horned and hollow-eyed** is associated with Achilleus more than any other of the items of his armour Patroklos is wearing, and when Zeus gives it to the victorious Hektor, the blood and dust which now defile it are a symbol that his **own death was close to him.**

816–28   **Patroklos, broken by the spear and the god's blow.** The description of Hektor's attack seems designed to cast him in the worst possible light, in particular the previous emphasis (cf. 792, 805, 806) on the effect on Patroklos of Apollo's and Euphorbos' attacks. **As a lion overpowers a weariless boar**: Hektor may be compared to the lion, but attention is concentrated on the boar, and then on **the fighting son of Menoitios who had killed so many**, and the effect is to emphasize the courage of the dying man in face of such odds.

834–42   **I with my own spear am conspicuous.** Hektor's perception of his role in Patroklos' defeat also puts him in an unfavourable light, for in reality he held back until Patroklos was fatally weakened. **see that you do not come back to me**: there is irony in the instructions Hektor imagines Achilleus giving to Patroklos when he sent him out to battle, because his instructions were in fact just the opposite (cf. 87–100), and it is Patroklos' inability to control his headstrong nature that has brought his undoing.

852   **You yourself are not one who shall live long.** In predicting Hektor's own death, Patroklos calls attention to the unbreakable link between the deaths of major figures in these later books—of Sarpedon, of Patroklos, and next, of Hektor (cf. 419–507n).

855–7   **the end of death closed in upon him.** There is great pathos in the description of the departure of Patroklos' soul, but these lines also link the deaths of Patroklos and Hektor, for they appear on only one other occasion in the poem, to describe the death of Hektor (22. 361–3).

ILIAD 17

This book provides an unbroken continuation of the previous Book 16 as Euphorbos, who with Apollo and Hektor was the killer of Patroklos, is in turn killed by Menelaos, and there is much general fighting with rally and counter-rally. News of Patroklos' death is eventually despatched to Achilleus, though the Achaians only finally succeed in carrying his body from the battle in the following book. The effect of this prolonged struggle is to defer the moment of revelation to Achilleus of his friend's death and so to heighten anticipation of his reaction to the appalling news. At the end of Book 16 Hektor was in hot pursuit of the immortal horses of Achilleus, but, as the disguised Apollo informs him, only Achilleus himself, the son of a divine mother, is able to control them (75–8): in his parentage, as in all else, Hektor is inferior to Achilleus, and his failure to capture and control the horses is an indication of this. Hektor's headlong pursuit of them serves the narrative purpose of removing him temporarily from the battlefield, and this permits the vengeance for the death of Patroklos to begin; Hektor's own death must wait some time yet.

4–5   as over a first-born calf the mother cow stands lowing. In picturing Patroklos as a young calf, the simile recalls the image of vulnerability and dependence on Achilleus that emerged when he himself compared Patroklos to a little girl running after her mother and begging to be picked up (cf. 16. 6–10n); but it is Menelaos who now holds his shield protectively over Patroklos' body, and this marks Achilleus' absence and its devastating consequence.

14–15   since before me no one of the Trojans. Euphorbos' boast is a typical heroic one, but it is also true: Apollo was the first to hit Patroklos, but it was only after Euphorbos wounded him that Hektor made the final blow. Like the manner of the killing itself, this boast detracts from Hektor's heroic stature (cf. 16. 816–28n).

24–8 Menelaos killed Euphorbos' brother **Hyperenor** at 14. 516–17, but there was no mention of his boasts and taunts: clearly Menelaos is embroidering with his own boasts what had been an insignificant encounter.

32 **Once a thing has been done, the fool sees it,** that is, it takes a wise man to see the event before it happens.

34–5 As the following lines make clear, by **penalty for my brother** Euphorbos means the *poine*, the blood-price (cf. 9. 632–6n), in the form of Menelaos' own death. The *poine* features in the next book also, in one of the scenes pictured by Hephaistos on Achilleus' new shield (18. 498).

51–8 Euphorbos' hair is defiled, **splattered with blood**, and the image seems consciously to recall the moment when Patroklos was struck by Apollo and the plumes on Achilleus' helmet for the first time were defiled by blood and dust (cf. 16. 792–804n), and so to make the connexion between the two deaths. **As some slip of an olive tree strong-growing**: this justly famous simile adds much to the pathos of the description of Euphorbos' death, especially the picture of his youth and beauty, and the loving care of his father; that the olive tree is raised **in a lonely place** recalls the loneliness the death of his brother brought to Euphorbos and to his father.

61–7 The **lion hill-reared** describes Menelaos' fighting strength, but the point of the simile is to illustrate the fear of the other Trojans, like the **dogs and the herdsmen**, and so to bring Hektor to the action as the only Trojan equal to the task.

71–81 **Phoibos Apollo begrudged him and stirred up Hektor,** that is, the two who shared in the killing of Patroklos now come to rescue the body of the third, Euphorbos; and Apollo implicitly blames Hektor for his death when he talks of his pursuit of **the horses of valiant Aiakides**. Achilleus' immortal horses, Xanthos and Balios, were an indication of Patroklos' mortality and that he would be unequal to the task of replacing Achilleus (cf. 16. 149–54n); and here they show that Hektor too is inferior, in anticipation of his meeting with Achilleus at the climax of the poem.

91–105 Menelaos debates with himself and decides not to face Hektor: for similar debates, cf. Odysseus (11. 403–10), Agenor (21. 550–70), and Hektor (22. 98–130); of these, only Menelaos here decides not to face his opponent. **for the sake of my honour** acknowledges that Patroklos died trying to regain Helen for him, and that he bears some responsibility for his death. Menelaos is able to overcome his sense of shame (*aidos*, cf. 6. 441–2n), because Hektor **fights from god**. His decision to flee is quite at odds with normal heroic behaviour, as typified by Aias' famous cry (645–7) when confronted by the hand of Zeus himself; but it does foreshadow Hektor's own flight from Achilleus in Book 22.

109–12 like some great bearded lion. Earlier Menelaos was like a lion which breaks the neck of the finest cow in the herd and holds at bay the terrified dogs and herdsmen (cf. 61–7n), but now the lion is driven off from a steading by the men and dogs. The reversal of the image reflects the reversal in his situation.

126 meaning to cut his head from his shoulders with the sharp bronze is a worse fate than Hektor promised Patroklos, that the vultures would have him (16. 836), and later he is 'urgent to cut the head from the soft neck and set it on sharp stakes' (18. 176–7): 'this vindictive violence, for which the ugly destruction of the opponent's dead body is the perfection of victory, is another mark of the change which overcomes Hektor's character during the Great Day of Battle' (Redfield 1975.169), and it culminates in the violence his own corpse suffers at Achilleus' hands.

133–6 stood fast, like a lion over his young recalls the beginning of this book when Menelaos also stood over Patroklos' body, like a mother cow lowing over its first-born calf (4–5n), and this contrast in imagery enhances Aias' warrior stature in comparison to that of Menelaos (cf. 91–105n).

142–68 Hektor, splendid to look at. Glaukos' words recall the insult Hektor himself hurled at his brother Paris (3. 39; 13. 769) with the implication of effeminacy and cowardice, and this is made explicit when he calls him **a runner,** that is, a deserter. Glaukos' charge against Hektor, **since after all we got no gratitude,** repeats that of Achilleus against Agamemnon when he rejected the embassy (9. 316–17). His charge, **you have abandoned Sarpedon, your guest-friend,** is that Hektor has failed in his heroic duty to reciprocate the favours rendered him by a guest-friend (cf. 6. 215–25n), and it is appropriate that this should be voiced by Glaukos, who shared with Sarpedon the account of heroic honour and responsibilities (12. 310–28). Glaukos considers Patroklos' body, **dead man though he be,** the best bargaining counter for the return of Sarpedon, unaware that Zeus has had Sarpedon's body safely conveyed home to Lykia (16. 676–83). His final charge, **you could not bring yourself to stand up against Aias,** forgets that Hektor fought an honourable draw with Aias, which was only ended by nightfall (7. 279–82).

187   **which I stripped from Patroklos the strong** is at odds with the account of Apollo knocking the armour from Patroklos' body (16. 793–804) before Hektor killed him, and the boast may be seen as Hektor's attempt to defend himself against Glaukos' accusations.

192–7   **changed his armour.** Homer here looks forward to the theme of the following Book 18, the making of new armour for Achilleus by Hephaistos, and to its aftermath, when Achilleus in his new arms will confront and kill Hektor wearing his old. Achilleus' old armour is **armour immortal** because it was given by the gods to his father Peleus when he married Thetis (18. 83–5), and there is a terrible irony in the phrase and in the description of Achilleus as **a son who never grew old in his father's armour,** for the immortality of the armour points up the mortality of all who wear it—Peleus, Achilleus, Patroklos, and now Hektor.

201–3   **death stands close beside you.** Zeus declares the significance of the moment, that the death of Patroklos will lead inexorably to that of Hektor, and that the arms of Achilleus bind the two deaths together: with the arms of Achilleus, Hektor 'puts on his own death' (Whitman 1958.201).

205   **taken the armour, as you should not have done.** The victor normally strips the armour from his enemy's body; Zeus' objection is that this is inappropriate in the case of armour which had been the gift of the gods.

210–12   **The armour was fitted to Hektor's skin** indicates that he is not suited to it, that he is an inferior hero to its proper owner, Achilleus; so too Ares is needed to enhance his **force and fighting strength.**

220–32   Amongst the leaders of the Trojan allies is **Glaukos,** and Hektor's speech is a response to his accusations: by implication, he accuses the allies of holding back from battle, just as he was accused by Glaukos; and he claims that the Trojan people are having to suffer hardships so he can offer gifts to the allies, though with little by way of return, just as Glaukos accused him of not returning the efforts of Sarpedon (150–3). Hektor ignores the obligation he should feel to his allies for their ten years of effort and concentrates only on the obligation they should feel to him, for all the rewards he has given them. Glaukos proposed that Patroklos' body be exchanged for Sarpedon's, but Hektor responds with a proposal to ransom it and give **half the spoils** to the man who can secure it.

250   **drink the community's wine.** Menelaos gently, and by implication only, points to the fact that by accepting benefits from his community, each hero owes in return service to the community, very much as Sarpedon himself explained to Glaukos (cf. 12. 310–21n).

263–7   **As when at the outpouring place of a rain-glutted river.** The simile introduces a prolonged battle description, as not for the first time the Trojans are characterized by the noise they make: elsewhere this feature represents their lack of discipline and their many languages, and so their lack of unity (cf. 3. 2–9n), whereas the Achaians are pictured standing firm **in a single courage.**

268–70   Zeus sends a **deepening mist** which in part represents his sorrow at Patroklos' death, but also serves the very practical purpose of concealing the death from Achilleus (368–70); in time Aias will pray for this mist to be removed (645–7).

288–90   Hippothoös' attempt to drag off Patroklos' body by means of a shield-sling fastened around the ankle prefigures Achilleus' treatment of Hektor's body, which he drags behind his chariot by means of a thong through the ankle (22. 396–8).

300–2   The pathos of Hippothoos' death is heightened by the combination of details, of his home in **generous Larisa**, and the **care of his dear parents.**

321   **the Argives, even beyond Zeus' destiny, might have won glory,** that is, contrary to Zeus' promise, which dictates that it will be Achilleus who will save the Achaians.

327–30   **how could you be the men to defend sheer Ilion.** Apollo's rather overstated meaning is simply, how would you hope to defend Troy when a god was opposing you, if you hold back now when Zeus is on your side?

364   **far fewer of them went down.** In terms of named warriors killed, the recent battle has been even, with three dead on each side since Aias killed Hippothoös (293).

366–7   **nor would you have thought the sun was still secure.** Homer conveys the confusion of the scene more dramatically by inviting the listener to imagine himself as part of it: 'Such passages, by addressing the reader directly, place him in the middle of the action

... By thus directly addressing your reader, you will enlist his feelings more effectively, secure his attention, and make the situation completely real to him' (Longinus, *On Great Writing* 26) (Grube 1991).

378 Homer here begins the long transition to the account of Achilleus' reaction to his friend's death, for it will be **Antilochos** who will carry to him the sad news, while **Thrasymedes** will replace him in the battle.

389–93 **As when a man gives the hide of a great ox.** As so often in the poem, the everyday activity from the peaceful world lends contrast and increases the horror of an event in the battle narrative.

402–11 **Achilleus did not yet know at all that Patroklos had fallen.** There has been frequent mention of Achilleus throughout this book (75–8, 105, 121, 271, 280, 388), as well as references to his armour captured by Hektor (187, 191, 195, 199, 208, 214); the effect is to keep him continually in the listener's mind, and so to heighten the anticipation of his receiving the news of Patroklos' death. Achilleus **had no expectation that Patroklos was dead** because of the order he gave him when he sent him out to battle (16. 87–96). Achilleus did not believe Patroklos would attack Troy **without himself** because he trusted his loyalty and obedience, **nor with himself either** because he believed that he would himself die first and that Patroklos would be saved to return home to Phthia (cf. 19. 328–30). There is irony in the statement that Achilleus' mother **was ever telling him what was the will of great Zeus,** for it is the will of Zeus that has brought about the tragedy of Patroklos' death, as yet unknown to Achilleus, as the climax of his plan to honour him.

424–5 The series of no fewer than three metaphors, **iron tumult, brazen sky,** and **barren bright air,** conveys effectively the turmoil of battle.

426–40 The most important, and the most affecting, of the many allusions to the absent Achilleus is the lament of **the horses of Aiakides** for the death of Patroklos, a common theme of heroic poetry (Bowra 1952.168). The horses stand motionless as **a grave monument which is set over the mounded tomb of a dead man or lady**; it may be that this recalls the engraved headstones (*stelai*) placed over the shaft graves at Mykenai (Edwards 1991.106), but in the present context it prefigures the tomb in which Patroklos will shortly be laid. The horses weep, not just for Patroklos, but also in anticipation of Achilleus' death, which they themselves will predict (19. 408–17). **their bright manes were made dirty,** just like Achilleus' helmet when it was knocked from Patroklos' head and rolled under the feet of these same horses: the horses and the helmet were originally wedding gifts from the gods to the mortal Peleus and were inherited by his son Achilleus, and both are now associated with the death of Patroklos (cf. 16. 792–804n).

453–5   **until they win to the strong-benched vessels.** In fact this high point in Trojan fortunes has already been reached at the end of Book 15, but this is still an important restatement of the limit Zeus has placed on the Trojans and Hektor, and of Hektor's impending doom (cf. 11. 191–4n).

460–3   **yet could kill no men when he swept in in chase of them.** Automedon's repeated attacks are ineffectual and also irrational, quite unlike any other warrior's behaviour in the poem, and probably are meant to demonstrate his grief at Patroklos' death.

485–90   Hektor entertains fresh hopes of winning **the horses of swift-footed Aiakides.** In fact he fails, but the scene is important in rounding off an episode which began when Hektor hurled a spear at the retreating Automedon as he drove off the horses immediately after the death of Patroklos (16. 864): his failure to capture the horses is another indication of his inadequacy for the task of facing Achilleus in their looming encounter (cf. 210–12n).

514   **these are things that are lying upon the gods' knees** most likely refers to the practice of placing offerings, to win the favour of a god, in the lap of its (seated) statue.

546   **for now his purpose had shifted.** The Achaian defeat Zeus promised in Book 1 has taken place, Achilleus is soon to return, and Trojan defeat and Hektor's death will follow; and Homer now marks the shift in the narrative. The rest of this book is concerned with bringing about the sending of a messenger to Achilleus with news of Patroklos' death, and so Homer now describes an Achaian defeat which will be sufficient to put them in mind of Achilleus.

548–50   **As when in the sky Zeus strings for mortals the shimmering rainbow.** Zeus' rainbow is a portent of the evil of war and of winter storm: similarly the three serpents of cobalt decorating Agamemnon's corselet were like rainbows 'which the son of Kronos has marked upon the clouds, to be a portent to mortals' (11. 27–8).

570–2 The **mosquito** hardly seems a suitable comparison for a hero: the point of it is that Menelaos' urge to taste the enemy's blood allows him to overcome his inferior status.

594 For the **aegis** of Zeus, cf. 15. 308–10n.

608–24 **Idomeneus** is the son of Deukalion, the son of Minos of Krete (cf. 13. 450–2). His flight from the battle is the signal for the Achaian defeat; in his earlier appearance, he was also forced to retreat when his strength failed (cf. 13. 484–515n).

640–7 **there should be some companion who could carry the message quickly to Peleus' son.** It is significant that it is Aias who makes this declaration, for ever since Achilleus' withdrawal from battle he has been the acknowledged champion of the Achaians. He it was who made the final unsuccessful appeal to Achilleus (9. 624–42) and despaired of ever winning him back to the battle. So his realization now of their need for Achilleus reflects the Achaians' despair at Patroklos' death and their subsequent defeat. His cry to Zeus, **draw free from the mist the sons of the Achaians**, is one of acceptance of man's helplessness in face of Zeus, and of a wish to confront death head-on.

653 Homer has already established a close relationship between Menelaos and **Antilochos**: he came to Menelaos' assistance when he was faced by Aineias (5. 565–70), and Menelaos was complimentary about his prowess when encouraging him to great deeds (15. 568–71); and later there will be a scene of great chivalry between them during the Funeral Games for Patroklos (23. 566–611).

657–64 **as from a mid-fenced ground some lion.** The simile was also used to described Aias when he too was reluctantly retreating (11. 545–54), and the two occurrences seem to bracket together these two sections of the narrative. After the first occurrence, Achilleus sent Patroklos to Nestor's tent and that was the moment the disastrous chain of events began, and now this second occurrence describes the withdrawal of Menelaos, whose purpose is to bring word to Achilleus of the terrible consequence of sending his friend.

674–8 **like an eagle.** This is a fine example of a simile that takes on a life of its own, apart from the narrative: the eagle is a good point of comparison for Menelaos as he searches for Antilochos, but its final action of tearing the life from a hare is clearly unsuited to the context, and serves to complete the story of the simile, not the narrative.

685–99   **Antilochos** is a young and outstanding warrior, fast on his feet (cf. 15. 569–70) and a close friend of Achilleus, well qualified for the thankless task of carrying the news to him. Throughout these later books of the poem Homer seems intent on keeping his relationship with Achilleus to the fore. There was a tradition that, after Patroklos' death, Antilochos took on his role of Achilleus' companion and suffered the same fate, so it is appropriate that it should be he who is chosen to bring Achilleus news of the death.

711   Menelaos has already spoken of the loss of Achilleus' armour (693), and now he declares that Achilleus cannot **fight bare of armour against the Trojans**: this marks the transition to the theme of the next book, the forging of new armour for Achilleus.

720   **we, who have the same name, the same spirit.** For the Aiantes, cf. 13. 701–18n.

722–59   The book ends with a vivid cluster of similes, which is matched only by the series used to introduce the Catalogue of the Ships (2. 455–83). Each of the similes highlights a different aspect of the Achaians' withdrawal with Patroklos' body and of the Trojans' pursuit of them: the Trojans are like dogs rushing against a wounded boar; the fight itself is like a fire roaring through a city, an image which prefigures the final outcome for Troy itself; the Achaians are like mules determinedly dragging timber from the high ground to make a beam or a ship's timber, an image which anticipates the mules which drag wood from the mountains for the funeral pyre of Patroklos (23. 120–2); the Aiantes are like a rocky ridge holding back flood water; and the noise of the retreating Achaians is like the terror of daws or starlings at the approach of a hawk. The series marks the climax of a book which has set the scene for the return of Achilleus, and of a day of battle which began long ago in Book 11.

760   **Many fine pieces of armour littered the ground.** The book ends, appropriately, with the image which has dominated it, the loss of armour.

ILIAD 18

In antiquity this book was given the title Hoplopoiïa, *The Making of Arms, referring to lines 468–616 where Homer describes the forging by Hephaistos of new armour for Achilleus, and in particular his decoration of the great shield. In its descriptive detail this is a passage quite without parallel in the poem: its closest relative is the description of Alkinoös' palace and garden in Scherie, the land of the Phaiakians* (Odyssey 7. 81–132). *The importance of the Shield to the poem as a whole is indicated both by the space given over to its description and by the immense care with which the poet has built it into the narrative: it may well be that the theme of Patroklos donning Achilleus' armour in Book 16 was designed, in part at least, to deprive Achilleus of his old armour and so introduce the need for new. Important recent work in English on the illustrations on the Shield of Achilleus and their relation to the remainder of the poem includes Shannon 1975; Andersen 1976; Atchity 1978; Taplin 1980; Edwards 1991; Byre 1992; Hubbard 1992; Stanley 1993; Becker 1995. Yet the importance of this book goes beyond the description of the Shield, for it also marks a momentous shift in the development of the narrative. The quarrel in Book 1 and the subsequent anger of Achilleus, which have resulted in the death of Patroklos, are now relegated to the background: where previously Achilleus acted out of heroic pride and a sense of outrage at the injury done to his personal honour, now he is driven by a single-minded quest for vengeance on the killer of his loved one. This is accompanied by a second, equally important, shift: the presence of his mother Thetis continually points to Achilleus' own approaching death which, she declares, will rapidly follow that of Hektor. Achilleus accepts his death as a necessary price for his vengeance upon Hektor: the man who told the ambassadors that all of Agamemnon's gifts were not worth the risk to his own life (9. 400–9) now readily embraces his own death in return for avenging Patroklos.*

3–4   Achilleus' position, **sitting in front of the steep-horned ships,** reveals his anxiety; in contrast, when the ambassadors came to visit him, he was taking his ease and singing unconcernedly (9. 186). Even before Achilleus voices his apprehension, Homer suggests that he is already contemplating the unthinkable and has a premonition **of things which had now been accomplished.**

8–14   **in the way my mother once made it clear to me.** This is the only mention of this prophecy from Achilleus' mother, but it reveals his state of mind: earlier he had no thought that Patroklos might be dead, because it never occurred to him that he would defy his orders and attack Troy without him (17. 406–7), but now begins his gradual realization of his mistake in allowing Patroklos to enter the battle in his place. So at the very outset Achilleus rehearses the dominant motif of the scene, his sense of his own responsibility in sending his friend to his death.

18–21   Antilochos' announcement of Patroklos' death contrasts with the long and detailed preparations for it: two lines apologizing for the news he brings, two lines reporting the death, the fight over the body, the loss of the armour. The curtness of his message expresses Antilochos' own grief, his fear of and for Achilleus, his anxiety about the fate of them all.

22–7   **the black cloud of sorrow closed on Achilleus.** Achilleus' demonstration of his grief follows a standard pattern: the showering of dust over the head and body, and the tearing of the hair, find many parallels in both literature and art. However the final part of the description, **he himself, mightily in his might, in the dust lay at length** suggests not just grief, but death itself: the formula was used of the dead Kebriones (16. 776n), and it is used also of the dead Achilleus (*Odyssey* 24. 40). Its meaning is of a hero's corpse measuring its length on the ground, and although it is an entirely fitting description of the mighty Achilleus stretched out in the dust and dirt, its association with death suggests that his posture is an indication of his own impending death.

36   Thetis' aged father is **Nereus** (cf. 1. 358n).

38–49   **all who along the depth of the sea were daughters of Nereus.** This catalogue of Nereids—no fewer than thirty-three named, and fifty in total—is similar, though not identical, to the catalogue of Nereus' daughters given by Hesiod (*Theogony* 243–62). Macleod (1982.110) suggests that the length of the list may lend "a feel of history" to it, or it may be that the sheer scale of the numbers is designed to add to the pathos of the scene. The Nereids attend upon Thetis as part of Achilleus' burial (*Odyssey* 24. 47).

52–64   Thetis' lament clearly indicates that the mourning for Patroklos is intended to anticipate Achilleus' death, for not only does she not name Patroklos, but she laments exclusively for her son and for herself. **the bitterness in this best of child-bearing** translates an extraordinary compound word *dusaristotokeia*, conveying a three-fold meaning: that he is best of the Achaians, that she bore him as a mortal, and that the bitterness (for her) of his death is approaching. **he shot up like a young tree** recalls the many young men destroyed by the war, such as Simoeisios, compared in death to a poplar tree felled to make a chariot wheel (cf. 4. 473–89n). Her lament that she will never receive him back **into the house of Peleus** suggests a homely idyll in which she and Peleus live together and raise their son, in contrast to the tradition that she left Peleus after their wedding night and henceforth lived beneath the waves—where indeed she is at present (36).

71   **took her son's head in her arms.** Thetis' gesture will be echoed in the description of Achilleus cradling Patroklos' head (23. 136), and Andromache cradling Hektor's (24. 724): it is the intimate gesture of the principal mourner at a funeral (Alexiou 1974.6). So both by her words and by her actions Thetis makes clear the significance of Patroklos' death: like Hektor (6. 500), Achilleus is mourned while he is still alive.

72–7   **Why then, child, do you lament.** Thetis' speech recalls her first meeting with Achilleus (72–4 = 1. 361–3), and signals that the present scene is the culmination of the request he put to her then. So there is great irony in Thetis thus reminding him of their first meeting, but there is palpable tragedy too, for Achilleus went much further than Thetis' account, that the Achaians should **suffer things that are shameful**; rather his request was for Achaian deaths to teach them and their king a lesson (1. 409–10). Deaths aplenty he has had, but his request has brought the death of Patroklos too, and that is the essence of what his mother is now telling him, that he has brought about his friend's death.

82–5   Achilleus' cry **I have lost him** (*apolesa*) may equally well be translated 'I have destroyed him', and it is reasonable to suppose that both Achilleus and Thetis, and Homer's audience, would hear both meanings. Achilleus associates his companion's death with the loss of his **gigantic armour**, and so acknowledges the significance of that armour, that it is a symbol of mortality, that death comes to all who wear it; and so he recalls that it was originally a gift to his mortal father Peleus **on that day they drove you to the marriage bed of a mortal.**

96–100   **your death must come soon after Hektor's.** Thetis grants Achilleus insight into his own fate, that only if he declines to exact revenge on Hektor will he extend his own life: and so at last he confronts the meaning of the choice he told the ambassadors his mother had offered him, a brief life of glory at Troy or a long life of anonymity at home (9. 410–16). He willingly accepts his own death: **I must die soon, then; since I was not to stand by my companion,** and his words recall two similes in the previous book, when Menelaos (17. 4–5n) and then Aias (17. 133–6n) stood protectively over the corpse of Patroklos; now Achilleus speaks of Patroklos' dependence, and his own absence in his moment of need.

112–13   **we will let all this be a thing of the past** contains the terrible irony that Achilleus said just the same thing when he agreed to let Patroklos return to the battle (16. 60): had he really let bygones be bygones then, he would not now be facing his present tragedy. Achilleus does not renounce his anger against Agamemnon so much as relegate it: when he says he will **beat down by force the anger deeply within us,** he does not present a forgiving or even conciliatory attitude, but rather a willingness to bow to circumstances and to relegate his anger in face of the more important task of killing Hektor.

117   **Herakles** died when he put on a cloak given to him by his wife Deianeira: believing that the blood of the Centaur Nessus could be used to win back her husband's love, she soaked the cloak in it, but in the event the blood was a poison which killed Herakles.

123–4   The **Dardanian woman, lifting up to her soft cheeks both hands** inevitably calls to mind the grieving widow of Hektor, Andromache, whose lament (22. 477–514) stands for the lament of all the women of Troy, just as Hektor's death stands for the destruction of Troy itself.

135–7   **not before with your own eyes you see me come back to you.** Thetis knows that her son is going to his death, but she seeks only to delay him long enough for her to bring new armour from

Hephaistos: just as she visited Olympos in Book 1 to put the request that has resulted in Patroklos' death, so now she makes her way there to bring the armour which will herald the final act of Achilleus' tragedy.

155–60   This description of the battle stretched evenly over Patroklos' body clearly differs from the previous book's scene of Menelaos and Meriones carrying the body back to the Achaian ships (17. 735–6).

177   For **to cut the head from the soft neck,** cf. 17. 126n.

193   For the **great shield of Telamonian Aias,** cf. 7. 219–23n. If Achilleus were to take it he would take on Aias' defensive role, and so it is quite unsuitable for his task ahead.

204   **the fluttering aegis** is Achilleus' temporary defence, but it is also an item of offence: Apollo led the Trojan advance bearing it in his hands to bring terror to mortals (15. 308–10n), and earlier it was described as betasselled and terrible and garlanded with the figures of Terror, Hatred, Battle Strength, Onslaught and the Gorgon's head, 'a thing of fear and horror' (5. 734–47n). So by her action Athene is enhancing Achilleus' terrifying aspect.

207–13   **As when a flare goes up into the high air from a city.** The besieged city in the simile is on an island and this illustrates the isolation of the Achaians for whom Achilleus is now a beacon of hope. The light recalls Achilleus' self-recrimination that he 'was no light of safety' to Patroklos or his other companions (18. 102–3).

219–20   **As loud as comes the voice that is screamed out by a trumpet.** This simile is closely associated with the previous one, in which the besieged people represent the Achaians, a role in which they have been cast since they built their defensive wall around the ships in Book 7. But in this second simile the Achaians have become the besiegers, and from this point it is the Trojans who are once more associated with defensive walls. The imagery of the two similes marks out the transformation brought by Achilleus' appearance, what Whitman (1958.137) calls the *peripeteia* of the poem's narrative.

222   The metaphor of **the brazen voice of Aiakides** enhances the force of the previous simile by continuing the image of the trumpet.

239–41   Hera forces the **unwilling weariless sun god to sink in the depth of the Ocean,** and so brings an end to this day of catastrophe for the Achaians. Zeus promised Hektor 'power... to kill men' during this day, but only 'until the sun goes down and the blessed darkness comes over' (11. 192–4). The sun will next rise on the day of Hektor's death.

249 It is a measure of Homer's artistry that he prepared for the debate between Hektor and **the careful Poulydamas** as long ago as Book 12, where he presented Poulydamas as a kind of *alter ego* of Hektor, as the voice of sense and sanity cautioning against the excesses of his headstrong nature (12. 50–80n), and in particular he showed the danger of ignoring Poulydamas' advice (12. 110–17n).

254–6 **I myself urge you to go back into the city.** Poulydamas' earlier advice was that the Trojans should not attack the Achaian wall (12. 216–22), and it was rejected by Hektor; now he goes much further by urging that they forego all their successes of the day and barricade themselves once more inside their own wall. Again Hektor rejects it, and as a result he will stand alone outside Troy's wall to await his death, and when he does so, he will recall Poulydamas' words now (22. 100–3).

290–6 **the lovely treasures that lay away in our houses have vanished.** Hektor earlier claimed that he was taking from his own people in order to maintain his allies at Troy (17. 225–6). **Not one of the Trojans will obey you. I shall not allow it**: Hektor claims absolute power over the Trojans and he demands to exercise that power, not to protect his people as Poulydamas urged, but to gain his own personal glory, since **the son of devious-devising Kronos has given me the winning of glory by the ships.** It is significant that Hektor's reassertion of the heroic ethos should follow so soon after Achilleus' declaration of the communal ethos, of his responsibility both to his loved one, Patroklos, and to his people (102–3).

317 **manslaughtering hands** is a formula particularly associated with Hektor (cf. 1. 242; 6. 498; 9. 351), and its ironic transfer to Achilleus as he mourns his companion killed by Hektor prefigures Hektor's own impending death at his hands. The formula is also transferred to Achilleus when Priam kisses these same manslaughtering hands (24. 478–9).

318–22 **As some great bearded lion.** Patroklos is like the lion cubs stolen by a deer hunter (Hektor), and Achilleus is like the lion which returns to find them gone: the simile suggests Patroklos' vulnerability, and the return of the lion **too late** reiterates Achilleus' failure to protect him; like the lion's, Achilleus' anguish is transformed into bitter anger against Hektor.

334–7   till I bring to this place the armour and the head of Hektor. The violence of Achilleus' threat is a measure of his sense of his own responsibility for Patroklos' death, and it echoes Hektor's own intention to behead Patroklos (17. 126n). Achilleus carries out his threat to kill the Trojan children at 23. 175, in a unique act of human sacrifice.

356–67   The following scene, a disagreement between Zeus and Hera, matches their quarrel in Book 1, but is a reversal of it: then, Hera complained about Zeus' continual secret plotting and he declared his right to act as he saw fit (1. 540–50); now, Zeus complains of her scheming to bring Achilleus back into the battle and she declares her right to continue her persecution of the Trojans. Zeus makes no attempt to reverse Hera's actions, and this is a clear indication that his plan for Trojan success begun in Book 1 is now at an end, and that the doom of Hektor and the Trojans is sealed.

369–467   The visit of Thetis to **Hephaistos** and his wife is a scene of great charm, of hospitality and civilized behaviour. In order to achieve this, Homer names Hephaistos' wife as **Charis** (Grace), rather than following the tradition of his marriage to Aphrodite, which was a rather less happy union, as demonstrated by her adultery with the war-god Ares (*Odyssey* 8. 267–366). Hephaistos is called **the god of the dragging footsteps** because of his shrunken legs (411).

395–405   when I suffered much at the time of my great fall. Hephaistos' story of his ejection from heaven by his mother Hera is very similar to the one he told at 1. 590–4, although then it was his father Zeus who threw him out. The story of his rescue by Thetis is designed to provide a reason for his now assisting her. **the stream of Ocean** was envisaged as surrounding the world; likewise Hephaistos fashions it round the edge of the shield he makes for Achilleus (606–7).

418   golden, and in appearance like living young women. Hephaistos' golden attendants are neither human nor divine, but are his magical creations of the same order as the automatic tripods he was working on when Thetis arrived (373–7).

432–41   Of all the other sisters of the sea he gave me to a mortal recalls the myth, which is not told in the *Iliad*, that Thetis was forced by Zeus to marry the mortal Peleus because of a prophecy that she would produce a son who would be greater than his father (cf. 1. 352n). The sight of her husband **broken by mournful old age** serves to emphasize her own immortality, and in turn the mortality of Achilleus.

464　**I wish that I could hide him away from death and its sorrow.** In assuring Thetis that he will make new armour, Hephaistos is declaring his sympathy for her and for Achilleus, but the effect of his words is to stress the inevitability of Achilleus' death and of his helplessness to do anything about it.

474–82　For the new armour for Achilleus Hephaistos uses bronze and tin, gold and silver, and this marks the great shield as a work of literary imagination, rather than a description of a real object. The description has been shown to mirror many aspects of the poem's narrative, and commentators have often remarked on the easy transition from description of the scenes displayed on it, immobile as works of art, to the narrative development of those scenes, suddenly full of life and movement. The Shield of Achilleus is made up of **five folds** (*ptuches*). It is best seen as round, though it is not actually described as such, with the five folds arranged concentrically and the description of the decorations working from the centre to the rim. The five sections represent: (i) at the centre, the constellations (483–9); (ii) two cities, one at peace, the other at war (490–540); (iii) the countryside (541–89); (iv) the dance (590–605); (v) on the outer rim, the Ocean River (606–7). The first and last of these pictures bracket the main body of the description: on the inside the universe, and on the outside man's physical boundary, the Ocean, and between them, in carefully balanced counterpoise, a summation of human life—the city (fifty-one lines) and the countryside (forty-nine lines). Whitman (1958.205) has called it 'a summary picture of the world', and Edwards (1991.209) speaks of 'the irony of the doomed hero of the past who bears into battle the depiction of the continuing life of ordinary human folk'. But it presents only a limited summation of life, for there is no mention of rituals for the gods, or of trades, or even of such important features of Greek life as the sea and shipping (Taplin 1980.12).

483–9　The presence of **the constellations that festoon the heavens** at the centre of the shield is in keeping with much of the peaceful content of the remainder, for they announce the beginning and end of the farming year; but **the strength of Orion** has significance within the poem for, when Priam sees Achilleus carrying this very shield in his hand charging to attack his son Hektor, he pictures him as

> . . . Orion's Dog, which is brightest
> among the stars, and yet is wrought as a sign of evil
> and brings on the great fever for unfortunate mortals.
>   (22. 29–31)

490–540 On the first of the three inner sections of the shield, the second 'fold' that is, **two cities of mortal men** are depicted, a City at Peace (490–508), and a City at War (509–40). There is no indication of how the two are arranged, either in their geography or in the organization of the shield, but their descriptions are clearly intended to contrast with each other.

491–6 The first of two scenes in the City at Peace is one of **marriages** and **festivals**, a scene of both family and community in harmony. The contrast with the narrative of the *Iliad* seems clear: the Trojan War was caused by the betrayal of marital harmony, the adultery of Helen and Paris, and the war is being fought against a backcloth of the marital harmony of Hektor and Andromache described in Book 6, a harmony which Achilleus will destroy when he confronts Hektor in Book 22 carrying this very shield. So the scene represents the harmony and stability of peace which Troy enjoyed before the Achaians came; but home and marital harmony, and the enjoyment of the city at peace, are also precisely what Achilleus has given up in exchange for heroic glory, and for vengeance upon Hektor (cf. 9. 393–400).

497–508 The second scene in the City at Peace is a scene **in the market place, where a quarrel had arisen,** which has long provoked debate about what precisely is happening (Westbrook 1992.53). Some believe that the quarrel is about whether a blood price (*poine*) has been paid for a murder: the murderer says he has paid it, the relative of the victim claims he has received nothing. A more likely reading of the passage, in line with Lattimore's translation, is that the murderer is claiming the right to pay the blood price, rather than pay with his own life, but that the relative of the victim refuses to accept it, and presumably demands blood in return. The Greek will allow both readings, but in neither case is there any dispute over the fact of the murder, or the murderer's guilt. The quarrel reflects closely the poem's events: the man who refuses to follow his society's convention (cf. 9. 632–6) of accepting the blood price for a dead relative recalls Achilleus' rejection of the embassy, when Agamemnon offered compensation to buy him off but he refused to accept anything (cf. 9. 379); and earlier (335–7) Achilleus promised Patroklos' body, not the blood price, but the head of Hektor and twelve Trojan youths (cf. 22. 349–54). The lawsuit on the shield recapitulates both Achilleus' rejection of the embassy and his recently declared vendetta against Hektor.

509–40   The representation of the City at War balances that of the City at Peace and is contained within the same section of the shield; it too presents two scenes, a siege (509–19), and an ambush (520–40).

509–19   In this first scene in the City at War there are two besieging forces, though they may well be two halves of the same army, and there is a difference of view between going for all-out victory or negotiating a settlement and accepting just part of the city's spoils. This reflects the poem's narrative, for earlier Antenor proposed a settlement of the war, that Helen be returned to the Achaians, but Paris refused (7. 345–64); and in time Hektor contemplates parleying with Achilleus and offering to share Troy's possessions (22. 114–21). The picture of **beloved wives and their children** and **with them the men with age upon them** recalls Priam and the Trojan elders on the tower of the Skaian gates (3. 146–53), and prefigures Priam and Hekabe on the walls of Troy pleading with Hektor to come inside before it is too late (22. 25–89).

520–40   The second scene in the City at War is one in which the besieged leave their city to ambush the sheep and cattle of their besiegers. A parallel is pointed with the Trojans' success in Book 8, for as part of the preparations for spending the night on the plain Hektor ordered that oxen and sheep be brought with all speed out of the city (8. 505–6). On the shield the besieged are able to come out of their city to steal the cattle of their attackers: in the main narrative the besieged Trojans were able to leave Troy, bring their cattle with them and besiege the Achaians by their ships. So the scenes of the City at War recapitulate the Trojan victory which resulted in the embassy to Achilleus, just as the scenes of the City at Peace recall the rejection of that embassy. The image of the dead man dragged **by the feet through the carnage** recalls the battle over the body of Patroklos in the previous book and in the earlier part of this, and it prefigures the dragging of Hektor by the feet behind the chariot of Achilleus.

541–72   The second of the three inner sections of the shield, the third 'fold', is made up of scenes depicting the countryside through the four seasons—Spring (541–9), Summer (550–60), Autumn (561–72), and Winter (573–89). The images are of the Countryside at Peace, the counterpart of the City at Peace; they represent a world of harmony and joyful co-operation, and the prosperity of this countryside provides a pathetic insight into the world of Troy as it was before the war came.

541–9   Spring is represented by ploughing, and the **many ploughmen upon it** perhaps suggests the harmony of a communal ploughing to prepare the common land; this picture of mutual help is then enhanced by the figure bringing wine to refresh the ploughmen.

550–60   The summer scene is reaping the crops of **the precinct of a king**, with children lending a hand and a feast being prepared for the labourers. The precinct is the *temenos*, the best piece of land which is set aside by the people for the king in return for his leadership. In his memorable speech on the hero's responsibilities, Sarpedon spoke of the *temenos* as one of the benefits he enjoyed because of his status (12. 313–14); so Hephaistos is picturing on the Shield of Achilleus one of the prizes of heroism he has so recently rejected. It is not clear how the workmen eat the **abundant white barley**: it may have been made into a kind of porridge, or perhaps scattered on meat (cf. *Odyssey* 14. 77); barley is scattered over the victim just before it is sacrificed (1. 458), and when Hekamede prepares a potion for Nestor and Patroklos containing wine and grated goat's milk cheese, she scatters white barley into it (11. 639).

561–72   Autumn is represented by harvesting in **a great vineyard heavy with clusters,** by young girls and young men who dance and sing to the accompaniment of a lyre-player; the joy and innocence of the young people and the idyllic scene recall a recurring theme in the poem, of young men barely in their prime destroyed by the war (cf. 4. 473–89n), and they prefigure the young men killed by Achilleus in the coming books, including Lykaon whom he once took prisoner in a similar pastoral setting as he 'was cutting young branches from a fig tree' (21. 37–8). Various accounts of the death of **Linos** survive: one said that he was a son of Apollo who was ripped to death by dogs near Argos, another that he taught both Orpheus and Herakles, and was struck and killed with a lyre by Herakles, and a third that he was killed by Apollo for claiming to rival him in song. He was a god of vegetation, whose death represented the dying season, and so **the beautiful song for Linos** was sung at the time of harvesting. So the actions of the young reapers represent the death of the god and, amidst a scene of celebration of life and happiness, again evoke a picture of the death of youth.

573–89 Winter is represented by the movement of cattle from farmyard to pasture, but two lions attack and disrupt the peaceful scene. The scene finds a close parallel in an earlier simile (17. 61–7) describing Menelaos' attack.

590–605 The final inner scene on the shield is the dance, a scene which echoes the marriage occasion earlier (494–6). Taplin (1980.9) has suggested that the emphasis on the fine clothes of the dancers is designed to recall the prosperity of Troy before the war's destruction. **Daidalos** was the great craftsman of Minoan Crete: he devised a structure which allowed Pasiphaë, wife of king Minos, to indulge her infatuation for the bull which Poseidon had given to Minos; he built the labyrinth at Knossos to house the offspring of that infatuation, the Minotaur; he devised the thread given by **Ariadne** to Theseus, which allowed the hero to retrace his route out of the labyrinth after he killed the Minotaur; he devised the dancing area for Ariadne, the daughter of Minos; and he invented the wings on which he and his son Ikaros tried to flee from Minos, only to see his son fly too close to the sun and drown in the Ikarian sea, when the wax of the wings was melted by the heat. The dancing young men and girls on the shield recall the tradition that, after Theseus had killed the Minotaur, he and Ariadne performed a dance in imitation of the winding route he had taken through the labyrinth. Joining in this dance were the seven boys and seven girls from Athens whom Theseus had rescued from death at the hands of the Minotaur. So, like others on the Shield, this picture of youthful beauty and joyful expression recalls a story of young people cruelly destroyed.

606–7 The **Ocean** was conceived as a river which encircled the land, and so it forms a natural boundary on the rim of the shield too.

ILIAD 19

The theme of this book is Achilleus' transfer of his anger from Agamemnon to Hektor: first, he formally renounces his anger in front of a full assembly of the Achaians, and this is followed by a description of his arming to face Hektor, though their battle does not take place until Book 22. So in antiquity the book was given the title Renunciation of the Wrath (menidos aporresis). However, Achilleus declares that it is only 'by constraint' that he swallows his anger with Agamemnon (66), and so it may fairly be asked whether he is truly reconciled in this book, or in any subsequent book, to his enemy; it is certainly the case that he foregoes his anger in order to hasten his revenge on Hektor, but there are indications that he never forgets it. From this point Achilleus assumes the dominant role in the Achaian army, Agamemnon fades into the background, and it is Achilleus who exercises authority over his fellow leaders.

1 **Dawn the yellow-robed arose from the river of Ocean** provides a transition from the previous scene, for the Ocean River was the final fold on the Shield of Achilleus (18. 606–7n). This marks an important new day, during which Achilleus will receive his new armour and return to the battle to kill Hektor.

4 Achilleus' position, **lying in the arms of Patroklos**, recalls Thetis' visit to him, when she took his head in her hands (18. 71n).

17 **his eyes glittered terribly under his lids, like sunflare** is the first of numerous fire images which will be associated with Achilleus through this and the following books (Whitman 1958.137), and recalls the flame kindled around his head by Athene which marked his reappearance at the Achaians' defensive ditch (18. 206).

23–33 **Yet I am sadly afraid.** Swift disposal of the corpse is important in the climate of the Mediterranean region but Patroklos' burial is to be postponed, and Thetis' undertaking to preserve it is the first indication of a recurring theme, that nothing must be allowed to stand in the way of Achilleus' pursuit of vengeance.

35   Thetis commands Achilleus to **unsay your anger against Agamemnon** before an assembly of the Achaians, because it was before the assembly that he made his original declaration. Thetis calls his anger *menis*, the very first word of the poem: the story of the anger has reached its turning point, and this is indicated by this echo of the poem's beginning.

40–6   **he, brilliant Achilleus, walked along by the sea-shore** echoes the beginning of his anger, when he was also pictured on the sea-shore after the loss of his other loved one, Briseis (1. 350n). The significance of this occasion in redirecting the wrath of Achilleus is shown by the presence of even **helmsmen** and **stewards**.

47–53   **there were two who came limping**: Diomedes, **Tydeus' son**, was wounded in the foot (11. 377) and Odysseus in the ribs (11. 437); Agamemnon is also still suffering from his wound, to the lower arm (11. 252). That it is Achilleus who summons this assembly is an important detail, since its purpose is to repair the damage caused by the assembly in Book 1, which he also summoned (1. 54). Odysseus and Diomedes are the leaders Agamemnon insulted during the *Epipolesis* (4. 338–400), as he had insulted Achilleus during the quarrel, so it is significant that they, as well as Achilleus, are now witnesses as the tables are turned on Agamemnon and he is forced to acknowledge his error.

56–64   **was this after all the better way for both, for you and me.** Achilleus' question is heavily ironical, allowing him to accept some blame without in any way excusing Agamemnon, and his wish that Briseis had been killed rather than taken prisoner is an expression of his grief and anger, a forlorn wish that events had been different. His acceptance of blame is no more than regret for the consequences of his anger: at no point does he say, or even imply, that his anger was unjustified, and his tone is one of recrimination that, had Agamemnon not provoked the anger, many men would still be alive.

65–8   **Still, we will let all this be a thing of the past.** It is by an act of will, **by constraint** (*anagke*), that Achilleus swallows his anger, just as he earlier told his mother (18. 112–13n): the constraint is the need to pursue vengeance and this overrides all other considerations, though even as he speaks he feels the anger surge once more. There is no acceptance of Agamemnon's standpoint, nor is there reconciliation, rather there is a declaration that Hektor is now a far more pressing object of his anger: his anger with Agamemnon stands in the way of his vengeance and so, for this reason only, he abandons it. In a mere line and a half, **Now I am making an end of my anger. It does not become me unrelentingly to rage on,** Achilleus renounces the anger which has dictated his actions in the previous eighteen books.

76–82 Agamemnon speaks **from the place where he was sitting,** perhaps to draw attention to his wound or perhaps out of embarrassment at the support shown for Achilleus' words. Unlike Achilleus', his speech is rambling and confused, particularly his desperate appeal for a quiet hearing which serves to illustrate how much he has been unnerved by the army's response to Achilleus.

86–94 **yet I am not responsible but Zeus is, and Destiny, and Erinys the mist-walking.** For Erinys the avenging deity, cf. 3. 278–80n; she is 'mist-walking' because she comes upon mortals unseen and unexpectedly. Agamemnon's defence is that he was overcome by *ate*, delusion (cf. 1. 412n): the word appears here three times, as also at 126–8 and 136–7. By showing that *ate*, like Erinys, descends on mortals unseen, he tries to shift some blame from himself.

95–133 By telling at length how **Hera who is female deluded even Zeus,** Agamemnon seeks to show that he too was helpless in the face of *ate*. The thrust of the tale is that because of Zeus' *ate* the greatest of heroes **Herakles** was forced to serve **Eurystheus,** the king of Mykenai, even though he was his superior as a warrior, by performing the Labours he set him. For **Alkmene,** mother of Herakles, cf. 14. 317–28n. **Perseus** was the ancestor of the kings of Mykenai before the family of Atreus ruled there. In fact Homer mentions only one of the twelve labours of Herakles in the *Iliad*, bringing from Hades the three-headed dog Kerberos (8. 367–69).

137–44 **But since I was deluded and Zeus took my wits away from me** echoes Agamemnon's reply to Nestor in the scene which introduced the embassy (9. 119–20), and his aim remains, as before, to justify his action during the quarrel. He continues to press his wish **to give you all those gifts,** even though Achilleus vigorously rejected them in Book 9, and in doing so he continues to assert his authority (cf. 9. 120–1n). So in many respects he is repeating his earlier speech: he offers no apology, attempts to shift the blame onto Zeus, and again assumes that Achilleus, like every man, has his price, though he does not repeat his demand that Achilleus acknowledge his inferiority (9.160–1).

147–8   the gifts are yours to give if you wish, and as it is proper, or to keep with yourself. The curtness of Achilleus' answer to Agamemnon's offer of gifts contrasts with his lengthy reply to Odysseus when he reported the offer in Book 9: then he responded with angry rejection of the gifts, now with complete indifference, and both reactions show his refusal to acknowledge Agamemnon's superiority and his declaration of his own.

154–83   Odysseus plays an important role in this assembly because it covers the same issue as the embassy in Book 9 in which he also had a significant role. He has two functions in this scene: to urge Achilleus to be restrained while the army are fed and refreshed (155–72), and to urge Agamemnon to accept responsibility and appease Achilleus (172–83).

155–72   Do not drive the sons of the Achaians on Ilion when they are hungry. Odysseus' repeated demand that the army should fight on a full stomach has upset many readers and was responsible for his reputation in antiquity for gluttony (Stanford 1954.69). Willcock's comment that it shows him as 'the practical, experienced soldier in contrast to Achilleus' heroic idealism' (1976.218) is more to the point.

175–7   swear an oath to you that he never entered into her bed. In part this is designed to ease Achilleus' jealousy, but the fact that Agamemnon is able to swear this oath (261–3) shows that Briseis was not taken for any sexual purpose but as a symbol of the authority the two were disputing: so her return intact signifies Agamemnon's acknowledgment of defeat.

179–80   let him appease you with a generous meal maintains Odysseus' preoccupation with food, but it also reflects the significance of the feast at the heart of heroic society (cf. 12. 310–21n). When Odysseus urges Achilleus to sit in Agamemnon's shelter and eat with him, he represents the Achaians' wish for his return to the heroic fold. Achilleus' steadfast refusal to touch food or drink until Hektor is dead represents his continued position at the margins of his society, and his indifference to Agamemnon's gifts and his refusal to feast show that he is unwilling to respect the requirements of heroic reciprocity.

181–2   son of Atreus, after this be more righteous to another man. Odysseus' demand and his condemnation of Agamemnon's past attitude, particularly during the quarrel, should be heard against the background of Agamemnon's instruction that Odysseus demand Achilleus' subservience during the embassy, a demand Odysseus tactfully omitted (9. 300–6n).

185–98   Agamemnon's reply to Odysseus is placatory, though **I give you this errand, this order** recalls his arrogance of old, and his references to Achilleus seem almost to ignore his presence. For **cut our oaths of fidelity**, cf. 2. 124n. **bring the women back also:** for the role of women in the gifts offered by Agamemnon, cf. 9. 122–56n.

208–12   when we have paid off our defilement means when they have taken vengeance on Hektor; the defilement is that done to the body of Patroklos in death. Although he maintains his own position, **neither drink nor food shall go down my very throat**, Achilleus has changed his stance and when Odysseus again repeats the need to feed the army (225–31) he does not disagree. **turned against the forecourt** means with his feet pointing towards the door, that is, in preparation for burial.

219   since I was born before you and have learned more things is subtle characterization, for Agamemnon too claimed that he was older than Achilleus (9. 160–1) and, as a result, entitled to obedience; Odysseus on the other hand points out that it is wisdom that comes with age, and so points a lesson to the listening Agamemnon.

222–3   when the bronze scatters on the ground the straw in most numbers. The metaphor of the harvest continues Odysseus' message of the need to provide proper provisions if the army is to give of its best: the bronze refers to both the sickle and the sword, and the straw which is cut refers also to the soldiers killed; and the thin harvest refers to the scant rewards which the surviving soldiers reap for their efforts (Moulton 1979.286).

243–56   Just as he had his way in the matter of the army's meal, so too Odysseus prevails in the matter of the gifts. He sees the need, from the standpoint of heroic society, to observe all the proprieties, and so it is stressed that all the gifts Agamemnon had promised are brought from his shelter; the gifts are brought **into the midst of assembly** for all must see that reparation is given to Achilleus because all witnessed the insult he suffered; and Agamemnon's oath is accompanied by the sacrifice of a boar which, along with all the Achaians' ills, is then cast into the sea.

258–65 Let Zeus first be my witness: 'Zeus is supreme; Helios sees and hears everything (3. 277); Earth is mother of all and in physical contact with all mankind; and the Erinues act against those who break an oath' (Edwards 1991.265). Agamemnon's speech here is his last speaking role in the poem.

270–4 Father Zeus, great are the delusions with which you visit men. The theme of the quarrel is now wound up and this is Achilleus' epilogue to it. He accepts the role of Zeus and *ate* in what has occurred, though he does not claim to understand it and can only assume that 'somehow' Zeus wanted the death of many Achaians; but of course it was in response to his own request that Zeus has dealt so many deaths to the Achaians (1. 409–10). **and be in helplessness** translates *amechanos*, but 'be stubborn' gives better sense: Achilleus' final words on the subject of the quarrel and its consequences are neither words of forgiveness nor reconciliation, but of regret.

282–300 Despite the importance of **Briseis** to the story, her speech here is her first in the poem and her emotions have for the most part been concealed by the poet: this silence accentuates the pathos of her speech now, for she reveals that she has been much more than a captured object, and that it was the man whose body she now embraces who ensured that she was. Her lament contains some of the features of Andromache's plea to Hektor in Book 6, which was itself as much a lament as a parting. Briseis recalls that her husband and her three brothers were killed by Achilleus, and this was during the same expedition on which he killed Andromache's father and seven brothers (6. 414–24). **said you would make me godlike Achilleus' wedded lawful wife:** Patroklos' death has robbed Briseis of that marriage, just as Andromache laments Hektor's death will rob her; and her account of her former husband's death increases the pathos of this second widowhood.

313 The striking metaphor of **the jaws of the bleeding battle** conjures a picture of a wild beast fresh from the slaughter. It is used to good effect by Virgil (*Aeneid* 1. 296) to represent the frenzied beast of Civil War.

316   when you yourself would set the desirable dinner before me is in part a description of Patroklos' role as Achilleus' henchman and helps to establish the origins of their intimacy, their military service together under canvas; but it should also to be viewed against the background of Achilleus' refusal, just repeated (305–8), to take food or drink.

322–4   not even if I were to hear of the death of my father. Just as he has failed to protect Patroklos, so too by reason of his early death Achilleus will fail to protect his father. This theme will be taken up again at the poem's climax when, in response to Priam's appeal to him in the name of his father, he will weep 'now for his own father, now again for Patroklos' (24. 511–12). **for bereavement of such a son, for me** draws the explicit connection betweeen Patroklos' death and the imminent death of Achilleus himself (cf. 18. 22–7n).

326–7   godlike Neoptolemos appears nowhere else in the *Iliad*, except possibly for a passing reference to him unnamed (24. 467). In the Underworld, Odysseus tells the ghost of Achilleus that after his death his son was brought from Skyros, that he played a leading role in the strategy of the Trojan Horse, and that he was to the forefront during the sack of Troy (*Odyssey* 11. 506–37), but there is no mention of the tale in the *Iliad*. The later tradition told how before the expedition to Troy Achilleus was concealed, dressed as a girl, on Skyros by his parents, because they knew that he was to die at Troy: there Deïdameia, daughter of the king of the island, bore him Neoptolemos. There is good reason for the introduction of Neoptolemos here, for as the story moves towards its denouement, to the death of Hektor and the subsequent death of Achilleus, Homer presents the meaning of the coming tragedy in human terms: Andromache and Briseis, wives bereft of husbands (282–300n); Priam and Peleus, fathers bereft of sons (322–4n); Astyanax and Neoptolemos, sons bereft of fathers.

352–4   the delicate ambrosia and the nectar associates Achilleus with the dead Patroklos whose corpse was similarly treated to preserve it from decay (38–9). Sarpedon's corpse too was treated with ambrosia (16. 680), so it is clear that Achilleus is being treated as though already dead.

362–6   The metaphor **all earth was laughing about them** represents the shimmering glitter of the Achaians' armour, but it is also an indication of the soldiers' high spirits, despite Patroklos' death, at having Achilleus once more at their head. Achilleus' description matches that of his army: **his eyes glowed as if they were the stare of a fire** echoes the shining glitter of their armour, and the **clash went from the grinding of his teeth** echoes the thunder of their marching feet. For the fire image, cf. 375–8n.

368–91   After the renunciation of his anger, the second major theme of this book is the arming of Achilleus, and this in turn introduces his *aristeia* which will continue until the death of Hektor in Book 22. The arming of the hero (Armstrong 1958) is a traditional theme in the poet's repertoire, which he adapts to suit the hero or the context (cf. 16. 130–42n): in the present case the adaptation is the fact that the armour has been fashioned by the god Hephaistos.

375–8   **as when from across water a light shines to mariners from a blazing fire.** Fire imagery is an important feature of Achilleus' arming scene: his eyes glow like fire (366); the light glimmers from his shield like the moon or a fire (374–6); his helmet shines like a star (382); the armour becomes like wings (386) which may represent the swiftness of fire; fully armed he shines like the sun (398); and of course the armour was forged by the fire god himself. Whitman (1958.139) concludes that 'throughout the arming scene, the single symbol of fire connotes directly all the anguish, semidivine glory, and utter isolation of Achilles. Less directly, it still flickers with intimations of rage, loss, and imminent death'. The light flickering across the sea comes from high in the mountains in a desolate steading, and the sailors who observe it are being carried by the storm far away from their loved ones: so what might have been a symbol of hope to the Achaians in reality is pointing the isolation of Achilleus.

387–91   The ease with which Achilleus handles the **Pelian ash spear** contrasts with Patroklos' failure to arm himself with it (cf. 16. 130–42n), and its description, **to be death for fighters in battle,** marks it out as the weapon which will deal death to Hektor (22. 326–7). For **Cheiron**, cf. 11. 831n.

400   For Achilleus' immortal horses, **Xanthos** and **Balios**, cf. 16. 149–54n.

404–17   As when the horses mourned Patroklos (17. 426–40n), the effect of the speaking horse **Xanthos** is startling and adds force to what it says: that just as Patroklos died at the hands of Apollo and Hektor, so **for you there is destiny to be killed in force by a god and a mortal**. Once more the refrain of Achilleus' approaching death is heard: throughout the poem it has been associated with the appearance of his mother Thetis, and in time he will also hear it prophesied by the dying Hektor (22. 358–60). The predictions become ever more specific the closer death approaches, and culminate in Hektor naming Achilleus' killers as Apollo and Paris. Just as the mortal horse Pedasos pointed the mortality of Patroklos (16. 467–9n), so now the immortal Xanthos makes explicit the mortality of Achilleus, and it drags its mane in the dust just as it did in mourning for Patroklos (17. 426–40n).

421–3   I myself know well it is destined for me to die here. Achilleus again accepts the inevitability of his death, just as in his reply to his mother's prediction (18. 96–100n). In time he will reply similarly to the predictions of Lykaon (21. 110–13) and Hektor (22. 365–6).

ILIAD 20

The previous book ended with Achilleus, in his divinely made armour, declaring that he would not stop until the Trojans had had enough of his fighting. His arming scene and his words announced the beginning of his aristeia *and his urgency for the battle, but the present book frustrates the expected development, his vengeance upon Hektor, firstly by introducing an assembly of the gods on Olympos, and then by describing duels between Achilleus and Aineias, and Achilleus and Hektor, which come to nothing. The assembly of the gods matches the assembly of the Achaians in the previous book and, just as in Book 1 the beginning of the anger was followed by a declaration of Zeus' plan (1. 523–7), so Achilleus' renunciation of his anger in the previous book is now followed by Zeus' declaration that he is removing his control over events and that the gods are free to act as they wish. For their part, the duels of this book defer and anticipate the final duel of Achilleus and Hektor.*

5 **Themis** is the personification of righteousness and justice (cf. 15. 87n). The summoning of **all the gods into assembly** matches the assembly of the gods in Book 8, in which Zeus forbade them to enter the battle. The purpose of this assembly is to remove the prohibition and to return to the gods their independence to intervene on their favourites' behalf, for otherwise Achilleus might take Troy itself 'against destiny' (30).

7–9 **There was no river who was not there.** The presence of even the most minor deities at the divine assembly matches that of even the most humble of the Achaians at the the human assembly (cf. 19. 40–6n) and is an indication of its importance. The significance of the two assemblies is similar: Zeus' withdrawal of his prohibition matches Achilleus' abandonment of his anger.

18 **the onset of battle is almost broken to flame.** Poseidon means that the critical moment is approaching.

30   **I fear against destiny he may storm their fortress.** In reality,
nothing ever happens contrary to fate (cf. 16. 433–43n): here the
poetic fiction of Achilleus' anger, withdrawal and return confronts
the unalterable reality of the traditional account of Troy's fall, from
which Achilleus was absent because he was already dead.

32–40   **the gods went down to enter the fighting.** The catalogue of
gods now lined up against each other shows that, following Zeus'
declaration (25), the divine *status quo* has been restored; but it is
anomalous that they do not in fact join battle fully until the following
book. **Xanthos** is the god of Troy's river, known to mortals as
Skamandros (74), and he is included because Achilleus will soon
fight against him; by the same token, **Hephaistos** is named as
supporter of the Achaians because he will help Achilleus during
that fight.

47–74   There is a fine symmetry in the gods' battle-lines: **Athene's**
bellow is matched by that of **Ares** on the other side, and while she
stands by the Achaians' ditch and by the sea, he stands on the
Trojans' citadel and runs beside their river Simoeis. Similarly Zeus'
thunder on high is matched by Poseidon, god of the earthquake,
who **shuddered** below. **Aïdoneus** is Hades, god of the Underworld,
who was allotted his area of authority, along with his brothers Zeus
and Poseidon, after the overthrow of Kronos (15. 187–92). **Enyalios**
is the war god Ares. Artemis' brother, **the far striker**, is Apollo.

83–5   **Where are those threats gone which as you drank your wine
you made** recalls Sarpedon's words to Glaukos, that a hero receives
the choice meats at the feast and the filled cups in return for fighting
at the forefront of the battle (12. 310–21). Apollo/Lykaon reminds
Aineias of his heroic responsibilities, a common theme in the poem
(cf. 4. 338–48; 8. 228–34).

89–96   **this will not be the first time I stand up against swift-footed
Achilleus.** Aineias' recollection of his previous meeting with
Achilleus and of his rescue by Zeus anticipates the outcome of this
duel when he will be saved by Poseidon (321–7); the help he says
Athene gave Achilleus foreshadows the help Achilleus will receive
from her against Hektor also. **the time he sacked Lyrnessos and
Pedasos** was the occasion Achilleus took Briseis prisoner (2. 689–
91)

101–2   The metaphor in **pull out even the issue of war** is of stretching
a rope between the two sides. The metaphor in **claims to be made**

all of bronze, denoting Achilleus' new armour, signifies his invincibility: it may reflect the tale that his mother dipped him as a child, except for his ankle, in the river Styx to make him invulnerable.

106–23 **Achilleus was born of a lesser goddess.** Achilleus' mother Thetis, a sea nymph, is daughter of **the sea's ancient,** Nereus (18. 38). The response to Apollo's argument is given by Hera: Achilleus' divine parentage may be humbler than Aineias', but he is loved by those **who are the highest of the immortals.** This scene amongst the gods serves to confirm Aineias' own conclusion, that no man should face Achilleus, and this points up Hektor's foolishness in doing so.

127–31 **such things as Destiny wove with the strand of his birth.** A human's fate was spun out at the moment of birth by the Moirai (Fates): Klotho who spun the thread of life, Lachesis who decided upon its length, and Atropos who cut it. In the role normally taken by his mother, Hera emphasizes the shortness of Achilleus' life and the imminence of his death. **when a god puts out his strength against him in the fighting** foreshadows Achilleus' battle with the river Xanthos, and **It is hard for gods to be shown in their true shape** suggests the ambiguous form of the river god (cf. 21. 212n).

145–8 **the stronghold of godlike Herakles.** Poseidon built the walls of Troy for the Trojan ancestor Laomedon but was then cheated of payment by him, and so he sent a **Sea Beast** to terrorize Troy; Herakles, under the protection of this stronghold, killed the monster but was himself then cheated of payment by Laomedon (5. 640–2n). The story explains Poseidon's hatred and opposition to Troy, and is a reminder of Trojan dishonesty at the very moment he has restated the gods' support for Achilleus.

164–73 **the son of Peleus rose like a lion against him.** This simile, the longest of the poem's many lion similes, marks the dramatic moment of Achilleus' first battle, but it also recalls the moment when he heard of Patroklos' death and was compared to a lion returning, 'too late', to find that its cubs had been stolen by a hunter (18. 318–22n). Here the lion's indifference to the hunters matches Achilleus' indifference before the death of Patroklos; that death has now brought him into the battle, just as the lion's wound at last draws its attention to the hunters; and the lion's groan matches the grief of Achilleus. The hunters bring disaster on themselves because of **one of the impetuous young men,** just as the impetuosity of Hektor has brought Achilleus back into the battle. The simile's power lies in its representation of Achilleus' psychology, for the lion's rage is expressed through its physical appearance, and this then describes Achilleus' inner turmoil as he returns to the battle.

178–98   As a warrior, **Aineias** is second only to Hektor on the Trojan side. He is the son of Aphrodite and Anchises (208–9), and is descended from the Trojan ancestor Tros; his descent is traced through Tros' son Assarakos, Hektor's is through Tros' son Ilos, and it is Ilos' descendants who occupy the Trojan throne: so Aineias is second to Hektor in royal standing too, and Achilleus' taunt **in hope you will be lord of the Trojans** reflects the fact that he is not of the ruling family of Troy, nor will be because Priam has sons of his own to succeed him. One other passage (13. 460n) suggests an animosity between these two branches of the Trojan royal family. The duel of Achilleus and Aineias here prefigures the final duel of Achilleus and Hektor, when Hektor's death will symbolize Troy's fall; Aineias' survival of his meeting with Achilleus itself prefigures his survival of the war, so there is irony in Achilleus' taunt that Priam will never allow Aineias to be king of Troy. **have the men of Troy promised you a piece of land** recalls that Sarpedon included just such a plot of land in his account of the privileges accorded to a hero by his community (12. 313–14). **Another time before this** recalls the meeting Aineias spoke of (89–96n), but Achilleus' recollection is more detailed and registers his contempt for his opponent.

200–9   **never hope by words to frighten me as if I were a baby.** Aineias is following to the letter Apollo's advice not to be deterred by 'blustering words and his threats of terror' (108–9), but the louder he protests that he should not be treated as a child (cf. 211–12, 244–5), the more he calls attention to his obvious inadequacy and to his awareness of it. He also takes his lead from Apollo (105–7) in telling Achilleus that his mother is Aphrodite.

213–14   **if you wish to learn all this and be certain of my genealogy** recalls Glaukos' introduction of his account of his pedigree (6. 150–1), when he too found himself isolated and confronted by a superior opponent, Diomedes.

215–41   Aineias gives his pedigree. After Zeus, four generations of founding fathers are named: **Dardanos,** who founded the city of

Dardania for the tribe of Dardanians, the tribe now led by Aineias
(2. 819); Dardanos' son **Erichthonios**; Erichthonios' son **Tros,** who
was the ancestor of the Trojan race; and Tros' son **Ilos,** who was
the founder of the city of Ilion, or Troy. The poem makes no use of
the tradition that **Ganymedes** was caught away by Zeus for sexual
purposes, though **for the sake of his beauty** may be an allusion; it
was jealousy at Zeus' action which in part caused Hera's relentless
hatred of the Trojans. For **Tithonos,** cf. 11. 1n.

242–3 **Zeus builds up and Zeus diminishes the strength in men** is
partly a response to Achilleus' taunt that he had fled from their
earlier encounter but, coming at the end of his account of his
pedigree, it may show an intuition that one day his branch of the
royal family will be supreme.

247–58 The combination of the two metaphors, the **ship of a
hundred locks** (that is, oars) and the **tongue of man,** and the simile
of the two squabbling wives who **go out in the street and say abusive
things to each other,** confirms the impression of the nervous chatter
of the man trying to steel himself for the coming battle: and when,
after fifty-five lines of babble to a silent Achilleus, Aineias declares
you will not by talking turn me back from the strain of my warcraft,
there is a moment of true humour.

261–3 There is never any doubt that Achilleus is the superior fighter;
in fright refers to the awe Achilleus feels fighting in his divine armour
for the first time, not to fear of Aineias.

270 **the god of the dragging feet** is Hephaistos, who earlier told
how he was thrown from Olympos by Zeus and fell to earth on the
island of Lemnos (1. 591–4), and this may account for his lameness.
In *Odyssey* 8 he is the cuckolded husband of Aphrodite, and his
lameness is contrasted with the physical perfection of her lover,
the war god Ares.

286 **a stone, a huge thing which no two men could carry** recalls
Aineias' earlier fight with Diomedes: as he stood and defended the
body of his companion Pandaros, he was wounded when Diomedes
struck him on the hip with a stone, described by the same formula
(5. 303–4). The description serves to distance the action from the
audience's own time, to a time when men were greater and stronger.

291 **had not the shaker of the earth Poseidon sharply perceived all.**
In his earlier fight with Diomedes, Aineias was also in danger of his
life 'had not Aphrodite, Zeus' daughter, been quick to perceive

253

him' (5. 312), and he was then saved by Apollo. Diomedes' victory was part of his *aristeia*, which established him as the replacement for Achilleus; now Achilleus' own *aristeia* celebrates his return to the battle, and it is marked by victory over the same hero Diomedes defeated, Aineias.

297–9 why does this man, who is guiltless, suffer his sorrows in part is an acknowledgment of Aineias' piety to the gods, but it is also an assertion that it was not he and his branch of the royal family who had brought about the war by the abduction of Helen, but Hektor's and Priam's side, in the person of Paris (cf. 178–98n). The future of the Trojan race is concentrated on two characters, Hektor and Aineias, and so both are brought into combat with Achilleus, the one to die, the other to survive.

300 let us ourselves get him away from death. In contemplating, and then accomplishing, Aineias' rescue from his fight with Achilleus, Poseidon foreshadows the outcome of Hektor's fight with Achilleus, when Zeus similarly contemplates saving him (22. 174–6), just he also contemplated saving Sarpedon (16. 435–8). In both these cases Zeus considers altering destiny to save a mortal, but in the present case Poseidon contemplates, and effects, action to ensure that destiny is fulfilled and that Aineias does not die: this reworking of the traditional theme focuses attention on Aineias' destiny and the destiny of Troy he embodies.

306–8 Poseidon does not say when, or why, Zeus **has cursed the generation of Priam**, but it is one more assertion of the guilt of Priam's family through the actions of Laomedon (cf. 145–8n) and Paris; it also looks back to his granting to the gods the freedom to support their favourites which will result soon in the death of Hektor and the fall of Troy. His prediction that **the might of Aineias shall be lord over the Trojans, and his sons' sons** will in time culminate in the Roman belief that their imperial family was descended from Aineias.

324 laid it down again before the feet of Achilleus. Poseidon's action of returning Achilleus' spear foreshadows his duel with Hektor, when he has his spear returned to him by Athene (22. 276–7).

344–6 Here is a strange thing I see with my own eyes. Achilleus' confusion at Aineias' sudden disappearance recalls Menelaos' when he was robbed of his opponent Paris by Aphrodite (3. 448–50).

354–63 Achilleus' speech introduces an *aristeia* in which he kills a series of minor Trojan figures. He urges the Achaians to fight man to man and says that he is unable to do it all alone, but this seems designed to draw attention to the fact that this is precisely what he proceeds to do. In the Greek text the metaphor in **take the edge of such masses of men** actually refers to the mouth or the jaws of battle (cf. 19. 313n).

366–72 Hektor's sentiment that words are easy but actions hard, **I myself could fight in words against the immortals**, recalls Aineias' nervous prattling when facing Achilleus (247–58n). The repetition (epanalepsis) of **though his hands are like flame** highlights the effect of fire imagery in Achilleus' *aristeia* (cf. 19. 375–8n), and the effect is heightened here by the fact that it is his opponent's perception; the same effect is conveyed by the simile of **his heart like the shining of iron.**

376 Apollo's warning **do not go out all alone to fight with Achilleus** is designed to postpone Hektor's fight with Achilleus until the climax of his *aristeia*, but it also heightens the audience's anticipation of that fight, when this same god finally abandons Hektor (22. 213).

381–418 In this first part of Achilleus' *aristeia* he kills four Trojans, but Homer varies his description by means of some brief details. **Iphition**'s death gains pathos from the detail of his birth, and from the mention of his ancestral **lake waters of Gyge** in Maionia; **Hippodamas** is compared to a bellowing bull sacrificed to Poseidon, very appropriately in view of the god's prominent role in this book. In the case of **Polydoros**, it is his youth and the fact that he is his father Priam's favourite that enhances the pathos of his death: he has the speed of youth, but also the impetuosity, and the combination is the death of him, even though his father had forbidden him to enter the battle because of these very qualities. The death of this son of Priam anticipates that of another of his sons, Lykaon, in the next book (21. 116–27), and together they anticipate that of Hektor: so Polydoros' **display of his running** may look forward to Hektor's final moments, fleeing from Achilleus around the walls of Troy.

425–9 This meeting of Achilleus and Hektor is very brief, because Achilleus' *aristeia* is to run a much longer course before its climax, but it sets the scene for their later meeting and it heightens the audience's anticipation. The curtness of Achilleus' challenge, three lines followed by the peremptory **Come nearer, so that sooner you may reach your appointed destruction,** conveys both his impatience and his loathing.

431–7   **never hope by words to frighten me as if I were a baby** recalls Aineias' words to Achilleus (431–3 = 200–2), and Hektor acknowledges that **I am far weaker than you are,** while insisting that the issue is in the lap of the gods: in this preliminary skirmish a distinctive picture is being painted of the Trojan champion as inferior, like Aineias before him, to his Achaian opponent, and this prepares for their final meeting.

444   Hektor is saved from Achilleus by Apollo who **wrapped him in thick mist,** just as Aineias too was saved when Poseidon drew a mist over Achilleus' eyes (321). This is Hektor's final appearance before his fight with Achilleus in Book 22, and this departure from the battlefield is the impression the listener carries of him through all the following scenes of Achilleus' *aristeia*.

452–3   **if beside me also there is some god who will help me** foreshadows the next meeting of Achilleus and Hektor when there will indeed be a god, Athene, beside him to play a crucial role by deceiving Hektor.

455–89   Achilleus continues his rampage and kills no fewer than ten named Trojans. The death of **Tros** gains significance from the fact that he adopts the position of suppliant, **with his hands was reaching for the knees.** Like all such appeals on the battlefield, his fails and Achilleus rips out his liver, and so the episode serves to establish the mood of Achilleus; but like Polydoros' death (381–418n), it too may foreshadow the death of Lykaon in the next book after he also has supplicated Achilleus (21. 68–74). The result of both appeals is the same and both point forward to a third, also unsuccessful, appeal to Achilleus, that of Hektor.

490–2   **As inhuman fire sweeps on in fury.** The simile provides one final association in this book of Achilleus with fire (cf. 366–72n): the imagery evokes both the approaching fire which will engulf Troy and, more immediately, the supernatural conflict of fire and water which will feature in the next book.

495–7   **as when a man yokes male broad-foreheaded oxen.** As so often during battle descriptions, a peacetime activity illustrates by contrast the savagery of war, as the life-promoting work of the farmer is compared to the deadly actions of the hero.

ILIAD 21

In antiquity this book was given the title Battle by the River. It begins in the realm of mortals, with Achilleus' aristeia, but this brings him into conflict with the river Xanthos, or Skamandros; in turn this leads to a battle between the river god and Hephaistos, between water and fire, and then to a general battle amongst the gods. In Achilleus' battle beside, and then against, the river, he proves no match for its power and he is forced to summon divine assistance: he has been associated with images of fire since the very beginning of his return to battle (cf. 19. 375–8n), when Athene kindled a flame from the cloud surrounding his head (18. 205–6), but this is of no avail against the river, and it takes the fire of Hephaistos himself to save him. Leaf (1902.383) acknowledged 'the wild grandeur of this splendid scene', but he nevertheless dismissed the fight with the river as 'added as an afterthought', and even the Unitarian Owen felt that: 'an alien atmosphere comes into the poem . . . we are in a different artistic world from that we have been moving in . . . we seem to have passed back to an earlier, more primitive type of story, into the world of fairy- and folk-tale' (1947.211). The effect of the episode is to extend and intensify Achilleus' aristeia, but also to delay, and so arouse expectation of, his fight with Hektor. By the end of this book the gods who support the Trojans, like the Trojans themselves, have been routed, and only Apollo and Hektor stand between Troy and its doom.

1–2 **the fair-running river of whirling Xanthos** is the gods' name for Troy's river Skamandros: Homer begins the book with the river which is to be the focus of much of its action.

12–14 **As before the blast of a fire the locusts escaping.** The simile introduces the image of fire which will play a major role in this book. It recalls the comparison of Achilleus to fire sweeping through a mountain forest (20. 490–2n), and it looks forward to the moment when Hephaistos' fire will fight with Xanthos' water. The swarm

257

of the locusts represents the panic and confusion of the Trojans, and their huddling in the river represents the Trojans' helplessness; for his part, Achilleus is characterized through the description of the fire as **unwearied** and having blazed up **from a sudden start**.

22–4 **As before a huge-gaping dolphin the other fishes escaping** also portrays the Trojans' panic. This simile is the first of three descriptions in this book illustrating the increasing violence of Achilleus (Segal 1971.30): later on he taunts the body of Lykaon that fish will lick the blood from it and feed on its shining fat (122–3), and then eels and other fish tear at the body of Asteropaios and nibble the fat around his kidneys (202–4). This development, of fish eating the flesh of other fish to eating Achilleus' victims, is a measure of the increasing barbarity of his actions.

27–9 **took twelve young men alive from the river** recalls Achilleus' promise to Patroklos' corpse that he would behead twelve Trojan youths (18. 336). The sacrifice of these youths (23. 175) is a further escalation of his savagery. **vengeance** translates Greek *poine,* which featured in the picture of the trial scene on the Shield of Achilleus, translated there by Lattimore 'blood price': Achilleus here demonstrates his commitment to blood revenge for Patroklos' death rather than the compensation of the blood price (cf. 18. 497–508n). **fawns** are often used to indicate fear and cowardice (cf. 22. 1n).

34–48 **Lykaon** is a son of Priam by Laothoë (85–8), and so a half-brother to Hektor and a blood-brother to Polydoros, who was killed by Achilleus in the previous book (20. 381–418n). Lykaon pleads for his life, in an episode recalling the earlier scene in which Tros also begged Achilleus in vain for his life (20. 455–89n); that earlier scene resonates in the present and guides the audience's reaction to the appeal and its rejection, the pitifulness of the suppliant, and the continued heartlessness of the supplicated. The Lykaon episode itself prefigures a third unsuccessful appeal to Achilleus, that of Hektor in Book 22. Lykaon is one of a rare breed, a warrior who has encountered Achilleus and lived: his experience recalls a time when Achilleus took pity on prisoners (100–2), so his treatment here is a measure of the change Achilleus has undergone. When he was captured by Achilleus on that earlier occasion, Lykaon was preparing for the war, cutting the branches of a fig-tree to fashion the rails for a chariot (cf. Simoeisios, 4. 473–89n). This enhances the pathos of his capture, as does the extended chain of events that have brought him to this moment of terror. The **son of Jason** is Euneos (7. 467–9).

54–63   Here is a strange thing that my eyes look on. Achilleus' speech is heavily ironical and plays on the illusion that Lykaon has returned from the dead to confront him a second time. Achilleus muses that he must discover, since the grey sea could not hold Lykaon, whether a covering of earth will be any more successful, and the irony is maintained by the **prospering earth** (*ge phusizoos*) that is to cover Lykaon's body, for it is more literally translated 'the life-giving earth': that it is, after all, in the sea that Lykaon will find his final resting place completes the dark humour of this speech.

70–2   Lykaon with one hand had taken him by the knees. Lykaon's dramatic pose is a variation of the suppliant's normal pose of grasping the knees with one hand and the chin with the other to demonstrate that he accepts his inferiority (cf. 1. 500–1n): instead Lykaon vainly grasps the instrument of his death, Achilleus' spear.

73–96   you were the first beside whom I tasted the yield of Demeter, that is, bread. Lykaon claims that his eating with Achilleus after his capture established a relationship of guest friendship (cf. 6. 215–25n), and that this, as well as being a suppliant, entitles him to be spared; but in fact it was as captor, not host, that Achilleus entertained him before selling him into slavery. **my mother bore me to a short life** recalls the many references to Achilleus' own short life, and in particular his lament to his mother (1. 352), but this attempt by Lykaon to associate himself with Achilleus also fails. By naming his mother as **Laothoë** and by his reference to **Priam, who had many wives beside her,** Lykaon is aiming to show that he is not tainted with the guilt of Hektor, who is Hekabe's son; the resulting picture of Troy's king is of a polygamist.

103–13   Now there is not one who can escape death. In their savagery, Achilleus' words echo those of Agamemnon when he urged his brother Menelaos to 'let not one of them go free of sudden death and our hands; not the young man child that the mother carries still in her body' (6. 57–9). The calmness with which he announces Lykaon's fate matches that with which he accepts his own mortality, despite his greatness and despite his parentage, and in addressing Lykaon as **friend,** he shares with his abject opponent the lesson in mortality he has learned from the death of Patroklos: that no man may escape death, so he should accept it when it comes, without fear or complaint. This is similar to Sarpedon's conclusions about the hero's life of fighting, that no man can escape death, so it is better to fight 'and win glory for ourselves, or yield it to others' (12. 328). Achilleus accepts the inevitability of his own early death, but he does not draw Sarpedon's conclusion about the winning of glory.

122–35   Lie there now among the fish. The treatment of Lykaon's body is a grotesque parody of the hero's death rights: the fish with their tongues will perform the task of washing the body, and the river carrying the body will serve as his funeral procession (Richardson 1993.64). Achilleus' words illustrate his transformation from the man who in the time before Patroklos' death once honoured his enemy's body with the full ceremonial of burial (6. 416–19). His declaration, that the sacrifice of **the numbers of bulls** and **single-foot horses alive** will not be enough to win the river's protection for Troy, will stir the river to anger so that, when it throws the corpses out on to dry land, the river itself bellows like a bull (cf. 237n). His final words, that Patroklos and the other Achaians died **when I was not with them,** indicates that he accepts his responsibility for the Achaians' loss.

140–60   Achilleus' fight with **Asteropaios** is similar to that with Lykaon, in that they have both only recently arrived at Troy (cf. 81) and, like Lykaon, Asteropaios has just emerged from the river (cf. 35). So both can be seen as mortal representatives of the river against Achilleus, and the fight with Asteropaios can be seen as an important introduction to Achilleus' fight with the river itself: Xanthos is Troy's river and its defence, and Asteropaios, himself the grandson of the **wide-running river Axios** (the modern river Vardar), is sent by and from the river to defend the city against Achilleus, and when he fails, as all mortals must in face of Achilleus, then the river will itself rise up to oppose him. **this for me is the eleventh day since I arrived in Ilion** heightens the pathos of Asteropaios' death.

167   **the blood gushed out in a dark cloud.** The wounding of Achilleus runs counter to the tradition that he was invulnerable, except for his heel. The wound is a graze and has no consequence, and he offers no reaction to it; but in his entire fighting career in the poem it is the only wound he sustains, and so it gives an intimation of what Achilleus has now accepted, his own imminent death.

175   **Achilleus' ash spear** acts as a symbol of his superiority to all
other mortals (16. 130–42n); here Asteropaios does not have the
strength to withdraw it from the river bank, though Achilleus
himself will remove it effortlessly (200). The motif **Three times he
struggled straining to wrench it clear** describes both the desperation
and the courage of Asteropaios in face of Achilleus, and there is an
air of nightmare in his feverish attempts to withdraw the spear as
Achilleus closes in for the kill. His action contrasts with Lykaon's
passive supplication while grasping this same spear (70–2n), but
the outcome is the same for both of them.

189–99   **Peleus, Aiakos' son, but Zeus was the father of Aiakos.**
Aiakos was king of the island of Aegina. Legend told that he asked
Zeus to increase the depleted population of his island, and in
response the god turned a colony of ants into humans, who were
known thereafter as Myrmidons. With Minos and Rhadamanthys,
Aiakos was a judge of souls in the Underworld. Achilleus claims
that, as a descendant of Zeus, he is superior to one descended from
a mere river; but when he boasts that Zeus is greater than any
river, including **Acheloios**, the longest river in Greece, and the river
of Ocean, he only highlights the irony of his own mortality, that
Zeus and Thetis are unable to save him (1. 352n).

202–3   **about Asteropaios the eels and the other fish were busy.** Cf.
22–4n.

212   **the deep-whirling river spoke to him in anger.** The
anthropomorphism of the river during its fight with Achilleus is at
times so vivid that the distinction between Xanthos as surging river
and Xanthos as a minor deity seems completely removed. First the
river felt anger (136), then was given power of thought (137), and
now it has the power of speech.

223   **All this, illustrious Skamandros, shall be as you order.** Achilleus
agrees to the river's demand, but then promptly leaps into it to
continue his slaughter of the Trojans. So the scene highlights his
defiance of the god, and he almost pays with his life for doing so.

237   The description of the river **bellowing like a bull** gives a vivid
impression of the roar of a torrent heard by a man overwhelmed
within it, by Achilleus that is. The bull-like river recalls the bulls
which were sacrificed to it to win its protection for Troy (122–
35n).

252–3   **running with the speed of the black eagle.** The eagle is normally presented as a paradigm of speed and aggression, and this is the only time in the poem it is associated with a figure in retreat: this is entirely appropriate, since this is the only occasion on which Achilleus flees.

257–62   as a man running a channel from a spring of dark water. Like the farmer, Achilleus thought to control the river but is overwhelmed by it; like the rush of water scattering the pebbles in its course, the river has thrown up the corpses lying in it; and like the garden, the plain is inundated and its crops ruined. Just as the farmer loses his control over nature, so Achilleus, who has just been wounded for the first time, now for the first time also loses control and is threatened with destruction: and this has happened because he has confronted an immortal.

273–83   Father Zeus, no god could endure to save me from the river. Achilleus' lament is not that he is going to die, but that the manner of his death, by drowning, will rob him of the renown he would have gained from death in battle before Troy (cf. *Odyssey* 5. 306–12); death by drowning in a river smacks of foolishness. His courage in face of death is important because his present action, flight, is precisely the action Hektor will take in the following book when he confronts his death, and Homer is careful to distinguish between the two, by having Achilleus wish he could have been killed by Hektor. **I should be destroyed by the flying shafts of Apollo** looks forward to his death, shot by Paris' bow.

296–7   when you have taken Hektor's life go back again to the ships recalls Achilleus' own order to Patroklos to return when he had driven the Trojans from the ships (16. 87). Patroklos disobeyed and died as a result; now Achilleus is told he must not go beyond penning the Trojans inside the city, and this is an indication that he will not take part in the sack of the city.

305–23   Xanthos is now called by its Trojan name **Skamandros**, because the battle beside it foreshadows the sack of the Trojan city: for this reason also it summons assistance from Troy's other river, Simoeis, whom it calls **beloved brother**. The defeat of the immortal defender of Troy (Xanthos) by the immortal force of fire (Hephaistos) prefigures the defeat in the next book of the mortal defender of Troy (Hektor) by the mortal force of fire (Achilleus) wearing the arms made by Hephaistos. Xanthos' threat, that he will cover Achilleus' body **with abundance of sands and rubble,** is a distortion of normal burial practice and matches the burial Achilleus promised Lykaon (122–35n) (Richardson 1993.78).

332 whirling Xanthos would be fit antagonist for you in battle. When the gods lined up against each other in the previous book, 'against Hephaistos stood the great deep-eddying river who is called Xanthos by the gods' (20. 73–4). That battle was suspended and Homer instead described Achilleus' *aristeia*; now at last he reverts to the position as he left it at that point.

346–7 As when the north wind of autumn suddenly makes dry. Hephaistos' victory over the river is swift and total. The simile matches the earlier one comparing the inundation of the plain to the uncontrolled irrigation water in a garden (257–62n); it describes the restoration of order and the saving of Achilleus, who remains unharmed and whose relief is shown in the reaction of the farmer.

373–6 I will swear you a promise not ever to drive the day of evil away from the Trojans recalls the river's declaration to Hephaistos that he will no longer protect Troy from Achilleus (359–60): the complete surrender of Troy's river to Hephaistos' fire explicitly prefigures the sack of Troy itself.

385–513 The Battle of the Gods (*Theomachia*). This long scene has been generally dismissed by readers, on the grounds that it interrupts and detracts from Achilleus' *aristeia*. It is comical and at times even slapstick: the battling gods are presented as though they are mortal heroes, with all the usual challenges and boasts, but then their fights remain unresolved, because of course neither party can be killed; the result is a sense of anticlimax. However the scene does serve a proper purpose in the narrative. Firstly, the triviality of the gods' battles with each other illustrates, by contrast, the horrors of the battlefield and the deadly seriousness of the mortals' battles. Secondly this episode, along with the defeat of the river Xanthos, removes Troy's protecting gods and so prefigures the city's fall. The gods lined up against each other in the previous book: on the Achaian side were Hera, Athene, Poseidon, Hermes and Hephaistos; on the side of the Trojans were Ares, Apollo, Artemis, Leto and Xanthos (20. 33–40). Hephaistos and Xanthos have fought already, and so there are five encounters: Athene–Ares, Athene–Aphrodite, Poseidon–Apollo, Hera–Artemis and Hermes–Leto. Of these, only three lead to a fight, as Poseidon–Apollo and Hermes–Leto are resolved without violence. The result, with or without combat, is victory for the Achaians' supporters, with Leto the sole winner on the Trojan side.

388   the huge sky sounded as with trumpets. Similarly Achilleus' return to battle was heralded by his great shout, as loud as 'the voice that is screamed out by a trumpet' (18. 219).

391–414   Ares began it, the shield-stabber, and rose up against Athene. The battles of the gods are obviously parodies of those of mortal heroes: the motive for this first one is at best strained, for Ares is seeking revenge for the wound he received from Diomedes with Athene's support (5. 855–8). Ares stabs with his spear, ineffectually of course; Athene, who has the standard warrior's **heavy hand,** picks up a huge stone—just as Diomedes did against Aineias (5. 302–4n), as Hektor did against Aias (7. 264), and as Aineias did against Achilleus (20. 286n)—and sends Ares crashing to the ground; his hair drags in the dust and his armour clashes, just like a fallen hero's; and he measures his length on the ground— seven acres of it! At the end there is no tragedy, but a chortling Athene who calls the mighty war god a child. **because you abandoned the Achaians** recalls Ares' treachery in first promising that he would support the Achaians, but then going over to the Trojans (5. 832–4).

415–17   By **taking Ares by the hand** and leading him away, Aphrodite is repaying a debt to her brother, who arranged her escape in his chariot back to the safety of Olympos when she was wounded by Diomedes (5. 355–63).

435–67   The meeting of Poseidon and Apollo echoes the meeting of Glaukos and Diomedes (6. 119–236): like Glaukos recalling the long story of Bellerophontes, Poseidon recalls the time he and Apollo favoured the early Trojans but were then cheated by Laomedon (cf. 20. 145–8n); and Apollo's comparison of **insignificant mortals, who are as leaves are** recalls Glaukos' comparison of the generations of men to dying leaves (6. 146–50). The similarities emphasize the difference between the two scenes, for the earlier scene stresses the chivalry of the heroes' guest-friendship (6. 215–25n), but the scene amongst the gods serves merely to highlight the insignificance of man in their eyes. The paradox of Apollo's assertion **let the mortals fight their own battles** is that throughout the poem the gods fight by proxy, by supporting their own favourites against the favourites of others; but it also looks forward ominously to the moment

Hektor will stand alone, deserted by his divine protector, to face Achilleus (22. 213)

481–96 It will be hard for you to match your strength with mine may have the appearance of an heroic challenge to battle, but it is just a small step to comedy, as Artemis has her ears boxed and dashes off to Zeus for consolation, just as Aphrodite, when wounded by Diomedes, sought comfort from her mother Dione (509–10 = 5. 373–4). The episode raises a smile from the reader as well as from Hera, and yet there was nothing remotely amusing in the scene when a god, Apollo, laid low a hero, Patroklos with a blow (16. 791–2): it is their immortality which makes the situations of Artemis and Aphrodite comical, when set against the fall of Patroklos. **Zeus has made you a lion among women** recalls that Artemis brings death with her arrows to women, just as her brother Apollo brings death to men with his (1. 51); the picture of Artemis as the beast that kills women is then reversed, and she is pictured as one who hunts down ravening beasts in the mountains.

497 For Hermes **Argeïphontes**, cf. 2. 103n; he is **the Guide** because he conducts the souls of the dead in the Underworld. Leto, one of **the brides of Zeus,** is mother, by him, of Apollo and Artemis.

515–17 The end result of the Battle of the Gods may be comical, but underlying it is the serious point that Troy has been abandoned by all its protecting gods except Apollo. He enters Troy, but he no longer looks to save it, merely to ensure that it does not fall to the Achaians, **before they were fated.**

522–4 and as when smoke ascending goes up into the wide sky. The simile continues the association of Achilleus with fire, and it foreshadows the final destruction of Troy. The description of the city, following immediately upon the abandonment of Troy by its gods, as **with the anger of the gods let loose upon it,** may be taken to refer to the gods of the Achaians whose anger has been demonstrated so recently.

526 Priam's position **on the god-built bastion** is significant, in recalling the *Teichoskopia* when he sat on the tower at the Skaian Gate while Helen identified the Achaian leaders (3. 162–242), and in looking forward to the death of Hektor which Priam will witness from this position.

538 the gates opening let in daylight illustrates vividly the claustrophobic atmosphere and the fear within Troy.

545   **Agenor** is no random choice as Trojan champion, for he was
      the first man on the Trojan side to kill an Achaian (4. 467); and
      when Apollo disguises himself as him and flees with Achilleus in
      close pursuit, the scene foreshadows Achilleus' pursuit of Hektor
      in the following book.

552   **deeply disturbed he spoke to his own great-hearted spirit** also
      described Odysseus facing the Trojans all alone (11. 403) and
      Menelaos facing Hektor (17. 90), and it will appear again when
      Hektor confronts Achilleus (22. 98): in each of these cases, except
      the last, the hero is rescued from the ensuing fight. So this Achilleus–
      Agenor meeting foreshadows the Achilleus–Hektor combat, and
      highlights the desertion of Hektor by Apollo (22. 213), the very
      god who here rescues Agenor.

556–61   The accumulated details in this speech by Agenor convey
      effectively the impression of a rapidly evolving fantasy of escape
      from Achilleus' clutches; this too foreshadows Hektor's combat
      with Achilleus, when he too escapes temporarily into a fantasy in
      which he and Achilleus calmly and rationally resolve the cause of
      the war (22. 111–21).

573–8   **as a leopard emerges out of her timbered cover.** The simile
      describes the leopard's courage, but also its stubbornness in fighting
      on and its unwillingness to retreat: so also Agenor, and then Hektor
      in the next book, refuse to join the other Trojans within the
      protection of the city.

586   By asserting that **there are many of us inside,** defending from
      within Troy's walls, Agenor is demonstrating the renewed siege
      mentality of the Trojans; and his decision to confront Achilleus
      outside the walls anticipates Hektor's fateful encounter with him.

593   **back from the struck greave the bronze rebounded.** Similarly
      in Hektor's fight with Achilleus, his spear will rebound ineffectually
      from Achilleus' new shield (22. 291).

597   **caught Agenor away closing him in a dense mist.** So also
      Aphrodite rescued Paris (3. 380–2), and Apollo rescued Hektor
      (20. 443–4), though in the present case Apollo's purpose is not so
      much to rescue Agenor as to deceive Achilleus and so grant the
      Trojans a breathing space. This divine mist helping the Trojans at
      the end of the book balances the mist Hera sent to help Achilleus
      at its beginning (6–7).

ILIAD 22

This book marks the climax of Achilleus' anger, which from the beginning was directed at Agamemnon but since the death of Patroklos in Book 16 has had Hektor as its object. The subject of the book is the death of Hektor in single combat with Achilleus, a death which Patroklos predicted to Hektor with his own dying breath (16. 852-4), and which it has been made clear will be followed by that of Achilleus (18. 96). The book has a carefully balanced structure with the combat of the two champions at its centre, framed by three speeches on either side: before it, there are appeals to Hektor from his parents, Priam and Hekabe, and a speech of his own pondering his possible courses of action in face of Achilleus; after the combat, there are speeches of lamentation for the dead Hektor, again from his father and mother, and the third from his wife Andromache. So it is from a Trojan perspective, and particularly that of Hektor's family, that events are viewed, and the result is a book of great pathos, but at the same time one of surprising rapidity of movement. Much of the book's impact results from the picture of Troy and of Hektor and his family which was painted in Books 3 and 6, and there is a marked consistency in the development of that picture here. The central figure nevertheless remains Achilleus, who in this book validates his claim to the title 'best of the Achaians'.

1   the Trojans, who had run like fawns. The fawn is an image of fear and helplessness throughout the poem, for example the twelve Trojan youths Achilleus captured to be a sacrifice to Patroklos (21. 27–29n) and Hektor fleeing from Achilleus later in this book (189–92). So this brief simile is part of a series illustrating the result of Achilleus' *aristeia*.

5–6   he stood fast in front of Ilion and the Skaian gates. This is

Hektor's first appearance since his earlier duel with Achilleus, when he was rescued by Apollo and concealed in a mist (20. 444n). It was on the Skaian gate that his wife Andromache made her appeal to him (6. 392–439), and it is from there also that his father and mother will make their appeals; as a result, and in spite of the intervening narrative, these three appeals appear as a unit. Andromache implored him to stay on the Skaian gate with her and to forsake the world of war (6. 237n); now that gate is firmly shut, and inside are the women and the fighting men who have survived Achilleus' onslaught, but Hektor alone stands outside, in line with the reply he gave Andromache (6. 440–65).

7–10   **Apollo** disguised himself as Agenor in order to fool Achilleus and allow the Trojans to escape from him (21. 600–11).

22–3   **like a racehorse with his chariot.** The translation misses some of the meaning, for the horse is called *aethlophoros*, prize-winning, and this indicates the outcome of Achilleus' encounter with Hektor; the speed of the horse, and so of Achilleus, contrasts with Hektor's static pose (5). The simile recalls Hektor's comparison to a horse breaking its tether and galloping across the plain (15. 263–8n), and it foreshadows his pursuit by Achilleus, when the two of them are compared to a couple of racehorses as they run 'for the life of Hektor' (161–6).

26–31   **like that star which comes on in the autumn** recalls the simile introducing the *aristeia* of Diomedes, Achilleus' substitute (5. 4–6n), and also the many associations of Achilleus with fire since his return to battle (19. 17n); it looks forward to the climax of Achilleus' fight with Hektor, when the gleam from the tip of his spear is like the shining of Hesper, the evening star (317–20). **Orion's Dog** is Sirius, and the **great fever** is the merciless heat of summer which the dog-star brings, and they represent the catastrophe which Priam envisages Achilleus' approach will bring upon the Trojans.

33–4   **with both hands high uplifted beat his head, and groaned amain.** Priam is lamenting the death of Hektor while he is still alive, just as Andromache and the women of Troy did when Hektor left the city for the last time to return to battle (6. 500n).

42–3   The beginning of Priam's appeal contrasts with its end, for the fate he wishes on Achilleus now, that **the dogs and the vultures would eat him,** becomes the fate he imagines Hektor's death will bring on himself (66–7).

45–55   **sold them away among the far-lying islands** recalls the fate
of Lykaon, captured by Achilleus but spared by him and sold on
the island of Lemnos (21. 79). **Lykaon and Polydoros** have of course
already fallen to Achilleus (20. 417; 21. 114); there is pathos in
Priam's reverie, that he might ransom his sons for bronze and gold,
for Lykaon made just such an appeal, in vain, to Achilleus, and
Priam will shortly offer ransom for another of his sons, for the
body of Hektor.

56–7   **Come then inside the wall, my child** echoes Andromache's
appeal to Hektor that he defend his relatives and his people from
within Troy's wall (6. 431–4n), and will be repeated by Hekabe
(84–5). All three of his relatives urge the same viewpoint upon
him, that his should be a role of duty and devotion to those who
are dependent upon him. Hektor rejected his wife's appeal because
he felt deep shame before the Trojans (6. 441–3), and he will reject
his parents' appeals, and will demonstrate the same heroic concern
for his reputation (105) and for glory (129–30).

60–5   Priam's premonitions will be realized, but not in the *Iliad*. **my
sons destroyed and my daughters dragged away captive**: his son
Hektor will be killed, and his daughter Kassandra taken by
Agamemnon; **the chambers of marriage wrecked** recalls the fifty
bedrooms of his sons and their wives and the twelve bedrooms of
his daughters and their husbands (6. 244–50), and represents the
destruction of his family; **innocent children taken and dashed to
the ground**: his grandson Astyanax will be hurled from Troy's wall;
the wives of my sons dragged off: his son's wife Andromache will
be taken by Achilleus' son Neoptolemos. Priam personalizes the
fall of Troy to make his appeal to Hektor the more persuasive, a
technique Virgil used in *Aeneid* 2, in presenting the effect on Aineias
of the fall of Troy and of the death of Priam himself.

66–76   **my dogs in front of my doorway will rip me raw** goes much
further than the conventional picture of the hero's corpse left as
carrion for wild dogs (cf. 1. 4–5): it is an apocalyptic vision of a
future in which even tame household creatures will revert to savage
beasts. Priam's words are full of pathos and irony, for even as he
declares that **a young man all is decorous when he is cut down in
battle**, his son Lykaon lies in the Skamandros river with the fish
tearing at his 'shining fat' (21. 127).

83–9   **if ever I gave you the breast to quiet your sorrow.** Hekabe begs repayment for the nourishment and comfort she gave Hektor as a baby; she calls her breast *lathikedea*, literally forgetful of cares, and so highlights her helplessness now as he confronts death. **sweet branch, o child of my bearing** stresses her role as life-giver and so emphasizes the pathos that his death at Achilleus' hands will deprive her of her final mother's duty, to mourn him on his death-bed.

93–6   **as a snake waits for a man by his hole** conveys a picture of Hektor's courage and determination in face of Achilleus; it recalls and contrasts with the simile comparing his brother Paris to a man startled by a snake (3. 33–5n). The snake coiling outside its hole and around it illustrates Hektor's defence of the circle of Troy's wall; it acts aggressively because it is glutted with evil poisons, just as Hektor is in the grip of unquenched fury, *asbeston menos*, and so fails to heed his parents. Virgil makes use of this simile (*Aeneid* 2. 471–5), where the symbolism of the snake identifies Neoptolemos as the reincarnation of his murderous father Achilleus.

98–110   **Deeply troubled he spoke to his own great-hearted spirit,** cf. 21. 552n. Hektor rejected the advice of **Poulydamas** and the Trojans supported his decision (18. 249–309) because 'Pallas Athene had taken away the wits from them' (18. 311–12); now Hektor acknowledges his **own recklessness**. Priam urged Hektor to fight from within the walls and so save Troy (56–7n), but Hektor says he will fight outside the walls because he has failed to save his people: where Priam spoke of duty, Hektor speaks of his shame, and the reproaches of Poulydamas and the Trojans outweigh his duty to mother and father, wife and son. He repeats the words he spoke to his wife, **I feel shame before the Trojans and the Trojan women with trailing robes** (6. 442), but the circumstances are very different, for on that earlier occasion he was driven by the shame he would feel if he failed to act, but now he is driven by the shame he feels at the failure of his actions.

111–21   **Or if again I set down my shield massive in the middle.** During this brief moment of fantasy, Hektor's thoughts follow each other in rapid succession, and his excitement in his self-delusion is palpable. The proposal **to give back Helen, and with her all her possessions** was made by Antenor during the earlier truce, but was rejected by Paris who refused to surrender Helen (7. 347–64); Priam's appeasement of his son on that occasion and his refusal to impose Antenor's suggestion in effect sealed Troy's fate (7. 373–

4n); and in his fantasy Hektor seems to recall that moment and the lost opportunity to resolve the dispute, as he now faces the consequences of it.

122–30   I might go up to him, and he take no pity upon me. Supplicating Achilleus was the course Hektor's brother Lykaon took (21. 70–5) in a scene which prepared the ground for Hektor's speech here, and he received no pity. The origins of the obscure expression **from a tree or a rock** have long since disappeared, but it seems clear that it was a proverbial phrase for impossibility. There is pathos in Hektor's repetition of **a young man and a young maiden,** for as he imagines all this, he is standing below the Skaian gates where he spoke for the last time to his wife Andromache (cf. 5–6n), and to underline the connection between the two scenes, Homer uses the same verb *oarizemenai,* **whisper together** (6. 516). So Homer recalls that earlier scene at the very moment Hektor decides finally to abandon his wife and family and the recollection emphasizes his isolation as he awaits Achilleus' attack.

133–5   The **Pelian ash spear was used earlier to signify the inferiority of both Patroklos (16. 130–42n) and Asteropaios (21. 175n); now, by contrast, it is in Achilleus' hands, as the supreme symbol of his warrior prowess. **like the flare of blazing fire or the sun in its rising:** Achilleus' armour is again associated with the fire-god Hephaistos and his victory over Troy's river in the previous book, and is the immortal symbol of Achilleus' power and coming victory (21. 305–23n); but the simile also recalls his comparison to the dog-star and so continues his association with celestial bodies, harking back to his arming, when his shield glimmered like the light of the moon (19. 374) and his helmet shone like a star (19. 382).

137   **Hektor's behaviour, **left the gates behind, and fled, frightened, is quite unique in the poem: there are strategic withdrawals in face of the enemy, for example Aias (11. 555), and a hero may contemplate flight, for example Agenor (21. 553–70), but nowhere else is a hero portrayed in full flight before another warrior, though Achilleus of course fled before the river god.

139–42   As when a hawk in the mountains. This simile should be read in conjunction with a second one from the natural world illustrating Hektor's flight (189–92): first he is like a trembling dove and then a deer's fawn (cf. 1n), and Achilleus is like a hawk and then a dog in the mountains. The picture is less one of cowardice than of helplessness, a picture Hektor himself drew when he compared himself, naked (unarmed) before Achilleus, to a woman (124–5).

145   **the windy fig tree** is where Andromache urged Hektor to draw up his men, 'where the city is openest to attack' (6. 433–4), while himself remaining on the rampart: the first of the city's landmarks Hektor comes to in his flight is precisely that vulnerable place the city most needs him to defend. The **two sweet-running well springs** are also symbols of Troy's vulnerability, for they lie outside its besieged walls. Homer here foreshadows the moment when Hektor's fate will be settled, for when he and Achilleus pass this point for the fourth time, Zeus will place their fates in his scales and the balance will come down against Hektor (208–13).

162–4   **As when about the turnposts racing single-foot horses** recalls the description of Achilleus as a prize-winning racehorse, which anticipated his victory in the present race (22–3n); the simile leads naturally to the gods watching the spectacle of the race, and then to their debate about Hektor's fate. The laps around the turnposts which the two horses cover match the circuits of Troy the two heroes will complete before Hektor dies. The **games for a man's funeral** foreshadow the funeral games Achilleus will host for Patroklos in the next book, so this race for Hektor's life, at the end of which he will pay the ultimate price for killing Patroklos, itself looks forward to the honour which will be paid to the dead Patroklos.

170   For the offering of **thigh pieces of oxen**, cf. 1. 458–66n.

174–85   **whether to rescue this man** recalls that Zeus also contemplated postponing the death of Sarpedon at Patroklos' hands (16. 433–43n), but was persuaded not to by the consolation that the dead hero would be transported by Death and Sleep to his home in Lykia and given due burial; no such consolation is offered this time, and the gods appear quite detached from the mortal struggle, illustrated by Zeus' almost glib remark **I say this not in outright anger, and my meaning toward you is kindly.**

199–200   **As in a dream a man is not able** is a striking comparison of the pursuit to a nightmare, but whereas awakening brings escape from a dream, for Hektor no such route exists.

203   **for this last and uttermost time** points a contrast with the Achilleus–Agenor scene in the previous book (cf. 21. 552n), for

although he was an inferior fighter Agenor survived his meeting with Achilleus because of Apollo's help; and now that Hektor is deserted by Apollo, his fate is sealed.

208–13 But when for the fourth time seems deliberately to recall the killing of Patroklos by Hektor (cf. 16. 784–7). The weighing of the heroes' fates in Zeus' **golden scales** is merely symbolic, a dramatic representation of an outcome already decided: just as the defeat of the Trojans, represented by the death of Hektor, is marked in this way, so too was the beginning of their victory (cf. 8. 69n).

216–17 you and I will take back great glory to the ships of the Achaians. Athene's role in helping Achilleus and deceiving Hektor during their fight has caused many readers discomfort: 'so revolting and so needless' (Leaf 1902.429). In fact Achilleus has Athene's support for the very good reason that he is going to win: granted that he wins, then he must have the support of Athene, otherwise he would not win; granted that he could not catch up with Hektor, then Hektor must have had the help of Apollo; and granted that Achilleus does finally catch up with him, then Apollo must have withdrawn his help. The gods' actions are manifestations of what does, or does not, happen.

232 Hektor of the shining helm is the first of three appearances of this common formula in a short section of narrative (cf. 249, 337) and this may be designed to recall, at the moment of his death, the scene in which he symbolically replaced on his head the helmet which caused such terror to his son (6. 468n).

239–41 our father and the lady our mother, taking my knees in turn is of course part of the fiction to fool Hektor by stressing his brother's devotion, but it is also intended to remind Hektor of the appeal from his father and mother which he so recently rejected.

254–9 Come then, shall we swear before the gods. Hektor's words may be no more than a desperate attempt to avoid what in the event Achilleus inflicts on his corpse; but once previously he proposed conditions for a duel, between himself and Aias, and then too he proposed the return of the loser's body for burial (7. 76–84). So he is in fact proposing a formal heroic duel with Achilleus.

261–72 Achilleus' reply, **argue me no agreements**, finds no place for Hektor's chivalrous contest, with its emphasis on honour and respect for the defeated; it is the ultimate expression of the contrast between Hektor's pursuit of heroic glory and Achilleus' pursuit of vengeance, as Moulton (1977.85) comments 'Achilleus' grim words on enmity contrast pointedly with Hektor's vision of young lovers'.

281   you are someone clever in speech and spoke to swindle me contains the intense irony that Hektor is now standing to face Achilleus precisely because he has been swindled by someone clever in speech, the disguised Athene.

293–5   He stood discouraged, and had no other ash spear. Hektor's position is in marked contrast to Achilleus', whose spear has just been returned by Athene. His desertion, **Deïphobos was not near him,** is as briefly stated, and as final, as his abandonment by Apollo (213).

301–5   So it must have long since been pleasing to Zeus marks Hektor's realization that all his achievements have been merely a means to a different end, to the granting of glory, not to himself, but to Achilleus, that is, the fulfilment of Zeus' promise to Thetis in Book 1. **Let me at least not die without a struggle, inglorious** recalls Sarpedon's sentiments on the subject of heroic glory (12. 326–8): as he confronts his death, Hektor's last thoughts are not of his mother or father, nor even of his wife, but rather he embraces the heroic axiom of death in everlasting renown (cf. 56–7n).

308–10   he made his swoop, like a high-flown eagle. The simile describes the speed and the new found courage of Hektor, though the image of the victim, lamb or hare, is hardly appropriate to Achilleus; the simile reverses that used of Achilleus, when he was like a hawk swooping on a trembling dove (139–42n).

317–18   Hesper is the evening star; at the beginning of this contest Achilleus was like the dog-star which 'brings on the great fever for unfortunate mortals' and now he is like the star which brings an end to the day, in this case Hektor's last day. **the fairest star who stands in the sky** indicates both the beauty of the divine armour and the supremacy of the warrior who wears it.

321–3   the armour, brazen and splendid is Achilleus' old armour which he lent to Patroklos for his fight with Hektor (cf. 17. 192–7n).

331–6   surely you thought as you killed Patroklos. Similarly Hektor boasted to the dying Patroklos by imagining his thoughts and Achilleus' words to him when he set out for the battle (16. 834–42n).

339   do not let the dogs feed on me recalls the image with which the poem began (1. 4–5n), and which looms large in this book. Priam declared that his son's death would result in his being torn by his own dogs (66–76n); in reply to Hektor, Achilleus calls him 'you dog' (345), says he wishes to take on the dogs' role by eating Hektor's flesh himself, and twice says the dogs will tear his body (348, 354).

347–50   Achilleus' wish **to hack your meat away and eat it raw** is taken up by Hekabe in her grief and rage (24. 212–13). His wish is all the more dramatic because of his steadfast refusal in the past to eat anything until he has taken vengeance on Hektor (19. 179–80n). In his quest for vengeance he has reached 'the outermost limits of barbarism' (Motto and Clark 1969.112). The forcefulness of **ten times and twenty times the ransom** is reminiscent of his rejection of the embassy (9. 379–80), but it foreshadows the moment in Book 24 when Priam will come to him with ransom.

360   Hektor's final words, spoken with his dying breath, are **Skaian gates**: his prediction of Achilleus' death there, at the hands of Paris and Apollo, recalls the security the gates afford Troy, even as he perishes outside them; perhaps too there is a wistful reminiscence of his parting from Andromache (cf. 5–6n).

361–3   These three lines link Hektor's death to that of Patroklos, for they are used, on these two occasions only, to describe the death of them both (cf. 16. 855–7n).

365–6   **I will take my own death at whatever time.** Cf 18. 115–16. Achilleus accepts without question the inevitability of his own death now that he has killed Hektor, and he does so in exactly the same words, though with slight variation in Lattimore's translation, as he addressed to his mother when she told him of the link between Hektor's death and his own.

369–74   **none stood beside him who did not stab him** enhances the stature of Hektor, for it is only in death that they dare come close to him. The repeated stabbing of the body is compulsive, and almost ritualized, and the very mutilation of it emphasizes its **stature** and **imposing beauty**. The awe they feel looking at the corpse makes their need to defile and mutilate all the greater.

381   **let us go in armour about the city.** Like Patroklos before him, Achilleus is overtaken by the euphoria of victory, and appears to contemplate the attack on Troy which in time will bring about his death.

391–3   let us go back, singing a victory song Although his fight has been single-handed, Achilleus invites the **young men of the Achaians** to join him in raising the victory song and bearing Hektor's body back to the ships. Since Achilleus renounced his anger in Book 19, Agamemnon has been relegated to the background, and Achilleus has assumed authority. Here too he exercises that authority, as he first decides strategy—whether or not there will be an immediate attack on the city—and then returns to the ships in triumph, surrounded by *his* victorious army.

395   It is often assumed that **shameful treatment** is Homer's moral judgment on Achilleus' treatment of Hektor's body, but it is more likely that it represents Achilleus' own view, his intention in acting as he does. He has already declared that he would like to eat Hektor raw (347), and now he judges that the best way to vaunt his triumph, the most serious dishonour he can inflict, is to drag his enemy's corpse in full view of his family and the Trojans who had depended on him.

401–4   all that head that was once so handsome was tumbled in the dust recalls the death of Patroklos whose helmet was defiled by blood and dust: the defilement of Patroklos' (Achilleus') helmet is now avenged by the defilement of Hektor's head. Hektor's defilement is also the defilement of **the land of his fathers,** and this evokes the pathos of his parents standing on the walls as grieving witnesses to the event, but it also points up the failure which it represents, his failure to defend his ancestral land.

406   Hekabe's gesture, **threw the shining veil far from her,** is matched by that of Hektor's widow Andromache when she learns of his death (468–72n).

410–11   if all lowering Ilion had been burning top to bottom in fire makes the significance of Hektor's death palpable: it represents the fall of Troy, and the fire which will destroy it is personified in his killer, who has twice been associated in similes with fire destroying a city (18. 207–13n; 21. 522–4n).

412–28   His people could scarcely keep the old man in his impatience characterizes Priam's brief lament for his son, and it foreshadows the events of Book 24 when he will make his way to the Achaian ships to beg for the return of his son's body. **since I am old, and his father also is old** anticipates Priam's first words as suppliant to Achilleus, when he appeals to him to remember his father, 'one

who is of years like mine, and on the door-sill of sorrowful old age'
(24. 486–7), in a scene which will be underpinned by the shared
suffering of the two fathers. Priam's recollection of **the number of
my flowering sons he has cut down** heightens the pathos of his loss
of this the greatest of his sons, but it also recalls the futility of the
dying Hektor's appeal to Achilleus and, before him, that of another
son of Priam, Lykaon (21. 70–2n), and this too heightens the pathos
of the old king's desperation to supplicate Achilleus.

430–6   Hekabe's appeal to Hektor concentrated on her life-giving
role (83–9n), but now she laments that his death has taken away
her own life. Her sentiment that the Trojans **adored you as if you
were a god** is the same as Achilleus' (394), though her tone is very
different; her grief is tinged with a mother's pride in his stature,
and this points the depth of his fall and the catastrophe it represents
for the Trojans.

437–41   Throughout the present episode Andromache is not named,
but is called **the wife of Hektor.** She was last seen at the end of
Book 6, fondly looking backwards as Hektor made his way into
the battle and she returned to their home; since then she has been
mentioned twice (8. 187–9, 17. 207–8), but she has not appeared.
Hektor had told her to return to 'the loom and the distaff' (6.
491), so her appearance now working at her loom effectively
conveys a picture of obedience to her husband and duty to his
household. The addition of **for no sure messenger had come to her**
enhances the pathos of her situation, for the entire city has witnessed
Hektor's death but the one dearest to him alone has not yet heard
of it. Andromache is weaving **a red folding robe, and inworking
elaborate figures,** as too was Helen (3. 125–8n), and it has been
suggested that the function of the queens' weaving is to represent
and commemorate the achievements of the royal households
(Atchity and Barber 1987.31): so there is the further pathos that
Andromache is weaving the tale of Hektor's household at the very
moment he has perished.

443–5   **so that there would be hot water for Hektor's bath** contains
the irony that it will be as a corpse that Hektor will be bathed, and
that Andromache will be denied even this consolation by Achilleus'
continued abuse of the body.

457–9   **put an end to that bitter pride of courage,** that is, Hektor's
pride is 'bitter' in its consequences for his family. Andromache's

sentiment that Hektor **would never stay back where the men were in numbers** recalls her vain attempt to persuade him to stay within the wall and direct his troops from there (6. 431–4n).

460   The description of Andromache as **like a raving women** recalls her earlier description as 'like a woman gone mad' when she heard that the Trojans were losing and rushed to the wall (6. 388–9n). That earlier scene heralded her final meeting with Hektor and her appeal to him to stay within Troy's wall, and the similarity of her reaction here effectively connects the two scenes and invites the reader to view the coming events against that earlier background.

468–72   **threw from her head the shining gear that ordered her headdress.** Andromache casts aside her **circlet** (*kredemnon*), the symbol of the bride's chastity, and so of marriage. The same word is used of the battlement or crenellation of a city, and Nagler (1974.48) has suggested a connection of idea between the destruction of the city's *kredemnon* and the loss of the female's *kredemnon*, that the removal of the veil is symbolic of sexual violation: so by her gesture Andromache prefigures the fall of Troy and the consequent violation of the females. Her gesture also evokes her earlier meeting with Hektor, when he too removed his headdress, his helmet, to calm the fears of their son (6. 468n). As the gift of Aphrodite, the circlet is the symbol of the love of Andromache for Hektor and of their marriage. **the house of Eëtion** recalls that Andromache's father and his city were also victims of Achilleus, and his death and its fall prefigured the death of Hektor and the fall of Troy (6. 425n).

484   **a widow in your house, and the boy is only a baby** recalls Andromache's final, desperate, plea to Hektor not to 'leave your child an orphan, your wife a widow' (6. 432).

487–507   Andromache's account of the suffering of his orphaned son Astyanax parallels Hektor's own account of the suffering of his widow (6. 454–65), as she is led by some Achaian into slavery. Both illustrate the consequence of his death, by showing the transformation in his family's life, but here the picture is hardly an accurate one since many members of Hektor's family remain to offer the child protection; it does nevertheless convey effectively Andromache's emotional response. **one whose parents are living beats him out of the banquet**: exclusion from the feast in effect would represent exclusion from heroic society (cf. 19. 179–80n). For the origin of the name **Astyanax**, cf. 6. 402n.

512–14   all of these I will burn up in the fire's blazing. Andromache laments that Hektor will not receive burial because his body is held by the Achaians and that the cremation of his clothes is the only burial she can give him. Taplin (1992.249) has suggested that 'her burning of Hektor's clothes will be a symbolic pre-enactment, not so much of his funeral pyre, as of the burning of Troy as a whole'. When Hektor refused Andromache's appeal to protect his family by remaining within Troy, he declared that he 'would feel deep shame before the Trojans, and the Trojan women with trailing garments' (6. 441–2), and he left his family for the last time and returned to the battle in pursuit of glory. Now his widow recalls that fateful decision, perhaps in consolation, but with a hint of bitterness, as she speaks of the heroic **honour** (*kleos*) he has won **from the men of Troy and the Trojan women.**

ILIAD 23

This book recounts the funeral of Patroklos, first the ceremony itself (1–257), and then the funeral games held in his honour by Achilleus (257–897). Whitman (1958.262) has described the architecture of the poem in which the later books mirror the earlier, and he has argued that this book mirrors Book 2, in that the Funeral Games present a final picture of the major Achaian heroes to balance their introduction in the Catalogue of the Ships. By his display of good-will and courtesy towards the participants in the games, Achilleus encourages an atmosphere of harmony and co-operation, albeit against a background of fiercely contested competition; and he contributes to the restoration of good order in place of the disharmony which has characterized his relations with the Achaians during the course of the poem. He adjudicates and he awards prizes and, by doing so, he affirms that that is his right: his is the power to grant or withold reward, and he exercises that power with tact and good humour. The other heroes are able, under the conditions of a temporary peace, to exercise the competitive qualities they have displayed in the narrative; and, by accepting from Achilleus the prizes he awards, they acknowledge his authority.

1   **So they were mourning through the city** links back to the mourning for Hektor by the Trojan women and by Andromache (22. 515), and forwards to the mourning for Patroklos in the Achaian camp (12).

13–15   The honour the Achaians show Patroklos, by **Three times, mourning, they drove their horses** around his body, is matched by the dishonour Achilleus heaps on Hektor by dragging his body behind his chariot three times around the burial mound of Patroklos (24. 14–17). **Thetis stirred the passion for weeping:** Thetis also led the mourning of her sister Nereïds, ostensibly for the dead Patroklos,

280

but in reality for her doomed son Achilleus (18. 52–64n). **The sands were wet**: the sea-shore is to be the location of Patroklos' grave mound (125–6), so it is appropriate that his body has been placed there; but the location also recalls Achilleus' prayer to his mother 'beside the beach of the grey sea', which set in motion the whole tragic course of events (1. 350n).

18 **Peleus' son laid his manslaughtering hands over the chest of his dear friend,** cf. 18. 317n. The formula 'manslaughtering hands' commonly refers to Hektor, so it is a particularly appropriate description as Achilleus lays the hands which have killed Hektor on his victim Patroklos.

20 **All that I promised you in time past.** Achilleus promised that he would bring the armour and head of Hektor, and that he would offer up twelve Trojan children to assuage his anger (18. 334–7).

24 For **shameful treatment,** cf. 22. 395n. Here too it is more likely that the phrase indicates Achilleus' intention rather than the poet's moral judgment on his act. The shameful treatment involves leaving Hektor's body face down in the dust, to contrast with the honour paid to Patroklos who lies alongside him on his back on his bier (18).

29–30 Achilleus **set the funeral feast in abundance before them,** but there is no indication that he takes part in it himself. Similarly when he comes to the shelter of Agamemnon, there is an implicit reluctance in his words 'let us now give way to the gloomy feast' (48), and it is again unclear whether he takes part. In this case, he is maintaining his reluctance to be reconciled with his society, and with Agamemnon in particular (cf. 19. 179–80n).

34 **The blood ran and was caught in cups,** and is then presumably poured on the ground as offering to the spirit of Patroklos. At *Odyssey* 10. 526–40 Kirke instructs Odysseus that the spirits in the Underworld who approach him will be able to speak to him when they have drunk the blood offering he makes: so it may not be entirely coincidental that in the following scene the ghost of Patroklos appears to Achilleus in his sleep and speaks to him.

40–1 **to set a great cauldron over the fire** recalls Achilleus' instructions for the washing of Patroklos' blood-stained corpse (18. 343–53). Achilleus' refusal to wash the filth of the bloodstains from his own body places him in the attitude of Patroklos' corpse.

47 **cut my hair for him** is the usual sign of grief (135). Hair is normally

worn long in Homer, whereas in later times this is itself a sign of grief.

59–64   the beach of the thunderous sea, cf. 13–15n. **lay down, groaning heavily** contrasts Achilleus' restlessness with the sleep of all the others; he is reluctant to sleep, as he was reluctant to eat and to wash, and sleep catches him unawares (cf. 232).

65–7   the ghost of unhappy Patroklos all in his likeness appears almost to be an idealization, taking the appearance Patroklos had in life, not displaying the wounds he received in death.

72–6   Passage of the dead into the Underworld means to **cross the river**, that is, the river Styx, and to **pass through the gates of Hades**, and so to enter Hades' house. The ghost complains that Achilleus' neglect of burial is preventing it doing either: this is the first time the connection is made between burial and entry into the Underworld.

80–1   And you, Achilleus like the gods, have your own destiny. The theme of Achilleus' approaching death has appeared frequently in the poem, since he first declared that his mother bore him 'to be a man with a short life' (1. 352); he predicted his own death as he dealt Lykaon his (21. 103–13n), and the dying Hektor predicted that he would die at the hands of Paris and Phoibos Apollo at the Skaian gates (22. 359–60). Achilleus' death will be the last in an unbreakable chain, begun with the death of Sarpedon, and continued through those of Patroklos and Hektor (16. 419–507n): so the ghost's prediction, and the speech generally, reinforces the connection between the deaths of Patroklos and Achilleus.

85–90   when Menoitios brought me there from Opous. The ghost's story recalls Phoinix' account of how, having stolen his own father's concubine and then fled his anger, he too came to Phthia and was received with kindness by Peleus (9. 447–82); and, where Patroklos was made Achilleus' henchman, Phoinix was made his tutor. Both Phoinix and Patroklos' ghost appeal to Achilleus' memory of his father and the kindness he displayed to them, and this in turn foreshadows the appeal Priam will make in the final book, also in the name of Achilleus' father Peleus (24. 486).

91–2   the golden two-handled urn which Thetis, always conscious of Achilleus' fate, has provided to hold his ashes, recalls the goblet she provided, from which he poured a libation and prayed to Zeus for Patroklos' safe return when he sent him into the battle (16.

225–7); both objects are symbols of the two companions' unity in death.

103–7   Even in the house of Hades there is left something is a reflection of the pathos of the moment, of the contrast between the apparent reality of the ghost when first it appeared (66–7) and its evanescence when he tries to embrace it, rather than some metaphysical observation on Achilleus' part. As he starts awake, the scene has more the appearance of a dream than a visitation by a ghost.

116–22   They went many ways, uphill, downhill, sidehill and slantwise is a unique line, to emphasize the men's enormous physical effort and so enhance the honour paid to Patroklos; it is matched by the energy and eagerness of **the mules** pulling the timbers, who thus join in the honouring of the hero.

125–6   along the beach, where Achilleus had chosen place for a huge grave mound continues Achilleus' association, even in death, with the sea-shore (59–64n). In later times, the Tomb of Achilleus was one of the landmarks pointed out on the Trojan coast (Rubens and Taplin 1989.82–4).

135–42   They covered all the corpse under the locks of hair, so that a part of each of them may accompany Patroklos in death (Seaford 1994.168). Achilleus' gesture, **held the head sorrowing,** is the same as his mother's, who held his own head when he heard the news of Patroklos' death (18. 71n). **cut off a lock of fair hair**: traditionally boys dedicated a lock of hair on coming of age, and **Spercheios** would have received Achilleus' as being the principal river of his homeland, Phthia. His gesture of offering up the hair to be consumed in the funeral pyre instead is a gesture of affection towards his companion, but it is also a symbolic acknowledgment that he will not return home to dedicate it to the river itself; the burning of the lock ensures that Achilleus too will share figuratively in the cremation of his friend.

156–60   Now cause them to scatter. To a large extent the circumstances of this book dictate that Achilleus takes the dominant role in performing the burial of Patroklos, but it is noticeable that he continually demands that Agamemnon be the one who carries out his wishes; his tone appears accommodating, but it is clear that he is very firmly in control of proceedings.

166–76   The offerings placed on the funeral pyre will, after cremation, accompany Patroklos to the Underworld. The sacrifice of two **dogs of the table** recalls one of the scenes on the famous fourteenth-century BC limestone sarcophagos from Hagia Triadha in Crete (Warren 1989.106), in which a dead man is approached by three men bearing offerings: two carry animals, possibly hounds, and one carries a boat, probably for transportation across the river of the Underworld. The sacrifice of **twelve noble sons of the great-hearted Trojans** was foreshadowed at the time they were captured (21. 27–9n). This human sacrifice (Hughes 1991.49) is an extension of Achilleus' violence towards Lykaon (21. 120) and Asteropaios (21. 202–4); but he also promised Patroklos the head of Hektor (18. 335) and that Hektor's body would be devoured raw by the dogs (21), and he even said that he wished to eat Hektor's flesh himself (22. 347). In fact none of these things happen, and this slaughter of Trojan prisoners marks the climax of his violence.

177–83   let loose the iron fury of the fire to feed on them The metaphor of fire as the consumer of bodies is predominant, and the 'fury of fire' is taken up later to describe the still-glowing embers of the pyre (238). However, in the present context, the description of the fury of fire as 'iron' intensifies the image, perhaps by transfer from the common metaphor of the heart of iron (e.g. 22. 357), and so it may be that 'the iron fury of the fire' is suggestive of the fury in Achilleus' heart.

185–7   drove the dogs back from him. Aphrodite's protection of the body from being torn by the dogs recalls that it was with just this terrible fate that Achilleus taunted Hektor (22. 354); and **anointed him with rosy immortal oil** recalls that Thetis protected the body of Patroklos by distilling ambrosia and nectar through his nostrils (19. 38–9), but it also anticipates the dispute amongst the gods about the disposal of Hektor's body (24. 33–63).

192–216   the pyre of dead Patroklos would not light. Achilleus' inability to light the funeral pyre and his need for the winds to intervene, Iris' help and the winds' response to her, all contribute to the significance of the kindling of the pyre. The **Aithiopians** provide a convenient reason why Iris cannot stay and enjoy the winds' hospitality; they were also brought in to explain why Thetis could not put into immediate effect Achilleus' request that she go to enlist Zeus' help, namely, that Zeus was on a visit to them at the time (1. 423–4).

221–3   as a father mourns as he burns the bones of a son. The simile comparing Achilleus to a grieving parent and Patroklos to a dead son recalls a number of scenes: Achilleus' words when Patroklos approached him with the plan which was to cost him his life (16. 6–10n), the simile describing Achilleus' reaction to his friend's death (18. 318–22n), and Achilleus' comparison, during the embassy, of himself to the mother bird struggling to feed its young while itself going hungry (9. 323–4n). The simile also looks forward to the meeting of Achilleus and Priam in the following book; for Priam has been portrayed in Book 22 as the paradigm of the grieving parent, and so by associating Achilleus' emotions here with those of Priam, Homer is anticipating the scene of mutual understanding and compassion that closes the poem.

236–7   first put out with gleaming wine the pyre is another example of Achilleus issuing orders to Agamemnon (cf. 156–60n), who obeys silently (249).

243–8   The grave mound which is not very great will be a temporary structure to mark the place of Patroklos' cremation, but his remains will be kept in a golden jar in Achilleus' shelter; he will only be buried after Achilleus' death, when the mound will be extended to receive the bones of them both. Achilleus will continue to honour Patroklos by dragging Hektor's body behind his chariot around this mound (24. 16).

257–897   The Funeral Games for Patroklos. Of the eight events, the first, the chariot race, is described at greater length than the other seven combined (261–650): the other competitions are boxing (651–99), wrestling (700–39), the foot-race (740–97), the armed combat (798–825), weight throwing (826–49), archery (850–83), and spear throwing (884–97). The Funeral Games have been thought by some to be a later addition to the poem; in particular, it has been claimed that the armed combat, weight throwing and archery 'rival each other in absurdity and obscurity' (Leaf 1902.469).

261–70   Achilleus announces five glorious prizes for speed of foot for the horsemen, and subsequently five competitors are named (288–351): that all the participants are to receive a prize is in keeping with the atmosphere of the games, of fiercely contested competition resolved in comradely co-operation. The richness of the prizes offered by Achilleus recalls the striking catalogue of gifts he was offered by Agamemnon (9. 121–57), but his generosity on this occasion contrasts with the violence of his rejection then, and illustrates the very different spirit now underlying the heroes' actions. Nevertheless, Achilleus' distribution of the prizes is an assertion of his social superiority (Donlan 1993.160), and their acceptance by his companions, including Agamemnon, demonstrates that they accept that superiority. That **a woman faultless in the work of her hands** is a prize is in keeping with the role of women in the poem as the disposable assets of the heroes, though it is a little surprising that she is to be first prize, for in the wrestling contest a woman is the loser's prize.

277   The **immortal horses** of Achilleus are Xanthos and Balios (cf. 16. 149–54n).

280–4   There is pathos in Achilleus thus remembering Patroklos as **the gentle one** and his tender care of the horses, when his ghost has so recently accused him of neglect (69–70). Patroklos' pampering of Achilleus' horses recalls the care Andromache lavished on the horses of Hektor (8. 185–90n). In **these two horses stand here and grieve**, Achilleus is crediting the horses with his own sadness, and this matches the grief they themselves displayed earlier (17. 426–40n; 19. 404–17n).

291–2   Diomedes **had taken by force** Aineias' horses (5. 323–4), which were descended from the horses Zeus gave to Tros in compensation for the loss of his son Ganymedes to the god (5. 265–6).

296–9   **so as not to have to go with him to windy Ilion.** The Achaian heroes followed Agamemnon and Menelaos to Troy in line with their mutual obligations to lend assistance in time of trouble; there was also a tradition that all Helen's suitors swore an oath to her father to fight for her return if ever she was abducted (1. 159n). Echepolos' actions suggest that such obligations could also be met by payment of a gift, and this confirms the story of Euchenor (13. 663–72n).

306–48   **in this race your horses should run slowest.** Nestor's horses epitomize the old man himself as he appears throughout the poem, slower than all the rest; but his advice to his son, **have your mind full of every resource of skill**, defines his role in the poem, for what he lacks in strength and speed he compensates in experience and intelligence, like the **woodcutter** or the **sea captain**. Nestor's advice seems little more than common sense, that a tight turn at the turning-point will give a chariot a good advantage, and that with this advantage it will be impossible for Antilochos to be caught in the straight. In fact Antilochos completely disregards his father's advice during the race and risks a serious collision, so it seems likely that it is included in order to characterize his headstrong nature. The divine horse **Arion** was the offspring of Poseidon and Demeter when they mated in the form of a stallion and a mare; by its speed it saved its rider **Adrestos**, the king of Argos and leader of the Seven against Thebes, when their expedition ended in failure. For **Laomedon's horses,** cf. 5. 265–70.

373–6   **as the rapid horses were running the last of the race-course back** describes the return leg. No account is given of the charioteers' technique in rounding the turning-post, so it is not clear whether Antilochos in fact took Nestor's advice, but as he appears to be in fourth place at this point, he probably did not. The **son of Pheres** is Admetos (cf. 289).

383–90   **dashed the shining whip from his hands.** Neither the loss of Diomedes' whip nor its return to him by Athene is actually required by the narrative, so the story is probably included to give honour to Diomedes who goes on to win the race.

431–2   **As far as is the range of a discus swung from the shoulder.** The simile accords well with the present context of sporting competition.

441   **you will not get this prize without having to take oath.** Menelaos has already accused Antilochos of recklessness (426), and now he angrily anticipates his demand that Antilochos swear on oath that he used no guile to defeat him (584–5); but his blustering accusation of cheating cannot disguise the fact that he was the one who lost his nerve at the crucial moment (434–6).

457–72   **am I the only one who can see the horses.** Idomeneus' speech conveys the excitement of the moment as the chariots come into view, and he both reports and interprets the scene, offering a suggestion for what might have happened to the original leader Eumelos. The issue is trivial and the resulting disagreement is typical of any spectator sport, as within moments the air is thick with traded insults and the occasion is soured. It seems to be Idomeneus' tone of self-congratulation, that he alone can observe the scene clearly, which upsets Aias, rather than the actual news he is offering.

474–81   Idomeneus' speech hardly justifies the tone of Aias' reply, **what was all this windy talk?**, which is quite at odds with the friendly spirit of the games. The speed with which the quarrel develops may reflect the tensions of the Achaians, though the scene appears strained and the emotions forced; the quarrel draws attention to the role of peace-maker, to Achilleus, who succeeds in calming their passions, and so the scene confirms his authority and the responsibility with which he exercises it.

492–8   **If another acted so, you yourselves would be angry.** Achilleus counsels common sense, patience and self-control, taking neither side but offering a spirit of co-operation and tolerance. The contrast with his actions and demeanour in Book 1 could scarcely be greater.

515   **not by speed but by taking advantage.** A contrast is being drawn with speed, so the meaning of Greek *kerdesi* ('by taking advantage') should rather be 'wiliness'.

523–4   **he was left behind the length of a discus thrown** is another simile ideally suited to the context of the funeral games (cf. 431–2n).

536–8   **The best man is driving his single-foot horses in last.** Achilleus' proposal to award second prize to Eumelos, even though he finished last, is an acknowledgment of his excellence as a horseman, and is in keeping with the heroic principle of rewarding merit, for example in the distribution of booty from a sacked city (cf. 1. 99n); but in this case it serves to rile the heroic temper of the man who came second, Antilochos.

548–52   **there is abundant gold in your shelter.** Antilochos' suggestion, that Eumelos be given an alternative prize, recalls Agamemnon's demand during the quarrel (1. 118), though on that occasion Achilleus replied that there were no spare prizes with which to compensate him; now he readily hands over the corselet he took from Asteropaios (21. 183), and a situation fraught with difficulty and danger is resolved by his surrender of his own hard-won spoil.

555–62   **swift-footed Achilleus, favouring Antilochos, smiled.** No clearer indication could there be of the change in Achilleus in this scene than this, his only smile in the entire poem, and the humanity he has displayed is illustrated by the recollection of his contrasting treatment of **Asteropaios**, whose body he hurled into the river Xanthos to be consumed by the eels and the other fish (21. 203–4).

570–85   Menelaos in fact owes a substantial debt to **Antilochos,** whom he now berates, for he stood by him and saw off Aineias when Menelaos was in very real danger of his life (5. 565n). Menelaos puts into the mouth of the anonymous Achaian the same charge against himself, of **using lies and force,** as he is lodging against Antilochos, and he echoes the charge in the oath he demands his opponent swears, that **you used no guile to baffle my chariot.** The sanctity of the oath is indicated by the invocation of **him who encircles the earth,** that is, Poseidon, and by gripping the horses and the whip, the very object with which Menelaos claims he has cheated.

587–95   **you are the greater and go before me.** Antilochos takes his lead from the generosity of spirit Achilleus has just displayed, but in fact he addresses none of Menelaos' points: not only does he not admit to cheating or take the oath as demanded, he continues to assert his victory and presents his action of handing over the mare as one of unreserved generosity rather than one of apology.

601–11   **I myself, who was angry, now will give way before you.** Menelaos is touched by Antilochos' magnanimity, and tries to outdo him in generosity of spirit, though he continues to insist the prize is by rights his; Achilleus plays no direct role in the scene, yet his positive effect on those around him is clear. **you have suffered much for me, and done much hard work,** cf. 570–85n; Antilochos also had the thankless task of carrying, at Menelaos' request, the news of Patroklos' death to Achilleus (17. 691).

615–23   **the fifth prize, the two-handled jar, was left** because Eumelos was given the special extra prize, and Achilleus gives it as a special honour to Nestor as consolation for his old age which now denies him his true heroic portion. By giving Nestor a prize, Achilleus does more than make an old man happy; he acknowledges the honour and dignity due to old age, a theme that reaches its climax in his meeting with the aged Priam in the next book.

629–42   **I wish I were young again.** Nestor recalls his exploits as a youth so as to show himself the equal of any of the competitors and so legitimize the award of a prize even though he has not competed. The occasion was also one of funeral games, when **Amaryngkeus was buried by the Epeians at Bouprasion** (cf. 2. 615–24). His sole defeat, in the chariot race, seems to have resulted from aggressive driving similar to that of his son in his struggle with Menelaos; for his victors, the **sons of Aktor,** who may have been Siamese twins, cf. 11. 749–50n.

650   **May the gods, for what you have done for me, give you great happiness.** Achilleus has generously given a prize to the competitor who came last and has soothed the anger of the one who came second, he has settled the quarrel which arose from the accusation of cheating and has presented a prize to one who has not competed at all, so he has shown himself the very model of diplomacy in his role as arbiter of the games. It was Nestor who took, unsuccessfully, the role of arbiter during Achilleus' quarrel with Agamemnon (1. 247–84), so his words here are a true indication of the transformation Achilleus has undergone since that quarrel.

653–99   The description of this second competition, the **painful boxing,** is very much shorter than that of the chariot race, partly because narrative economy demands that not all the games are described in equal detail, but also because it provides rather less scope for tension and dramatic description. The prizes are much less valuable than in the first contest.

665–77   **Epeios** is associated with Odysseus, though not in the *Iliad*, as the man who built the Trojan Horse (cf. *Odyssey* 8. 492). His boasting is a strange amalgam of self-assertiveness and self-defence, so that he presents a picture of a rather inadequate man, who covers up his inadequacies with a show of bombast and violence. He admits his shortcomings in battle, quite unlike the typical hero, but his threat to smash his opponent's skin apart and to break his bones is enough to deter all but one opponent. **Euryalos** is one of those who successfully attacked Thebes, the Epigonoi, the sons of the Seven against Thebes.

679–80   **who came once to Thebes and the tomb of Oidipous after his downfall** implies a very different version of the story of Oidipous from that found in Sophokles' *Oidipous at Kolonos,* where the self-blinded Theban king goes into exile and dies at Athens.

695   It is entirely in keeping with the friendly but competitive spirit of the games that, after lifting Euryalos off the ground with the force of his punch, Epeios **took him in his arms and set him upright.**

700–39   The third contest is the **painful wrestling,** and the contestants are **huge Telamonian Aias** and **resourceful Odysseus,** traditional descriptions which contrast the brute strength of the one and the cunning of the other and which is reflected in the evenness of the contest: 'versed in cunning' gives better sense than **versed in every advantage**. After the death of Achilleus, these same two heroes competed for his armour and, when it was awarded to Odysseus, Aias committed suicide, and this tradition may be recalled in Achilleus' declaration of a draw and his proposal, **take the prizes in equal division**.

740–97 The fourth contest is the **foot-race**. The description of the prize, a silver mixing-bowl, contains the only mention in the poem of the name **Phoenicians**: in their own land (today Syria) they are called Sidonians, taking the name of their greatest city Sidon. They are represented as great craftsmen and traders: Paris brought home examples of their woven robes on the expedition which brought Helen from Sparta (6. 289–92). **Thoas** was the king of Lemnos, whose daughter Hypsipyle married **Jason** and bore him **Euneos**. **Lykaon** told how he was bought **out of slavery** (21. 77–9), but he claimed that it was Achilleus who sold him and for the price of a hundred oxen, whereas the account here says it was Patroklos who did so and for the bowl here described; the effect of the change is to connect the account more closely with the present occasion, the games in honour of the dead Patroklos.

765 **Great Odysseus was breathing on the back of the head of Aias** recalls the closeness between the chariots of Eumelos and Diomedes during the chariot race (377–81), when Eumelos could feel the heat of the pursuing horses on his back.

774 **Aias slipped in his running, for Athene unbalanced him.** Athene's two-fold assistance for Odysseus, lightening his limbs, and then causing Aias to slip in the ox dung, matches her actions during the chariot race, when she returned Diomedes' whip, and then wrecked Eumelos' chariot in order to give victory to Diomedes (383–90n).

784 **all the rest of them laughed happily** at the sight, of course, of the great man covered in ox dung and spitting it out of his mouth; but Aias' indignity is compounded by his pose, grasping the horns— of an ox (780).

787–92 Antilochos covers his embarrassment at coming third, since Aias has had time to pick himself up from the pile of dung and still beat him for second place. His mockery of Odysseus, that he is so old that he **is out of another age than ours**, is gentle; his flattery, that with a god's help Odysseus has defeated a man much his junior, leads naturally to his final, almost obsequious, reference to Achilleus.

798–825   The fifth contest is the armed combat, and the prize is the
armour of Sarpedon, which Patroklos captured when he killed him
(16. 663–5): like the oxen slaughtered to honour Patroklos (776),
this detail summons up the figure of Patroklos whose death has led
to these games and lends pathos to the occasion. The winner is the
one who manages to **get through armour and dark blood and reach
to the vitals** of the other, and this makes this contest far more
serious than any of the other games. The contest seems to be adapted
from the formal duel between enemies, for example that between
Aias and Hektor in Book 7; here it is between the two Achaians
who can claim to be the best after Achilleus, Aias and Diomedes,
and as in Aias' earlier contest, the wrestling, his opponent appears
to get the better of the fight even though a draw is called.

826–49   The sixth contest is weight-throwing, and the prize is a **lump
of pig-iron, which had once been the throwing-weight of Eëtion;**
so this object is connected with other objects captured when
Achilleus sacked Thebe, the city of Andromache's father Eëtion
(cf. 16. 149–54n). In an age when weapons are made of bronze,
iron is a valuable commodity, but it is clearly not uncommon, as
shepherd and ploughman have the use of it, and there is a source
of supply in the city. The contest is one of great physical strength,
as is indicated by the presence of **Polypoites** and **Leonteus,** leaders
of the Lapithai, whose mighty efforts in defence of the Achaian
ships (12. 127–194) actually induced Poulydamas to urge Hektor
to call off the entire Trojan attack; the contest is probably a kind of
putting the shot. For the third time Aias is beaten into second place,
which may reflect the tradition that he also came second, to
Odysseus, in the contest for the arms of Achilleus (700–39n).

845–7   **as far as an ox-herd can cast with his throwing stick.** The
purpose of the throwing stick is not made clear, but it is to be
assumed that it is used to herd the cattle.

850–83   The seventh contest is archery, and again **gloomy iron** is the
prize. The **thin string attached to her foot** is of course a smaller
target than the bird itself, and so cutting it would be a better shot
than hitting the bird. In the event, Teukros does cut the string and,
because the bird has then flown high, it takes an exceptional shot
from Meriones to kill it; there is considerable narrative weakness
in Achilleus thus providing a separate prize to be awarded in the

case of the chance cutting of the string, only for this to happen the next moment. **The lord of archery** is Apollo.

884–97 The eighth, and final, contest is spear-throwing. Achilleus sets down **a far-shadowing spear and an unfired cauldron,** which suggests that both objects are prizes, with the spear being first prize as it is mentioned first. **take this prize and keep it:** Achilleus awards the prizes without the contest ever taking place, and it is generally accepted that he is seen here at his most tactful: he realizes the intolerable position Agamemnon as commander would be placed in if he were defeated by an inferior, and so he awards him the prize for being best without having to prove it, and graciously completes the reconciliation begun in Book 19, by accepting Agamemnon's superiority, **for we know how much you surpass all others** (Macleod 1982.31). Yet Agamemnon has proved far from a great fighter throughout, so it is more likely that Achilleus' statement is ironical, and contains the unspoken premise that he would lose if the contest were to go ahead. **let us give the spear to the hero Meriones:** if the spear is first prize, then Meriones is the winner in this non-event. Achilleus has awarded prizes throughout the games as an assertion of his own superiority (261–70n), and now he makes the ultimate assertion of his authority; Agamemnon acknowledges that authority by his wordless acceptance of Achilleus' award, and his acceptance reverses Achilleus' pointed refusal in Book 9 to accept Agamemnon's gifts and authority. This is the final meeting in the poem of the two antagonists of Book 1, and it neatly reverses the crucial event of that book, Agamemnon's arrogant abuse of power in removing Achilleus' prize (Postlethwaite 1995).

ILIAD 24

The poem concludes with the ransoming of Hektor's body by his father Priam; conducted by Hermes, he travels to the Achaian camp and, in exchange for gifts, receives from Achilleus the body of his son which has been preserved by divine intervention. Faced by the old king, whose suffering in bereavement matches his own, Achilleus at last abandons his anger. Priam returns to the city, and the book ends with the lamentations of Hektor's family and with his funeral. Many of the events of this final book reverse those of the first: just as Book 1, and the poem, began with the refusal of the autocratic Agamemnon to accept ransom for the daughter of the aged Chryses, so Book 24, and the poem, end with Achilleus' acceptance of ransom for the son of the aged Priam; the resulting quarrel of Achilleus and Agamemnon in Book 1 is reversed in Book 24, in the mutual sympathy and understanding of Achilleus and Priam; and just as the development of Achilleus' anger resulted from his mother Thetis' visit to him, and then to Zeus to put his request, so in Book 24 his anger is assuaged when his mother is sent to him by Zeus to demand that he release Hektor's body. The poem which began with the violence of Achilleus' quarrel with his ally concludes in the harmony of his reconciliation with his enemy.

1–8 **the people scattered to go away.** The end of the games marks the end of the Achaians', but not Achilleus', mourning for Patroklos, and they now return to life's routines. He **wept still as he remembered** recalls the beginning of the previous book, when all his companions slept, but Achilleus lay down on the shore groaning for his lost companion. It is Patroklos' **manhood and his great strength** that Achilleus laments, his very presence beside him as companion in arms. Once more the image of Achilleus on **the beach of the sea** portrays his isolation (cf. 1. 350n): the games of Book 23 have been merely an interlude, and his grief and anger remain as violent as ever.

16–18 **draw him three times round the tomb** echoes the action of the Myrmidons who drove their chariots three times around Patroklos' body to honour him (23. 13–15n), but Achilleus' action is a parody of the Myrmidons', for behind his chariot he drags the body of Hektor. His action of leaving Hektor **to lie sprawled on his face in the dust** similarly dishonours the body (cf. 23. 24n).

18–21 **guarded the body from all ugliness** draws attention to the figure of Apollo who will soon take a leading role in urging the gods to deny Achilleus by granting Hektor burial. Earlier Aphrodite preserved the body by anointing it with immortal oil, and Apollo covered it in mist to keep the withering sun from it (23. 185–91).

24 For Hermes **Argeïphontes**, the slayer of Argos, cf. 2. 103n. His epithet **clear-sighted** recalls the close look-out he had to keep for the hundred-eyed Argos, but it is also in keeping with his role as god of thieving, the role the other gods urge him to undertake here.

25–30 The reason for **Poseidon's** hatred of the Trojans was that Laomedon refused to pay him for the construction of Troy's wall (20. 145–8n); the hatred of **Hera** and of **the girl of the grey eyes,** Athene, arose from the Judgment of Paris when he **favoured her who supplied the lust that led to disaster,** Aphrodite. This is the first direct mention in the poem of the Judgment of Paris, the ultimate origin of the Trojan War; of the three contestants, Hera as queen of the gods offered Paris power, Athene offered him warrior prowess, and Aphrodite offered him sex. The effect is to concentrate responsibility for Troy's disaster on Paris, and so to emphasize the innocence of Hektor, but this does nothing to lessen the unremitting hatred of the three gods.

41–3 The lion that **has given way to his own great strength and his haughty spirit** recalls the picture of the Achilleus that Aias railed against after the failed embassy, 'Achilleus has made savage the proud-hearted spirit within his body' (9. 628–9), and this picture contrasts with the Achilleus displayed later in this book.

46–54 **For a man must some day lose one who was even closer than this** is a further echo of Aias' speech during the embassy, when he too spoke of the loss of a brother or of a child (9. 632–6); he was speaking in the wake of Achilleus' loss of Briseis, as Apollo now speaks of his loss of Patroklos, and both voice the concern that his reaction is too intense. The **Destinies** are the three Fates (Moirai), cf. 20. 127–31n. The **dumb earth** means Hektor's body.

56–63   Hera gives precedence to Achilleus because he is **the child of a goddess**, while Hektor was **suckled at the breast of a woman**; but in fact Achilleus' position is ambivalent, for his father Peleus is a mortal, and so he himself is constrained by the limitations of mortality (cf. 1. 352n). It was during the **wedding** of Peleus and Thetis that the discord arose which led to the Judgment of Paris; the presence of the gods at the wedding provided for the honour of its offspring, Achilleus, and so Apollo's favouring of Hektor is seen by Hera as a betrayal, **faithless forever.**

74–6   Once more **Thetis** is to be intermediary between the greatest of gods, Zeus, and the greatest of mortals, Achilleus: Achilleus asked her to visit Zeus to ensure that he grant him honour (1. 407–12), and now Zeus is to ask her to visit Achilleus to ensure that Hektor's body is ransomed.

84   **she in their midst was mourning the death of her blameless son** recalls the lamentation beneath the waves when Thetis heard Achilleus' terrible cry of grief, and she and the other goddesses of the sea cried in unison. Once more Thetis' presence introduces the theme of her son's early death, and she weeps as though he is dead already (cf. 18. 52–64n).

90–1   **I feel shamefast to mingle with the immortals** partly reflects Thetis' grief at her son's approaching death, but it may also recall her earlier visit to Zeus and her appeal to him, and her realization that present circumstances are the result of that visit.

94   **her black veil, and there is no darker garment** is an indication of the depth of Thetis' grief. In early Greek epic only one other character is associated with such a garment, the grieving Demeter after the abduction of her daughter Persephone by Hades (*Homeric Hymn to Demeter*, 42).

101   **Hera put into her hand a beautiful golden goblet** is in marked contrast to Thetis' earlier visit to Olympos, when Zeus was anxious that he and Thetis should not be seen by Hera (1. 522–3).

107   **For nine days there has risen a quarrel among the immortals** mirrors the poem's opening, for the plague sent by Apollo to punish Agamemnon and the Achaians for the treatment of his priest similarly lasted for nine days (1. 53).

110 **but I still put upon Achilleus the honour that he has** recalls
Zeus' promise to Thetis (1. 524), and by contrasting his own support
for Achilleus with the opposition of the other gods he lends a
spurious authority to his request to Thetis.

124–9 **were busy at their work and made ready the morning meal**
implies that the companions prepare the meal for their own
consumption, not for Achilleus, and this is confirmed by Thetis'
remember neither your food nor going to bed. Achilleus' abstention
from the normal routines of life, eating and sleeping, has marked
his remoteness from the community of his fellows since Patroklos'
death (23. 29–30n); both of these routines will be restored later in
this book when he and Priam eat together (601) and then retire to
their beds (673–6).

130–1 **It is a good thing even to lie with a woman in love.** Many
have objected that it is inappropriate for Thetis, as his goddess
mother, to encourage Achilleus to take a woman into his bed, and
it has even been suggested that her words imply that he should
take a woman because he no longer has Patroklos as lover (Clarke
1978.386)! In fact Thetis is drawing attention to the person of
Briseis, for with Patroklos dead, and his father Peleus fated never
to see him again, the one remaining object of his affection is the
girl over whom the quarrel took place; just as in time he will eat
once more as a token of reconciliation, so his final appearance will
be sleeping with Briseis by his side (676).

139 **He can bring the ransom and take off the body.** Achilleus'
immediate obedience suggests that he was already disposed to return
the body before Thetis told him to.

148–9 **alone, let no other man of the Trojans go with him** ensures
that greater tension will attach to Priam's journey to Achilleus'
shelter, and is taken up in Hekabe's vain appeal to her husband
(203–8). **let one elder herald attend him** suggests that the sanctity
of the herald's office will protect the old king, just as Chryses'
office of priest should have ensured Agamemnon's respect (1. 11–
14n), and this points the contrast between Agamemnon's violent
rejection of the suppliant parent Chryses and Achilleus' generous
reception of the suppliant parent Priam later in this book.

156–8 Zeus portrays Achilleus as he was, before he was so twisted
by grief that he even tried to defile Hektor's body: **but will hold
back all the others** recalls the way he leapt to the defence of the

seer Kalchas and in effect offered to lay down his life to protect him from Agamemnon (1. 86–91n).

162–5 **the old man sat veiled, beaten into his mantle** means that the mantle is drawn so tight around him that it appears to have been moulded to his shape. **Dung lay thick on the head and neck of the aged man**: for self-defilement, see Parker (1983.68). Priam also wallowed in the muck when he proposed to go as suppliant to the Achaian ships but was restrained by his people (22. 414), and Achilleus lamented the death of Patroklos by covering his head and face with dust and scattering ashes over his tunic (18. 23–5).

194–9 **What does it seem best to your own mind for me to do?** In fact Priam refuses to accept Hekabe's advice when she gives it as requested, and the result is a portrait of a man of determination, unwilling to be deterred even by the soundest advice. Priam makes no mention to her of the promise that Hermes would accompany him to guide and protect him, so Hekabe sees only her husband's foolish wish to enter the Achaian camp.

203 **How can you wish to go alone** is Hekabe's own intuition, as Priam said nothing about going alone, and it reveals her anxiety, as she visualizes him alone and vulnerable before Achilleus.

212–16 **I wish I could set teeth in the middle of his liver and eat it** echoes Hekabe's description of Achilleus as 'savage' (207), *omestes*, which more literally means 'eater of raw flesh'. Hekabe's wish recalls Achilleus' violence as he took vengeance on Hektor (22. 346–8), and it throws into relief Priam's determination to be done with revenge and violence. Similarly Zeus accused Hera of harbouring such hatred of the Trojans that she would only be able to glut it if she could eat Priam and his children raw (4. 31–6n). Hekabe remembers that Hektor **was no coward** and had **no thought in his mind of flight,** forgetting his temporary panic when he faced Achilleus; she seems consciously to echo Hektor's own declared determination to avoid the charge of cowardice 'before the Trojans and the Trojan women with trailing garments' (6. 442).

226–7 **with my own son caught in my arms.** Virgil, perhaps with this scene in mind, pictured Priam killed by Achilleus' son, Pyrrhus, in a pool of the blood of his son Polites (*Aeneid* 2. 551).

239–46 **Get out, you failures, you disgraces.** Priam's grief is well observed. First came pain and self-pity when he saw Hektor's body dragged behind Achilleus' chariot, and he felt only death could bring relief (22. 425–6); now he expresses the anger of grief, through his contempt for his surviving sons who bring him no consolation; and finally will come the acceptance of his grief, urged on him by Achilleus (549–51).

248–62 Most of these sons of Priam are unknown, but their names highlight the loss of the greatest of them, Hektor. In the later tradition, **Troilos** was one of the more famous: it was foretold that if he survived to age twenty Troy would never be taken, but he fell as one of Achilleus' many victims. **the liars and the dancers** best characterizes Paris, who was described by Aphrodite as looking as though he was on his way to a dance (3. 390–4n).

266–80 The wealth of detail provided in this description of the **wagon for mules** emphasizes the importance of the mission; similarly the horses reared and tended by Priam's own hand, and the fine detail of their **polished manger**, shows how special they are and the occasion in which they are involved. The description effectively separates two scenes of high emotion, Priam's angry indictment of his sons, and his prayer to Zeus for his safe return from the Achaian camp. For interpretation of the wagon's details, see Wace and Stubbings (1962.540).

287–95 For **pour a libation to Zeus father**, cf. 1. 458–66n. To pour a libation and pray for safe return is standard practice, as, for example, when Achilleus sent Patroklos into battle to fight in his place (16. 230–484); but nowhere else does a character pray for a prodigy, and this reveals the depth of Hekabe's anxiety and distrust of her husband's claim to have been visited by Zeus' messenger.

303–5 **to pour unstained water over his hands.** For ritual purification before the sacrifice, cf. 1. 449n.

309 **grant that I come to Achilleus for love and pity** is a very different request to the one Hekabe has just suggested: she said he should pray for safe return from the ships (287–8), but in fact he prays for Achilleus' love and pity, and so confirms his earlier declaration that he only wishes to hold his son one last time, and does not care what may then happen (224–7).

327–8 **all his kinsmen were following much lamenting, as if he went to his death** recalls the last time Hektor left Troy to return to the battle, when he was mourned by the people in his house 'while he was living still' (6. 500–1), in anticipation of his imminent death. On this occasion, however, the lamentation is premature, for Priam is to return safe.

332–3   He saw the old man. There is pathos in the continual emphasis on Priam's old age (cf. 162, 164, 217, 235, 248, 252, 265, 279, 302, 322, 326), which matches the emphasis placed on the old age of Chryses in the poem's opening (cf. 1. 35n). Priam prayed that he might receive love and pity from Achilleus, and Zeus **took pity upon him** sets the tone for their meeting.

334–5   to you beyond all other gods it is dearest to be man's companion. Hermes appears, for example, to Odysseus as he makes his way to meet Kirke, and gives him good advice and the magic herb *moly* (*Odyssey* 10. 277–306). But Hermes also guides the spirits of the dead to the Underworld with his wand (*Odyssey* 24. 1–5), and so it has been thought that his guiding of Priam to Achilleus' shelter may have originated in a Journey to the Dead (Whitman 1958.217), for he is able to provide safe conduct by putting the guards to sleep (445–6).

347–8   the likeness of a young man, a noble, with beard new grown. Hermes' youthful disguise contrasts with the emphasis on Priam's old age, and this contrast prefigures Priam's meeting with the youthful Achilleus, for the relationship of mutual trust now established between the old man and the stranger prefigures the developing relationship between him and the Achaian champion.

349–52   by this time darkness had descended on the land fosters the illusion that Priam and the herald Idaios have travelled a great distance, as does their need to water the horses in the river. Homer is carefully setting the scene for Priam's meeting with the disguised Hermes—**the great tomb of Ilos** (cf. 10. 415n), the river-crossing point, the darkness descending, the loneliness—and this emphasizes his vulnerability and hence his fear at the god's sudden appearance.

362–71   Hermes' greeting, **my father**, is echoed in Priam's reply 'dear child' (373), and Hermes ends his promise of protection with **You seem to me like a [my] beloved father**. This is more than just politeness, but indicates the development of a kind of father-son bond, and the theme of parenthood is taken up by Priam (377), by Hermes (385), and by Priam again (387–8). This same bond is developed in the meeting of Priam and Achilleus, for it is by remembering his own father that Achilleus will come to recognize and to appreciate the suffering of the father of Hektor (511). Hermes' warning of what might happen **if one of these** [Achaians] **were to see you** also finds a parallel in Priam's meeting with Achilleus (cf. 648–55n), and prepares the listener for Achilleus' anxiety for the enemy king.

396–400 By identifying himself as **Achilleus' henchman** (*therapon*), the disguised Hermes is claiming the privileged status enjoyed by Patroklos until his death, and so a unique insight into Achilleus' mind. The details he adds about his background are unnecessary, but they have the effect of increasing his familiarity with Priam, for his father too is old and wealthy, and they lend credibility to the story he is telling and the advice he is offering. His story that his six brothers stayed at home, while **it was my lot to come on this venture**, suggests that his father may have bought exemption from the war for his brothers and recalls the story of Echepolos, who bought exemption from serving with Agamemnon at Troy by the gift of a horse (23. 296–9).

413–14 **now here is the twelfth dawn he has lain there.** Three days were taken up with Patroklos' funeral and were followed by nine days of quarrelling amongst the gods. For the divine preservation of Hektor's body, cf. 18–21n.

425–31 **to give the immortals their due gifts,** cf. 1. 40n. Mention of man's reciprocal relations with god leads naturally to Priam's wish to establish reciprocal bonds with a fellow hero by means of a gift. **if ever I had one** is a rare idiom, used to lament the passage of time, or the loss of a loved one (cf. 3. 173–80n).

448–56 **a towering shelter the Myrmidons had built for their king.** There has been no previous indication that Achilleus' shelter is such an impressive building; Homer is portraying Priam's apprehension, as he is about to come face to face with the greatest of all the heroes, the killer of so many of his sons, by presenting this intimidating structure through the old man's eyes as he stands in front of it.

465–7 Hermes' instruction to **clasp the knees of Peleion** ensures that it will be a proper supplication and so will be successful (cf. 1. 500–1n). In fact Priam will appeal only in the name of Achilleus' father, but the mention of his mother and son heightens the emotional force of the passage. The rare mention of **his child**, Neoptolemos, recalls Achilleus' lament at the height of his grief for Patroklos that his friend's death had robbed the boy of his protection (19. 326–7n).

471–6 The theme of Achilleus' isolation is continued as he sits apart from his companions, but **He had just now got through with his dinner** indicates that the theme of his fasting has been abandoned (124–9n). He has followed his mother's advice that nothing was to be gained from it and accepted her words on the nature of grief and mortality, and in turn he will pass on the lesson to Priam before they sit down together and feast (549–51).

478–80 Priam performs the set ritual of supplication. Kissing the knees of the supplicated is a part of the ritual which Athene said Thetis performed (8. 371), and which is here adapted to memorable effect, **kissed the hands that were dangerous and manslaughtering**, for kissing the hands of his son's killer is the supreme act of forgiveness and reconciliation. For 'manslaughtering hands', cf. 18. 317n.

480–2 **As when dense disaster closes on one who has murdered a man.** The sense of the simile is inverted: Priam is not a fugitive, for he is in his own land, nor is he a murderer, but rather he is supplicating a murderer, that of his own son; in addition, he is himself a man of substance, as the wealth of the ransom he bears indicates. The simile asserts the authority of Achilleus, by comparing him to the man of substance with power of life and death, and it points up the status of Priam as suppliant by making him an exile in his own land. The simile recalls, amongst others, the stories of Phoinix (9. 447–84) and Patroklos (23. 84–90), both of whom fled to Phthia as suppliants and were taken in by Peleus; so Priam is here associated with the men Achilleus holds dearest, and through them Homer evokes the spirit of forgiveness and humanity his father showed them.

486 **Achilleus like the gods, remember your father.** As Achilleus lamented Patroklos' death, he was compared to a father mourning as he burns the bones of his son (23. 221–3n), and earlier he characterized himself as parent to the weeping Patroklos (16. 6–10n). In his loss of Patroklos, Achilleus suffers the most devastating of griefs, like that of a parent; and through it he comes to understand Priam's grief and, by extension, that of his own father Peleus, at home alone and unprotected against his enemies.

490–2 There is irony in Priam's misconception that Peleus **is hopeful**

that he will see his beloved son come home, for Achilleus knows that he will never return home (cf. 18. 98); and therein lies his tragedy, for by killing Priam's son he has robbed his own father of his son.

495–506   Fifty were my sons corresponds to the fifty bedchambers Priam had built for his sons in his palace, as well as twelve chambers for his daughters (6. 244n). The number of Priam's sons highlights the one son who remained to protect him and so match the one son who still protects Peleus, and having invented a rounded number of sons, the invention of extra mothers follows naturally. The point is not that Priam is a 'polygamous Eastern potentate' (Willcock 1976.271), but a tragic father of war dead. Only two of his other wives are named in the poem, Kastianeira, the mother of Gorgythion (8. 304), and Laothoë, the mother of Lykaon (21. 85). Like Hekabe (212–16n), Priam remembers his son's actions with pride, **he fought in defence of his country,** but in fact it was shame for his past failure that Hektor declared was his reason for standing alone to face Achilleus (22. 98–110n).

508–9   Achilleus' action, **took the old man's hand and pushed him gently away,** breaks the bond of physical intimacy Priam established by kissing his hands, and replaces it with a bond of emotional intimacy which allows them both to indulge their grief openly (Lateiner 1995.38). Achilleus' gentleness towards Priam contrasts with Agamemnon's roughness towards Chryses (1. 25).

515–16   By raising Priam to his feet, Achilleus confirms he is accepting his supplication. The pathos of **in pity for the grey head and the grey beard** results from the great care with which Priam has been portrayed as an old man (332–3n). It is a scene of great simplicity and tenderness and contrasts, not just with Agamemnon's treatment of Chryses, but with Achilleus' rejection earlier of the supplications of Lykaon (21. 99–113) and of Hektor (22. 345–54).

522   **sit down upon this chair** is Achilleus' third gesture: having first gently pushed Priam away, and then having raised him from his suppliant position, this invitation to sit is his first act of hospitality, to be followed by the gift of food and of a bed.

525   **Such is the way the gods spun life for unfortunate mortals.** For the Moirai, cf. 20. 127–31n. Zeus himself declared that 'among all creatures that breathe on earth and crawl on it there is not anywhere a thing more dismal than man is' (17. 446–7), and Dodds (1951.29) believed that Achilleus here 'pronounces the tragic moral of the whole poem'. It is not just the tragic fates of Priam and Peleus that move Achilleus, but his acceptance that his own death is unavoidable and imminent.

527–33   an urn of evils, an urn of blessings. No man receives gifts from the urn of blessings alone: either he receives a mixture of evils and blessings, or he receives evils alone. The gifts, be they mixed or wholly evil, are bestowed by Zeus, but there is no suggestion that they come as a reward or as a punishment. Elsewhere in the poem man's relations with his gods are based on a system of reciprocity (425–31n), so it seems certain that this passage is designed for its context, so that the picture of man's portion assigned at the whim of Zeus confirms the pessimism of Achilleus' message to Priam, that man must simply endure that portion. The image of the wanderer driven over the earth by **the evil hunger** seems consciously to recall the image of the exiles Peleus welcomed into his home (480–2n).

534–42   Such were the shining gifts given by the gods to Peleus. Achilleus pictures his father as a man of power and substance comparable to Priam himself, and he presents marriage to the goddess Thetis as one of Peleus' blessings; yet this contains the bitter irony that the wedding was the occasion of the discord which has culminated in the Trojan War, and that marriage to a mortal was the cause of Thetis' suffering. **a single all-untimely child** is Achilleus' response to Priam's lament that he has lost all his sons (494), whereas Peleus has the consolation that he might one day welcome his son home (490): in fact it is Priam who has the consolation of surviving sons, whereas Peleus must lose the only son he ever had.

544–5   Lesbos is **Makar's hold** because he was its legendary king; in fact it lies south of Troy, and **Phrygia** lies to the east.

551   sooner you must go through yet another sorrow looks forward to the death of Priam and the fall of Troy, of which Hektor's death has stood throughout as the symbol (cf. 22. 410–11n).

560–70   No longer stir me up, old sir. Achilleus' brief lapse into anger is triggered by Priam's hope that he will return in safety to the land of his fathers (556–7), even though Achilleus has just declared himself 'all-untimely', and by Priam's mention of the ransom gifts: the ransom is irrelevant to Achilleus' decision, for he will release Hektor's body in accordance with the gods' will and out of respect for Priam himself, and so he instructs Priam not to make him conscious once more of his grief.

580–1 The clothing brought by Priam was all intended to be part of the ransom, so the **two great cloaks and a finespun tunic** that Achilleus reserves to shroud Hektor's body constitute a gift from himself to Priam; so there is gift-exchange between them, and this complements the hospitality Achilleus will provide.

587–91 Washing the corpse and anointing it with olive oil, and then clothing it for burial, are the first stages in Hektor's death ritual (Seaford 1994.177), which will be followed by the ritual lamentation over the body in Troy (720–2). **Achilleus himself lifted him and laid him on a litter**: the role of Achilleus is important in delivering up with his own hands Hektor's body for burial, for his action and his prayer to Patroklos bring to an end his quest for vengeance for his companion's death.

592–5 Be not angry with me, Patroklos. Patroklos' ghost had complained of Achilleus' neglect (23. 69–74), and now Achilleus appears afraid of a further accusation of betrayal, for when he greeted Patroklos for the last time on his funeral pyre, he promised him that 'I will not give Hektor, Priam's son, to the fire, but the dogs, to feast on' (23. 182–3).

601 When Priam arrived at his shelter, Achilleus had 'just now got through with his dinner' (471–6n); Achilleus' insistence now that **you and I must remember our supper** indicates his reconciliation with his enemy, just as his continual refusal to eat with the Achaian heroes indicated his isolation from them (124–9n).

602–20 The story of **Niobe** is told in the form of a ring composition (Introduction, 7(c)). Achilleus adapts the story in order to persuade Priam to eat with him, just as he was himself persuaded by his mother Thetis. Niobe, the daughter of Tantalos, offended Apollo and Artemis by boasting that she was superior to their mother Leto, on the grounds that she herself was the mother of twelve children, and in punishment the divine pair killed all her children; her grief was inconsolable, and she steadfastly refused to eat, and so Zeus turned her to stone, but her tears continued to flow. Pausanias (1.21.3) describes the natural feature on Mount Sipylos in Lydia which gave rise to the tale: 'Niobe from close up is a rock and a stream; but if you go further off you seem to see a woman downcast and in tears' (Levi 1984.59). Homer has changed the story to match the circumstances of his narrative, for Niobe, who traditionally was inconsolable, in his version was consoled and ate, and Achilleus urges Priam to do the same. **Nine days long they lay in their blood** is designed to match the arrangements for Hektor's funeral, that he will be mourned for nine days and, like the children of Niobe, buried on the tenth (664–5); in addition, the quarrel amongst the gods about the disposal of Hektor's body had lasted nine days when Thetis came to Zeus (107n). Homer has invented the detail that Zeus **made stones out of the people**, so that in the tale Niobe's children may lie unburied, just as Priam's son has lain unburied.

629–32 **wondering at his size and beauty.** The wonder with which Priam and Achilleus gaze at each other reflects their new-found respect; in Priam's case, it contrasts with the horror with which he viewed Achilleus, as he approached Hektor waiting outside Troy's walls, when he was like the dog-star (22. 30–1).

637–40 **my eyes have not closed underneath my lids.** Priam's sleeplessness through grief echoes that of Achilleus (cf. 4–5), and his wallowing in the muck in his courtyard (cf. 162–5n) recalls Achilleus' refusal to wash the dirt from his body until he had buried Patroklos (23. 40–5): the gesture is an attempt by the mourner to put himself in the place of the corpse.

644 **to make a bed in the porch's shelter.** The porch (*aithousa*) is the usual place for a stranger to be accommodated (cf. *Odyssey* 3. 399), though it is slightly curious that Achilleus' shelter should have one, as though it were a palace.

648–55 **Achilleus of the swift feet now looked at Priam and said, sarcastic.** The word *epikertomeon*, 'sarcastic', appears twice elsewhere in Homer to denote an unpleasant tone or manner (16. 744; *Odyssey* 22. 194), which is quite at odds with the atmosphere of harmony in this scene. Despite various attempts to change its meaning to suit the present context (Jones 1989), it is better to retain 'sarcastic' and to see it as referring, not to Achilleus' dealings with Priam, but rather his relations with Agamemnon to whom he refers scathingly for the last time in the poem. The reason Achilleus gives for Priam sleeping in the porch, **for fear some Achaian might come in here,** is incongruous since it is just the place he would be certain to be seen by a visitor. The incongruity arises from the need to include a final reference to Agamemnon: Achilleus wishes to contrast his own magnanimous actions with the likely behaviour of Agamemnon in similar circumstances, **there would be delay in the ransoming of the body**, and so Homer draws an explicit contrast between Achilleus' acceptance of supplication at the end of the poem and Agamemnon's rejection of it at the beginning.

664   **Nine days we would keep him in our palace and mourn him.** The period of mourning for Hektor which ends the poem matches the nine days of plague with which it began (1. 53).

669   **I will hold off our attack for as much time as you bid me** are Achilleus' final words in the poem, and they are a final assertion of his authority (cf. 22. 391–3n), as he commits the Achaian army to a truce of twelve days, without consultation with, or even acknowledgment of, Agamemnon.

675–6   Achilleus' final appearance in the poem, **slept in the inward corner of the strong-built shelter**, is marked by the end of the sleeplessness theme with which this book began (cf. 4–5), and this signals the end of his grief. That he sleeps beside **Briseis of the fair colouring** signifies that he has followed his mother's advice (130–1), but it also indicates finally his triumph over Agamemnon through the restoration of his prize.

683–8   **Aged sir, you can have no thought of evil.** After the gentleness and tranquillity of Priam's scene with Achilleus, Hermes' recollection of the danger Priam is in comes as a shock. Like Achilleus before him (648–55n), Hermes compares Achilleus' behaviour with that of Agamemnon and the other Achaians, **the sons you left behind would give three times as much ransom for you**: this is the final mention of Agamemnon in the poem, and the unfavourable comparison drawn completes the unfavourable picture of him throughout.

692–5   **when they came to the crossing-place of the fair-running river.** When Priam and the herald reached the river on their way from Troy to Achilleus' shelter, they stopped to water the horses, night fell, and they were joined by Hermes (350–2); now on the return journey, they have reached the same river, night ends, and Hermes leaves them. The parallel events effectively mark off the night during which the meeting of Priam and Achilleus has taken place.

699   The poem betrays no knowledge of the tradition that **Kassandra** was granted the gift of prophecy, but was fated never to be believed.

720–2   **the singers who were to lead the melody in the dirge** are

probably professional singers of the lament (*threnos*). Alongside
the formal lament are three laments, from the three women in
Hektor's life—his wife Andromache, his mother Hekabe, and his
brother's wife Helen—which parallel the appeals they made to him
during his visit to Troy, Hekabe (6. 253–62), Helen (6. 343–58),
Andromache (6. 406–39). There were also three laments for Hektor
at the moment of his death, by Priam (22. 415–28), Hekabe (22.
431–6), and Andromache (22. 477–514).

724   For the gesture, **held in her arms the head of manslaughtering
Hektor,** cf. 18. 71n.

725–45   The lament of Andromache echoes her appeal to him (6.
406–39) when, as here, she spoke of her fate and that of her child
after Hektor's death. **you, its defender, are gone, you who guarded
the city** echoes the irony of Homer's description of Astyanax, the
child of Hektor and Andromache, 'whom Hektor called
Skamandrios, but all of the others Astyanax—lord of the city; since
Hektor alone saved Ilion' (6. 402–3). **among them I shall also go**
prefigures Andromache's fate, given to Neoptolemos the son of
Achilleus, and **hurl you from the tower into horrible death** prefigures
Astyanax's death at the same man's hands (cf. Euripides *Troades*
1134–5). Her wish for **some last intimate word** recalls that they
shared the poem's most intimate moment, a moment Hektor
remembered as he faced Achilleus and death (22. 122–30n).

748–59   The lament of Hekabe recalls a time when Achilleus **would
sell** [her sons] **as slaves,** and so spare their lives; as he killed Lykaon,
one of those sons, Achilleus himself also recalled that time (21.
101–2). Hekabe's **but even so did not bring him back to life** recalls
Achilleus' declaration to Priam that there was nothing to be gained
for Hektor from his grief, for 'you will never bring him back' (550–
1): neither extremes of grief nor extremes of violence can untangle
the tragedies which have befallen them. **he of the silver bow, Apollo,
has attacked and killed with his gentle arrows** echoes the death of
Niobe's sons, killed by Apollo with arrows from his silver bow
(605); the pathos of Hekabe thus imagining her son's gentle death
is heightened by the savage reality of it.

762–75   The lament of Helen. **I should have died before I came
with him** recalls the curses Helen heaped upon herself during
Hektor's visit to Troy, the wish that she had been caught up by a
whirlwind on the day she was born or that she had been swept

away by the sea's waves (6. 343–58n). **now is the twentieth year upon me since I came** implies that Helen had already been at Troy for ten years before the ten-year siege began; the most likely explanation is that this is a standard formulation of a hero's absence, for example Odysseus' ten-year absence at the war followed by ten years of wanderings, which has been attached to Helen. **his father was gentle always** recalls the kindness Priam displayed towards Helen during the *Teichoskopia*, when he defended her and blamed the gods for what had befallen his city and people (3. 164n). **There was no other in all the wide Troad who was kind to me** also recalls her scene with Priam on the Skaian gate, when the chattering old men spoke admiringly of her beauty, but wished nonetheless that she would be gone from Troy (3. 154–60). Helen portrays the misery of her life at Troy, a foreigner and a figure of abhorrence to all, and this enhances her picture of Hektor as a figure of kindness.

783–4 **Nine days they spent bringing in an endless supply of timber** accords with Priam's request for nine days to gather wood for the pyre, because it had to be brought from distant hills and because the Trojans were afraid to venture out (663–4); similarly the wood for Patroklos' funeral pyre had to be transported down from the range of Ida (23. 113–26).

804 **Such was their burial of Hektor.** The first image of the poem was the multitude of strong souls of heroes hurled to the house of Hades, and the last is the burial of the greatest of the Trojan heroes: this in turn looks forward, beyond the confines of the poem, to the death of the greatest of the Achaians too.

BIBLIOGRAPHY

Adkins, A.W.H. (1960) *Merit and Responsibility*, Oxford.

Adkins, A.W.H. (1982) 'Values, goals, and emotions in the *Iliad*', *CP* 77, 292–326.

Ailshie, W.K. (1965) 'Phoenix rises again', *CJ* 61, 97–103.

Alexiou, M. (1974) *The Ritual Lament in Greek Tradition*, Cambridge.

Allen, S.H. (1999) *Finding the Walls of Troy*, Berkeley.

Andersen, O. (1976) 'Some thoughts on the Shield of Achilles', *SO* 51, 5–18.

Andersen, O. (1978) *Die Diomedesgestalt in der Ilias*, Oslo.

Andersen, O. and Dickie, M. (eds) (1995) *Homer's World: Fiction, Tradition, Reality*, Bergen.

Anderson, M.J. (1997) *The Fall of Troy in Early Greek Poetry and Art*, Oxford.

Arend, W. (1933) *Die typischen Scenen bei Homer*, Berlin.

Armstrong, J.I. (1958) 'The arming motif in the *Iliad*', *AJPh* 79, 337–54.

Arthur, M.B. (1981) 'The divided world of *Iliad* VI', in Foley, H.P. (1981).

Atchity, K.J. (1978) *Homer's Iliad: The Shield of Memory*, S. Illinois.

Atchity, K.J. (ed.) (1987) *Critical Essays on Homer*, Boston.

Atchity, K.J. and Barber, E.J.W . (1987) 'Greek princes and Aegean princesses: the role of women in the Homeric poems', in Atchity. (1987), 15–36.

Austin, N. (1994) *Helen of Troy and her Shameless Phantom*, Cornell.

Baldick, J. (1994) *Homer and the Indo-Europeans: Comparing Mythologies*, London.

Bardollet, L. (1997) *Les Mythes, les Dieux et l'Homme*, Paris.

Becker, A.S. (1995) *The Shield of Achilles and the Poetics of Ekphrasis*, Lanham.

Bennet, J. (1997) 'Homer and the Bronze Age', in Morris and Powell (1997), 511–34.

Bergold, W. (1977) *Der Zweikampf des Paris und Menelaos*, Bonn.

Bespaloff, R. (1947) *On the Iliad*. (tr. M. McCarthy), Princeton.

Beye, C.R. (1968) *The Iliad, the Odyssey, and the Epic Tradition*, London.

Boardman, J. and Vaphopoulou-Richardson, C.E. (eds) (1986) *Chios*, Oxford.

Bowersock, G.W., Burkert, W. and Putnam, M.C.J. (eds) (1979) *Arktouros*, Berlin.

311

Bowra, C.M. (1930) *Tradition and Design in the Iliad*, Oxford.

Bowra, C.M. (1952) *Heroic Poetry*, London.

Byre, C.S. (1992) 'Narration, description, and theme in the Shield of Achilles', *CJ* 88, 33–42.

Cairns, D.L. (1993) *Aidos: The Psychology and Ethics of Honour and Shame in Ancient Greek Literature*, Oxford.

Calder, W.M. (1984) 'Gold for bronze: *Iliad* 6.232–236', in Rigsby, K.J. (1984), 31–5.

Camps, W.A. (1980) *An Introduction to Homer*, Oxford.

Carlisle, M. and Levaniouk, O. (eds) (1999) *Nine Essays on Homer*, Lanham.

Clarke, W.M. (1978) 'Achilles and Patroclus in love', *Hermes* 106, 381–96.

Collins, D. (1998) *Immortal Armor: the Concept of ALKE in Archaic Greek Poetry*, Lanham.

Conche, M. (1999) *Essais sur Homère*, Paris.

Crielaard, J.P. (ed.) (1995a) *Homeric Questions*, Amsterdam.

Crielaard, J.P. (1995b) 'Homer, History and Archaeology', in Crielaard (1995a), 201–88.

Crotty, K. (1994) *The Poetics of Supplication*, Cornell.

Danek, G. (1988) *Studien zur Dolonie*, Wien.

Davison, J.A. (1962) 'The transmission of the text', in Wace and Stubbings. (1962), 215–33.

De Jong, I.J.F. (1987) *Narrators and Focalizers: the Presentation of the Story in the Iliad*, Amsterdam.

Dickinson, O. (1994) *The Aegean Bronze Age*, Cambridge.

Dodds, E.R. (1951) *The Greeks and the Irrational*, Berkeley.

Donlan, W. (1979) 'The structure of authority in the *Iliad*', *Arethusa* 12, 51–70.

Donlan, W. (1981) 'Reciprocities in Homer', *CW* 82, 137–75.

Donlan, W. (1989) 'The unequal exchange between Glaucus and Diomedes in light of the Homeric gift-economy', *Phoenix* 43, 1–15.

Donlan, W. (1993) 'Duelling with gifts', *Colby Quarterly* 3, 155–72.

Dorsch, T.S. (1965) *Aristotle, Horace, Longinus: Classical Literary Criticism*, Penguin.

Duckworth, G.E. (1966) *Foreshadowing and Suspense in the Epics of Homer, Apollonius, and Vergil*, New York.

Easterling, P.E. (1989) 'Agamemnon's skeptron in the *Iliad*', in Mackenzie and Roueche. (1989), 104–21.

Ebbott, M. (1999) 'The wrath of Helen: self-blame and nemesis in the *Iliad*', in Carlisle and Levaniouk (1999), 3–20.

Edwards, M.W. (1980) 'Convention and individuality in *Iliad* 1', *HSCP* 84, 1–28.

Edwards, M.W. (1987) *Homer Poet of the Iliad*, Baltimore.

Edwards, M.W. (1991) *The Iliad: A Commentary, vol. 5: Books 17–20*, Cambridge.

Emlyn-Jones, C. (1992) 'The Homeric gods: poetry, belief, and authority', in Emlyn-Jones et al.. (1992), 91–103.

Emlyn-Jones, C., Hardwick, L. and Purkis, J. (eds) (1992) *Homer: Readings and Images*, London.

Erbse, H. (1986) *Untersuchungen zur Funktion der Götter im homerischen Epos*, Berlin.

Evelyn-White, H.G. (1967) *Hesiod, Homeric Hymns, and Homerica*, Loeb.

Fagles, R. (1990) *The Iliad*, Penguin.

Farron, S. (1979) 'The portrayal of women in the *Iliad*', AC 22, 15–31.

Fenik, B. (1968) *Typical Battle Scenes in the Iliad*, Wiesbaden.

Finley, M.I. (1977), *The World of Odysseus. (*2nd ed.), London.

Finley, M.I. (1981) *Early Greece: the Bronze and Archaic Ages*, London.

Finnegan, R. (1977) *Oral Poetry*, Cambridge.

Fisher, N. and Van Wees, H. (eds) (1998) *Archaic Greece: New Approaches and New Evidence*, London.

Foley, H.P. (ed.) (1981) *Reflections of Women in Antiquity*, New York.

Foley, J.M. (1988) *The Theory of Oral Composition*, Indiana.

Foley, J.M. (1991) *Immanent Art: From Structure to Meaning in Traditional Oral Epic*, Bloomington.

Ford, A. (1992) *Homer: The Poetry of the Past*, Cornell.

Foxhall, L. and Davies, J.K. (eds) (1984) *The Trojan War*, Bristol.

Fränkel, H. (1921) *Die homerischen Gleichnisse*, in Wright and Jones (1997), 103–23.

Frazer, R.M. (1993) *A Reading of the Iliad*, Lanham.

Friis Johansen, K. (1967) *The Iliad in Early Greek Art*, Copenhagen.

Gill, C.J. (1996) *Personality in Greek Epic, Tragedy, and Philosophy*, Oxford.

Gill, C.J., Postlethwaite, N. and Seaford, R.A. (eds) (1998) *Reciprocity in Ancient Greece*, Oxford.

Godley, A.D. (1966) *Herodotus i*, Loeb.

Golden, L. (1989) 'Dios apate and the unity of *Iliad* 14', *Mnem* 42, 1–11.

Goldhill, S. (1991) *The Poet's Voice*, Cambridge.

Griffin, J. (1978) 'The divine audience and the religion of the *Iliad*', CQ 28, 1–22.

Griffin, J. (1980a) *Homer on Life and Death*, Oxford.

Griffin, J. (1980b) *Homer*, Oxford.

Griffin, J. (1995) *Iliad Book 9*, Oxford.

Grote, G. (1884) *A History of Greece*, London.

Grube, G.M.A. (1991) *Longinus. On Great Writing*, Indianapolis.

Hainsworth, J.B. (1968) *The Flexibility of the Homeric Formula*, Oxford.

Hainsworth, J.B. (1969) *Homer*, Oxford.

Hainsworth, J.B. (1993) *The Iliad: A Commentary, vol. 3: Books 9–12*, Cambridge.

Halperin, D.M. (1990) *One Hundred Years of Homosexuality*, New York.

Haslam, M. (1997) 'Homeric papyri and the transmission of the text', in Morris and Powell. (1997), 55–100.

Herman, G. (1987) *Ritualised Friendship and the Greek City*, Cambridge.

Heubeck, A. (1974) *Die homerische Frage*, Darmstadt.

Holoka, J.P. (1983) 'Looking darkly: reflections on status and decorum in Homer', *TAPA* 113, 1–16.

Hope Simpson, R. and Lazenby, J.F. (1970) *The Catalogue of the Ships in Homer's Iliad*, Oxford.

Hubbard, T.K. (1992) 'Nature and art in the Shield of Achilles', *Arion*. (3rd series) 2, 16–41.

Hughes, D.D. (1991) *Human Sacrifice in Ancient Greece*, London.

Janko, R. (1982) *Homer, Hesiod, and the Homeric Hymns*, Cambridge.

Janko, R. (1992) *The Iliad: A Commentary, vol. 4: Books 13–16*, Cambridge.

Jones, P.V. (1989) '*Iliad* 24. 649. Another solution', *CQ* 39, 247–50.

King, K.C. (1987) *Achilles: Paradigms of the War Hero from Homer to the Middle Ages*, California.

Kirk, G.S. (1962) *The Songs of Homer*, Cambridge.

Kirk, G.S. (1985) *The Iliad: A Commentary, vol. 1: Books 1–4*, Cambridge.

Kirk, G.S. (1990) *The Iliad: A Commentary, vol. 2: Books 5–8*, Cambridge.

Korfmann, M. (1986) 'Troy: topography and navigation', in Mellink (1986), 1–16.

Korfmann, M. (1998) *Troia: ein historischer Überblick und Rundgang*, Darmstadt.

Krischer, T. (1971) *Formale Konventionen der homerischen Epik*, Munich.

Kullmann, W. (1960) *Die Quellen der Ilias*, Wiesbaden.

Kullmann, W. (1984) 'Oral poetry theory and neoanalysis in Homeric research', in Kullmann (1992), 140–55.

Kullmann, W. (1985) 'Gods and men in the Iliad and Odyssey', in Kullmann (1992), 243–63.

Kullmann, W. (1992) *Homerische Motive*, Stuttgart.

Latacz, J. (1996) *Homer, der erste Dichter des Abendlands* (tr. J.T. Hooker), Ann Arbor.

Lateiner, D. (1995) *Sardonic Smile: Nonverbal Behavior in Homeric Epic*, Ann Arbor.

Leaf, W. (1900) *The Iliad, i*, London.

Leaf, W. (1902) *The Iliad, ii*, London.

Leinieks, V. (1986) 'The similes of *Iliad* two', *CandM* 37, 5–20.

Lesky, A. (1961) *Göttliche und menschliche Motivation in homerischen Epos*, Heidelberg.

Levi, P. (1984) *Pausanias Guide to Greece, i*, London.

Lohmann, D. (1970) *Die Komposition der Reden in der Ilias*, in Wright and Jones (1997), 71–102.

Lonsdale, S.H. (1990) *Creatures of Speech*, Stuttgart.

Lord, A.B. (1953) 'Homer's originality: oral dictated texts', *TAPA* 84, 124–34.

Lord, A.B. (1960) *The Singer of Tales*, Cambridge, Mass.

Lord, A.B. (1991) *Epic Singers and Oral Tradition*, Ithaca, N.Y.

Lord, A.B. (1995) *The Singer Resumes the Tale*, Cornell.

Lorimer, H.L. (1950) *Homer and the Monuments*, London.

Lowenstam, S. (1981) *The Death of Patroklos: A Study in Typology*, Königstein.

Mackenzie, M.M. and Roueche, C. (eds) (1989) *Images of Authority*, Cambridge.

Mackie, H.S. (1996) *Talking Trojan: Speech and Community in the Iliad*, London.

Macleod, C.W. (1982) *Homer Iliad Book XXIV*, Cambridge.

Manning, S.W. (1992) 'Archaeology and the world of Homer', in Emlyn-Jones et al. (1992), 117–42.

March, J.R. (1987) *The Creative Poet*, London.

Marg, W. (1956) *Homer über die Dichtung*, Münster.

Mee, C.B. (1984) 'The Mycenaeans and Troy', in Foxhall and Davies (1984), 45–56.

Meister, K. (1966) *Die homerische Kunstsprache*, Darmstadt.

Mellink, M.J. (ed.) (1986) *Troy and the Trojan War*, Bryn Mawr.

Morris, I. (1986) 'The use and abuse of Homer', *ClAnt* 5, 81–138.

Morris, I. (1997) 'Homer and the Iron Age', in Morris and Powell (1997), 535–59.

Morris, I. and Powell, B. (eds) (1997) *A New Companion to Homer*, Leiden.

Morrison, J.V. (1992) *Homeric Misdirection: False Predictions in the Iliad*, Ann Arbor.

Motto, A.L. and Clark, J.R. (1969) 'Ise Dais: the honor of Achilles', *Arethusa* 2, 109–25.

Moulton, C. (1977) *Similes in the Homeric Poems*, Göttingen.

Moulton, C. (1979) 'Homeric metaphor', *CP* 74, 279–93.

Mueller, M. (1984) *The Iliad*, London.

Muellner, L.C. (1996) *The Anger of Achilles: Menis in Greek Epic*, Cornell.

Murray, O. (1980) *Early Greece*, London.

Nagler, M. (1974) *Spontaneity and Tradition: A Study in the Oral Art of Homer*, Berkeley.

Nagy, G. (1974) *Comparative Studies in Greek and Indic Meter*, Harvard.

Nagy, G. (1979) *The Best of the Achaeans*, Baltimore.

Nagy, G. (1983) 'On the death of Sarpedon', in Rubino and Shelmerdine (1983), 189–217.

O'Brien, J.V. (1991) 'Homer's savage Hera', *CJ* 86, 105–25.

O'Brien, J.V. (1993) *The Transformation of Hera*, Maryland.

Owen, E.T. (1946) *The Story of the Iliad*, Toronto.

Page, D.L. (1959) *History and the Homeric Iliad*, Berkeley.

Parker, R.C.T. (1983) *Miasma: Pollution and Purification in Early Greek · Religion*, Oxford.

Parry, A. (ed.) (1971) *The Making of Homeric Verse*, Oxford.

Parry, A. (1972) 'Language and characterization in Homer', *HSCP* 76, 1–22.

Postlethwaite, N. (1988) 'Thersites in the *Iliad*', *G&R* 35, 123–36.

Postlethwaite, N. (1995) 'Agamemnon, best of spearmen?', *Phoenix* 49, 95–103.

Pucci, P. (1998) *The Song of the Sirens*, Lanham.

Raaflaub, K.A. (1997) 'Homeric society', in Morris and Powell. (1997), 624–48.

Rabel, R.J. (1997) *Plot and Point of View in the Iliad*, Ann Arbor.

Redfield, J.M. (1975) *Nature and Culture in the Iliad*, Chicago.

Reinhardt, K. (1960) *Tradition und Geist*, in Wright and Jones (1997), 170–91.

Reinhardt, K. (1961) *Die Ilias und ihr Dichter*, Göttingen.

Richardson, N.J. (1993) *The Iliad: A Commentary, vol. 6: Books 21–24*, Cambridge.

Richardson, S.D. (1990) *The Homeric Narrator*, Nashville.

Rieu, E.V. (1966) *Homer The Iliad*, London.

Rigsby, K.J. (ed.) (1984) *Studies Presented to Sterling Dow*, Durham, N.C.

Romilly, J. de. (1996) *Hector*, Paris .

Rose, P.W. (1988) 'Thersites and the plural voices of Homer', *Arethusa* 21, 5–25.

Rosner, J.A. (1976) 'The speech of Phoenix: *Iliad* 9.434–605', *Phoenix* 30, 314–27.

Rubens, B. and Taplin, O. (1989) *An Odyssey Round Odysseus*, London.

Rubino, C.A. (1979) 'A thousand shapes of death: heroic immortality in the *Iliad*', in Bowersock et al. (1979), 12–18.

Rubino, C.A. and Shelmerdine, C.W. (eds) (1983) *Approaches to Homer*, Austin.

Rutherford, R.B. (1996) *Homer*, Oxford.

Ryan, G.J. (1965) 'Helen in Homer', *CJ* 61, 115–17.

Schadewaldt, W. (1959) *Von Homers Welt und Werk*, in Wright and Jones (1997), 124–42.

Schein, S.L. (1984) *The Mortal Hero*, California.

Scodel, R. (1982) 'The autobiography of Phoenix: *Iliad* 9.444–495', *AJPh* 103, 128–36.

Scodel, R. (1992) 'The wits of Glaucus', *TAPA* 122, 73–84.

Scott, W.C. (1974) *The Oral Nature of the Homeric Simile*, Leiden.

Scully, S.P. (1986) 'Studies of narrative and speech in the *Iliad*', *Arethusa* 19, 135–53.

Scully, S.P. (1990) *Homer and the Sacred City*, Cornell.

Seaford, R.A. (1994) *Reciprocity and Ritual*, Oxford.

Segal, C. (1968) 'The embassy and the duals of *Iliad* 9. 182–198', *GRBS* 9, 101–14.

Segal, C. (1971) 'Nestor and the honor of Achilles', *SMEA* 13, 90–105.

Severyns, A. (1966) *Les Dieux d'Homère*, Paris.

Shannon, R. (1975) *The Arms of Achilles and Homeric Compositional Technique*, Leiden.

Sherratt, E.S. (1992) 'Reading the texts: archaeology and the Homeric question', in Emlyn-Jones et al.. (1992), 145–65.

Silk, M.S. (1987) *Homer, the Iliad*, Cambridge.

Sinos, D.S. (1980) *Achilles, Patroklos and the Meaning of Philos*, Innsbruck.

Slatkin, L.M. (1986) 'The wrath of Thetis', *TAPA* 116, 1–24.

Slatkin, L.M. (1991) *The Power of Thetis*, Berkeley.

Snodgrass, A.M. (1971) *The Dark Age of Greece*, Edinburgh.

Snodgrass, A.M. (1980) *Archaic Greece*, London.

Snodgrass, A.M. (1998) *Homer and the Artists*, Cambridge.

Stanford, W.B. (1954) *The Ulysses Theme*, Oxford.

Stanley, K. (1993) *The Shield of Homer*, Princeton.

Stella, L.A. (1978) *Tradizione Micinea e Poesia dell'Iliade*, Rome.

Taplin, O. (1980) 'The Shield of Achilles within the *Iliad*', *G&R* 27, 1–21.

Taplin, O. (1986) 'Homer's use of Achilles' earlier campaigns in the *Iliad*', in Boardman and Vaphopoulou-Richardson (1986), 15–19.

Taplin, O. (1992) *Homeric Soundings*, Oxford.

Thornton, A. (1984) *Homer's Iliad: its Composition and the Motif of Supplication*, Göttingen.

Thorpe, M. (1973) *Homer*, London.

Traill, D. (1989) 'Gold armour for bronze and Homer's use of compensatory time', *CP* 84, 301–5.

Traill, D.A. (1995) *Schliemann of Troy: Treasure and Deceit*, London.

Tsagarakis, O. (1979) 'Phoinix's social status and the Achaean Embassy', *Mnem* 32, 221–42.

Turner, F.M. (1997) 'The Homeric question', in Morris and Powell (1997), 123–45.

Van Nortwick, T. (1996) *Somewhere I Have Never Travelled*, Oxford.

Van Wees, H. (1992) *Status Warriors*, Amsterdam.

Visser, E. (1997) *Homers Katalog der Schiffe*, Stuttgart.

Vivante, P. (1990) *The Iliad: Action as Poetry*, Boston.

Wace, A.J.B. and Stubbings F.H. (eds) (1962) *A Companion to Homer*, London.

Warren, P.M. (1989) *The Aegean Civilizations*, Oxford.

West, M.L. (1995) 'The date of the *Iliad*', *Museum Helveticum* 52, 203–19.

Westbrook, R. (1992) 'The trial scene in the *Iliad*', *HSCP* 94, 53–76.

Whitman, C.H. (1958) *Homer and the Heroic Tradition*, Cambridge, Mass..

Whitman, C.H. and Scodel, R. (1981) 'Sequence and simultaneity in *Iliad* N, I, and O', *HSCP* 85, 1–15.

Willcock, M.M. (1970) 'Some aspects of the gods in the *Iliad*', *BICS* 17, 1–10.

Willcock, M.M. (1976) *A Companion to the Iliad*, Chicago.

Willcock, M.M. (1978) *The Iliad of Homer, Books I–XII*, London.

Willcock, M.M. (1984) *The Iliad of Homer, Books XIII–XXIV*, London.

Wilson, C.H. (1996) *Homer Iliad Books VIII and IX*, Warminster.

Winnifrith, T. and Murray, P. (eds) (1983) *Greece Old and New*, London.

Wood, M. (1985) *In Search of the Trojan War*, London.

Wright, G.M. and Jones, P.V. (eds) (1997) *Homer: German Scholarship in Translation*, Oxford.

Wyatt, W.F. (1985) 'The embassy and the duals in *Iliad* 9', *AJPh* 106, 399–408.

Zielinski, T. (1899) *Die Behandlung gleichzeitiger Ereignisse im antiken Epos*, Philologus Supp. 8.

INDEX